EVOLUTION

(Singularity to the Future)

> ***"The Big Bang theory postulates that 13.772 billion years ago our Universe emerged from a singularity – a point of infinite density and gravity – and that before this event space and time did not exist. (This means that the Big Bang occurred at no place and at no time!)"***
> ***www.space.com***

James F. Frayne

"We climb mountains not so much that the world can see us, but that we can see the world"

David McCullough Jr.

Milnesium tardigradum

M. tardigradum is microscopic eight-legged animal that has been to outer space and would likely survive the apocalypse.

PEDIGREE OF MAN

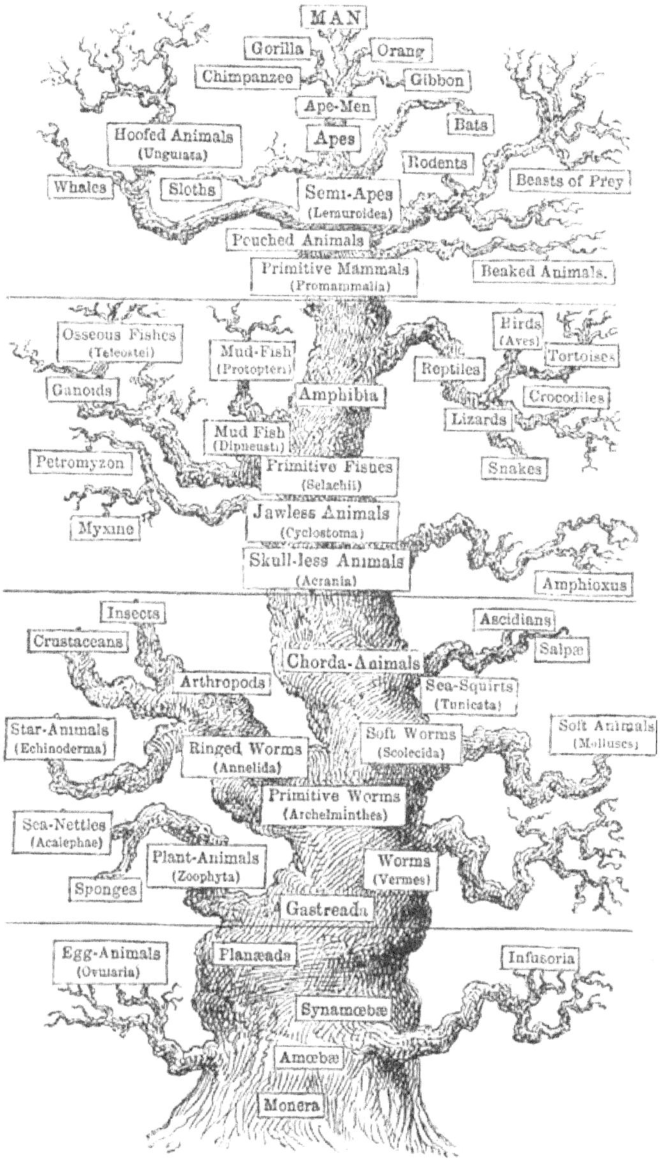

The tree of life as seen by Haeckel in The Evolution of Man (1879)

VOLUME TWO

This is **Volume Two** of two volumes. Whereas Volume One is devoted, in the main, to the Evolution of the Universe, galaxies, the Solar System, our Earth, and to the future and Volume Two is more directed to the Evolution of living things, this is by no means to suggest a clear cut division.

In fact whilst it is true to say that the two volumes are essentially mutually exclusive, there is a considerable degree of accordance between the two volumes. One volume supports the other

First Printing: 2023

979-8-8535-9691-7

Ordering information:
Special discounts are available on quantity purchases by corporations, associations, educators, and others.

U.S. trade bookstores and wholesalers:
Please contact author at:
e-mail: jamesfrayne2014@hotmail.com
or direct to www.jamesfrayne.co.uk

All tables, charts, maps and animal line drawings are available as prints in A4 at competitive prices.
For details, contact the author at the e-mail address detailed below.

Front Cover *Section of Charles R. Knight's 1920 reconstruction: Magdalenian painters at Font-de-Gaume, France.PD*

This classic Knight mural from the American Museum of Natural History depicts a Cro-Magnon artist painting mammoths near the entrance of Font-de-Gaume, France.

For more details please visit author's website at:
http://jamesfrayne.co.uk

By the same author:

Tall Grows the Grass (African Historical Novel)
First Son of Khui (Egyptian Historical Novel)

'SHE' (Anthology of Women in Mathematic and Science)

Easy as you Go! A Mathematical Companion
(Volume 1: A – L)
Easy as you Go! A Mathematical Companion
(Volume 2: M- Z)
A-Star Question Bank
(Mathematics with or without solutions)
Mathematics & Statistics for Biology, Psychology & Chemistry

Mathematics by Stages (Angles to Vectors)
Mathematics by Stages (Circles and Curves)
Mathematics by Stages (Advanced Topics)

Hell Bank Notes (A Pictorial Catalogue)
Romancing the Wood
(History behind the American Wooden Nickel)
The Indian Hundi
(Favourite negotiable instrument in days gone by)
Hidden Stories behind Paper Money around the World

Selected Biology Advance Level Topics (Volume 1: A – J)
Selected Biology Advance Level Topics (Volume 2: K – Z)

Greenhouse Effect
Mechanics (The Basics)

Jenny Two-tails and her Friends (Book for Young Children)

Applications of Genetics
Atoms and Fundamental Particles

Contents (Volume One)

Contents (Volume Two)

Raphus cucullatus

*The **dodo** is an extinct flightless bird that was endemic to the island of Mauritius. The closest living relative of the dodo is the Nicobar pigeon.*

Three Domain Tree of Life
(and Including VIRUS)

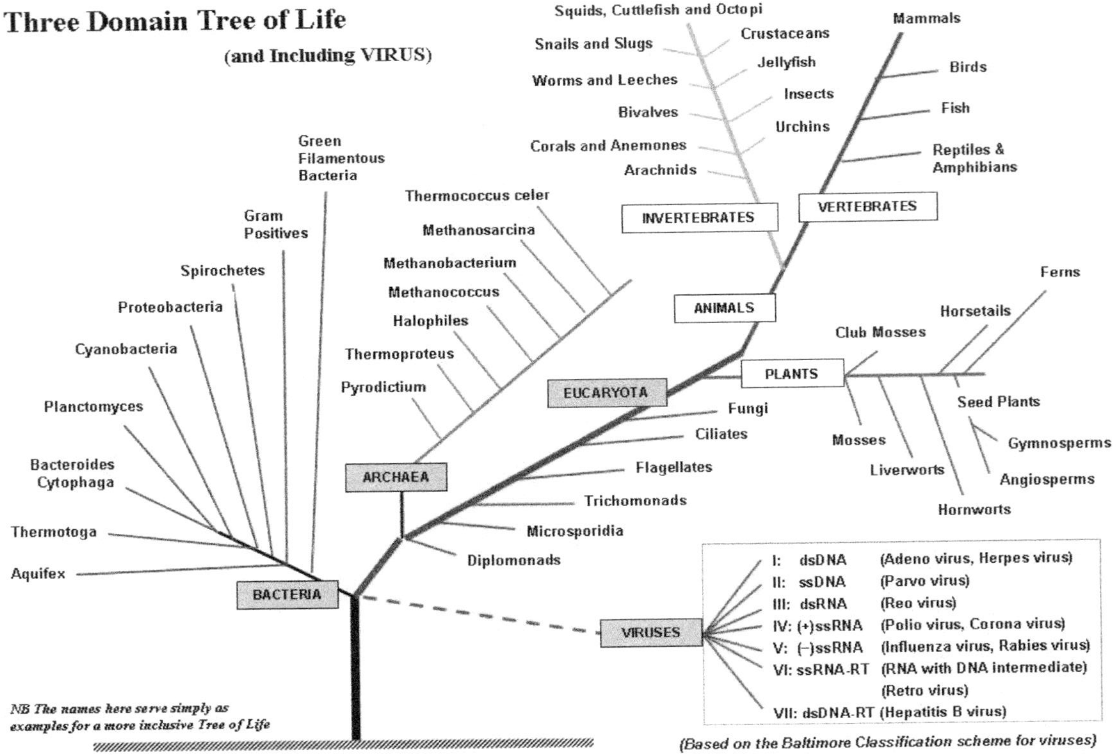

NB The names here serve simply as examples for a more inclusive Tree of Life

(Based on the Baltimore Classification scheme for viruses)

Tick off all those questions that you can answer with confidence before you read any further.

Come back when you have read <u>the two volumes</u> of 'EVOLUTION (Singularity to the Future)' and tick off all the questions for a second time!

☐ Are there such things as 'friendly viruses'?

☐ Are viruses alive?

☐ Did early Trilobites really have crystals for eyes?

☐ Did the Opabinia really have five eyes?

☐ Do humans have tails?

☐ How can 'flicker fusion rate' protect the Housefly?

☐ How fast does Earth travel through space?

☐ How is Teleology possibly significant to Evolution theory?

☐ How many eyes do Scallops have?

☐ How many teeth do snails have?

☐ How were prehistoric animals assisted in their breathing?

☐ Is the Planaria truly immortal?

☐ What animal had one single orifice to serve for both ingesting and excretion?

☐ What animal had properties far ahead of the evolutionary process?

☐ What animal has over two hundred separate eyes?

☐ What animal possessed tooth whorls?

☐ What are considered to be the closest living relatives to animals?

☐ What are the objections to Darwinian Theory of Natural Selection?

☐ What are the properties of all the greenhouse gases?

☐ What are the two major elements in the Sun?

☐ What are tomia?

□ What are Ur and Vaalbara?
□ What are vibrissae?
□ What damage will the collision of Milky Way with the Andromeda galaxy cause?
□ What does the Drake Equation imply?
□ What does the Malthusian Theory of Population predict?
□ What does Titus-Bode Law state?
□ What happened for the Miller-Urey Experiment to be so significant?
□ What important findings were made on the Galapagos Islands?
□ What important step was made by Leonardo da Vinci?
□ What is a Main Sequence star?
□ What is a nictitating membrane?
□ What is anoxic water?
□ What is Burgess Shale?
□ What is Cosmic Microwave Expansion?
□ What is de Sitter Expansion?
□ What is Grand Unified Theory and what are the four forces in nature?
□ What is Hachimoji DNA?
□ What is Hardy-Weinberg's contribution to Microevolution?
□ What is methane clathrate?
□ What is Methanosarcina?
□ What is so highly significant about the Charnia?
□ What is so important about the Precambrian Period?
□ What is so special about a Tardigrade?
□ What is so special about Iridium?
□ What is so special about the Gaia-Enceladus galaxy?
□ What species is believed to be the earliest example of a primate?

- □ What is the connection of Evolution to Global Warming and the Greenhouse Effect?
- □ What is the Escape Velocity from Earth?
- □ What is the essential idea behind the 'Out of Africa' Hypothesis?
- □ What is the Genetic Code?
- □ What is the Geologic Time Scale?
- □ What is the Kardashev Scale?
- □ What is the Multiregional Hypothesis?
- □ What is theorized to have happened to the planetoid called Theia?
- □ What makes Murchison meteorite special?
- □ What Prosimians were believed to be ancestral to Hominids?
- □ What significant event caused the Dinosaurs to become extinct?
- □ What term did Herbert Spencer introduce in his quest for an understanding of the origin and destiny of all living things?
- □ What were the first examples of prehistoric art?
- □ What were the functions of the 24 eyes of a Box Jellyfish?
- □ What were the key events in the Geological Timeline?
- □ What will happen to Homo sapiens in future years?
- □ What will happen to the Earth, the Solar System and the Milky Way in future years?
- □ When did Archbishop Usher calculate that God created man?
- □ When did Multi-cellular life first appear?
- □ When did the 'Great Dying' occur?
- □ When did the brain of Homo sapiens cease to grow?
- □ When did the Chicxulub Impact Event occur?
- □ When did the first warm-blooded animals appear?
- □ When was the Great Oxidation Event?
- □ When was the Solar System formed?
- □ When will oxygen run out?

☐ Where can Golden Jellyfish be found?

☐ Where did the water in all the oceans come from?

☐ Where do viruses come from?

☐ Who advanced the idea that the physical world's remote history can be inferred from evidence in present-day rocks?

☐ Who championed the idea of continuity and gradual change in early civilization?

☐ Who was Lucy?

☐ Who were the Cro Magnon?

☐ Why is the Sixth Extinction Event so significant to life on Earth?

Physalia physalis

*The name "**man o' war**" comes from the name of a sailing warship and the animal's resemblance to the Portuguese version (the caravel) at full sail.*

Preface

*'Evolution is the process of continuous developments over time and by which process such inherent changes are evidenced by positive traits leading to further enhancements and a combination of interrelated phenomena, or to **negative incompatible traits ending with extinction**.'*

Evolution in all its various forms has come a long way from the split second after the Big Bang until the present day.

In 'Metaphysics' Aristotle states 'the more you know, the more you know you don't know' and it is this principle that has goaded 'civilization' to greater ends. The knowledge that *Homo sapiens* has gained about the past 13.77 billion years of the Universe's existence has been unparalleled.

Yet there are probably more things we do not know now about life, our purpose in living, our destiny. Though not since the last Mass Extinction some 66 million years ago has life been in so much danger of extinction than it is right now.

Ever since the beginning of the Industrial Revolution around the 1750s technology has developed exponentially. But the knowledge that we have gained has come at a dreadful price. Industrialization and an incomplete appreciation of the effects it has had, and continues to have, on life and evolution in general cannot be ignored.

The current geological age, the so-called **Anthropocene Age**, is viewed somewhat magnanimously as the period during which human activity has been the dominant influence on climate and the environment. Rather more than this though, and one that has far more implications; it is as if the lights of present-day life are sadly and unquestionably going out one-by-one.

We have now begun to suffer from the effects of wanton pollution of our planet and lack of control in carbon emissions. The consequences of this are manifold: degradation of the environment, increased risk to the health of both fauna and flora (and that includes humans), ozone layer depletion, land infertility, global warming ... the list goes on...!

But all these consequences have a serious bearing on Evolution; they are all the '**negative incompatible traits which could well end in extinction**'.

There is ample evidence of the consequences, not least of all in widespread floods and forest fires that are now blighting large areas of the world. What is perhaps not so evident is the alarming loss of species, many of which are fundamental to the well-being of *H. sapiens* in one way or another.

It is sincerely hoped that this book will be instrumental in bringing home an awareness of the many paths, the twists and turns, the trials and tribulations that nature has gone through in order for *H. sapiens* to become the species it has become today.

But just as importantly, it is hoped that this book will leave the reader more appreciative of the Universe in which everybody and everything plays such a momentous part, and to the ever-changing nature of life which could perhaps hold such a wonderful fulfilling future for many billions of years to come were the present threats to world survival be addressed in earnest before it is too late.

James F Frayne
2023

PS The discerning reader will note repetitions in some areas – this is deliberate and is intended to help give a fuller picture of the specific topic then being addressed.

Index of Illustrations

(Volume Two)

Helicoprion (290 – 270 Mya)

Helicoprion had a tight, curled-up coil of triangular teeth, a bit like a Swiss roll, but considerably deadlier. As far as palaeontologists can tell, this bizarre structure was attached to the bottom part of Helicoprion's jaw.

Animals & Fossils

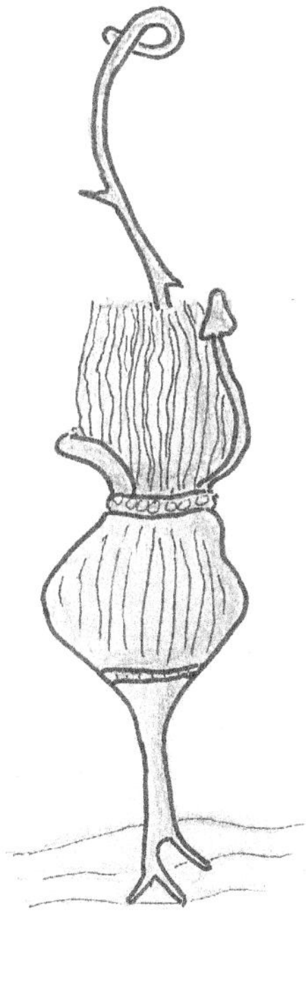

Choanoflagellate

The Choanoflagellates are a group of free-living unicellular and colonial flagellate eukaryotes considered to be the closest living relatives of the animals.

Early Primates

Dryopithecus fontani
Darwin briefly noted that Dryopithecus casts doubt on the African origin of ape.

Early Homo

Australopithecus afarensis (Lucy)

Bacteria

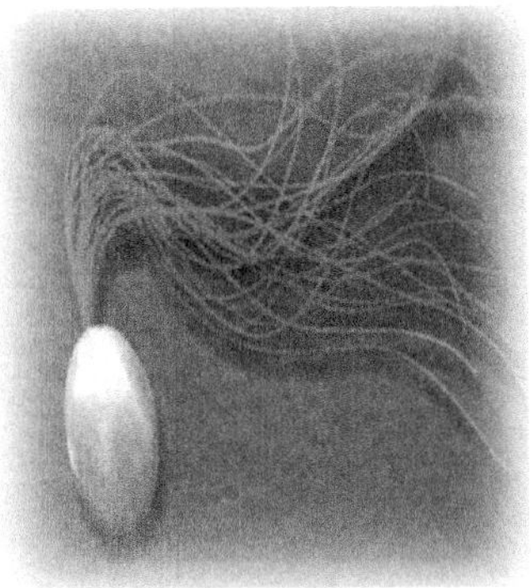

Pyrolobus fumarii

Virus

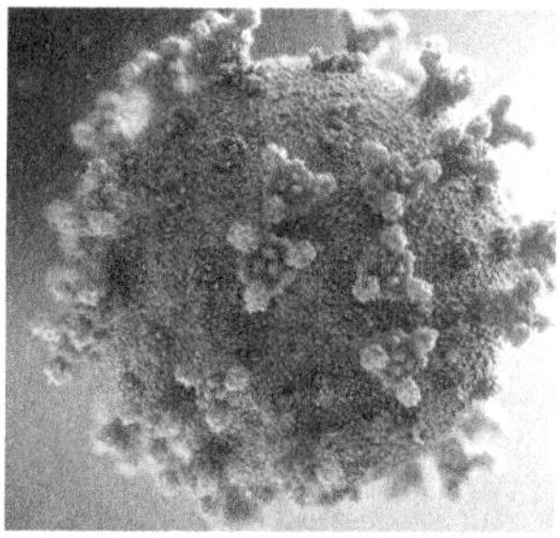

COVID-19 (SARS-CoV-2)

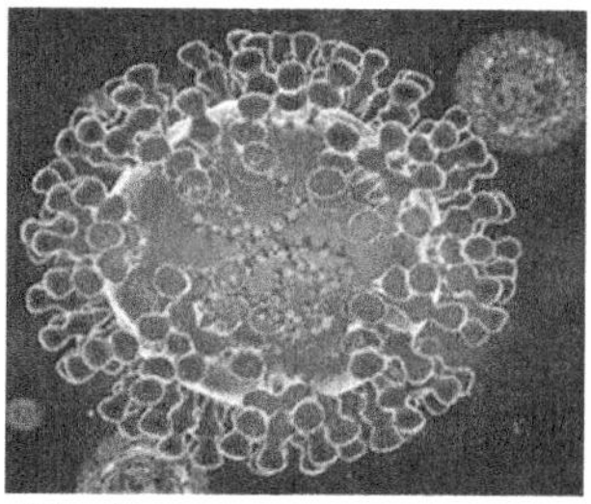

Monkeypox (Chimpanzee adenovirus)

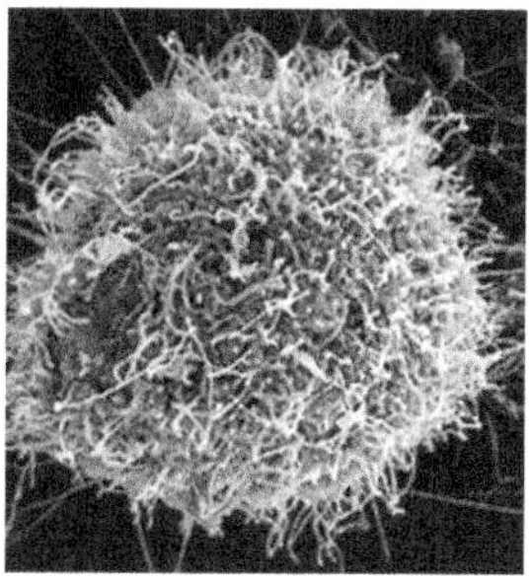

Ebola (Ebola hemorrhagic fever)

Information Sheets

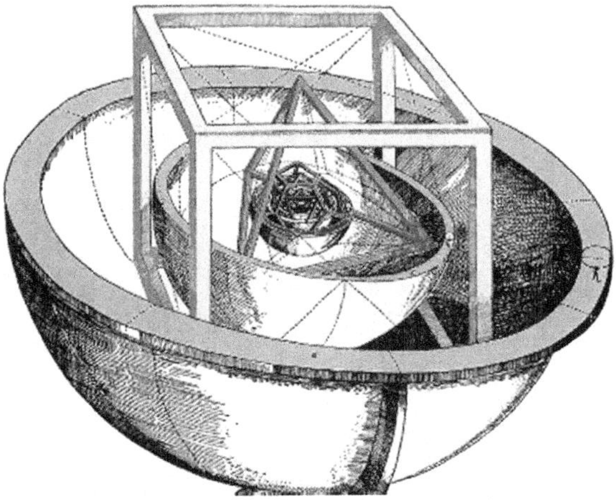

Johannes Kepler

was a German astronomer, mathematician, astrologer, natural philosopher and writer of music He is a key figure in the 17th-century Scientific Revolution, best known for his laws of planetary motion, and his books Astronomia nova, Harmonice Mundi, and Epitome Astronomiae Copernicanae. These works also provided one of the foundations for Newton's theory of universal gravitation.

Evolution of Living Things

The belief that living things are related to one another and that they have been derived from one or more common ancestors is now so generally accepted that it is well to realise that this concept of *organic revolution* is a fairly recent development of biological thought.

Historical Views on Evolution

The term 'evolution' was introduced by **Herbert Spencer** in **1852**, but the idea behind it arose very early in the history of man's quest for an understanding of the origin and destiny of all living things, including man himself.

The idea of continuity and gradual change originated in early civilisation which grew up in the Valley of the Nile.

From there it was brought to Greece by **Pythagoras**.

During the intervening period, most of the authority on scientific matters was in the hands of the clergy, and many of these believed that the variety of living things on the Earth were separately and simultaneously created, as is suggested by the Book of Genesis.

An important step was made when **Leonardo da Vinci** identified fossils as the remains of extinct creatures which must have lived during the actual formation of the rocks in which they are now embedded.

Previously, they had been dismissed as God's rejects, or possibly the handiwork of the Devil.

Theologists maintained that a theory of organic evolution would require that the Earth's age should be hundreds of millions of years.

They did not think this. In fact in the 17th century, **Archbishop Usher** had estimated by careful calculations that the Earth was less than 6000 years old and, moreover, God has specially created man on the **4th October, 4004 BC** at precisely 9:00 am!!!

Modern methods of dating rocks, however, have shown that the age of the Earth is to be measured in thousands of millions of years.

There is now evidence from approximately 3.5 billion year old ***Stromatolites*** in sedimentary rocks of Western Australia. These are currently regarded as the oldest evidence of life on Earth, and pushing the record further back in time had seemed unlikely because there is almost no rock remaining from the earliest period of Earth's history.

Stromatolites are the ***layered trace fossils of microbial life,*** *primarily cyanobacteria. Some of them date back an astounding 3.4 billion years, making them the oldest record of life on planet Earth.*

Fossilized stromatolite in Strelley Pool Chert, about 3.4 billion years old from Pilbara Craton, Western Australia
CC BY-SA 4.0

Evidence of this kind, which points to the great antiquity of living things, has supported the views of those who believe that a gradual evolution of living things has taken place and that for even the slightest change in each generation could bring about striking alterations during periods of millions of years.

Today, the evidence that organic evolution has occurred is overwhelming, and scientists have no hesitation in stating that the many and varied living things on the Earth are related to one another, and they have evolved from one or a few common ancestors.

Thus human beings and apes are believed to have evolved from some type of animal, now extinct, which may have had some of the features common to both man and apes.

Carrying this process still further back, it is most probable that humans, apes, dogs, cows and all other mammals have a common reptilian ancestor, which was probably not very unlike some of the lizards we find on the Earth today.

The reptiles are believed to have evolved from some simple amphibian, and amphibians from fishes.

The fishes in their turn seen to have evolved from some invertebrate animal, and within the invertebrate group we may trace various lines of descent from the simplest forms to the more complex types.

The ultimate ancestor of living things was probably something resembling the bacteria and viruses.

Some, though, believe that the first form to live was something like an amoeba, which was capable of photosynthesis, or in some way independent of other things for its food.

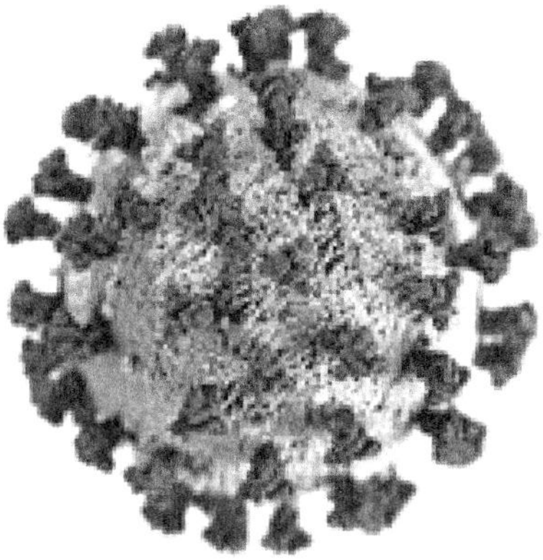

Amoeba

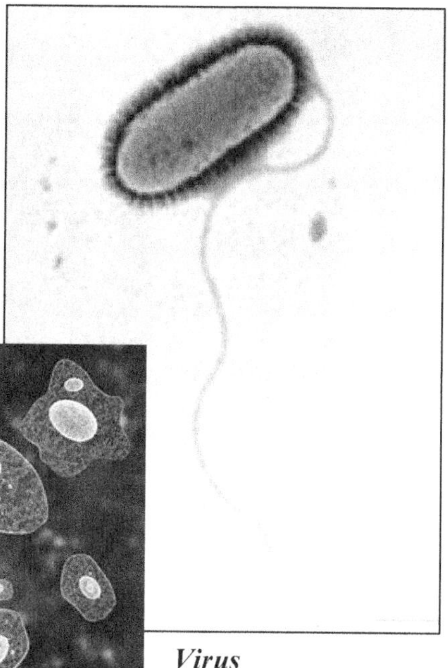

Virus

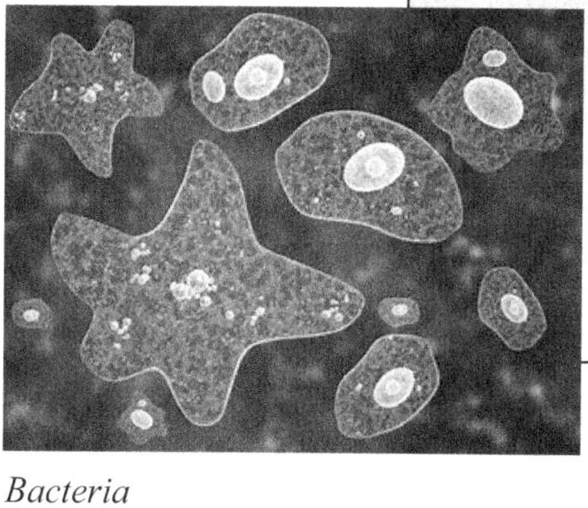

Bacteria

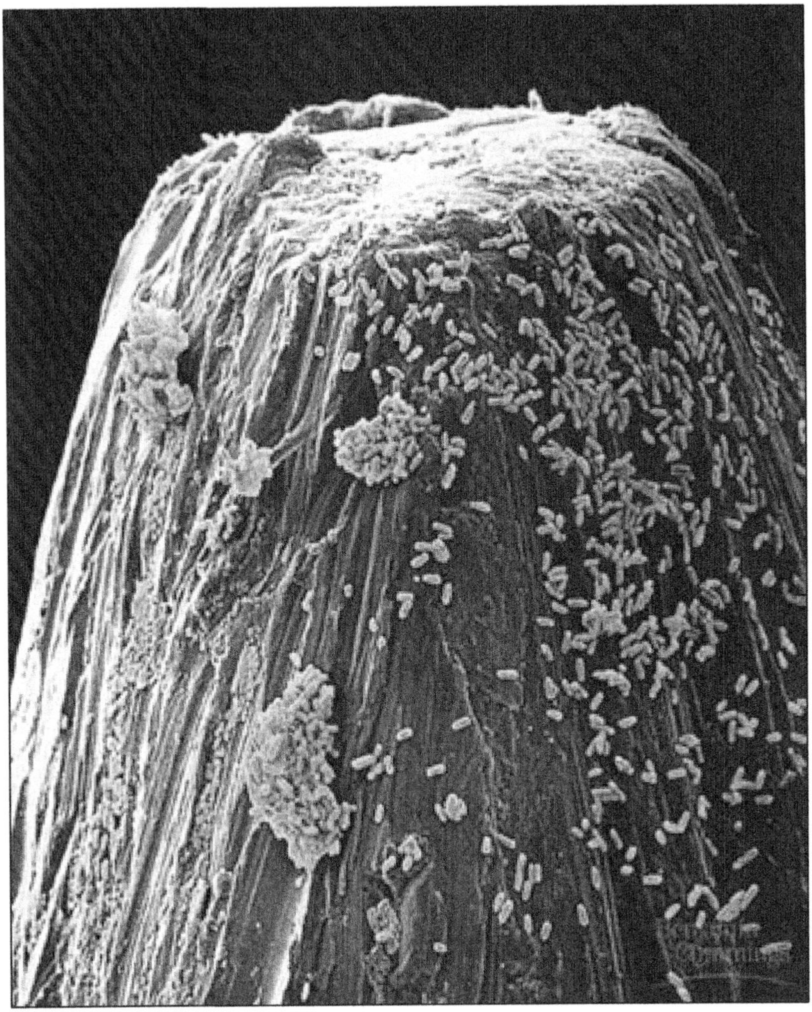

Bacteria on the point of a pin.

Origins of Evolutionary Thought

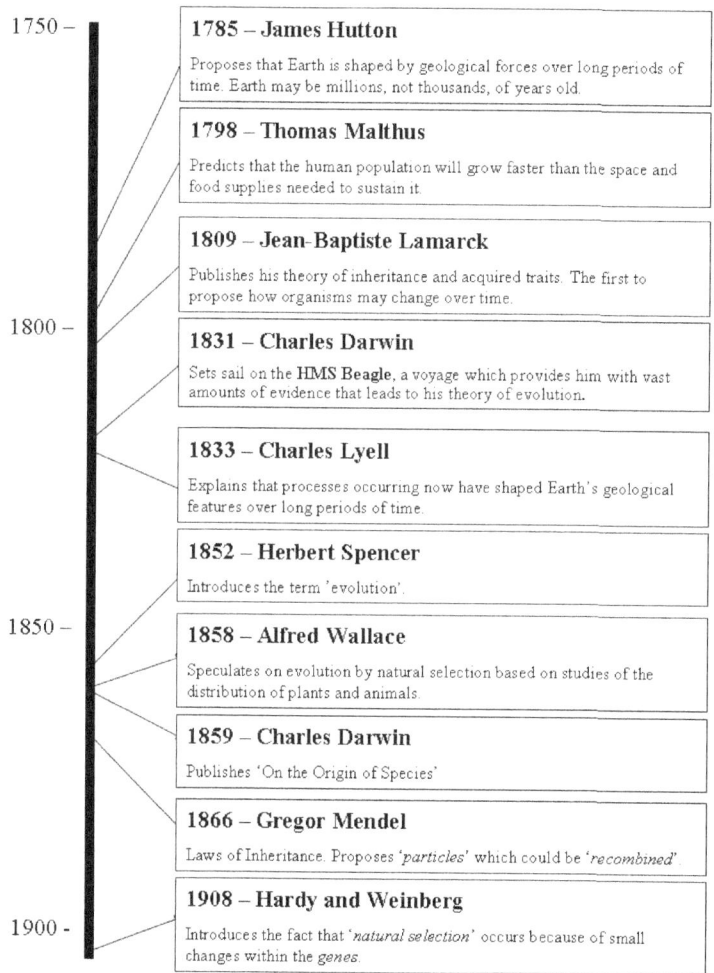

1750 –

1785 – James Hutton

Proposes that Earth is shaped by geological forces over long periods of time. Earth may be millions, not thousands, of years old.

1798 – Thomas Malthus

Predicts that the human population will grow faster than the space and food supplies needed to sustain it.

1809 – Jean-Baptiste Lamarck

Publishes his theory of inheritance and acquired traits. The first to propose how organisms may change over time.

1800 –

1831 – Charles Darwin

Sets sail on the **HMS Beagle**, a voyage which provides him with vast amounts of evidence that leads to his theory of evolution.

1833 – Charles Lyell

Explains that processes occurring now have shaped Earth's geological features over long periods of time.

1852 – Herbert Spencer

Introduces the term 'evolution'.

1850 –

1858 – Alfred Wallace

Speculates on evolution by natural selection based on studies of the distribution of plants and animals.

1859 – Charles Darwin

Publishes 'On the Origin of Species'

1866 – Gregor Mendel

Laws of Inheritance. Proposes '*particles*' which could be '*recombined*'.

1908 – Hardy and Weinberg

1900 -

Introduces the fact that '*natural selection*' occurs because of small changes within the *genes*.

Origins of Evolutionary Thought

James Hutton (1785)

James Hutton advanced the idea that the physical world's remote history can be inferred from evidence in present-day rocks. He developed the theory that geological features could not be static but underwent continuing transformation over indefinitely long periods of time. From this he argued, contrary to conventional religious tenets of his day, that the Earth could not be young.

He was one of the earliest proponents of what in the 1830s became known as *'uniformitarianism'*, the science which explains features of the Earth's crust as the outcome of continuing natural processes over the long geologic time scale.

He also advocated **evolution** in the form of *'uniformitarianism'* for living creatures and even suggested **natural selection** as a possible mechanism affecting them.

He distinguished between heritable variation as the result of breeding, and non-heritable variations caused by environmental differences such as soil and climate.

Hutton thought the mechanism allowed species to form varieties better adapted to particular conditions and provided evidence of benevolent design in nature.

Though Hutton circulated privately an abstract of his Theory '*Concerning the System of the Earth, its Duration, and Stability*' in 1785, it did not appear in full print until 1788.

Studies of Charles Darwin's notebooks have shown that Darwin might well have arrived separately to the idea of natural selection which he set out in his 1859 book *On the Origin of Species*.

Jean-Baptiste Lamark (1809)

The first serious attempt to provide a theory for the cause for evolution was that of Jean Baptiste de Lamark (1744 – 1829).

Lamark's Theory

Lamark assumed that heritable variations were produced in animals by a change in habit or by a change in the environment.

First Law:
Living things show a tendency to increase in size as they become more complex.

Second Law:
New organs arise in the body in response to new needs which the organism experiences.

Third Law: (Law of use and disuse)
The development and effectiveness of organs is promoted by the use of these organs, whereas disuse brings about their decline.

He stressed the effect of use and disuse as agents in modifying certain structures in such animals as the ostrich.

Here the long powerful legs and the poor developed wings means that the bird no longer flies but relies on its speed of running to escape from its enemies.

The development and effectiveness of organs is promoted by the use of these organs, whereas disuse brings about their decline.

He stressed the effect of use and disuse as agents in modifying certain structures in such animals as the ostrich.

Here the long powerful legs and the poor developed wings means that the bird no longer flies but relies on its speed of running to escape from its enemies.

Fourth Law:
(Law of inheritance and acquired characteristics)
Everything acquired or modified during the individual's lifetime is preserved by heredity and transmitted to the individual's offsprings.

The elongated neck of the giraffe, for example, has been produced by the short necked horse-like ancestors of the giraffe ceasing to feed on grass and feeding instead on the leaves of trees.

Constant stretching of the necks to reach leaves high up on the trees ultimately produced, in his view, the long necks of the present-day giraffes, each generation acquiring slightly longer necks and transmitting this acquired character to the offspring.

Objections to Lamark's Theory

The main objections are:

- The absence of experimental evidence in support of the use or disuse of an organ.
- The lack of evidence that modifications of structure acquired during the life of a organism can affect the germ cells in such a way that the modification can be transmitted to the offspring. For example mutilations practiced by man on domestic animals (such as 'docking' tails of sheep and horses), though continued for many generations, have produced no heritable effect.

Charles Darwin (1831)

Darwin's argument for his **Theory of Natural Selection** was based on three observable facts from which he made two deductions:

He observed that all organisms show a tendency to increase in a geometrical ratio so that young animals or plants of any species are always more numerous than their parents.

However, the number of adult individuals making up any species remains relatively constant over any period of time.

From these two facts, Darwin deducted that there must be a struggle for existence among young animals and plants.

Darwin observed that all members of a species exhibit variation. He believed that some of these variations might confer some advantage on the offspring which would help them to survive in the struggle for existence.

Other variations might prove unfavourable and bring the early death of the individual.

The individual which survives long enough to reproduce (either sexually or asexually) and to leave offsprings is 'biologically fit' in relation to its particular environment. ***We can therefore speak of 'survival of the fittest'***.

Darwin did not know of Mendel's theory of heredity, but he had observed that not only many large, but also slight variations are inherited.

If this is so, then the effects of differential survival are handed down and accumulated from generation to generation.

He therefore deducted that a mechanism is in operation by which new species can gradually originate by means of natural selection.

While elaborating the idea of Natural Selection as the main directing agent of evolution, Darwin also included secondary ones such as 'sexual selection', the effect of geographical location and, like Lamark, the effect of use and disuse on certain organs.

Sexual Selection

Darwin considered that sexual selection was responsible for the brighter plumage of male birds as compared with that of the hen of the same species, owing to the hen birds always choosing the more brightly coloured cock birds as mates in each generation.

On the other hand, the more sober coloured plumage of the hen birds would be due to a process of elimination of the brighter coloured ones since the sitting hen is more liable to be seen and attacked by predatory birds.

Hawks use this method, so that the less conspicuous ones stand a greater chance of escaping observation.

In this manner, generation by generation, the plumage of hen birds has become less and less conspicuous.

This is due more to Natural Selection than Sexual Selection

In polygamous species, such as the deer, the stronger males with the best developed antlers overcome their weakest rivals and mate with the females, so that their male offsprings inherit those features which in their turn enable them to overcome their rivals.

In this way, progressive increase in the size of the antlers has taken place.

Geographical Isolation

Due to mountains, sea barriers and other impediments, geographical isolation could induce, in Darwin's view, increased variation and hence favour the production of new species. This is due to the absence of 'swamping effects' by interbreeding, with other variations so as to produce a less varied population.

Darwin believed that if all the various varieties of pigeons produced by man's selective action were allowed to interbreed, reversion to the original wild type pigeon would result.

Also, during his visit to the **Galapagos Islands**, situated on the Equator, 1,000 miles southwest of Panama, he found that the flora and fauna of these islands were closely related to those of the mainland South America, yet the actual species were different on each island.

He made a study of the finches on these islands. These birds illustrate the divergence of species and Darwin believed *speciation* to be due also to natural selection operating independently on the stock of each island.

1. Geospiza magnirostris.
2. Geospiza fortis.
3. Geospiza parvula.
4. Certhidea olivacea.

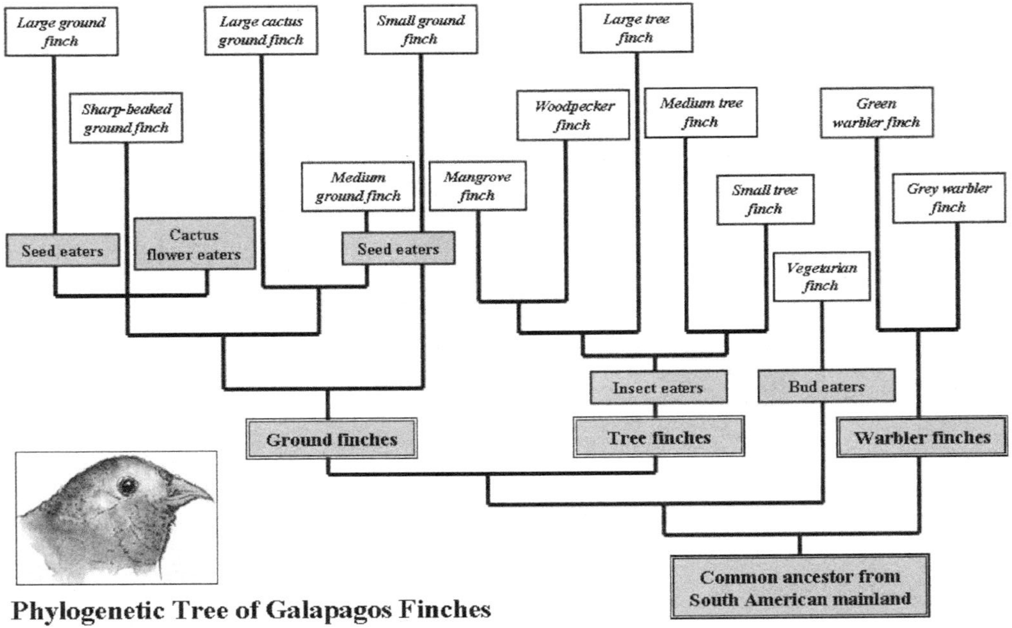

Phylogenetic Tree of Galapagos Finches

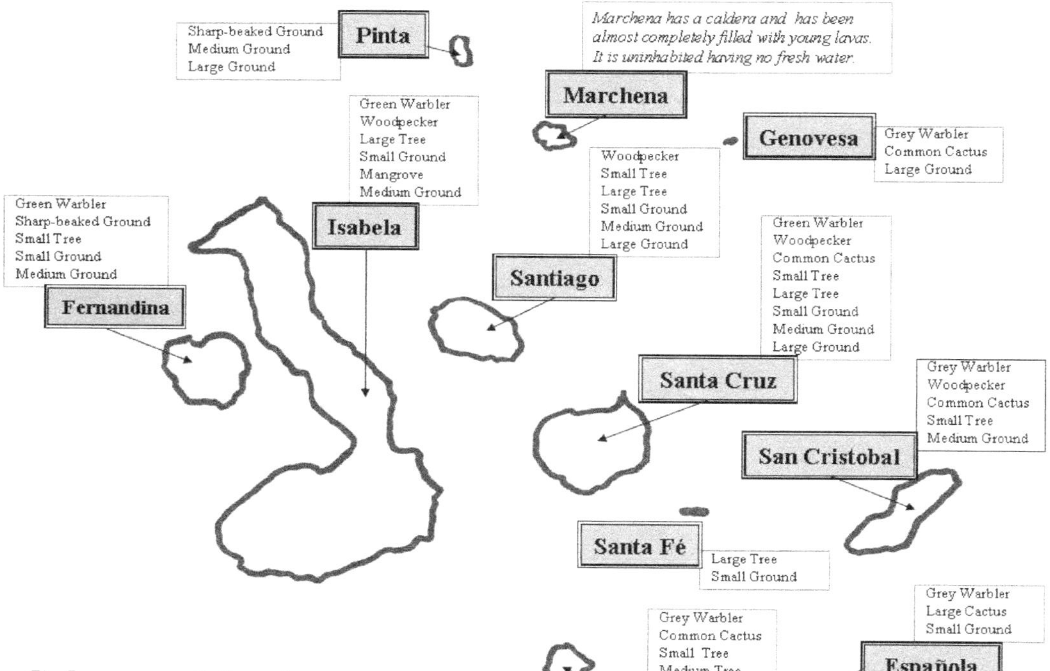

Galapagos Islands

Main Finch Distribution

An Example:

To illustrate the difference between Lamark's and Darwin's theories

The **Dodo** (*Raphus cucullatus)*, a type of pigeon with reduced powers of flight, until recently inhabited the islands of Mauritius. It could not have survived on the mainland of Africa, since its capture by predatory enemies would be easily accomplished owing to its inability to fly.

No such enemies existed on Mauritius until the arrival of the crews of sailing ships visiting the island to obtain fresh water. It was originally thought that indiscriminate killing of the dodos for food occurred during their visits, resulting eventually in their complete extermination.

(This belief has, however been somewhat overshadowed in recent years in favour of a **contributory factor** concerning **population theory**. The original precept is, however, still remains valid).

Darwin's theory would have accounted for the diminished power of flight and the poorly developed wings by Natural Selection.

Mauritius is exposed to high winds and those birds with well developed wings which flew well were liable to be swept out to sea, while those with poorly developed wings and unable to fly were preserved from this danger.

In this way Natural Selection by the agency of high winds evolved a breed of flightless dodos.

On Lamarkian lines, the absence of enemies would account for the diminished size of the wings as the result of their disuse over a long period of time, since the need to escape from enemies by flight was not present.

Charles Lyell (1833)

Sir Charles Lyell argued that the formation of Earth's crust took place through countless small changes occurring over vast periods of time, all according to known natural laws. His '*uniformitarian*' proposal was that the forces moulding the planet today have operated continuously throughout its history.

He offered a theory of evolution, some of which was based on his friend Darwin's observations. What made Lyell's theory unique was the fact that he is recognized as one of the first to believe that Earth could be more than 300 million years old. He made this decision based on geological anomalies that he observed.

It was his work in the field of Stratigraphy that would help him influence evolution as he examined at how fossils and shells were placed within the rock layers, or strata, in the ground. Lyell concluded that by categorizing the number of marine shells within a specific layer of rock, a picture of the planet at the time of formation could be created.

Lyell suggested that Darwin's theories were a modification of Lamarck's ideas about evolution, and much of Lyell's work is included with Darwin's theories. However, Darwin's work has more recognition and influence today than Lyell's own personal theories.

Mendel's Laws of Inheritance

Darwin's **Theory of Evolution** proposed that, with the natural variations that occur in populations, any trait that is beneficial would make that individual more likely to survive and pass on the trait to the next generation. This process of Natural Selection could result in completely new species. However, Darwin did not have an explanation for how the traits could be preserved over the succeeding generations. At the time, the prevailing theory of inheritance was that the traits of the parents were 'blended' in the offspring. But this would mean that any beneficial trait would be diluted out of the population within a few generations. This is because most of the 'blending' over the next generations would be with individuals that did not have the trait.

Darwin's Theory, often a symbol of the clash of religion and science, was revived through the work of **Gregor Mendel**. A Roman Catholic friar from Moravia, Gregor Mendel, had the answer to Darwin's problem. Traits were not 'blended', but 'inherited' whole. Modern Neo-Darwinism combines both Darwin's and Mendel's work.

Gregor Mendel provided a way for Darwin's *beneficial traits* to be preserved. Instead of mixtures that were 'blended', Mendel proposed *particles* that could be 'recombined'.

As long as the *particles* associated with a trait survived in the population there was some probability that the trait encoded by the *particles* would remain in the population.

Mendel's **Laws of Inheritance** helped revive Darwin's theory. They would also prove tremendously important to the future of biology and medicine, affecting the lives of billions of people. A completely new discipline within Biology, *Genetics*, arose from Mendel's work. New hybrid food strains were developed that were more productive, nutritious, disease resistant, or had better taste. The **Green Revolution** and foods that we now take for granted, such as canola oil, were largely the product of Mendelian genetics. He carried out experiments crossing (mating) plants with different characteristics. By observing the characteristics of the offspring produced, he was able to draw conclusions about the inheritance of characteristics. Even though he did not know about *chromosomes* or *genes* he was able to conclude the following:

- Characteristics are determined by factors within the organism (now known to be genes)
- That the factors (genes) can be present in two different forms (now known as alleles)
- That the two factors (alleles) in an individual separate during gamete formation (now known as meiosis).

Laws of Inheritance

- The **laws of inheritance** were proposed by Gregor Mendel after conducting experiments on pea plants for seven years.
- The Mendel's laws include law of dominance, law of segregation and law of independent assortment.
- Mendel's **first law** or the **law of segregation** states that every individual possesses two alleles and only one allele is passed on to the offspring. It describes the segregation of alleles and discrete inheritance of characteristics. The law further explains that during the production of gametes of an individual, chromosomes first separate and each gamete gets only one set of individual chromosome pair. Further, this allele segregation process occurs via meiotic cell division. Hence, Mendel's first law talks about a single trait and the **50:50** chance of getting the allele to each gamete during gametogenesis.

	D	r
D	DD	Dr
r	Dr	rr

- Mendel's **second law** or the **law of independent assortment** states that the inheritance of one pair of genes is independent of inheritance of another pair It describes the segregation of alleles and discrete inheritance of characteristics.

- The law further explains that during the production of gametes of an individual, chromosomes first separate and each gamete gets only one set of individual chromosome pair. Further, this allele segregation process occurs via meiotic cell division. The law considers the behaviour of independently assorting non-homologous chromosomes. It mainly explains the independent assortment of two or more traits. According to the second law, without the interference of the other trait, all the traits are independently transmitted to the daughter cells (**9:3:3:1** distribution).

	AB	Ab	aB	ab
AB	AABB	AABb	AaBB	AaBb
Ab	AABb	AAbb	AaBb	Aabb
aB	AaBB	AaBb	aaBB	aaBb
ab	AaBb	Aabb	aaBb	aabb

- Mendel's **third law** or the **law of dominance** states that one of the factors for a pair of inherited traits will be dominant and the other recessive, unless both factors are recessive. The law states that dominant alleles always mask the recessive alleles. The characters that appear in an F1 generation are called the dominant alleles and are not expressed; they are described as being recessive. For example, in a cross between any pair of contrasting characters, the dominant character is always expressed.

Although Mendel's Laws explain the inheritance pattern in sexually reproducing organisms, it does not hold true in all cases.

There are a few complex inheritance patterns that cannot be understood with Mendel's Laws alone. One such condition is the presence of multiple alleles that are found in blood types, which means that there are more than two alleles that code for a trait.

Breaking the Genetic Code

Marshall Warren Nirenberg was an American biochemist and geneticist. He shared a Nobel Prize in Physiology or Medicine in 1968 with Har Gobind Khorana and Robert W. Holley for "breaking the genetic code" and describing how it operates in protein synthesis.

The **genetic code** is the set of rules by which information encoded within genetic material (DNA or mRNA sequences) is translated into proteins by living cells. Biological decoding is done by the ribosome. This links amino acids together in an order specified by mRNA. It uses transfer RNA (tRNA) molecules to carry amino acids and to read the mRNA. The molecules read the mRNA three nucleotides at a time. These nucleotide triplets are called **codons**. A codon specifies which amino acid will be added next during protein synthesis. There are some exceptions, but usually a three-nucleotide codon represents a single amino acid.

The genetic code among all organisms is very similar. It can be expressed in a simple table with 64 entries.

The genetic code decides the protein sequence for a given coding region (gene). Other regions in the genome can influence when and where these proteins are produced.

Genetic Code - Synthesis of DNA

First letter \ Second letter	U	C	A	G	Third letter
U	UUU, UUC — Phe UUA, UUG — Leu	UCU, UCC, UCA, UCG — Ser	UAU, UAC — Tyr UAA — STOP UAG — STOP	UGU, UGC — Cys UGA — STOP UGG — Trp	**U** **C** **A** **G**
C	CUU, CUC, CUA, CUG — Leu	CCU, CCC, CCA, CCG — Pro	CAU, CAC — His CAA, CAG — Gln	CGU, CGC, CGA, CGG — Arg	**U** **C** **A** **G**
A	AUU, AUC, AUA — Ile AUG — Met	ACU, ACC, ACA, ACG — Thr	AAU, AAC — Asn AAA, AAG — Lys	AGU, AGC — Ser AGA, AGG — Arg	**U** **C** **A** **G**
G	GUU, GUC, GUA, GUG — Val	GCU, GCC, GCA, GCG — Ala	GAU, GAC — Asp GAA, GAG — Glu	GGU, GGC, GGA, GGG — Gly	**U** **C** **A** **G**

Series of Codons as part of an mRNA

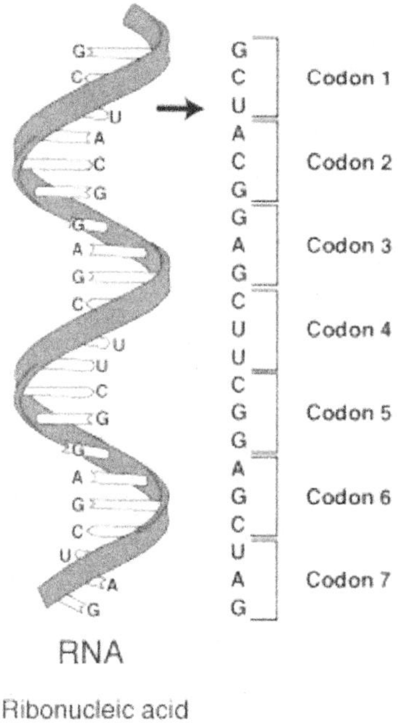

A series of codons in part of a messenger RNA (mRNA) molecule. Each codon consists of three nucleotides. This usually represents a single amino acid. The nucleotides are shown by the letters A, U, G and C. This is mRNA, which uses U (uracil). DNA uses T (thymine) instead.

Hachimoji DNA

Hachimoji DNA (from Japanese hachimoji, "eight letters") **is** a synthetic nucleic acid analog that uses four synthetic nucleotides in addition to the four present in the natural nucleic acids, DNA and RNA.

This leads to four allowed base pairs: two unnatural base pairs formed by the synthetic nucleobases in addition to the two normal pairs. Hachimoji bases have been demonstrated in both DNA and RNA analogs, using deoxyribose and ribose respectively as the backbone sugar.

Benefits of such a nucleic acid system may include an enhanced ability to store data, as well as insights into what may be possible in the search for extraterrestrial life.

The hachimoji DNA system produced one type of catalytic RNA (ribozyme or aptamer) in vitro.

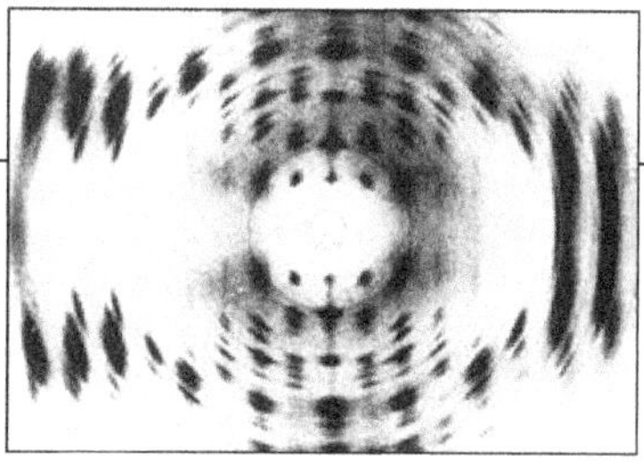

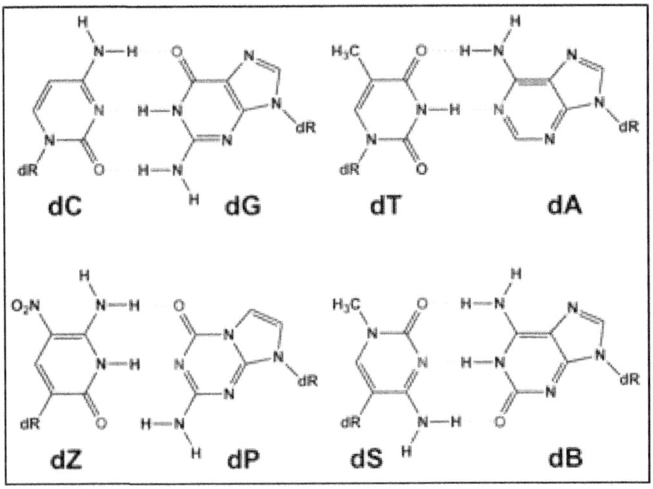

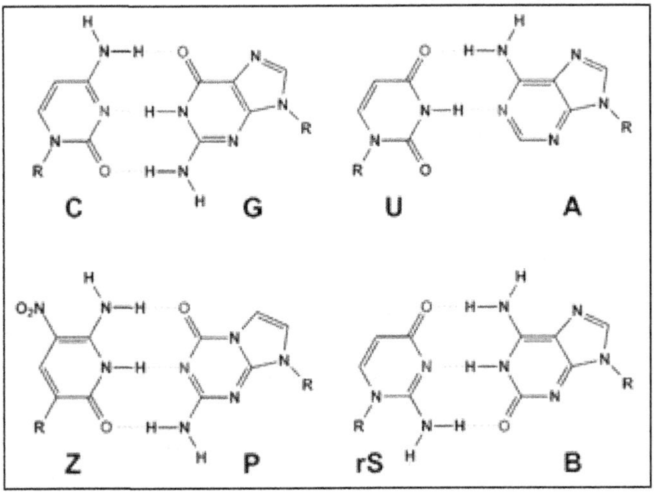

New Base Pairs

DNA and RNA are naturally composed of four nucleotide bases that form hydrogen bonds in order to pair. Hachimoji DNA uses an additional four synthetic nucleotides to form four types of base pairs, two of which are unnatural: **P** binds with **Z** and **B** binds with **S** (**dS** in DNA, **rS** in RNA).

Base		Name	Formula	Structure
P		2-Aminoimidazo[1,2a][1,3,5]triazin-4(1*H*)-one	$C_5H_5N_5O$	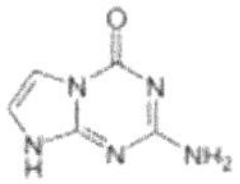
Z		6-Amino-5-nitropyridin-2-one	$C_5H_5N_3O_3$	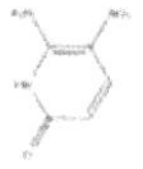
B		Isoguanine	$C_5H_5N_5O$	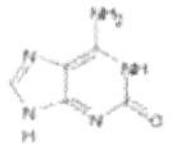
S	rS	Isocytosine	$C_4H_5N_3O$	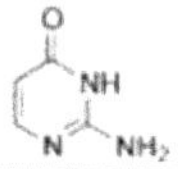
	dS	1-Methylcytosine	$C_5H_7N_3O$	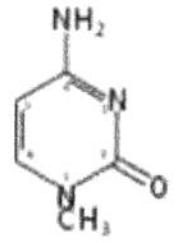

Hardy-Weinberg and Microevolution

Charles Darwin's Theory of Evolution touched briefly on favourable characteristics being passed down from parents to offspring. But the actual mechanism for that was flawed and **Gregor Mendel** did not publish his work until after Darwin's death to prove this. Both **Hardy** and **Weinberg** understood that natural selection occurred because of small changes within the genes of the species.

The focus of both Hardy's and Weinberg's work was on very small changes at a gene level, either due to chance or other circumstances that changed the gene pool of the population. The frequency at which certain alleles appeared changed over generations. This change in frequency of the alleles was the driving force behind evolution at a molecular level, or '***micro-evolution***'.

Hardy wanted to find an equation that would predict allele frequency in populations so he could find the probability of evolution occurring over a number of generations. Weinberg also independently worked toward the same solution. The **Hardy-Weinberg Equilibrium Equation** used the frequency of alleles to predict genotypes and track them over generations.

$$\mathbf{p^2 + 2pq + q^2 = 1} \quad \text{and} \quad \mathbf{p + q} = 1$$

where, in decimal format:

p = the frequency or percentage of the dominant allele
q = the frequency or percentage of the recessive allele

Since p is the frequency of all dominant alleles (**A**), it counts all of the homozygous dominant individuals (**AA**) and half of the heterozygous individuals (**A**a). Likewise, since q is the frequency of all recessive alleles (**a**), it counts all of the homozygous recessive individuals (**aa**) and half of the heterozygous individuals (A**a**). Therefore, p^2 stands for all homozygous dominant individuals, q^2 stands for all homozygous recessive individuals, and 2pq is all heterozygous individuals in a population. Everything is set equal to 1 because all individuals in a population equal 100 percent. This equation can accurately determine whether or not evolution has occurred between generations and in which direction the population is heading.

In order for this equation to work, it is assumed that all of the following conditions are not met at the same time:

- Mutation at a DNA level is not occurring.
- Natural selection is not occurring.
- The population is infinitely large.
- All members of the population are able to breed and do breed.
- All mating is totally random.
- All individuals produce the same number of offspring.
- There is no emigration or immigration occurring.

The list above describes causes of evolution. If all of these conditions are met at the same time, then there is no evolution occurring in a population. Since the Hardy-Weinberg **Equilibrium Equation** is used to predict evolution, a mechanism for evolution must be happening.

The **Hardy-Weinberg Law** states that 'In a large, random-mating population, the genotype and allele frequencies remain constant in the absence of any evolutionary influences from one to another generation'.

Burgess Shale

Burgess Shale is found in an area of the Canadian Rocky Mountains known as the Burgess Pass, and is located in British Columbia's Yoho National Park. Part of the ancient landmass called **Laurentia**, centred in Hudson Bay, the Burgess Shale represents one of the most diverse and well-preserved fossil localities in the world.

Burgess Shale contains the best record there is of Cambrian animal fossils. The locality reveals the presence of creatures originating from the Cambrian explosion, an evolutionary burst of animal origins dating **540 to 525 million years ago**.'

During this period, life was restricted to the world's oceans. The land was barren, uninhabited, and subject to erosion. These geologic conditions led to mudslides, where sediment periodically rolled into the seas and buried marine organisms. At the Burgess locality, sediment was deposited in a deep-water basin adjacent to an enormous **algal reef** with a vertical escarpment several hundred metres high.

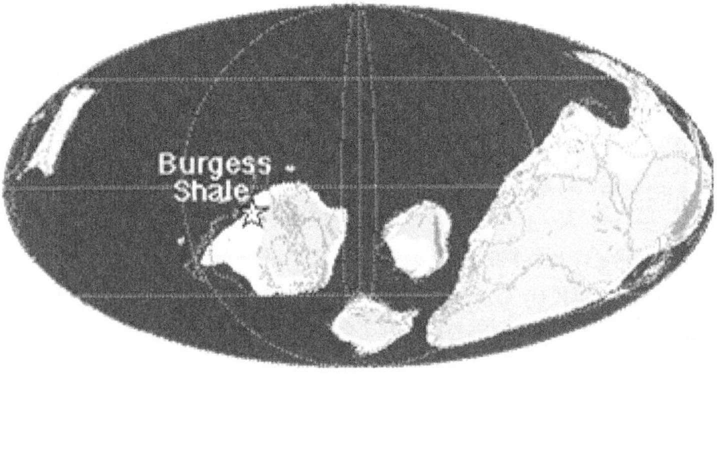

The map above shows the Earth as it was in the Cambrian (508 Mya). Location of the Burgess fauna is indicated by a star on the continent of Laurentia (western North America).

In 1909, Burgess Shale was discovered by Charles D. Walcott of the Smithsonian Institution. Walcott called Burgess Shale the 'fossil-bearing unit', but it received little attention until fifty years later.

Ultimately in 1960, there was a renewed interest to Walcott's work when members of Burgess Shale fauna were redefined. In 1967, a major project was initiated. Through additional work on the site, it was determined that Burgess Shale included multiple fossil bearing layers of about 2 metres thick stacked 150 metres high and over 60,000 unique fossils have been found.

The dominant fossils found are *arthropoda*, but other fossils are found in great abundance, including worms, *crinoids*, sea cucumbers, *chordates*, and other organisms with no mineralized shell. Most fossils were found in underwater banks known as the **'phyllopod beds'**.

Burgess fauna contains many fossils of **soft bodied animals** as well as those with hard parts. This is a tremendous opportunity for researchers because the soft bodied fossils are rarely found.

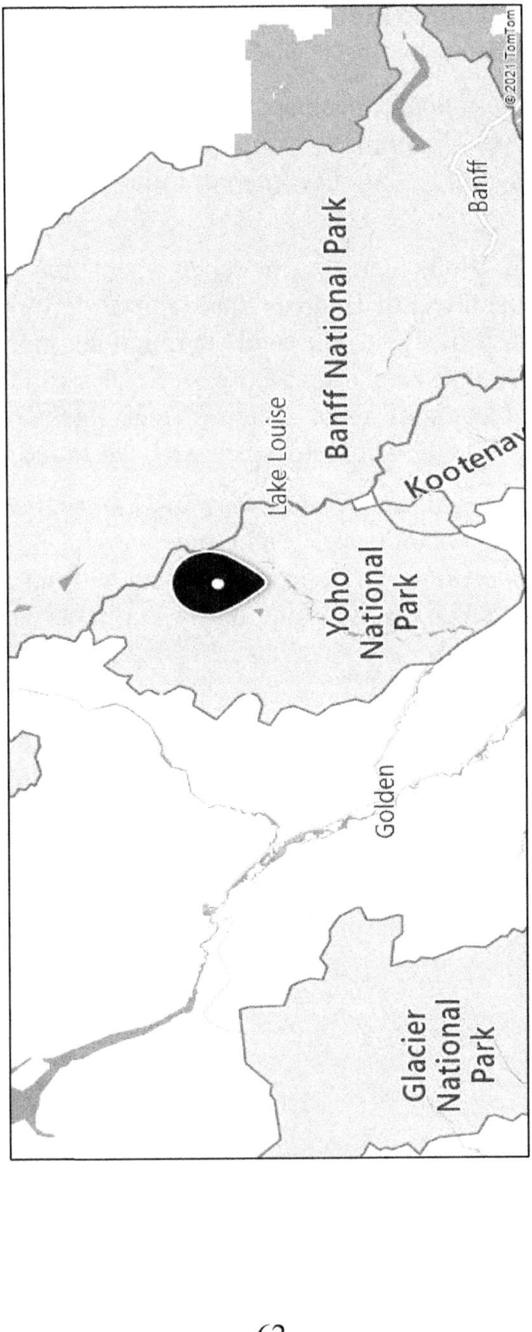

Banff National Park
Lake Louise
Banff
Yoho National Park
Golden
Glacier National Park
©2021 TomTom

Walcott's Classification of Burgess Arthropoda

1. Branchiopoda

Anostraca

Bidentia
Leanchoilia
Opabinia
Yohoia

Notostraca

Anomalocaris
Burgessia
Waptia

2. Malacostraca

Carnarvonia
Fieldia
Hurdia
Hymenocaris (Canadaspis)
Odaraia
Tuzoia

3. Trilobita

Marrella
Mollisonia
Naraoia
Nathorstia (Olenoides serratus)
Tontoia

4. Merostomata

Emeraldella
Habelia
Molaria
Sidneyia

Aysheaia pedunculata

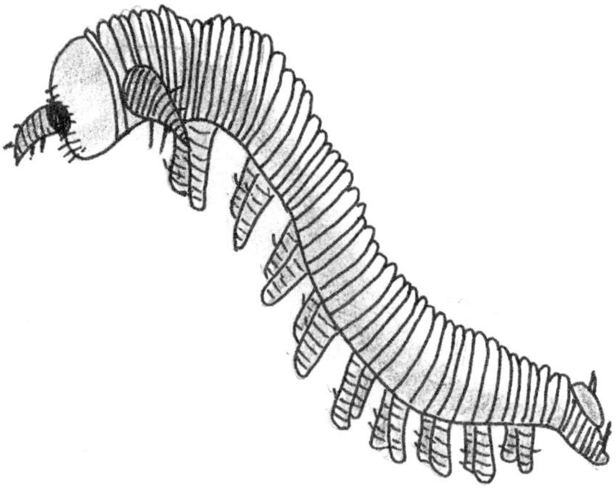

A. pedunculata has up to ten body segments, each of which has a pair of spiked, annulated legs. The animal is segmented, and looks somewhat like a bloated caterpillar with a few spines added on - including six finger-like projections around the mouth and two grasping legs on the 'head'. Each leg has a subterminal row of about six curved claws. No jaw apparatus is evident. A pair of legs marks the posterior end of the body, unlike in *onychophorans* where the anus projects posteriad; this may be an adaptation to the terrestrial habit.

Based on its association with sponge remains, it is believed that *A. pedunculata* was a sponge grazer and may have protected itself from predators by seeking refuge within sponge colonies. *A. pedunculata* probably used its claws to cling to sponges.

A terminal mouth is also seen in tardigrades that are omnivores or predators, but not detritovores or algivores. This may provide an ecological signal.

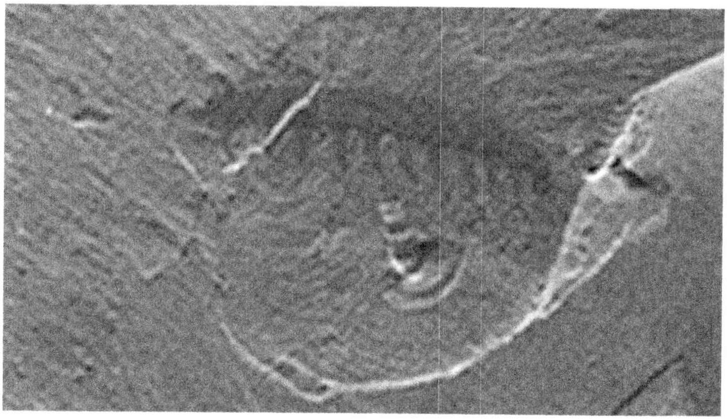

Fossil of A. pedunculata on display at NMNH   CC BY-SA 2.0

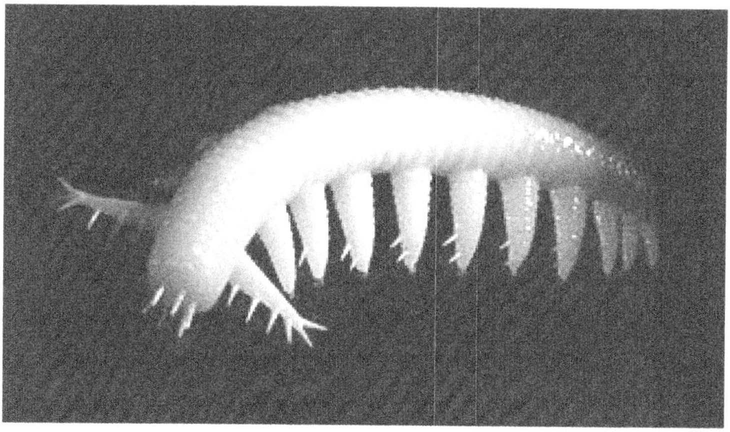

Reconstruction of A. pedunculata   CC BY-SA 2.0

Canadaspis perfecta

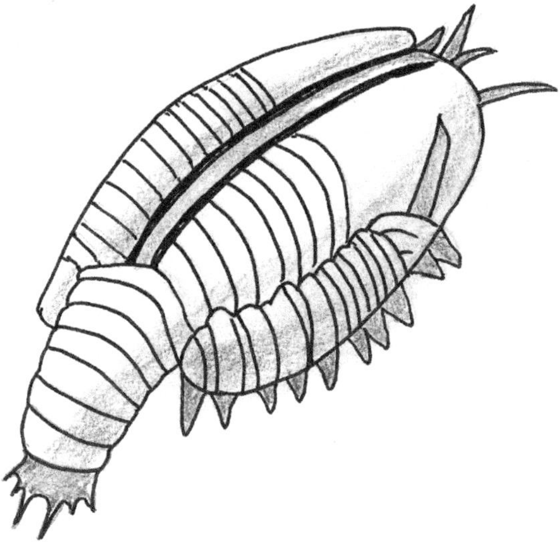

Canadaspis was an early representative of crabs, lobsters and shrimps. It was the second most common to be found in Burgess Shale and could be up to 7.5cms in length. The structure of the limbs indicated they were used primarily for walking.

The limbs allowed the animal to scrape and dig sediment in search of food. Outer flap-like limbs provide a mechanism for swimming by moving downwards in a wave like motion along the thorax.

These flaps were used in respiration by exchanging oxygen with the surroundings.

Specimen of Canadaspis perfecta from the Burgess Shale

Habelia

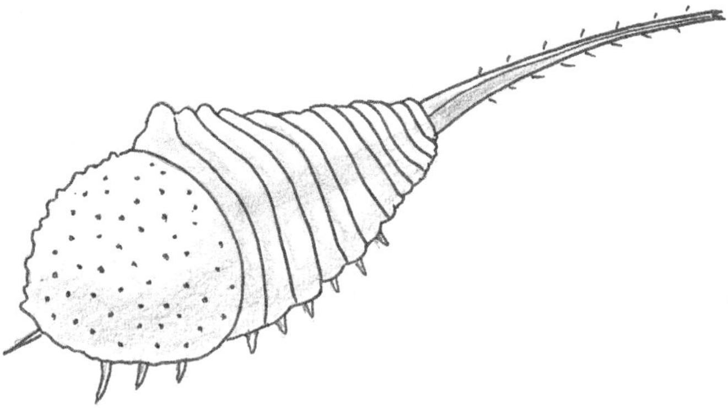

Habelia is a genus of extinct *arthropoda* from Middle Cambrian. Its fossils have been found in Burgess Shale. Fifty-four specimens of *Habelia* are known from the **greater phyllopod bed**, where they comprise 0.1% of the community.

While previously considered difficult to classify, a 2017 study found that this animal formed a clade (*Habeliida*) with *Sanctacaris, Utahcaris, Wisangocaris* and *Messorocaris* as a stem-group to *Chelicerata*.

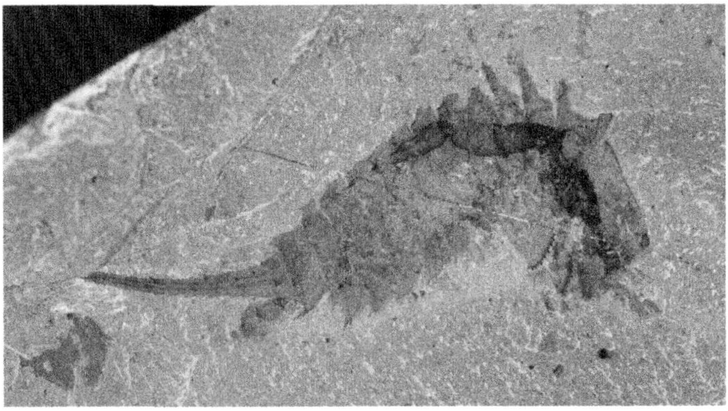

Hallucigenia

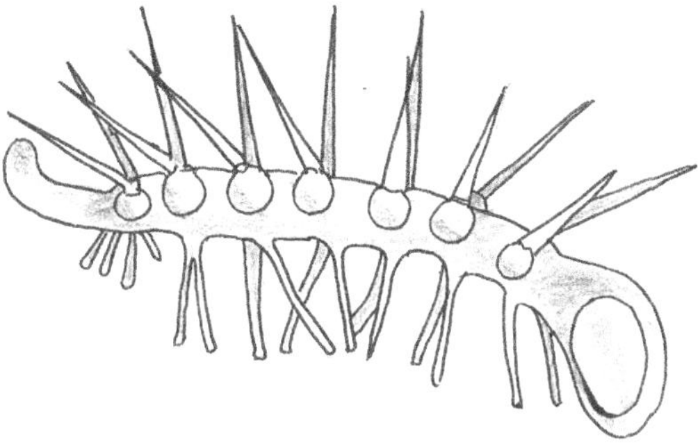

Hallucigenia is a genus of Cambrian animal known from articulated fossils both in Burgess Shale-type deposits as well as from isolated spines around the world.

The generic name reflects the type species unusual appearance and eccentric history of study. When it was classified as a genus, *H. sparsa* was reconstructed as an enigmatic animal upside down and back to front. *Hallucigenia* was later recognized as part of *lobopodians*, a grade of Paleozoic *panarthropods* where the velvet worms, water bears (*tardigrades)* and *arthropods* arose.

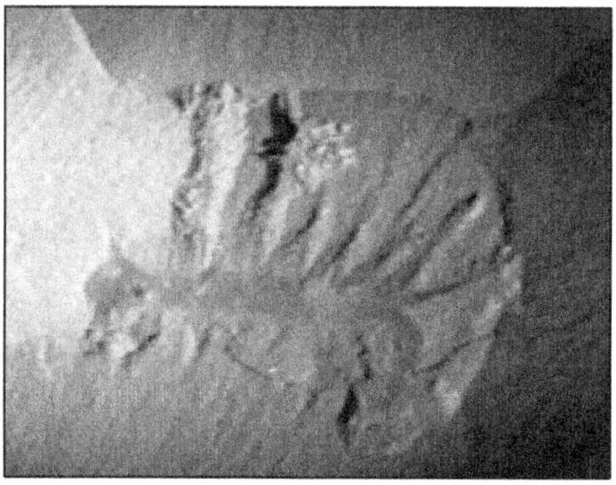

Fossil specimen of Hallucigenia from the Burgess Shale on display at the Smithsonian in Washington, DC

Marrella

Charles Walcott nicknamed this fossil the 'lace crab' and it is the most abundant of Burgess Shale animals.

Marrella itself is a small animal, 2cm or less in length. The head shield has two pairs of long rearward spikes. On the underside of the head are two pairs of antennae, one long and sweeping, the second shorter and stouter. *Marrella* has a body composed of 24–26 body segments, each with a pair of branched appendages.

The lower branch of each appendage is a leg for walking, while the upper branch is a long, feathery gill. There is a tiny, button-like *telson* at the end of the thorax. It is unclear how the unmineralized head and spines were stiffened.

Marrella has too many antennae, too few cephalic legs, and too few segments per leg to be a *trilobite*.

It lacks the three pairs of legs behind the mouth that are characteristic of *Crustacea*. The legs are also quite different from those of crustaceans, with the first pair modified into a single pair of pleopods with a copious blood supply.

The identification of a diffraction grating pattern on well-preserved *Marrella* specimens proves that it would have harboured an iridescent sheen - and thus would have appeared colourful. Dark stains are often present at the posterior regions of specimens, probably representing extruded waste matter or *hemolymph*.

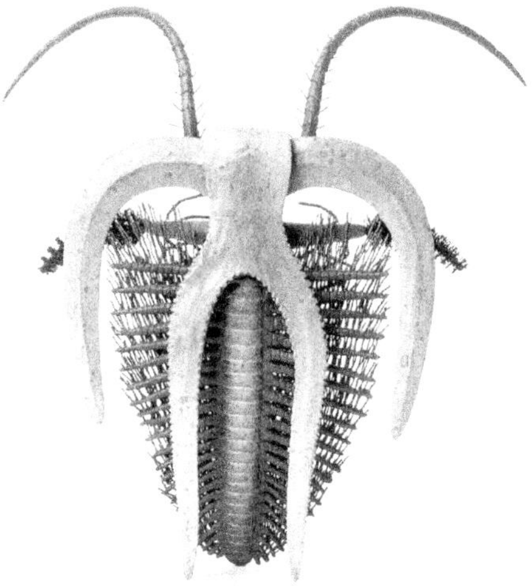

Life reconstruction of Marrella by the MUSE - Science Museum, in Trento
CC BY-SA 3.0

Marrella splendens

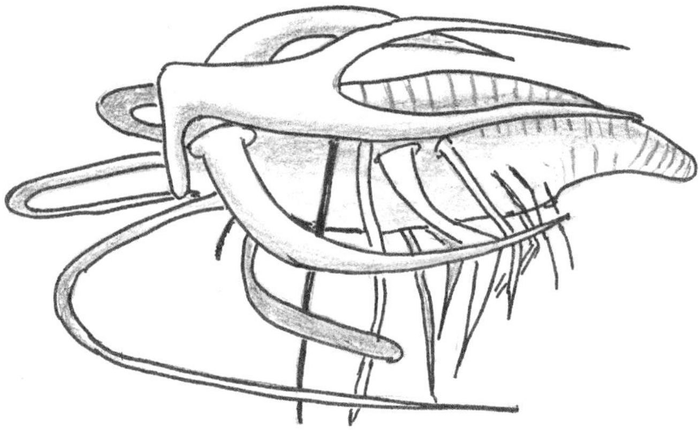

In the Burgess fauna ***Marrella*** is the most abundant creature found. The animal's length varied from 2.0mm to 1.9cm.

Marrella swam above the surface of the seabed feeding on organic material and small organisms.

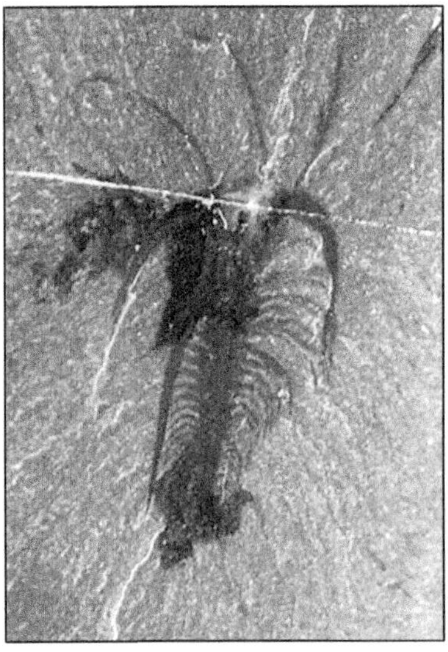

Marrella splendens *from the Middle Cambrian Burgess Shale in the collections of the Sedgwick Museum, Cambridge*
CC BY 2.5

Nectocaris pteryx

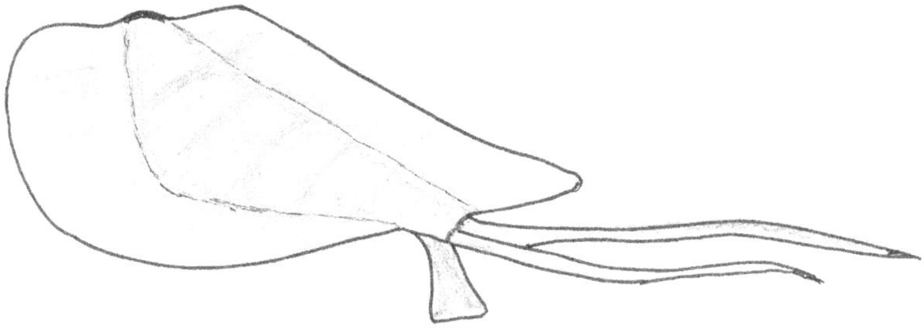

Nectocaris pteryx is a species of possible *cephalopod* known from the early Cambrian.

Nectocaris was a free-swimming, predatory or scavenging organism. This lifestyle is reflected in its binomial name: *Nectocaris* means ‘swimming shrimp’ (from the Ancient Greek νηκτόν, *nekton*, meaning ‘swimmer’ and καρίς, *karis*, ‘shrimp’; πτέρυξ, *pteryx*, means ‘wing’).

Two morphs are known, a small morph about an inch long, and a large morph anatomically identical but around four times longer.

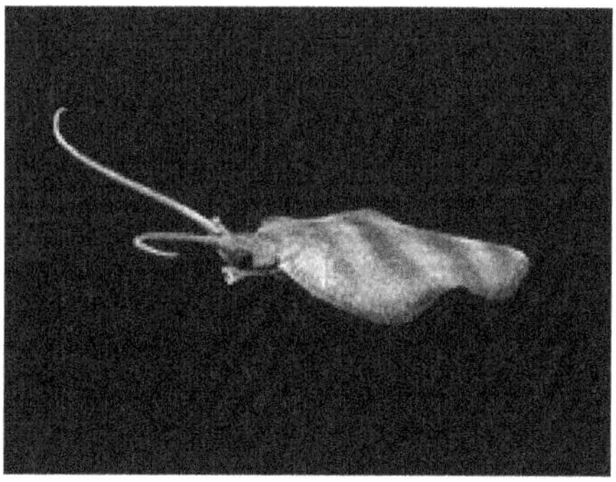

Life reconstruction of Nectocaris pteryx as a cephalopod

The closely related Ordovician taxon Nectocaris is a second genus, closely resembling Nectocaris, but possessing an internal skeletal element.

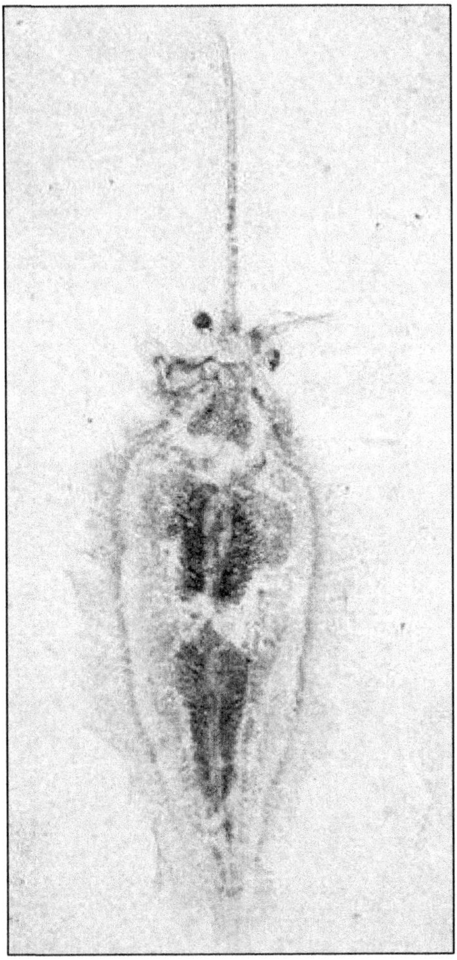

Nectocaris pteryx *from the Burgess Shale; funnel is visible folded to left of specimen. Image from Smith (2013). CC0*

Odontogriphus

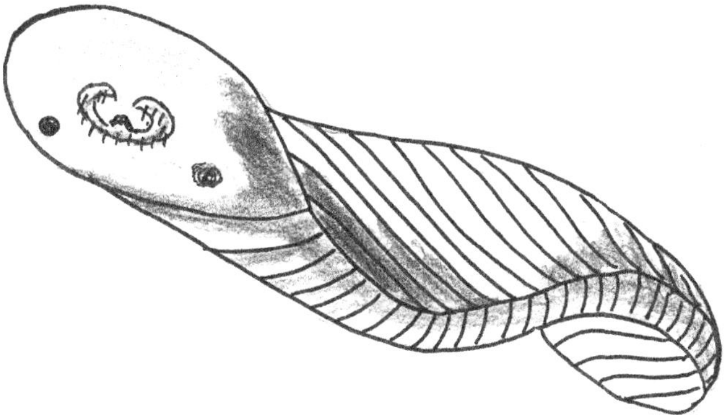

Odontogriphus (literally 'toothed riddle') is a genus of soft-bodied animals known from middle **Cambrian Lagerstätte**.

Reaching as much as 12.5cm in length, *Odontogriphus* is a flat, oval *bilaterian* which apparently had a single muscular foot and a 'shell' on its back that was moderately rigid but of a material unsuited to fossilization.

Odontogriphus from Burgess Shale ROM 57723 (Fig. 8B in Smith 2013) CC0

Olenoides

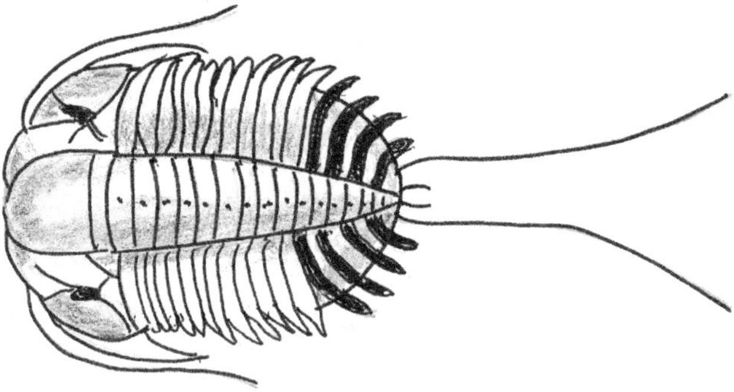

Olenoides followed the basic structure of all *trilobites* with a *cephalon* (head shield), a thorax with seven jointed parts, and finally a semicircular *pygidium*.

Its antennae were long, and curved back along its sides. Its thin legs show that it was no swimmer, instead crawling along the sea floor in search of prey.

Its major characteristics are a large parallel-sided *glabella*, deep interpleural furrows on the *pygidium*, and slender pygidial spines, as well as the fact that it is the most common limb-bearing *trilobite* species in Burgess Shale.

An exceptionally well preserved Olenoides serratus from the Burgess Shale. The antennae and legs are preserved as reflective carbon film CC BY 2.5

Opabinia regalis

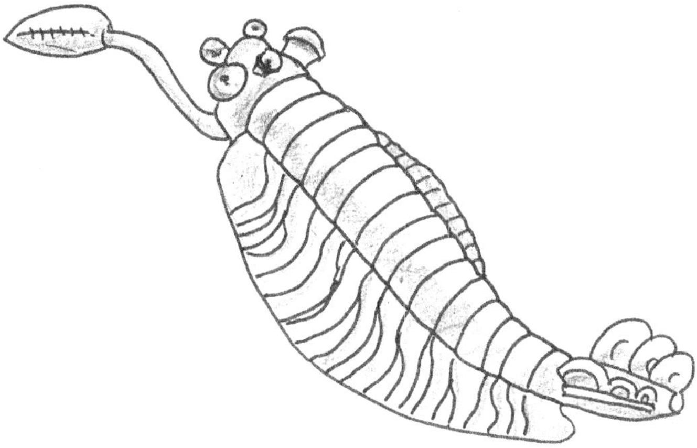

Opabinia existed on the soft sediment of the seafloor where it swam around using its lateral lobes.

The head consisted of **five eyes** on the dorsal section that were used to look for prey. The animal's length varied up to 7.5cm excluding the *proboscis* which was 2.5cm.

The *proboscis* was a long flexible appendage at the anterior of the body which ended in a spiny grasping structure. The creature could use its *proboscis* to search in sand burrows for worms.

With **five eyes** and a front-end 'nozzle', ***Opabinia*** remains an oddity. It swam with the help of its 15 pairs of paddle-shaped flaps, and it may have used its flexible 'trunk' to pull worms from their burrows.

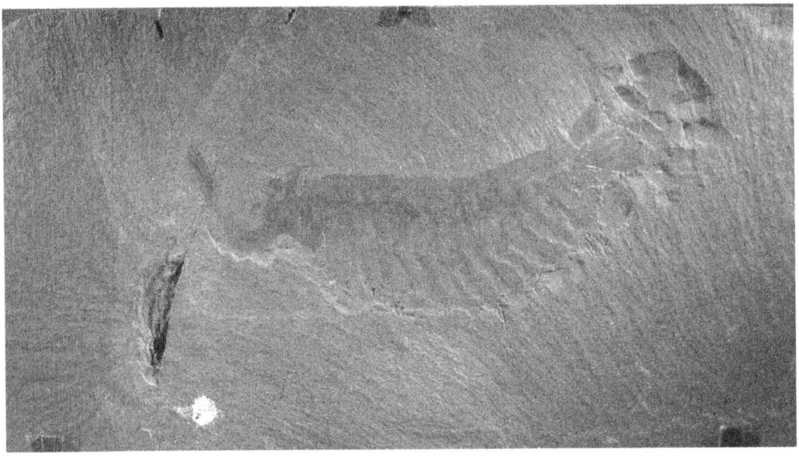

Fossil specimen of Opabinia regalis from the Burgess Shale on display at the Smithsonian in Washington, DC.

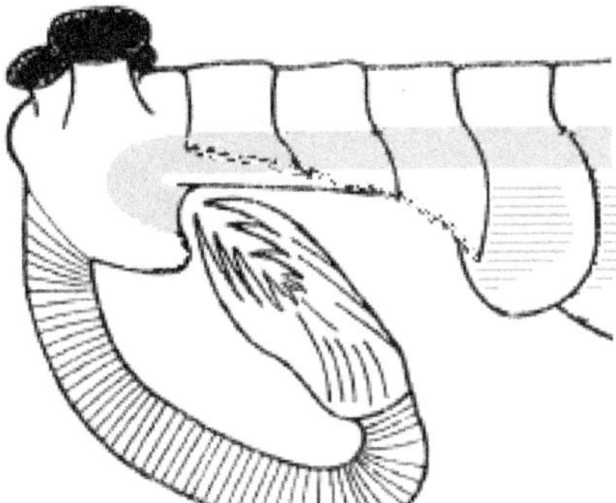

***Opabinia** head – foremost lobes and gills cut away to show proboscis passing food to mouth*

Ovatiovermis

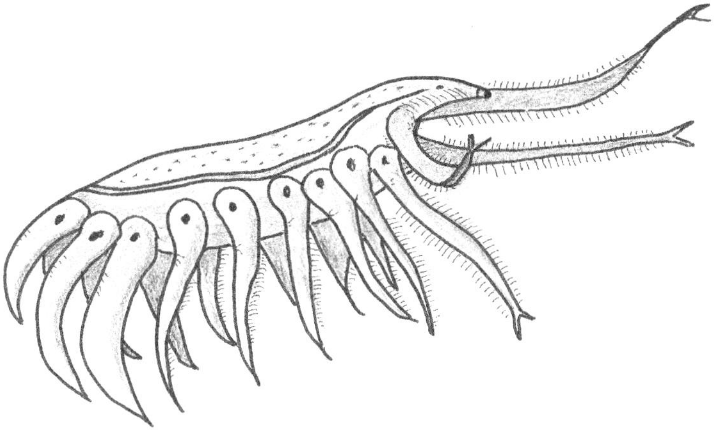

Ovatiovermis is a genus of filter-feeding *lobopodian*. It had nine pairs of *lobopods*; the first two pairs were elongate and had approximately 20 pairs of spines on each *lobopod,* with a *bifid claw* at each tip. The third to sixth pairs of *lobopods* were shorter and their paired spines were much smaller. On these four pairs of *lobopods* the spines were only large near the tip. The last three pairs of *lobopods* did not have the paired spines, showing that these spines were used for filter-feeding. Instead these *lobopods* had *talons* with which it could grip one of the *corals* or *sponges* found at the time and rear up into the current.

At the anterior end of the animal it had an *evertible proboscis*, with its mouth at the end. This would probably have been used to suck any particles of food which had been caught off the spines, possibly in a similar manner to a *sea cucumber*. Its head was not well separated from the body. Also on the head *Ovatiovermis* had two small and probably very primitive visual organs each measuring 0.1mm in diameter.

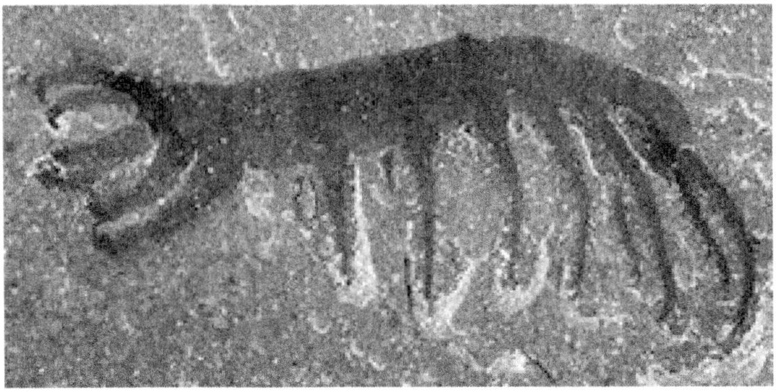

Life restoration of Ovatiovermis cribratus

Pikaia gracilens

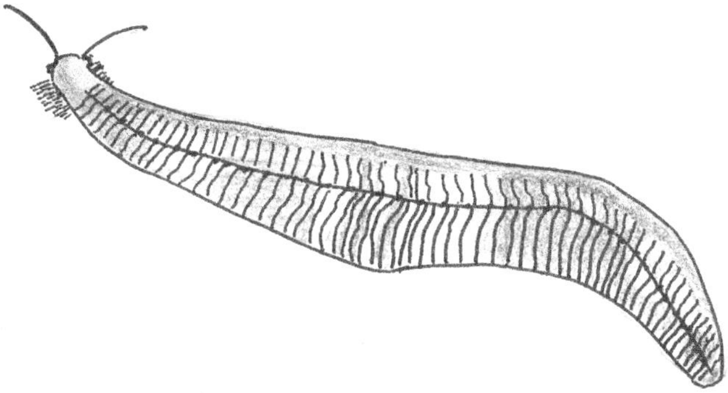

Pikaia is one of the earliest members of the phylum *Chordata*, the group to which all animals with backbones and spinal cords belong. It swam close to the sea floor and may have been a filter feeder.

Pikaia resembled the modern *lancelet*, and was the earliest known *chordate* until the discovery of the fish-like *Myllokunmingia* and *Haikouichthys* among the Chengjiang fauna.

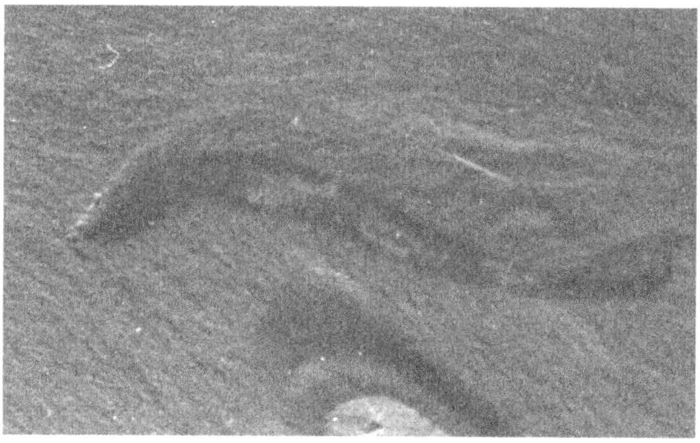

Fossil specimen on display at the Smithsonian in Washington, D.C.

Sanctacaris

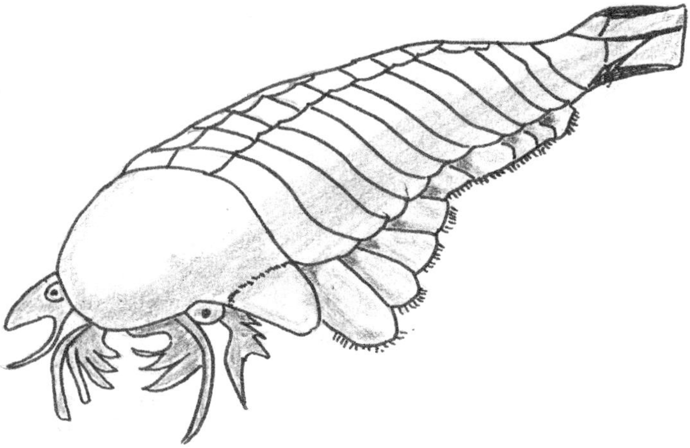

Sanctacaris grew up to 10cm in length and its body was made up of up to 11 segments each with a pair of legs and gills.

The first five spiny mouth appendages at the posterior allow the animal to capture prey.

The animal used the *telson* for balance and steering. This indicates swimming was the dominant form of movement.

Specimen of Sanctacaris Uncata on display in the Royal Ontario Museum, Toronto. Captmondo CC BY-SA 3.0

Wiwaxia corrugata

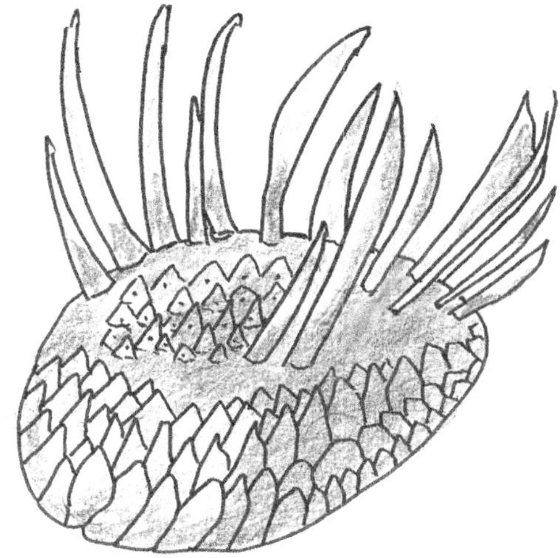

Wiwaxia is a genus of soft-bodied animals that were covered in carbonaceous scales and spines that protected it from predators.

Wiwaxia fossils are mainly in the form of isolated scales, but sometimes complete. Articulated fossils are known from early Cambrian and middle Cambrian fossil deposits across the globe.

Wiwaxia was *bilaterally symmetrical.* Viewed from the top the body was elliptical with no distinct head or tail, and from the front or rear it was almost rectangular. It reached 5cm in length.

Estimating their height is difficult because specimens were compressed after death. A typical specimen may have been 1cm high excluding the spines on their backs. The ratio of width to length does not appear to change as the animals grew.

Wiwaxia corrugata *from the Burgess Shale. Mature specimen, with incipient spines, and partial scleritome exposing underlying tissue. CC0 Smith.*

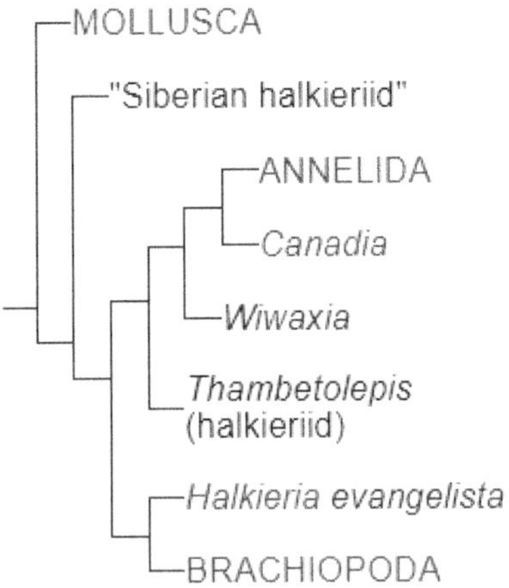

Cladogram:Conway Morris & Peel (1995)

Konservat-Lagerstätten

A ***Konservat-Lagerstätte*** (conservation 'storage place') is a sedimentary deposit that exhibits extraordinary fossils with exceptional preservation, sometimes including preserved soft tissues. These formations may have resulted from carcass burial in an anoxic environment with minimal bacteria.

Precambrian		
Bitter Springs	1000–850 Mya	South Australia
Doushantuo Formation	600–555 Mya	Guizhou Province, China
Mistaken Point	565 Mya	Newfoundland, Canada
Ediacara Hills	550–545? Mya	South Australia
Cambrian		
Qingjiang biota	518 Mya	Hubei province, China
Sirius Passet	518 Mya	Greenland
Maotianshan Shales (Chengjiang)	515 Mya	Yunnan Province, China
Emu Bay Shale	513 Mya	South Australia
Kaili Formation	513–501 Mya	Guizhou province, south-west China
Blackberry Hill	~510–500 Mya	Central Wisconsin, US
Burgess Shale	508 Mya	British Columbia, Canada
Spence Shale	507 Mya	Northeastern Utah, Southeastern Idaho, US
Wheeler Shale (House Range)	504 Mya	Western Utah, US
Marjum Formation	502 Mya	Western Utah, US
Weeks Formation	500 Mya	Western Utah, US
Kinnekulle Orsten and Alum Shale	500 Mya	Sweden
Ordovician		
Fezouata Formation	about 485 Mya	Draa Valley, Morocco
Douglas Dam Member	460 Mya	Douglas Dam, Tennessee
Beecher's Trilobite Bed	460? Mya	New York, US
Walcott-Rust Quarry	about 455? Mya	New York, US
Soom Shale	450? Mya	South Africa
Silurian		
Waukesha Biota	~435 Mya	Southeastern Wisconsin, US
Coalbrookdale Formation	~430 Mya	Herefordshire, England–Wales border, UK

Devonian

Rhynie chert	400 Mya	Scotland, UK
Hunsrück Slates (Bundenbach)	390 Mya	Rheinland-Pfalz, Germany
Gogo Formation	380 Mya (Frasnian)	Western Australia
Miguasha National Park	370 Mya	Québec, Canada
Canowindra, New South Wales	360 Mya	Australia
Waterloo Farm lagerstätte	360 Mya	South Africa

Carboniferous

Bear Gulch Limestone	320 Mya	Montana, US
Joggins Fossil Cliffs	315 Mya	Nova Scotia, Canada
Linton Diamond Coal Mine[	312 Mya	Ohio, US
Mazon Creek	310 Mya	Illinois, US
Montceau-les-Mines[	300 Mya	France
Hamilton Quarry	300 Mya	Kansas, US

Permian

Mangrullo Formation	about 285–275 Mya (Artinskian)	Uruguay

Triassic

Madygen Formation	230 Mya	Kyrgyzstan
Cow Branch Formation	230 Mya	Virginia, US
Ghost Ranch	205 Mya	New Mexico, US

Jurassic

Holzmaden/Posidonia Shale	183 Mya	Württemberg, Germany
Mesa Chelonia	164.6 Mya	Shanshan County, China
La Voulte-sur-Rhône	160 Mya	Ardèche, France
Karabastau Formation	155.7 Mya	Kazakhstan
Tiaojishan Formation	165-153 Mya	Liaoning Province, China
Cleveland-Lloyd Dinosaur Quarry	150 Mya	Utah, US
Solnhofen Limestone	145 Mya	Bavaria, Germany
Canjuers Limestone	145 Mya	France
Agardhfjellet Formation	150-140 Mya	Spitsbergen, Norway

Cretaceous

Las Hoyas	about 125 Mya (Barremian)	Cuenca, Spain
Yixian Formation	about 125–121 Mya	Liaoning, China
Shengjinkou Formation	about 120 Mya	Xinjiang, China
Xiagou Formation	about 120–115? Mya (mid-Apt.)	Gansu, China
Paja Formation	130-113 Mya	Colombia
Crato Formation	c117 Mya (Aptian)	northeast Brazil

Haqel/Hjoula/al-Nammoura	about 95 Mya	Lebanon
Santana Formation	108–92 Mya	Brazil
Smoky Hill Chalk	87–82 Mya	Kansas and Nebraska, US
Ingersoll Shale	85 Mya	Alabama, US
Auca Mahuevo	80 Mya	Patagonia, Argentina
Zhucheng	66 Mya	Shandong, China
Tanis	66 Mya	North Dakota, US
Eocene		
Fur Formation	55–53 Mya	Fur, Denmark
London Clay	54–48 Mya	England, UK
McAbee Fossil Beds	52.9 ± 0.83 Mya	British Columbia, Canada
Green River Formation	50 Mya	Colorado/Utah/Wyoming, US
Klondike Mountain Formation	49.4 ± .5 Mya	Washington, US
Monte Bolca	49 Mya	Verona, Italy
Messel Oil Shale	49 Mya	Hessen, Germany
Quercy Phosphorites Formation	25–45 Mya	South-Western France
Oligocene–Miocene		
Dominican amber	30–10 Mya	Dominican Republic
Riversleigh	25–15 Mya	Queensland, Australia
Miocene		
Foulden Maar	23 Mya	Otago, New Zealand
Chiapas amber	23-15 Mya	Chiapas, Mexico
Clarkia fossil beds	20-17 Mya	Idaho, US
Barstow Formation	19–13.4 Mya	California, US
Shanwang Formation	18-17 Mya	Shandong Province, China
Ashfall Fossil Beds	11.83 Mya	Nebraska, US
Pisco Formation	15-2 Mya	Arequipa & Ica, Peru
McGraths Flat	~11-16 Mya	NSW, Australia[12]
Pleistocene		
The Mammoth Site	26 Kya	South Dakota, US
Rancho La Brea Tar Pits	40–12 Kya	California, US
Waco Mammoth National Monument	65–51 Kya	Texas, US
El Breal de Orocual	2.5–1 Mya	Monagas, Venezuela
El Mene de Inciarte	25.5–28 Kya	Zulia, Venezuela

Evolution of the Eye

The basic light-processing unit of eyes is the photoreceptor cell, a specialized cell containing two types of molecules in a membrane: the **opsin**, a light-sensitive protein, surrounding the **chromophore**, a **pigment** that distinguishes colours. Groups of such cells are termed **'eyespots'**, and have evolved independently somewhere between 40 and 65 times. These eyespots permit animals to gain only a very basic sense of the direction and intensity of light, but not enough to discriminate an object from its surroundings.

Developing an optical system that can discriminate the direction of light to within a few degrees is apparently much more difficult, and only six of the thirty-some phyla possess such a system. However, these phyla account for 96% of living species.

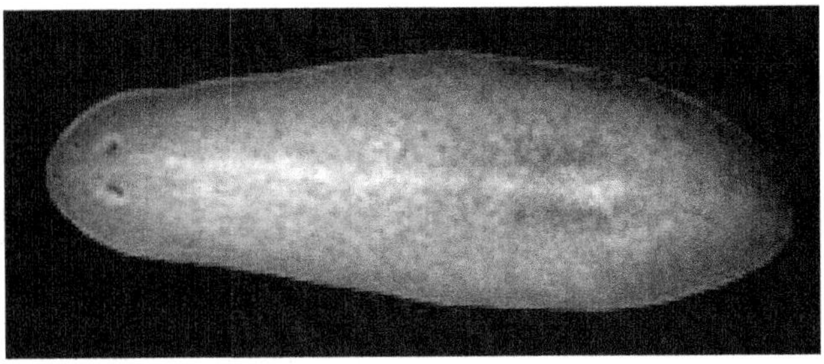

*The **planarian** has 'cup' eyespots that can slightly distinguish light direction.*

These complex optical systems started out as the multicellular eye-patch gradually depressed into a *cup*, which first granted the ability to discriminate brightness in directions, then in finer and finer directions as the pit deepened (a) (b).

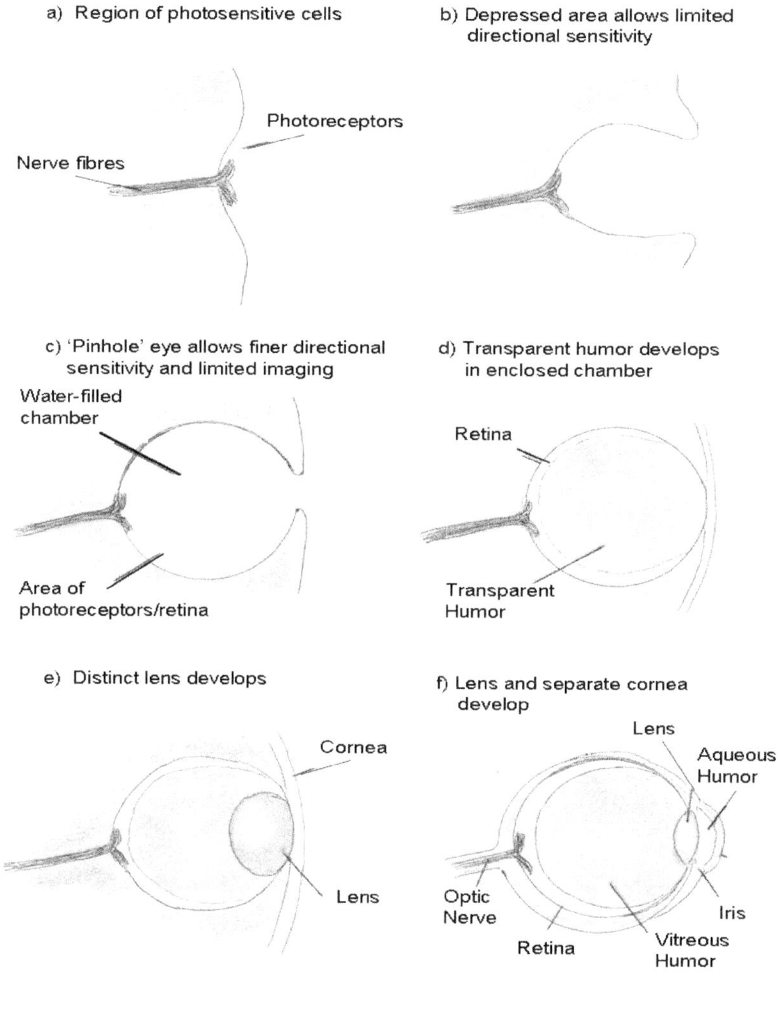
a) Region of photosensitive cells
Photoreceptors
Nerve fibres
b) Depressed area allows limited directional sensitivity
c) 'Pinhole' eye allows finer directional sensitivity and limited imaging
Water-filled chamber
Area of photoreceptors/retina
d) Transparent humor develops in enclosed chamber
Retina
Transparent Humor
e) Distinct lens develops
Cornea
Lens
f) Lens and separate cornea develop
Lens
Aqueous Humor
Optic Nerve
Iris
Retina
Vitreous Humor

While flat eye-patches were ineffective at determining the direction of light, as a beam of light would activate exactly the same patch of photo-sensitive cells regardless of its direction, the cup shape of the pit eyes allowed limited directional differentiation by changing which cells the lights would hit depending upon the light's angle. Pit eyes, which had arisen by the **Cambrian** period, were seen in ancient snails, and are found in some snails and other invertebrates living today, such as *Planaria*.

Planaria can slightly differentiate the direction and intensity of light because of their cup-shaped, heavily pigmented **retina cells**, which shield the light-sensitive cells from exposure in all directions except for the single opening for the light. However, this proto-eye is still much more useful for detecting the absence or presence of light than its direction; this gradually changes as the eye's pit deepens and the number of photoreceptive cells grows, allowing for increasingly precise visual information (c).

When a **photon** is absorbed by the **chromophore**, a chemical reaction causes the photon's energy to be transduced into electrical energy and relayed, in higher animals, to the **nervous system**. These photoreceptor cells form part of the **retina**, a thin layer of cells that relays visual information, including the light and day-length information needed by the **circadian rhythm system**, to the brain.

However, some jellyfish, such as *Cladonema*, have elaborate eyes, but no brain. Their eyes transmit a message directly to the muscles without the intermediate processing provided by a brain.

During the Cambrian explosion, the development of the eye accelerated rapidly, with radical improvements in image-processing and detection of light direction.

*A colony of **Cladonema radiatum**, magnified. The drawing has been made from the free variety of this hydroid.*

George James Allman - Allman G. J. The Monograph of the Gymnoblastic or Tubularian Hydroids. – Conclusion of Part I and Part II. – London: Robert Hardwicke, 1872.

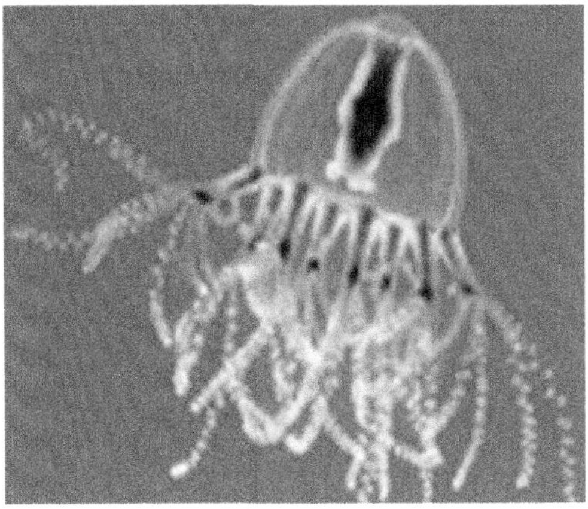

The primitive ***Nautilus*** *eye functions similar to a pinhole camera (c).*

After the photosensitive cell region invaginated, there came a point when reducing the width of the light opening became more efficient at increasing visual resolution than continued deepening of the cup. By reducing the size of the opening, organisms achieved true imaging, allowing for fine directional sensing and even some shape-sensing. Eyes of this nature are currently found in the *Nautilus*.

Lacking a cornea or lens, they provide poor resolution and dim imaging, but are still, for the purpose of vision, a major improvement over the early eye patches.

Overgrowths of transparent cells prevented contamination and parasitic infestation. The chamber contents, now segregated, could slowly specialize into a transparent humour, for optimizations such as colour filtering, higher **refractive index**, blocking of **ultraviolet** radiation, or the ability to operate in and out of water (d).

The layer may, in certain cases, be related to the 'molting' of the organism's shell or skin. An example of this can be observed in *Onychophorans* where the *cuticula* of the shell continues to the cornea.

The cornea is composed of either one or two cuticular layers depending on how recently the animal has molted (e).

Along with the lens and two humors, the cornea is responsible for converging light and aiding the focusing of it on the back of the retina. The cornea protects the eyeball while at the same time accounting for approximately 2/3 of the eye's total refractive power (f).

Head of ***Nautilus pompilius*** *showing the rudimentary eye, which functions similarly to a pinhole camera.* *CC BY-SA 4.0*

It is likely that a key reason eyes specialize in detecting a specific, narrow visible range of wavelengths on the electromagnetic spectrum is because the earliest species to develop photosensitivity were aquatic, and only two specific wavelength ranges of electromagnetic radiation, blue and green visible light, can travel through water.

This same light-filtering property of water also influenced the photosensitivity of plants.

Trilobite's Eyes

Even the earliest *trilobites* had complex, compound eyes with lenses made of calcite (calcium carbonate, $CaCO_3$). This is a characteristic of all *trilobite* eyes) which points to the fact that eyes of *arthropods* and probably other animals could have developed before the Cambrian.

Trilobite eyes were typically *compound*, with each lens being an elongated prism. The number of lenses in such an eye varied: some *trilobites* had only one, while some had thousands of lenses in a single eye. In compound eyes, the lenses were typically arranged hexagonally.

Lenses of *trilobite* eyes were made of pure forms of transparent calcite, and some trilobites used crystallographically oriented, clear calcite crystals to form lens of each eye.

Rigid calcite lenses would have been unable to accommodate to a change of focus like the soft lens in a human eye can. In some *trilobites*, the calcite formed an internal **doublet structure**, giving superb **depth of field** and minimal **spherical aberration**, according to optical principles discovered by French scientist **René Descartes** and Dutch physicist **Christiaan Huygens** in the 17th century.

In other *trilobites*, with a Huygens interface apparently missing, a **gradient-index lens** is invoked with the **refractive index** of the lens changing toward the centre.

Compound eyes in living *arthropods* such as **insects** are very **sensitive to motion**, and it is likely that they were similarly important in **predator detection** in *trilobites*.

It has also been suggested that **stereoscopic vision** was provided by closely spaced, but separate eyes. **Vertebrate lenses** can change shape (accommodate) to focus on objects at varying distances.

Trilobite eyes, in contrast, had **rigid, crystalline lenses**, and therefore no accommodation.

Instead, an internal '**doublet structure**' (two lens layers of different refractive indices acting in combination) corrected for focusing problems that resulted from rigid lenses.

The shapes of some *trilobite* lenses, in fact, match those derived by optical scientists over 300 million years later to answer similar needs. The result is that, even without the benefit of accommodation, the rigid *trilobite* doublet lens had remarkable **depth of field** (that is, allowed for objects both near and far to remain in relatively good focus) with minimal **spherical aberration** (distortion of image).

Photo credit: MLF

Box Jellyfish – Eye Structures

The eyes of Box Jellyfish can be divided into two broad categories according to their functions. The first category includes the complete eyes that are capable to form images and actually enable the box jellyfish to see specific light points. They are four in number.

Box Jellyfish can detect its habitat using these proper eyes from a distance of 10m. Beside the eyes that can form images, box jellyfish has twenty *ocelli* or simple eyes that are only capable to distinguish between darkness and light.

So, how do the jellyfish stay in the right place? They use their "upper lens eyes," four eyes which can see through the water's surface and into the space above. These eyes allow them to spot the mangrove canopy at distances of at least eight meters, and navigate towards them.

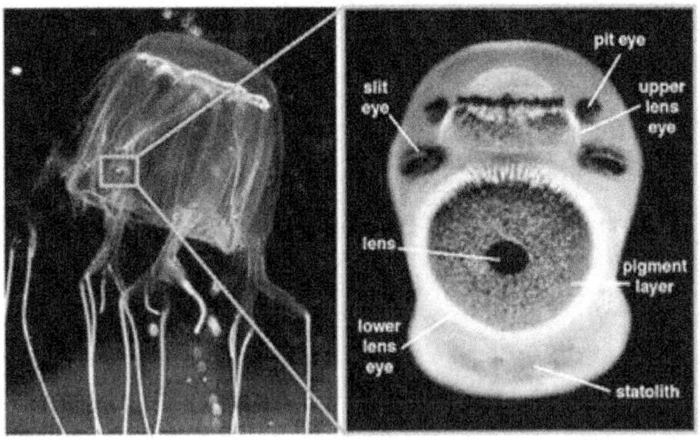

Ocelli

Ocelli (singular **Ocellus**) are simple photo-receptors (light detecting organs). They consist of a single lens and several sensory cells.

Unlike compound eyes, ocelli do not form a complex image of the environment but are used to detect movement. Most arthropods possess ocelli. Some species of arthropod do not possess compound eyes and only have ocelli.

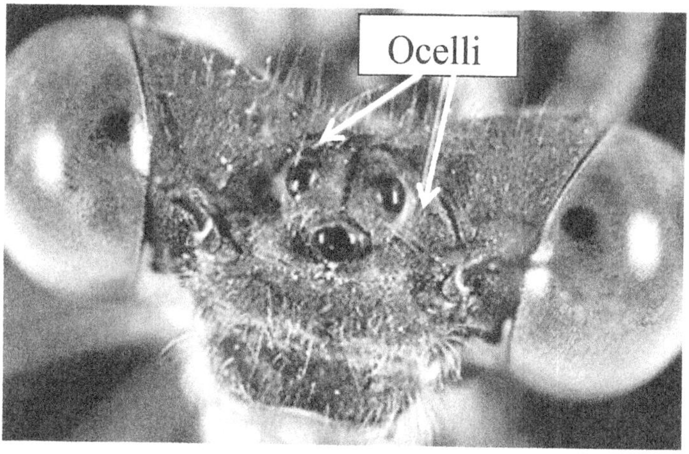

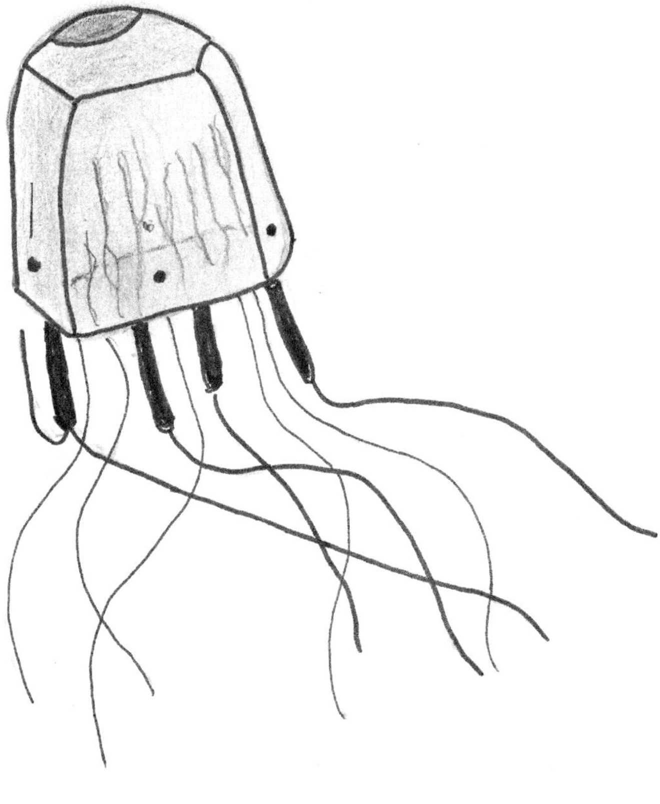

Chironex fleckeri (Box Jellyfish)
Tripedalia cystophora (Small Box Jellyfish)

Doublet Lens Structure

Christian Huygens (1629–95) and **Rene Descartes**, (1596-1650) were the first to independently solve the problem of spherical aberration in a lens, with a **doublet lens structure**.

However, evolution had already solved this problem millions of years earlier in the *trilobites*.

A **doublet** is a type of lens made up of two simple lenses paired together. It is this arrangement of lenses that provides remarkable depth of field with minimal spherical aberration

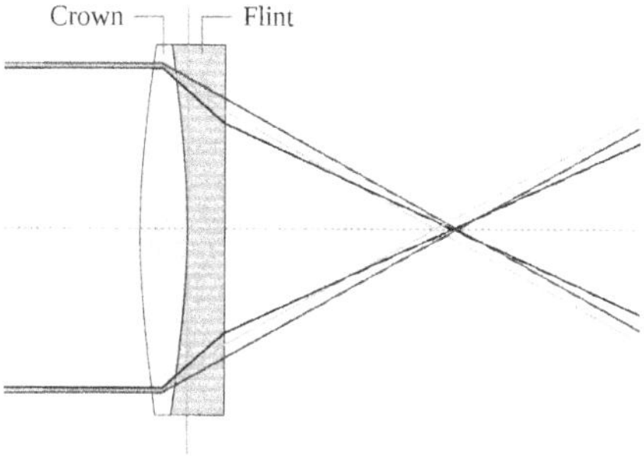

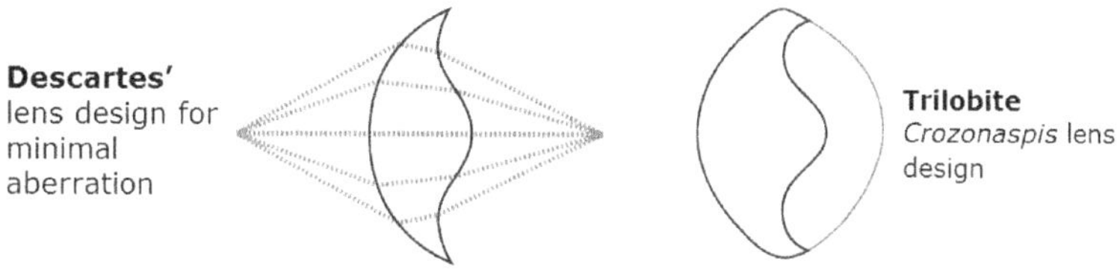

Light ray paths (dotted lines) entering the lens from the left come into focus a short distance to the right of the lens
In the eye of *Crozonaspis*, an intralensar body (white) further corrects focus after passing through the outer lens layer (grey).

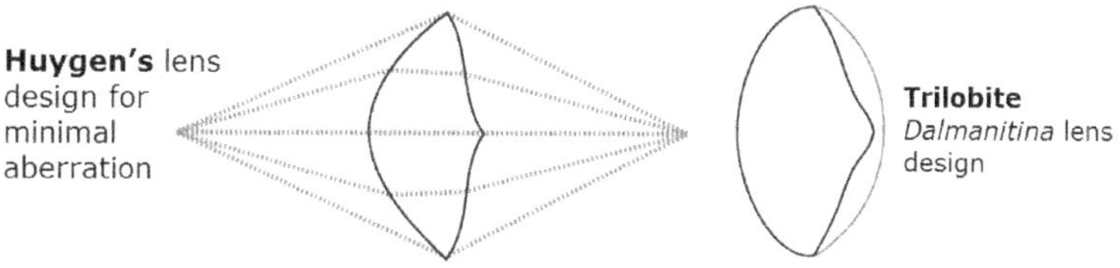

ref: ***Clarkson, E. N. K. 1975**. The evolution of the eye in trilobites. Fossils and Strata 4:7-31.*

Scallop's Eyes

The earliest known records of true scallops (*Argopecten irradians)* can be found from the Triassic, over 250 million years ago. The earliest species were divided into two groups, one with a nearly smooth exterior, *Pleuronectis*, while the other had radial ribs or *riblets* and auricles, *Praechlamys*. Fossil records also indicate that the abundance of species within the *Pectinidae* has varied greatly over time. Nearly 7,000 species and subspecies names have been introduced for both fossil and recent *Pectinidae*.

Fossil scallop Chlamys with encrusters. Nicosia Formation (Pliocene) of Cyprus CC0

Scallops have a large number (up to 200) of small (about 1mm) eyes arranged along the edge of their mantles.

These eyes represent a particular innovation among molluscs, relying on a concave, parabolic mirror of **guanine crystals** to focus and retro-reflect light instead of a lens as found in many other eye types.

Additionally, their eyes possess a double-layered retina, the outer retina responding most strongly to light and the inner to abrupt darkness.

While these eyes are unable to resolve shapes with high fidelity, the combined sensitivity of both retinas to light entering the eye and light retro-reflected from the mirror grants scallops exceptional contrast definition, as well as the ability to detect changing patterns of light and motion.

Scallops primarily rely on their eyes as an 'early-warning' threat detection system, scanning around them for movement and shadows which could potentially indicate predators. Additionally, some scallops alter their swimming or feeding behaviour based on the turbidity or clarity of the water, by detecting the movement of particulate matter in the water column.

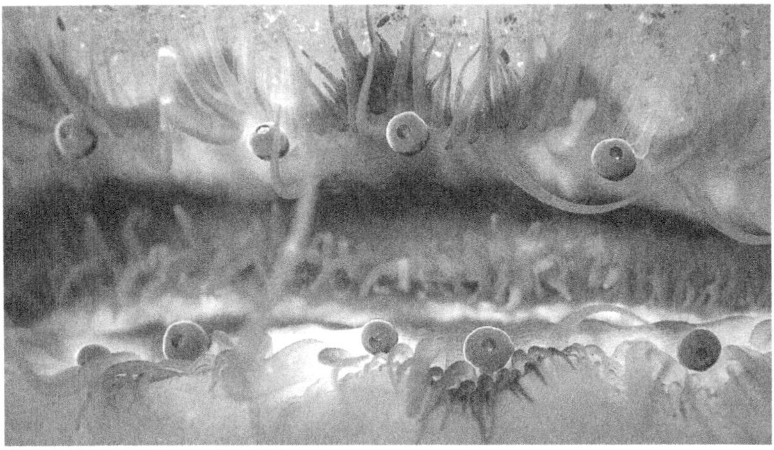

Close-up of the iridescent blue eyes of Argopecten irradians *Matthew Krummins* *CC-BY-2.0*

Argopecten irradians, photographed at the Marine Biological Laboratory in Woods Hole *PD*

Housefly's Eyes

The **housefly** (*Musca domestica)* is a fly of the suborder *Cyclorrhapha*, believed to have evolved in the Cenozoic.

The head is strongly convex in front and flat and slightly conical behind. The compound eyes each contain as many as 28,000 light-sensitive structures called *ommatidia* grouped under the *cornea*.

Each *ommatidium* contains a cluster of photoreceptor cells surrounded by support cells and pigment cells, and provides the fly's brain with one picture element.

The *cornea* in turn is composed of an equal number of hexagonal prism-shaped structures, each forming a separate image. The final image thus formed is actually like a mosaic image.

The pair of large compound eyes almost touch in the male, but are more widely separated in the female. Additionally, they have three simple eyes (*ocelli*) and a pair of short antennae.

Houseflies process visual information around seven times quicker than humans, enabling them to identify and avoid attempts to catch or swat them, since they effectively see the human's movements in slow motion with their higher *flicker fusion rate*.

Compound eyes are capable of detecting both the polarization of light and colour spectrums unseen by humans. The normal *flicker fusion rate* for humans averages about 60 flashes per second, but houseflies piece together 250 flashes or more.

Head of a female housefly with two large compound eyes and three ocelli clearly seen in the centre.

Evolution of the Head and Cephalization

The first sign of head development, **cephalization**, is seen in chordates such as *Pikaia* and *Branchiostoma*. It is thought that development of a head structure resulted from a long body shape, a swimming habit, and a mouth at the end that came into contact with the environment first, as the animal swam forward.

The search for food required ways of continually testing what lay ahead so it is thought that anatomical structures for seeing, feeling, and smelling developed around the mouth. The information these structures gathered was processed by a swelling of the nerve cord (*efflorescence*), the precursor of the brain. Altogether, these front-end structures formed the distinct part of the vertebrate body known as the head.

Cephalization is an evolutionary trend in which, over many generations, the mouth, sense organs, and nerve ganglia become concentrated at the front end of an animal, producing a head region. This is associated with movement and bilateral symmetry, such that the animal has a definite head end. This led to the formation of a highly sophisticated brain in three groups of animals, namely the arthropods, cephalopod molluscs, and vertebrates.

The philosopher Michael Trestman noted that three bilaterian phyla, namely the arthropods, the molluscs in the shape of the cephalopods, and the chordates, were distinctive in having 'complex active bodies', something that *acoela* and flatworms did not have. "Any such animal, whether predator or prey, has to be aware of its environment - to catch its prey, or to evade its predators. These groups are exactly those that are most highly cephalized".

These groups, however, are not closely related: in fact, they represent widely separated branches of the '*bilateria*', their lineages split hundreds of millions of years ago.

Cephalization

A *lobster* is heavily cephalized, with *eyes*, *antennae*, multiple *mouthparts*, *claws*, and the *brain* (inside the armored *exoskeleton*), all concentrated at the animal's head end.

Cephalization is an evolutionary trend in which, over many generations, the mouth, sense organs, and nerve ganglia become concentrated at the front end of an animal, producing a head region. This is associated with movement and bilateral symmetry, such that the animal has a definite head end. This led to the formation of a highly sophisticated brain in three groups of animals, namely the arthropods, cephalopod molluscs, and vertebrates.

***Lobster** (Homarus gammarus)*

Animals without bilateral symmetry

Cnidaria such as the radially symmetrical *Hydrozoa*, like *hydra* on the one hand and the *'Portuguese man o' war'* showing some degree of **cephalization** on the other.

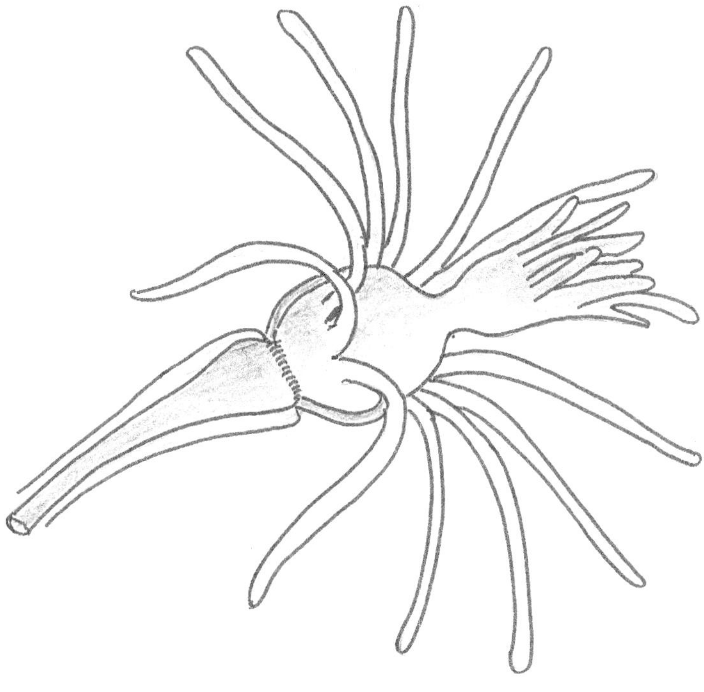

Hydra

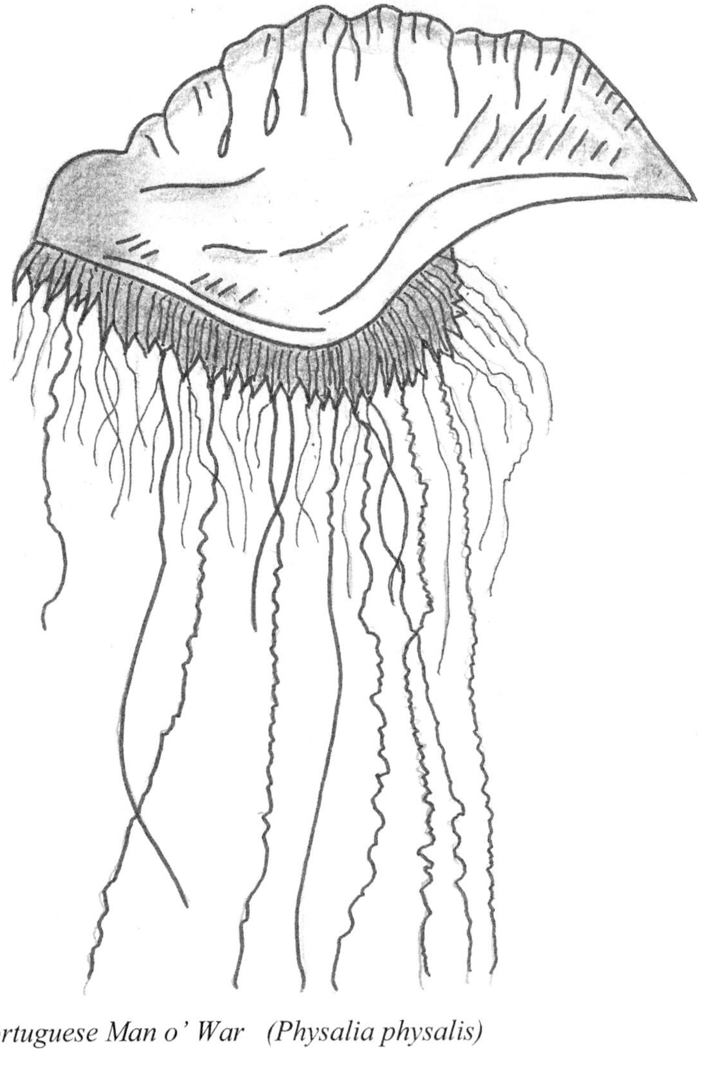

Portuguese Man o' War (Physalia physalis)

The *Anthomedusa* had a head end with its mouth, photoreceptive cells, and a concentration of neural cells.

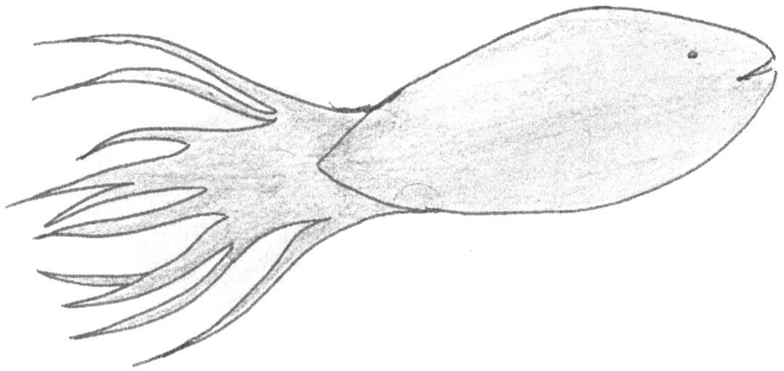

Cephalization is a characteristic feature of the '*bilateria*', a large group containing the majority of animal phyla. These have the ability to move, using muscles, and a body plan with a front end that encounters stimuli first as the animal moves forwards, and accordingly has evolved to contain many of the body's sense organs, able to detect light, chemicals, and often sound.

There is often also a collection of nerve cells able to process the data from these sense organs, forming a brain in several phyla and one or more ganglia in others.

The *acoelae* are basal bilaterians, part of the *xenacoelomorpha.* They are small and simple animals, and have very slightly more nerve cells at the head end than elsewhere, not forming a distinct and compact brain. This represents an early stage in **cephalization**.

The *platyhelminthes* (flatworms) have a more complex nervous system than the *acoelae*, and are lightly cephalized, for instance having an eyespot above the brain, near the front end.

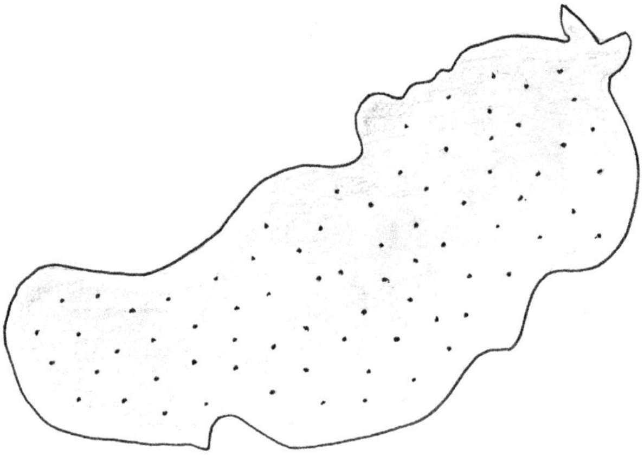

Platyhelminthes

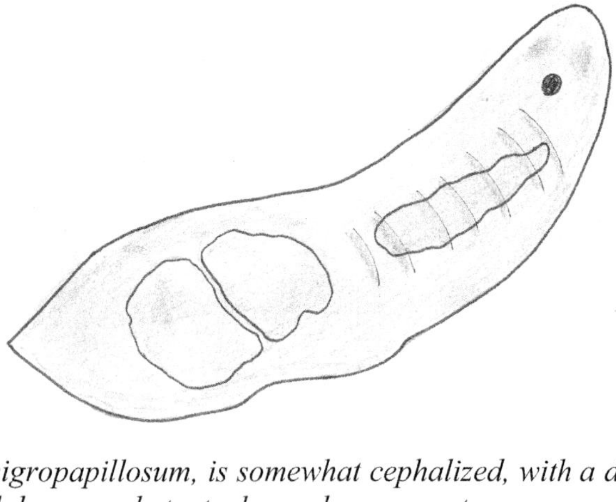

Thysanozoon nigropapillosum, is somewhat cephalized, with a distinct head end which has pseudo tentacles and an eyespot.

Vertebrates

Cephalization in vertebrates, the group that includes mammals, birds, and fishes, has been studied extensively. The heads of vertebrates are complex structures, with distinct sense organs, a large multi-lobed brain; jaws, often with teeth, and a tongue.

Cephalochordata like *Branchiostoma* are closely related to vertebrates but do not have these structures. These small vaguely eel- or snake-like animals are close relatives of vertebrates.

Unlike vertebrates, they do not have a true head (with a skull capsule, eyes, nose, a well-developed brain etc.), but merely a mouth adjacent to the gill-slits, with the slightly enlarged anterior end of the dorsal nerve cord above and in front of them.

A Lancelet (Amphioxus)
Subphylum: Cephalochordata
From coarse sand sediments on the Belgian continental shelf.
Total Length: approximately 22 mm.

Haikouichthys ercaicunensis (535 Mya)

Haikouichthys was an extinct genus of *craniate* (animals with *notochords* and distinct heads) believed to have lived 535 million years ago, during the Cambrian explosion of multicellular life. *Haikouichthys* had a defined skull and other characteristics that led paleontologists to label it a true craniate, and even to be popularly characterized as one of the earliest fishes. Cladistic analysis indicates that the animal is probably a *basal chordate* or a *basal craniate*, but it does not possess sufficient features to be included without due controversy even in either *stem group*. It was formally described in 1999.

Haikouichthys was about 2.5cm long and was narrower than *Myllokunmingia*, another putative *chordate* that comes from the same beds. The holotype of *H. ercaicunensis* was found near Haikou at Ercaicun, Yunnan, China, hence its name '*Haikou fish from Ercaicun*'. The fossil was recovered among the Chengjiang fauna, in one of a series of Lagerstätten sites where thousands of exquisitely preserved soft-bodied fossils have already been found.

Following the discovery of the holotype, additional Lower Cambrian fossils of *H. ercaicunensis* have been discovered.

The animal has a distinct head and tail. The head has at least six and perhaps nine probable gills. There are a number of segments (*myomeres*) with rear directed *chevrons* in the tail.

There is a *notochord.* There is also a prominent dorsal fin with fin radials similar, but not comparable, to those of **hagfish** and **lampreys**. The fin radials seem to angle 'forward' towards the end and are thought, on the basis of internal structures, to be the head. This happens with a few modern fish but is an uncommon arrangement. There are 13 circular structures along the bottom that may be gonads, slime organs, or something else entirely.

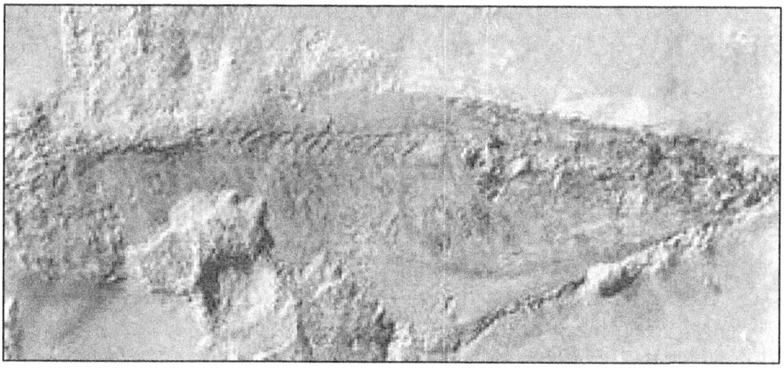

Pikaia (530 – 505 Mya)

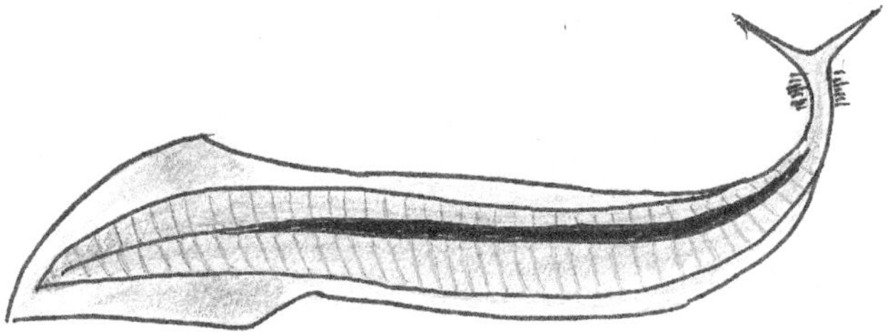

Pikaia was a primitive chordate that lacked a well-defined head and averaged about 38mm in length. Once thought to be closely related to the ancestor of all **vertebrates**, it has for that reason received particular attention among the multitude of animal fossils found in Burgess Shale. *Pikaia* had a pair of large, antenna-like 'tentacles' on its head, and a series of short appendages, which may be linked to gill slits, on either side of its head. In these ways, it differs from the modern *lancelet*.

Although primitive, *Pikaia* showed the essential prerequisites for vertebrates. When alive, *Pikaia* was a compressed, leaf-shaped animal with an expanded tail fin. The flattened body was divided into pairs of *segmented muscle blocks*, seen as faint vertical lines. The muscles were positioned on either side of a flexible structure resembling a rod that ran from the tip of the head to the tip of the tail.

It probably swam by throwing its body into a series of S-shaped, zigzag curves, similar to the movement of eels. Fish inherited the same swimming movement, but they generally have stiffer backbones. These adaptations may have allowed *Pikaia* to filter particles from the water as it swam along. *Pikaia* was probably a slow swimmer, since it lacked the fast-twitch fibres associated with rapid swimming in modern chordates.

Haikouella (521 – 514 Mya)

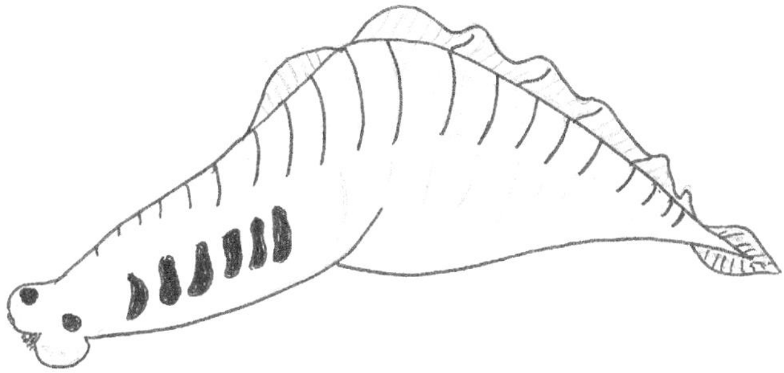

Haikouella was an *agnathan chordate* from the Lower Cambrian **Maotianshan shales** of in Yunnan Province, China.

It is similar to the form *Yunnanozoon*, which was possibly a *hemi-chordate*. There are, nevertheless, anatomical differences from *Yunnanozoon*, including a larger stomach and smaller (0.1mm) pharyngeal teeth. *Haikouella* does not have bones or a movable jaw, but it otherwise resembles vertebrates. *Haikouichthys* and *Myllokunmingia*, which seem to share significant fish-like characters, have been found in the same beds. Suspected *hemi-chordates* are also known from these deposits as well as from the Middle Cambrian of Burgess Shale. Other than possible fish scales/plates from the Upper Cambrian of Wyoming, these Chinese fish-like *chordates* are one of the only known pre-Ordovician *craniates*.

Haikouella is known from the many specimens mostly from a single bed in the Maotianshan shales. The animal is 20 to 30mm (40mm max) in length and has a head, gills, brain, *notochord*, well developed musculature, heart and circulatory system. It has a bent *caudal projection* of the *notochord* that might be a primitive tail fin. It might have a pair of lateral eyes. Very small (0.1mm) structures that are probably *pharyngeal teeth* are present in the body cavity. A few specimens display dorsal and ventral fins.

Myllokunmingia fengjiaoa (518 Mya)

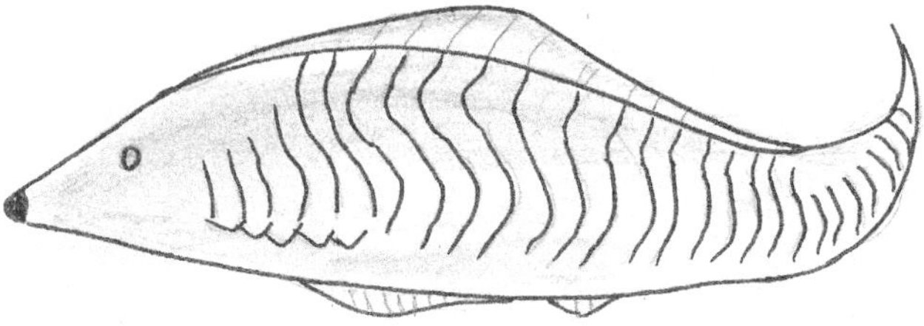

Myllokunmingia is a genus of *basal chordate* from the Lower Cambrian Maotianshan shales, thought to be a vertebrate although this is not conclusively proven. It is 28mm long and 6mm high.

It is among the oldest possible *craniates*, found in the lower Cambrian Chengjiang. It appears to have a skull and skeletal structures made of cartilage. There is no sign of bio mineralization of the skeletal elements.

The holotype was found in the Yuan Shan member of the Qiongzhusi Formation in the Eoredlichia Zone near Haikou at Ercaicun, Kunming City, Yunnan, China. The animal has a distinct head and trunk with a forward sail-like (1.5mm) dorsal fin and a ventral fin-fold (probably paired) further back. The head has five or six gill pouches with *hemibranchs*.

In the trunk there are 25 segments (*myomeres*) with rearward-facing chevrons. There is a *notochord*, a *pharynx* and a digestive tract that may run all the way to the rear tip of the animal. The mouth cannot be clearly identified. There may be a *pericardial cavity*. There are no fin radials.

There is only one specimen, which has the tip of the tail buried in sediment. Only one species is known – *Myllokunmingia fengjiaoa* (Shu, Zhang & Han).

Yunnanozoon lividum (514 Mya)

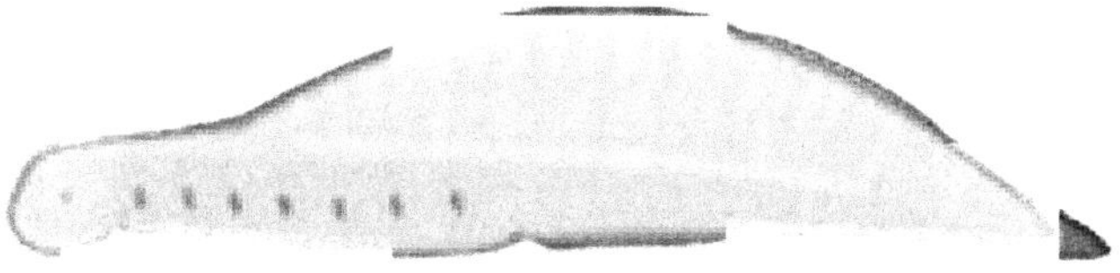

Yunnanozoon lividum, 'livid animal of Yunnan' is an extinct species from the Lower Cambrian, Chengjiang biota of Yunnan province, China. It is thought of as a *deuterostome* suspected of being either a *hemi-chordate* or *chordate*.

Yunnanozoon is similar to the form *Haikouella*, which is almost certainly a *chordate*. There are, though, anatomical differences from *Haikouella*, including a smaller stomach and much larger (1mm) pharyngeal teeth.

It is by no means certain whether *Yunnanozoon* possessed features such as a heart, gills, etc., which are seen in well-preserved specimens of *Haikouella*. *Yunnanozoon* somewhat resembles the Middle Cambrian *Pikaia* from the Burgess Shale.

Thirteen pairs of symmetrically arranged gonads have been identified, as have possible gill slits. However, some think that *Yunnanozoon* is closely related to the *chordate Haikouella* and that *Yunnanozoon* is probably a *chordate* rather than a *hemi-chordate*. A close relationship between *Yunnanozoon* and the taxon *Vetulicolia* has also been proposed.

Lancelet (509 Mya - present)

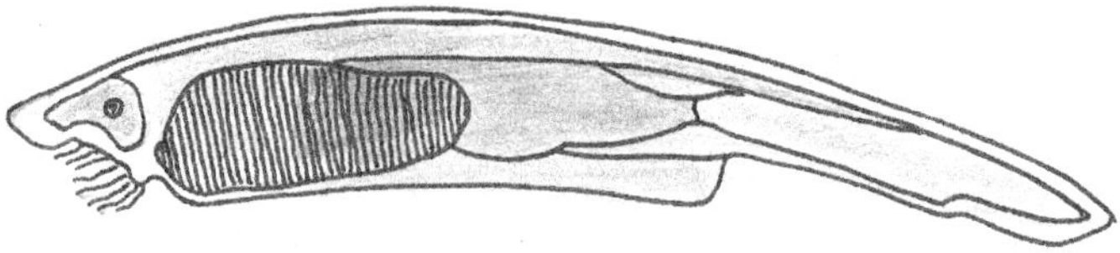

The ***lancelet***, also known as ***amphioxus*** consists of some 30 to 35 species of 'fish-like' *benthic* filter feeding chordates in the order *Amphioxiformes*. *Lancelets* closely resemble, and are considered to be related to *Pikaia*, fossils of which are known from the Burgess Shale.

Lancelets contain many organs and organ systems that are closely related to those of modern fish, but in more primitive form. Therefore, they provide a number of examples of possible evolutionary exaptation. For example, the gill-slits of lancelets are used for feeding only, and not for respiration. The frontal eye consists of a pigment cup, a group of putative photoreceptor cells, three rows of neurons, and glial cells. The circulatory system carries food throughout their body, but does not have red blood cells or haemoglobin for transporting oxygen.

A central, brain-like structure was present in the ancestors of the vertebrates. The brain of the lancelet barely stands out from the rest of the spinal cord, but specialised regions are nonetheless apparent. These specialised regions began to evolve slowly into more complex brains and to take on new roles.

By comparing genes from lancelets with the same genes in vertebrates, changes in gene expression, function and number as vertebrates evolved can be discovered. From such data it is now known that around 360 million years ago, such creatures already had a small neo-cortex in the form of extra layers of neural tissue on the surface of the brain responsible for the complexity and flexibility of mammalian behaviour.

Planaria torva

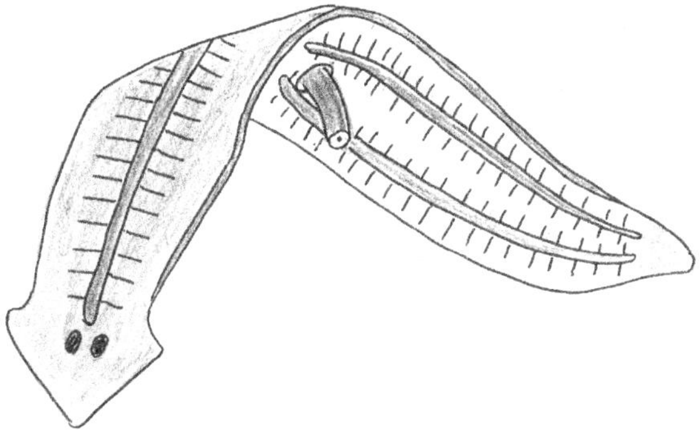

Planaria is a genus of *planarians* in the family *Planariidae*. It is currently represented by a single species, ***Planaria torva***, which is found in Europe.

Currently the genus *Planaria* is defined as freshwater *triclads* with oviducts that unite to form a common oviduct without embracing the *bursa copulatrix* and with an *adenodactyl* present in the male atrium. The testes occur along the whole body.

The food of *P. torva* consists of freshwater *gastropods*, *tubificid* worms, and freshwater *arthropods*, such as *isopods* of the genus *Asellus* and *chironomid* larvae, although it shows a clear preference for snails. In the United Kingdom, *P. torva* is a successful predator of the invasive New Zealand mud snail (*P. jenkinsi*).

The *triclads* are characterized by triply branched intestine and anteriorly situated ovaries, next to the brain. Planaria exhibit an extraordinary ability to regenerate lost body parts.

For example, a planarian split lengthwise or crosswise will regenerate into two separate individuals. Some planarian species have two eye-spots (also known as *ocelli*) that can detect the intensity of light, while others have several eye-spots.

The eye-spots act as photoreceptors and are used to move away from light sources.

Planarians move by beating cilia on the ventral dermis, allowing them to glide along on a film of mucus. Some also may move by undulations of the whole body by the contractions of muscles built into the body membrane.

Recent genetic screens utilizing double-stranded RNA technology have uncovered 240 genes that affect regeneration in *Schmidtea mediterranea (Platyhelminthes, Tricladida,* and *Continenticola).* Many of these genes have orthologs in the human genome.

The *planarian* has very simple organ systems. The digestive system consists of a mouth, *pharynx*, and a gastro-vascular cavity. The mouth is located in the centre of the underside of the body. Digestive enzymes are secreted from the mouth to begin external digestion.

Planarians receive oxygen and release carbon dioxide by diffusion. The excretory system is made of many tubes with many *flame cells* and excretory pores on them. Also, *flame cells* remove unwanted liquids from the body by passing them through ducts which lead to excretory pores, where waste is released on the dorsal surface of the *planarian.*

The triclads have an anterior end or head where sense organs, such as eyes and chemo-receptors, are usually found. Some species have *auricles* that protrude from the margins of the head. The *auricles* can contain chemical and mechanical sensory receptors.

The number of eyes in the *triclads* is variable depending on the species. While many species have two eyes (e.g. *Dugesia* or *Microplana*), others (e.g. *Polycelis felina*) have as many as 20 distributed along the body.

Sometimes, those species with two eyes may present smaller accessory or supernumerary eyes. The subterranean triclads are often eyeless or blind.

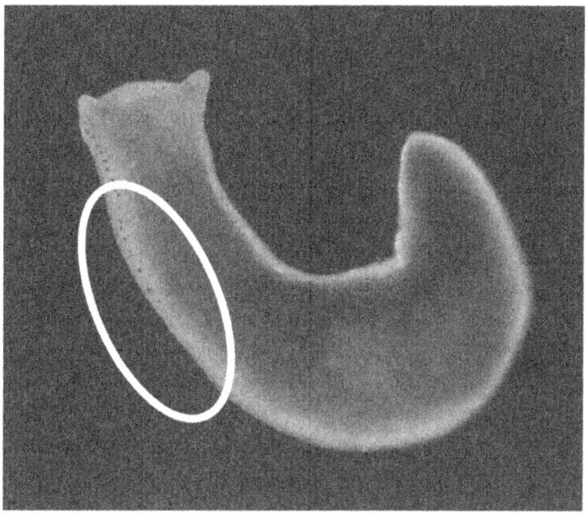

Polycelis felina can have more than 20 eyespots on its head
Office international de l'eau (Sandre)

Planaria and Immortality

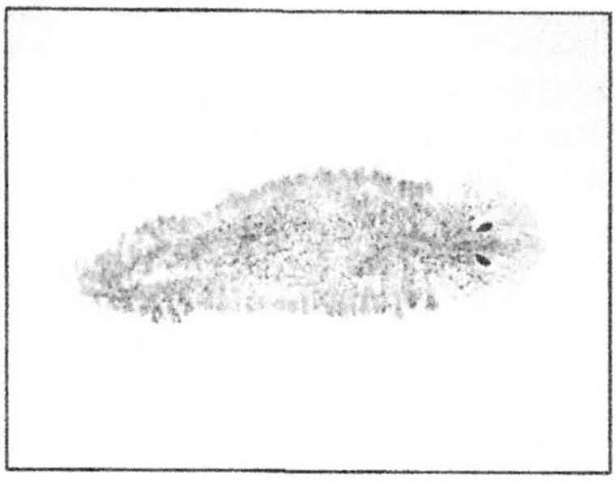

University of Nottingham scientists claim that *Planaria*, might actually be **immortal**, possessing an indefinite ability to regenerate their cells and thus practically never grow old. In fact, an important distinction must be made, it's not that the flatworm never grows old that is interesting, it is the fact that it stays forever young!

Most animal in the world gradually tend to lose this ability as they age, thus causing them to get older, function improperly and eventually die. *Planaria* not only is able to regenerate its old, dead cells, but it can literary grow a new brain, gut or tail when severed in two. Both cut ends grow into two new individuals.

Biologist Dr. Aboobaker explains "... Usually when stem cells divide - to heal wounds, or during reproduction or for growth - they start to show signs of aging. This means that the stem cells are no longer able to divide and so become less able to replace exhausted specialized cells in the tissues of our bodies. Our aging skin is perhaps the most visible example of this effect. *Planaria* and their stem cells are somehow able to avoid the aging process and to keep their cells dividing."

Each time a cell divides, the tip of its DNA, called the *telomere*, gets shorter. An enzyme called *telomerase* regenerates the *telomeres*. However in most sexually reproductive organisms it is only active during the organism's development. Once it reaches maturity, the enzyme stops functioning, and the telomeres become shorter and shorter until cell replication is made impossible, otherwise the DNA would become too severely damaged.

Immortality

An **immortal animal** is able to maintain *telomere* length indefinitely so that they can continue to replicate, and Aboobaker and colleagues were able to demonstrate that *Planaria* actively maintains the ends of its chromosomes in adult stem cells, leading to **theoretical immortality**.

The researchers claim that the next natural step is to study how this might apply to more complex organisms, like humans.

"The next goals for us are to understand the mechanisms in more detail and to understand more about how you evolve an immortal animal." said Aboobaker "*Planaria* is a model system in which we can ask questions, like whether it is possible for a multicellular animal [or human] to be **immorta**l and avoid the effects of aging."

The findings were published in the journal PNAS, University of Nottingham

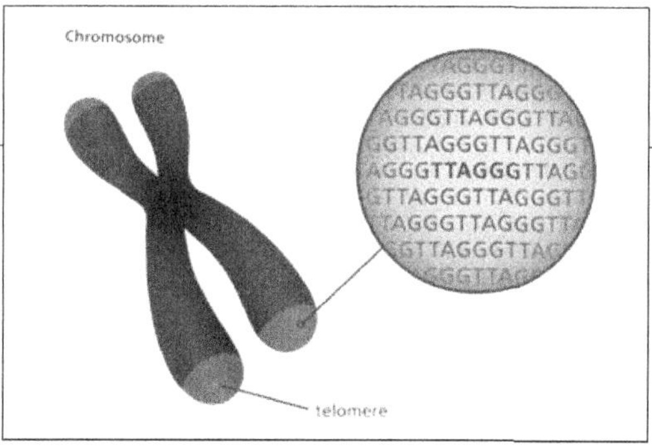

Bothriolepis (470 – 350 Mya)

Bothriolepis was a widespread, abundant and diverse genus of *antiarch placoderms* that lived during the Middle to Late Devonian of the Paleozoic.

Most species of *Bothriolepis* were characterized as relatively small, *benthic*, freshwater detritovores, averaging around 30cm in length. However, the largest species, *B. rex*, had an estimated body length of 170cm. Although expansive with over 60 species found worldwide comparatively, *Bothriolepis* is not unusually more diverse than most modern bottom dwelling species around today.

There are two openings through the head of *Bothriolepis*: a keyhole opening along the midline on the upper side for the eyes and nostrils and an opening for the mouth on the lower side near the anterior end of the head. A discovery regarding preserved structures that appear to be nasal capsules confirms the belief that the external nasal openings lay on the dorsal side of the head near the eyes. Additionally, the position of the mouth on the ventral side of the skull is consistent with the typical horizontal resting orientation of *Bothriolepis*.

It had a special feature on its skull, a separate partition of bone below the opening for the eyes and nostrils enclosing the nasal capsules called a *pre-orbital recess*.

Cast of a B. canadensis fossil CC BY-SA 3.0

Arandaspis prionotolepis (480 – 470 Mya)

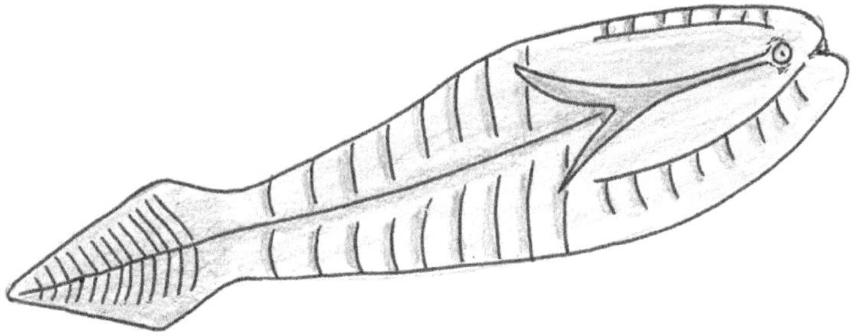

A. prionotolepis is an extinct species of jawless fish that lived in the Ordovician. Its remains were found in the **Stairway Sandstone** near Alice Springs, Australia in 1959, but it was not determined that they were the oldest known vertebrates until the late 1960s. *Arandaspis* is named after a local Aboriginal tribe, the Aranda (now currently called Arrernte).

Arandaspis was about 15cm long, with a streamlined body covered in rows of knobbly armoured *scutes*. The front of the body and the head were protected by hard plates with openings for the eyes, nostrils and gills. It probably was a filter-feeder.

It had no fins so its only method of propulsion was the use of its vertically flattened tail. As a result, it probably swam in a fashion similar to a modern tadpole.

Ostracoderms

Ostracoderms are the armoured jawless fish of the Paleozoic. The term does not often appear in classifications today because it is *paraphyletic* (or *polyphyletic)*, and thus does not correspond to one evolutionary lineage. However, the term is still used as an informal way of loosely grouping together the armoured jawless fishes.

An innovation of *ostracoderms* was the use of gills not for feeding, but exclusively for respiration. Earlier *chordates* with gill precursors used them for both respiration and feeding.

Ostracoderms had separate *pharyngeal* gill pouches along the side of the head, which were permanently open with no protective *operculum*.

Unlike invertebrates that use *ciliated motion* to move food, ostracoderms used their *muscular pharynx* to create a suction that pulled small and slow moving prey into their mouths.

Galeaspida (430 – 370 Mya)

Galeaspida is an extinct taxon of jawless marine and freshwater fish. The name is derived from *galea*, the Latin word for *helmet*, and refers to their massive bone shield on the head. Galeaspida lived in shallow, fresh water and marine environments during the Silurian and Devonian times in what are now Southern China, Tibet and Vietnam. Superficially, their morphology appears more similar to that of *Heterostraci* than *Osteostraci*, there being currently no evidence that the galeaspids had paired fins. However, Galeaspida are in fact regarded as being more closely related to *Osteostraci*, based on the closer similarity of the morphology of the braincase.

Their mouth and gill openings are situated on the ventral surface of the head (top right). In the most primitive forms, such as the Silurian genus *Hanyangaspis*, the median dorsal inhalant opening is broad and situated anteriorly. In other *galeaspids*, it is more posterior in position and can be oval, rounded, heart-shaped or slit-shaped. In some Devonian *galeaspids*, such as the *Lungmenshanaspis* and *Sanchaspis*, the head shield is produced laterally and anteriorly into slender processes. The *eugaleaspidiforms*, such as *Eugaleaspis* have a horseshoe-shaped head shield and a slit-shaped median dorsal opening, which imitates the aspect of the head shield of *osteostracans*.

The defining characteristic of all *galeaspids* was a large opening on the dorsal surface of the head shield, which was connected to the pharynx and gill chamber, and a scalloped pattern of the sensory-lines.

The opening appears to have served both the olfaction and the intake of the respiratory water similar to the nasopharyngeal duct of hagfishes. Galeaspids are also the vertebrates which have the largest number of gills, as some species of the order *Polybranchiaspidida* (literally 'many gills shields') had up to 45 gill openings!

The body is covered with minute scales arranged in oblique rows and there is no other fin besides the caudal fin. The mouth and gill openings are situated on the ventral side of the head, which is flat or flattened and suggests that they were bottom-dwellers.

A specimen of Nochelaspis maeandrine, on display at the Paleozoological Museum of China.
(Copyrighted free use)

Lungmenshanaspis (410 – 408 Mya)

Lungmenshanaspis is a genus of jawless fish from the Devonian period of China.

The gaping hole on its head helped it smell and breathe. A feature unique to this fish and its relatives. *Lungmenshanaspis* is one of the most extreme-shaped members of its group known for the long, slender projections on the front and sides.

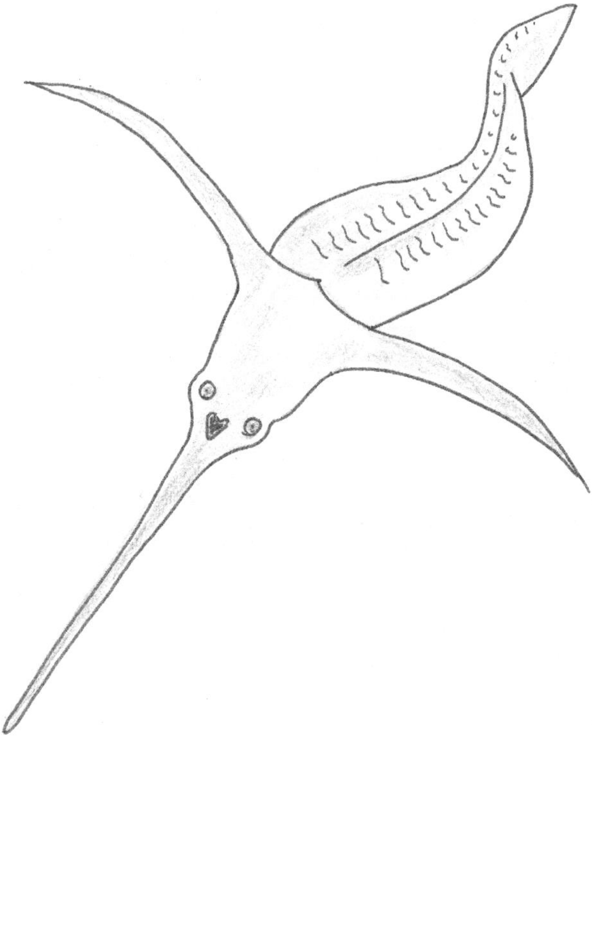

Sanchaspis megalorostrata (400 Mya)

S. megalorostrata is an extinct ***agnate fish,*** belonging to the ***galeaspids***. It lived in the Lower ***Devonian*** and its fossil remains have been found in China.

This fish was equipped with a *cephalic shield* of a decidedly unusual shape. In the front there was a long elongated *rostrum*, expanded in the final part in a bulb-shaped structure.

The *cephalic shield* was also equipped with two flattened and curved backwards lateral expansions, which gave the entire body the shape of a crescent. *Sanchaspis* was endowed, like all *galeaspids*, with a median opening placed dorsally on the cephalic shield; in *Sanchaspis,* this was elongated transversely and rather thin.

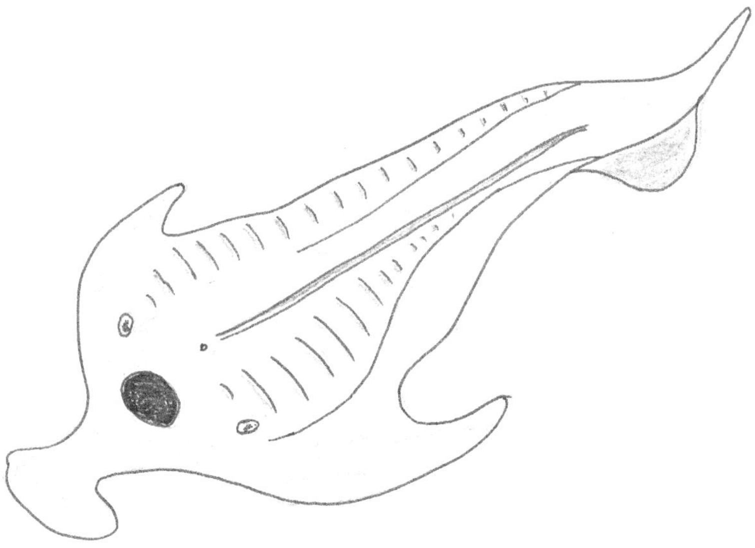

Pituriaspida (300 Mya)

The *Pituriaspida* are a small group of fossil, armoured jawless vertebrates, only known by two genera, *Pituriaspis* and *Neeyambaspis*, from the late Early Devonian or early Middle Devonian of Queensland, Australia.

The best documented form, however, is only *Pituriaspis*, which resembles the *Osteostraci*, although devoid of any median dorsal *nasohypophysial* opening. The nasal or nasohypophysial opening is supposed to lie ventrally, anteriorly to the mouth.

The head shield of *Pituriaspis* shows a ventral *oralobranchial* chamber, as in the *Osteostraci* and *Galeaspida*, a long anterior *rostral* process, and two lateral *corneal* processes which bound anteriorly the area for the attachment of the paired fins.

The head shield extends posteriorly to form a long abdominal division which probably reached the anal region.

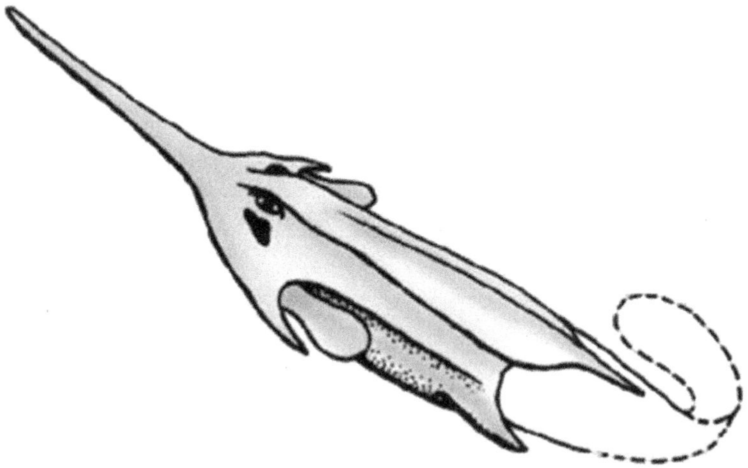

Osteostraci

The class ***Osteostraci*** is an extinct taxon of bony-armoured jawless fish, termed '*ostracoderms*' that lived in what are now North America, Europe and Russia from the Middle Silurian to Late Devonian.

Anatomically speaking, the *osteostracans*, especially the Devonian species, were among the most advanced of all known *agnathans*. This is due to the development of paired fins, and their complicated cranial anatomy.

The *osteostracans* were more similar to *lampreys* than to jawed vertebrates in possessing two pairs of semicircular canals in the inner ear, as opposed to the three pairs found in the inner ears of jawed vertebrates. They are thought to be the sister-group to *pituriaspids*, and together, these two taxa of jawless vertebrates are the sister-group of *gnathostomes*.

Most *osteostracans* had a massive cephalothorac shield, but all Middle and Late Devonian species appear to have had a reduced, thinner, and often micromeric dermal skeleton. This reduction may have occurred at least three times independently because the pattern of reduction is different in each taxon.

They were probably relatively good swimmers, possessing dorsal fins, paired pectoral fins, and a strong tail. The shield of bone covering the head formed a single piece, and so presumably did not grow during adult life. However, the way in which the bone was laid down makes it possible to examine the imprints of nerves and other soft tissues.

This reveals the presence of complex sensory organs and the sides and upper surface of the head, which may have been used to sense vibrations.

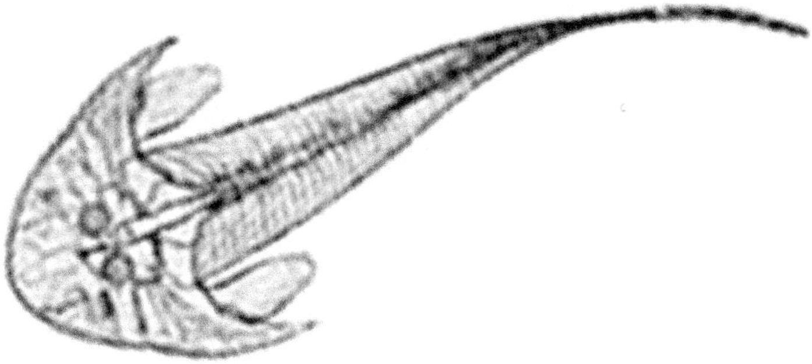

Zenaspidid osteostracan 1997 Philippe Janvier_ CC SA-BY 3.0

Pteraspidomorphi

Pteraspidomorphi is an extinct class of early jawless fish. They have long been regarded as closely related or even ancestral to jawed vertebrates, but the few characteristics they share with the latter are now considered as basal traits for all vertebrates. *Pteraspidomorphs* are characterized by their massive dermal head armour having large, median, ventral and dorsal plates or shields.

The fossils show extensive shielding of the head. Many had hypocercal tails in order to generate lift to increase ease of movement through the water for their armoured bodies, which were covered in dermal bone. They also had sucking mouth parts and some species may have lived in fresh water.

Most *pteraspidomorphs* were marine, but lived very near to the shore, in lagoons and deltas. Some groups are thought to have been fresh water-dwelling. They were certainly bottom-dwellers, as shown by traces of abrasion of the ventral surfaces of their head shields.

Pteraspidomorphs have been first regarded as related to bony fishes, then to sharks, then ancestral to hagfishes, and finally as the closest jawless relatives of the *gnathostomes*.

This last theory was based on the fact that they seem to have a paired olfactory organ and a sensory-line pattern which is quite similar to that of the *gnathostomes*. These characteristics are, however, likely to be general for either the vertebrates or, at any rate, for the ensemble of all *ostracoderms* and the *gnathostomes*.

Other *ostracoderms*, such as the *Galeaspida* are now known to have a paired olfactory organ. Current phylogenetic analysis using a large number of characteristics now place *pteraspidomorphs* as the sister-group of all other *ostracoderms* and the *gnathostomes*.

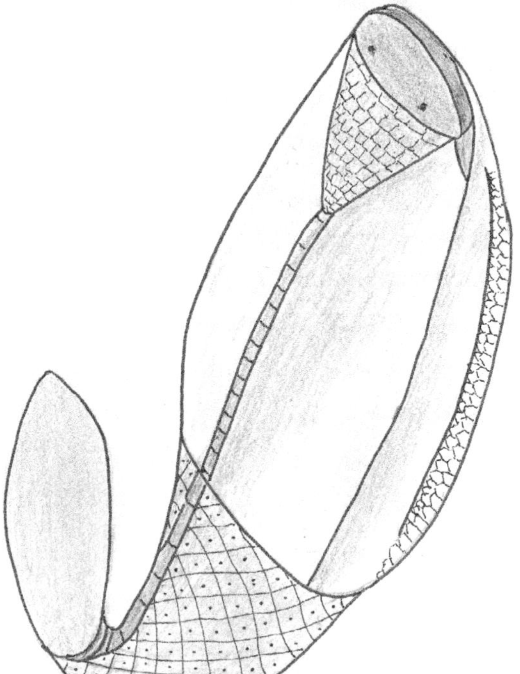

Larnovaspis stensioei (415 – 405 Mya)

The **Larnovaspis** is an extinct jawless fish, belonging to the *heterostraci*. It lived in the Lower Devonian and its fossil remains have been found in Europe.

This animal was quite similar to the well-known *Pteraspis*, and like the latter was equipped with armour consisting of two large plates (one upper and one lower) that enclosed the head and the front half of the body.

The body of *Larnovaspis* was spindle-shaped, and ended anteriorly in a robust but blunt *rostrum*, slightly flattened dorsoventrally. The eyes were small, and the head was wide.

Below and just behind this *rostrum* was the small mouth. Usually *Larnovaspis* did not exceed 20cm in length.

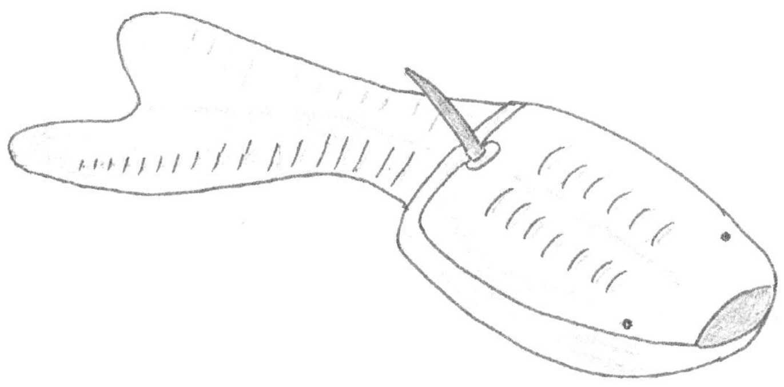

Boreaspis (407 Mya)

Boreaspis is an extinct genus of *osteostracan agnathan* vertebrate that lived in the early Devonian.

Fourteen different species of *Boreaspis* have been found in sandstone of the lagoons and estuaries of Devonian Spitsbergen, however some of these may well not belong to the genus.

Species of *Boreaspis* were very small, with head shields about 2cm long. All species possessed a long *spathe*-like *rostrum* derived from the anterior-most end of the head shield, which would have enhanced the fish's hydrodynamics and was probably also used to root out food buried beneath the substrate.

Pteraspis (400 Mya)

Pteraspis is an extinct genus of *pteraspidid heterostracan* agnathan vertebrate that lived from the Lochkovian to Eifelian epochs of the Devonian. The cephalic region of this primitive 'fish', about 25cm long, was flattened and covered with thick bone plates, which undoubtedly resulted from the fusion of numerous scales; there was a dorsal plate in the middle, one on the muzzle, one to cover the belly and a series of smaller plates on the sides. All the plates were covered with thin channels probably connected to the sense organs.

On the back there were various spines, the first of which was of considerable length, which acted both as a defence and as a dorsal fin. Two other lateral expansions of the 'shield' functioned as *ailerons*. The long *rostrum* helped the *Pteraspis* in swimming, and made it one of the most hydrodynamic *heterostracs*. The mouth, placed in a ventral position, was surrounded by small plates that perhaps helped the animal in feeding on the seabed or on the surface. The eyes were small and lateral, while the tail was very useful for pushing upwards and moving away from the seabed. The robust bony carapace, which substantially covered the entire anterior half of the *Pteraspis*, was of considerable protection against predators such as eurypterids, but could also be an important reserve of phosphate in times of food scarcity. (*See also page 254*)

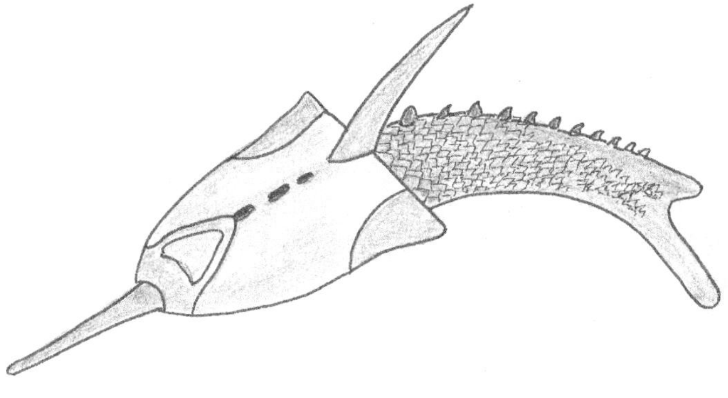

Evolution of the Brain

The evolution of the brain begins in the pre-historic oceans, long before the first animals appeared. The single-celled organisms that swam or crawled in them may not have had brains, but they did have sophisticated ways of sensing and responding to their environment.

Sponges

The evolution of multicellular animals depended on cells being able to sense and respond to other cells – to work together. **Sponges,** for example, filter food from the water they pump through the channels in their bodies. They can slowly inflate and constrict these channels to expel any sediment and prevent them clogging up. These movements are triggered when cells detect chemical messengers like **glutamate** or **GABA**, pumped out by other cells in the sponge. These chemicals play a similar role in our brains today. (*Journal of Experimental Biology, vol. 213, p 2310*)

Opening up channels that let ions flow freely across the membrane produces sudden changes in this potential. If nearby ion channels also open up in response, an electrical pulse can travel along a cell's surface at speeds of several metres a second.

Choanoflagellates

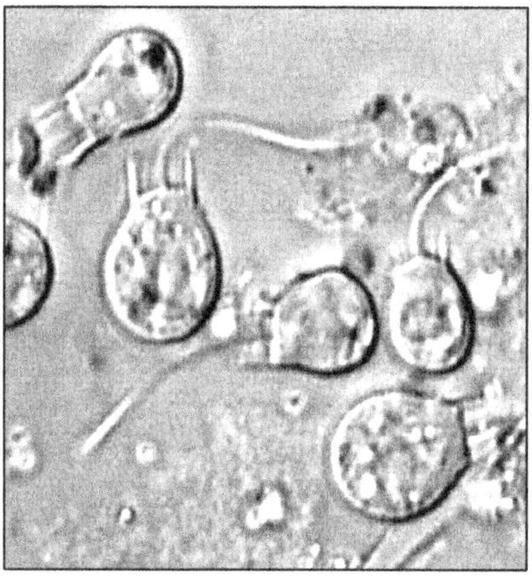

Recent studies have shown that many of the components needed to transmit electrical signals, and to release and detect chemical signals, are found in single-celled organisms known as ***Choanoflagellates***. That is significant because ancient *Choanoflagellates* are thought to have given rise to animals around 850 million years ago.

Almost from the start, the cells within early animals had the potential to communicate with one another using electrical pulses and chemical signals. From there, it was not a big leap for some cells to become specialised for carrying messages.

These nerve cells evolved long, wire-like extensions (*axons*) for carrying electrical signals over long distances. They still pass signals on to other cells by releasing chemicals such as **glutamate**, but they do so where they meet them, at *synapses*. That means the chemicals only have to diffuse across a tiny gap, greatly speeding things up. And so, very early on, the nervous system was born.

In other animals, groups of neurons also began to appear to develop into a **central nervous system**. This allowed data to be processed rather than merely relayed, enabling animals to move and respond to the environment in ever more sophisticated ways. The most specialised groups of neurons, the first brain-like structure, developed near the mouth and primitive eyes.

Mass Extinction Event (66 Mya)

After the demise of the dinosaurs following the K-Pg mass extinction event of 66 million years ago, the ancestors of the primates took to the trees. This led to an expansion of the visual part of the neo-cortex.

"We can only speculate about why their brains began to grow bigger around 2.5 million years ago, but it is possible that serendipity played a part. In other primates, the "bite" muscle exerts a strong force across the whole of the skull, constraining its growth. In our forebears, this muscle was weakened by a single mutation, perhaps opening the way for the skull to expand. This mutation occurred around the same time as the first hominids with weaker jaws and bigger skulls and brains appeared." (Nature, vol. 428, p 415).

260,000 – 125,000 years ago

Once early humans started to verbally communicate, there would be strong selection for mutations that improved this ability, such as the famous ***FOXP2*** gene, which enables the basal ganglia and the cerebellum to lay down the complex motor memories necessary for complex speech.

DNA sampling from *Homo neanderthalensis* bones indicates that their FOXP2 gene is a little different though largely similar to those of *Homo sapiens*. Previous genetic analysis had suggested that the *H. sapiens* FOXP2 gene became fixed in the population around 125,000 years ago. Some researchers consider the Neanderthal findings to indicate that the gene instead swept through the population over 260,000 years ago, before our most recent common ancestor with the Neanderthals.

The overall picture is one of a virtuous cycle involving our diet, culture, technology, social relationships and genes. It led to the modern human brain coming into existence in Africa from about 260,000 to 125,000 years ago.

Evolution never stops, though. According to one recent study, the visual cortex has grown larger in people who migrated out of Africa to northern latitudes. (Biology Letters, DOI: 10.1098/rsbl.2011.057).

200,000 years ago

The brain of *H. sapiens* burns 20 per cent of the food intake at a rate of about 15 watts. Any further improvements would be increasingly demanding. But there is an up-side to this. Not only did the growth in the size of *H. sapiens'* brain ceases around 200,000 years ago, but in the past 10,000 to 15,000 years the average size of the brain compared with body size has shrunk by 3 or 4 per cent.

But size is not everything, and it is perfectly possible that the brain has simply evolved to make better use of its processing matter. On the other hand this shrinkage may be a sign of a slight decline in our general mental abilities ... or, recently, too much reliance on the iPhone!

What is clear, though, is that the brain size of mammals increased relative to their bodies as they struggled for dominance over the dinosaurs. By this point, the brain filled the skull, leaving impressions that provide tell-tale signs of the changes leading to this neural expansion.

However, living amphibians and reptiles do not have a direct equivalent neurological system, and since their brains do not fill their entire skull cavity, fossils tell us little about the brains of our amphibian and reptilian ancestors.

Possible Hominid Ancestors

Choanoflagellates (1,050 – 0 Mya)

The ***Choanoflagellates*** are a group of free-living unicellular and colonial flagellate eukaryotes considered to be the **closest living relatives to animals**. *Choanoflagellates* are collared flagellates having a funnel shaped collar of interconnected microvilli at the base of a flagellum.

Choanoflagellates are capable of both asexual and sexual reproduction. They have a distinctive cell morphology characterized by an ovoid or spherical cell body 3–10μm in diameter with a single apical flagellum surrounded by a collar of 30–40 microvilli (*see figure*).

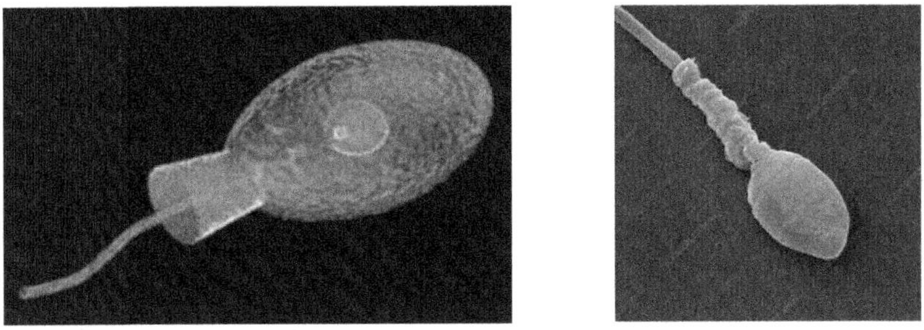

Note the anatomical similarity of Choanoflagellates (left) and human sperm cell (right)

Movement of the *flagellum* creates water currents that can propel free-swimming *Choanoflagellates* through the water column and trap bacteria and detritus against the collar of microvilli, where these foodstuffs are engulfed.

Each *Choanoflagellate* has a single flagellum, surrounded by a ring of actin-filled protrusions of these microvilli, forming a cylindrical or conical collar (*choanos* in Greek). Movement of the flagellum draws water through the collar, and bacteria and detritus are captured by the microvilli and ingested. Water currents generated by the *flagellum* also push free-swimming cells along, as in animal sperm. In contrast, most other flagellates are *pulled* by their *flagella*.

The nucleus occupies an apical-to-central position in the cell, and food vacuoles are positioned in the basal region of the cytoplasm. They apparently can coordinate to respond to light. The *Choanoflagellates* feed on bacteria and there is some evidence that they feast on viruses as well.

Choanoflagellates are either free-swimming in the water column or sessile, adhering to the substrate directly or through either the *periplast* or a thin *pedicel.* Although *Choanoflagellates* are thought to be strictly free-living and heterotrophic, a number of *Choanoflagellate* relatives, such as members of *Ichthyosporea* or *Mesomycetozoa*, follow a parasitic or pathogenic life style. The life histories of *Choanoflagellates* are poorly understood, but many species are thought to be solitary.

Coloniality seems to have arisen independently several times within the group and colonial species retain a solitary stage. Choanoflagellates grow 'vegetatively', with multiple species undergoing longitudinal fission. However, there is considerable evidence in some species that environmental changes, including the presence of certain bacteria, trigger the swarming and subsequent sexual reproduction (*Salpingoeca rosetta. Monosiga brevicollis* and *Monosiga ovata).*

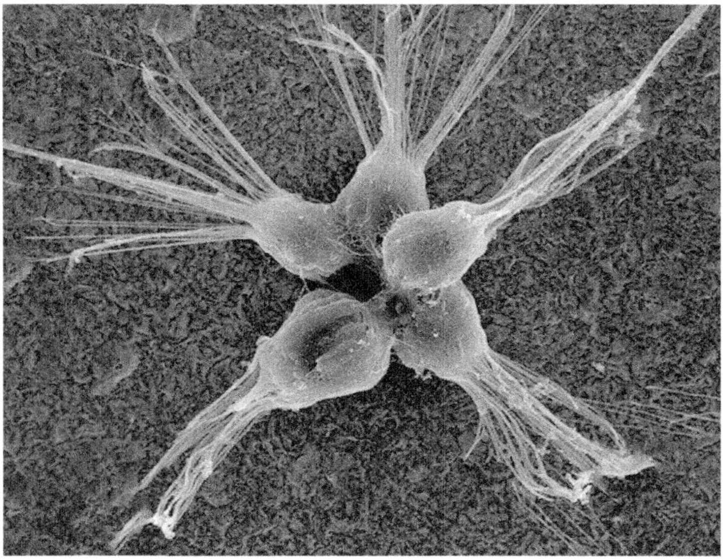

A choanoflagellate colony

Purgatorius (66 – 63 Mya)

Purgatorius is a genus of seven extinct species typically believed to be the earliest example of a primate or a proto-primate, a primatomorph precursor to the *Plesiadapiformes*, dating to as old as 66 million years ago.

It is thought to have been rat-sized, 15cm long, weighing about 37g and a diurnal insectivore, which burrowed through small holes in the ground.

Plesiadapis (58 – 55 Mya)

Plesiadapis is one of the oldest known primate-like mammal genera which existed about 55–58 million years ago in North America and Europe. *Plesiadapi* means 'near-Adapis', which is a reference to the *adapiform* primate of the Eocene, *Adapis*. *Plesiadapis tricuspidens*, the type specimen, is named after the three cusps present on its upper incisors.

Fossil of Plesiadapis, an extinct plesiadapiform
Musee d'Histoire Naturelle, Brussels
CC BY-SA 3.0

Paranthropus (2.7 – 1.2 Mya)

Paranthropus *i*s an extinct bipedal hominid genus which lived approximately 2.7 to 1.2 million years ago – from the Pliocene through the Pleistocene. This genus is actually composed of three different hominid species which have helped scientists to link modern humans to our earlier human ancestors. The three groups in this species include *Paranthropus aethiopicus, Paranthropus boisei* and *Paranthropus robustus*.

The first of these *hominids* to be found was *Paranthropus robustus* in 1938 when a jawbone fragment was found in a farm field in South Africa. This jaw bone was then sent to Robert Broom. After he decided it was an altogether different species than *Australopithecus africanus*, a known *hominid* at the time. He then set out to search for more bones and teeth of this species. He collected more and learned that they were about 0.9m tall, weighed around 64kg. They lived about 1.8 to 1.2 million years ago.

Paranthropus boisei was the next hominid species to be discovered. It was discovered in 1955 but much wasn't thought about it at the time because it was believed to have belonged to an existing species at the time. It would not be until fossils were found in 1959 by Mary Leakey that palaeontologists knew they had a new species. *Paranthropus* pictures of this species show them standing about 1.4m tall and weighing approximately 62kg, which is the average height and male of the males of this species. The female of this species was about 1.2m tall and weighed around 40kg. They lived about 2.3 to 1.3 million years ago.

Paranthropus aethiopicus was first discovered by French palaeontologists in 1967. However, like *Paranthropus boisei*, scientists did not realise this was a new species.

So even though hyperactive comets are rarer, the fact that they have similar isotope budgets to those seen on Earth put them back in the running for Earth's cosmic water bearer.

It would not be until 1985, when Alan Walker and Richard Leakey discovered a skull west of Lake Turkana in Kenya, that scientist realized this was a new species. An interesting fact about this species of *Paranthropus* is that little is currently known about its size. Hopefully, new fossils will be discovered so that palaeontologists can fill in the 'gaps' they have in their knowledge of this species.

Paranthropus by Roman Yevseyev

Evolution of Early Primates

Prosimians were the first type of primate to diverge from the ancestral primate line.

Surviving anthropoids are classified into three super-families.

- New World monkeys
- Old World monkeys
- Hominoids

Hominid proconsul is believed to be ancestral to *hominids*.

Skeleton of Monkey

Skeleton and skull of Hominid proconsul

Phylogenetic tree indicates humans are most closely related to African apes.

The last 'common ancestor' appears to have lived about 5-7 million years ago where genetic changes have been used as a molecular clock to measure relatedness of different groups.

Hominids

To be a *hominid*, a fossil must have an anatomy suitable for standing erect and walking on two feet.

Human anatomy differs from that of an ape largely because humans are bipedal while apes are quadrupedal.

Australopithecines

It is possible that one of the *australopithecines* that evolved and diversified in Africa 4 million years ago is a direct ancestor of humans.

- Southern Africa
  - *Australopithecus africanus*
- Eastern Africa
  - *Australopithecus afarensis (Lucy)*

However, whilst **bipedalism** was once thought to have evolved in *australopithecines*, it is now thought to have begun evolving much earlier in habitually **arboreal** primates.

The earliest claimed date for the beginnings of an upright spine and a primarily vertical body plan is 21.6 million years ago in the Early Miocene with *Morotopithecus bishopi*.

Morotopithecus bishopi (20.6 Mya)

Morotopithecus is a species of fossil ape discovered in Miocene-age deposits of Moroto, Uganda.

The phylogenetic status of *Morotopithecus bishopi* is debated to the extent that it challenges established views on the connection between Miocene primates and extant hominids (i.e. great apes).

Parsimonious phylogenetic analyses indicate *Morotopithecus* is more derived than *Proconsul*, *Afropithecus*, and *Kenyapithecus*, but less derived than *Oreopithecus*, *Sivapithecus*, and *Dryopithecus*. Under this arrangement, *Morotopithecus* would be a sister taxon to extant great apes while *Hylobates* (gibbons) seem to have branched off before this clade appeared. However, gibbons are believed to have branched off 18 million years ago while *Morotopithecus* is dated to more than 20.6 million years.

In a comparison of teeth characteristics of *Morotopithecus* to *Afropithecus* the results showed little difference, plus evidence gathered from cranial comparisons also indicate that the two genera may be the same complete anatomy for both (Patel, Grossman 2005).

Ghedoghedo
Fossil of jaw of
Morotopithecus, an extinct
mammal- Musee
d'Histoire Naturelle, Paris

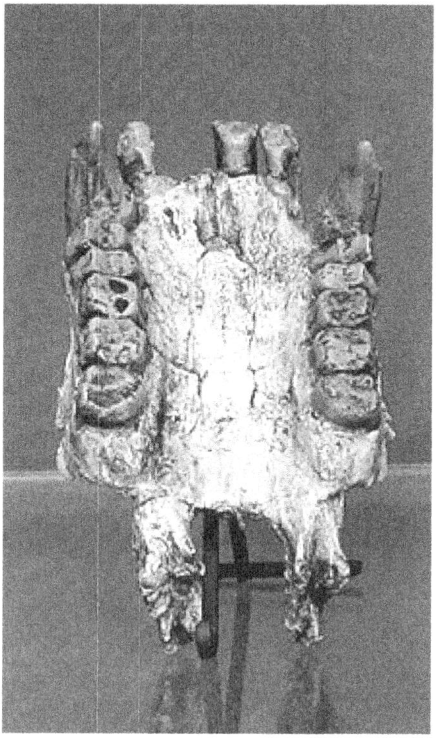

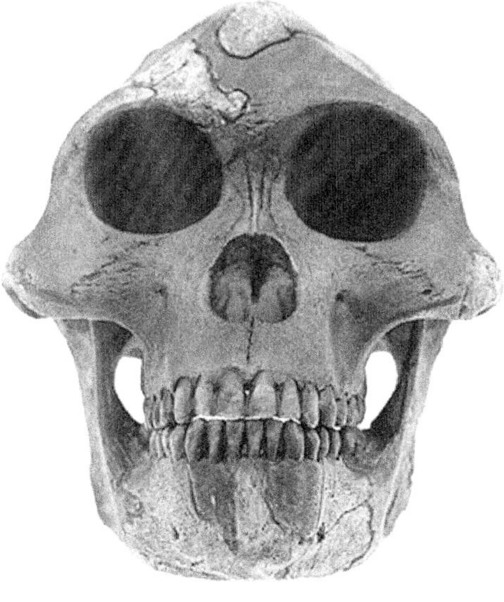

Nakalipithecus nakayama (9.9 – 9.8 Mya)

Nakalipithecus nakayamai is **an extinct species of great ape from Nakali, Kenya.** It is known from a right jawbone with 3 molars and from 11 isolated teeth, and the specimen is presumed female as the teeth are similar in size to those of female gorillas and orangutans.

Compared to other great apes, the canines are short, the enamel is thin, and the molars are flatter. *Nakalipithecus* is one of only three Late Miocene great apes known from Africa, the others being *Samburupithecus* and *Chororapithecus*. *Nakalipithecus* seems to have inhabited a sclerophyllous woodland environment.

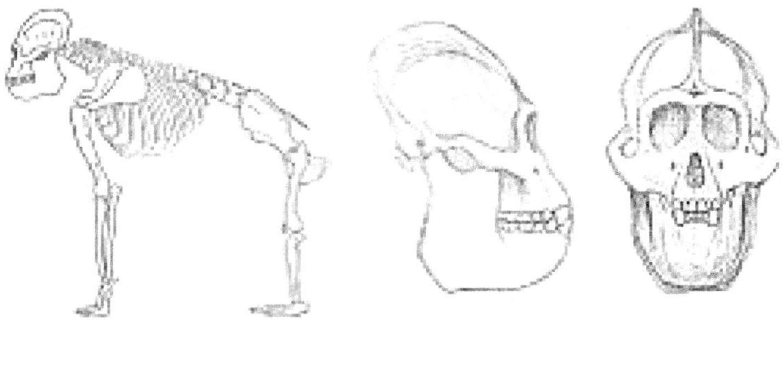

Ouranopithecus macedoniensis (9.6 – 8.7 Mya)

Ouranopithecus turkae (8.7 – 7.4 Mya)

Ouranopithecus is a genus of extinct Eurasian great ape represented by two species, a late Miocene hominoid from Greece and Turkey respectively, also from the late Miocene.

Some researchers consider *O. macedoniensis* to be the last common ancestor of humans (*hominini*) and the other apes, and a forerunner to *australopithecines* and humans, although this is very controversial and not widely accepted. It is true that *O. macedoniensis* shares derived features with some early hominins (such as the frontal sinus, a cavity in the forehead), but they are almost certainly not closely related species.

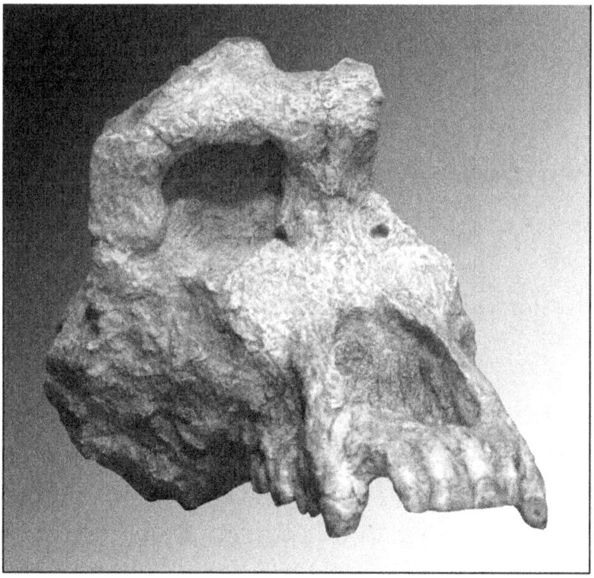

'Ouranopithecus macedoniensis' skull in the French National Museum of Natural History, Paris

Oreopithecus bambolii (9 - 7 Mya)

Oreopithecus is an extinct genus of *hominoid* primate from the Miocene whose fossils have been found in today's Tuscany and Sardinia in Italy. That was when this region was an isolated island in a chain of islands stretching from central Europe to northern Africa in what was becoming the Mediterranean Sea.

Oreopithecus bambolii had hominin-like hand proportions that allowed a firm, pad-to-pad precision grip. Features present in the hands of neither non-human-extant nor fossil apes include hand length, relative thumb length, a deep and large insertion for the *flexor pollicis longus*, and the shape of the *carp metacarpal* joint between the *metacarpal* bone of the index finger and the *capitate* bone.

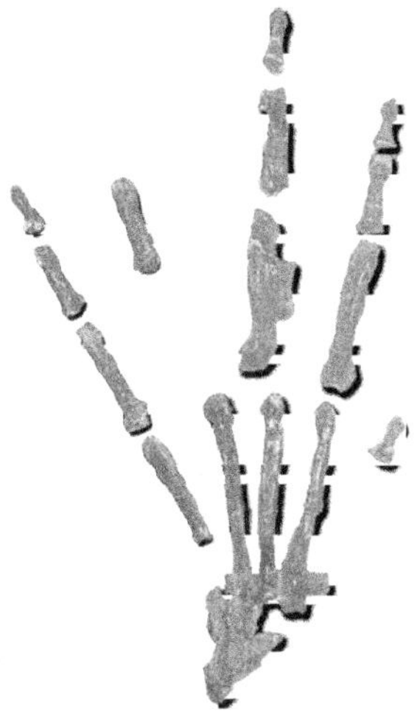

At the base of the second *metacarpal* bone, the facet for the *capitate* is oriented transversally, as in hominins. The capitate, on the other hand, lacks the waisting associated with apes and climbing, and still present in *Australopithecus*. *Oreopithecus* share the specialised orientation at the *carp metacarpal* joint with *A. afarenis* and the marked groove for the *flexor pollicis longus* with *A. africanus*. It is thus likely that the hand morphology of *Oreopithecus* is derived for apes and convergent for early *hominins*.

Its foot proportions are close to the unusual proportions of *Gorilla* and *Homo* but are distinct from those found in specialized climbers.

The lack of predators and the limitation of space and resources in *Oreopithecus'* insular environment favoured a locomotor system optimized for low energy expenditure rather than speed and mobility.

Oreopithecus has been claimed to exhibit features that are adaptations to upright walking, such as the presence of a lumbar curve, in distinction to otherwise similar species known from the same period. Since the fossils have been dated to about 8 million years ago, this would represent an unusually early appearance of upright posture. However, a re-evaluation of the spine from a skeleton of *Oreopithecus* has led to the conclusion that it lacked adaptations for habitual bipedality.

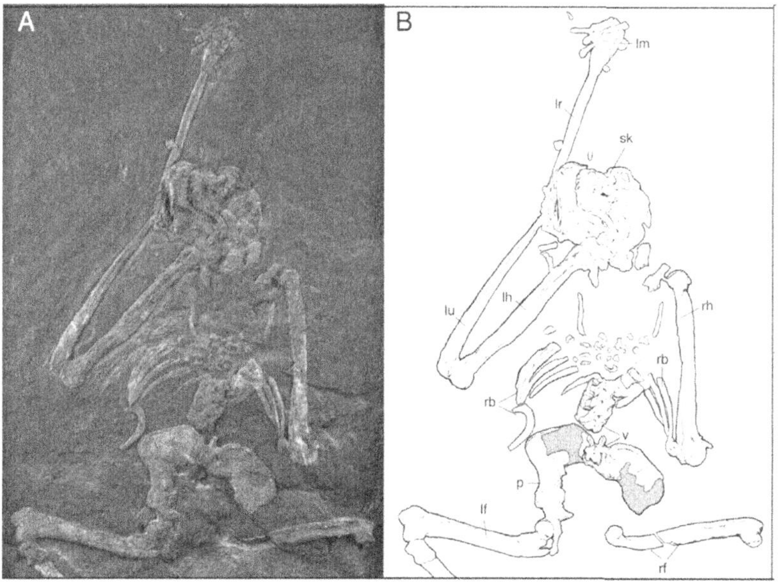

Anoiapithecus brevirostris (12 Mya)

Anoiapithecus is an extinct ape genus thought to be closely related to *Dryopithecus*.

The discoverers described ***Anoiapithecus brevirostris*** as a hominoid (super family *Hominoidea*) in the *Dryopithecine* tribe. They believe that it has more modern traits than the *Kenyapithecines* from which Kenya's *Kenyapithecus wickeri* brings fragmentary information. The African specimens are considered a sister taxon to the *hominids*, and 2 million years younger European specimens must be from the time after these two groups split. This means that *hominids* may have evolved in Europe.

The modern anatomical features that characterized the family *Hominidae* visible in the fossil of *A. brevirostris* among others are: unique facial pattern for *hominoids*, nasal aperture wide at the base, high cheek bone, and deep palate.

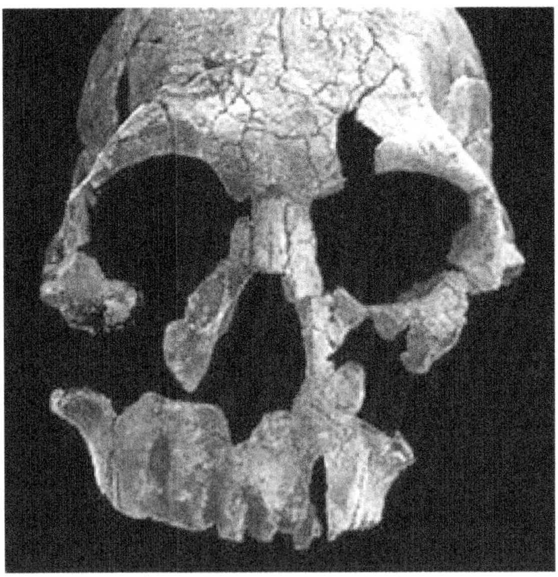

Chororapithecus abyssinicus (8 Mya)

Chororapithecus is an extinct great ape from the Afar region of Ethiopia roughly 8 million years ago during the late Miocene, comprising one species, namely *C. abyssinicus*.

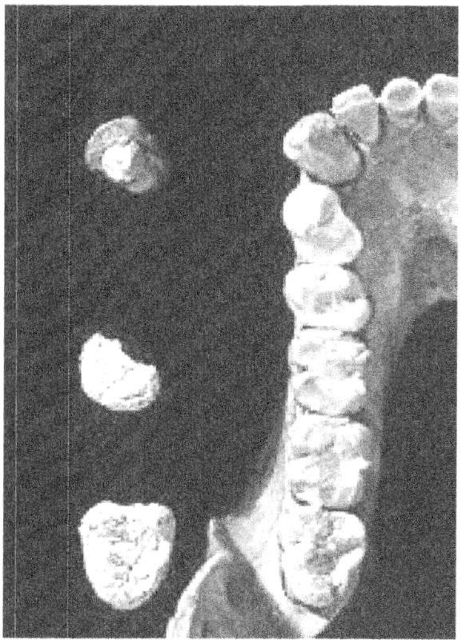

It is known from nine isolated teeth discovered in a 2005–2007 survey of the Chorora Formation. The teeth are indistinguishable from those of gorillas in terms of absolute size and relative proportions, and it has been proposed to be an early member of *Gorillini*.

However, this is controversial given the paucity of remains, and notable anatomical differences between *Chororapithecus* and gorilla teeth.

The Kenyan ape *Nakalipithecus* has been proposed to be an ancestor of *Chororapithecus* or at least closely related. If correct, they would be the only identified fossil members of any modern 'non-human' great ape lineage, and would push the 'gorilla human' last '**common ancestor**' from 8 million years ago (identified by molecular analysis) to 10 million years ago. The teeth are adapted for processing tough plant fibres as well as hard, brittle food, and the formation is thought to represent a forested lakeside habitat.

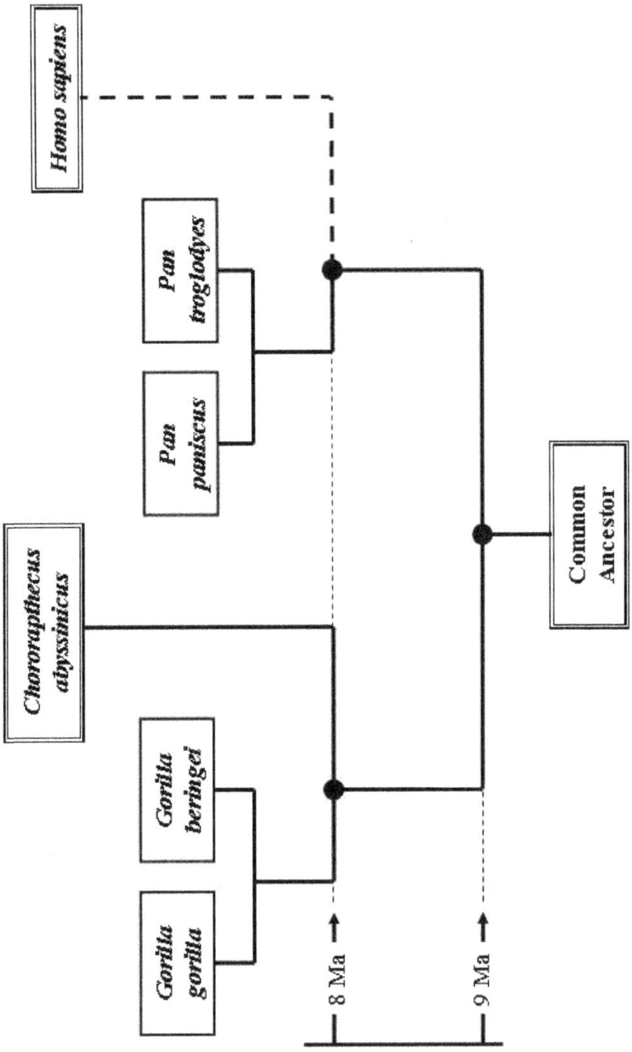

Homo sapiens
Pan troglodyes
Pan paniscus
Chororapthecus abyssinicus
Gorilla beringei
Gorilla gorilla
Common Ancestor
8 Ma
9 Ma

Dryopithecus fontani (12.5 – 11.1 Mya)

Dryopithecus is a genus of extinct great apes from the middle–late Miocene boundary of Europe.

Since its discovery in 1856, the genus has been subject to taxonomic turmoil, with numerous new species being described from single remains based on minute differences amongst each other, and the fragmentary nature of the holotype specimen makes differentiating remains difficult. There is currently only one uncontested species, the type species *D. fontani*, though there may be more.

The genus is placed into the tribe *Dryopithecini*, which is either an offshoot of orangutans, African apes, or is its own separate branch.

A male specimen was estimated to have weighed 44kg in life. *Dryopithecus* likely predominantly ate ripe fruit from trees, suggesting a degree of suspensory behaviour to reach them, though the anatomy of a *humerus* and *femur* suggest a greater reliance on walking on all fours (quadrupedalism). The face was similar to gorillas, and males had longer canines than females, which is typically correlated with high levels of aggression.

In the '*The Descent of Man*', Darwin briefly noted that *Dryopithecus* casts doubt on the African origin of apes:

> *"...it is somewhat more probable that our early progenitors lived on the African continent than elsewhere. But it is useless to speculate on this subject; for two or three anthropomorphous apes, one the Dryopithecus of Lartet, nearly as large as a man, and closely allied to Hylobates, existed in Europe during the Miocene age; and since so remote a period the earth has certainly undergone many great revolutions, and there has been ample time for migration on the largest scale."*

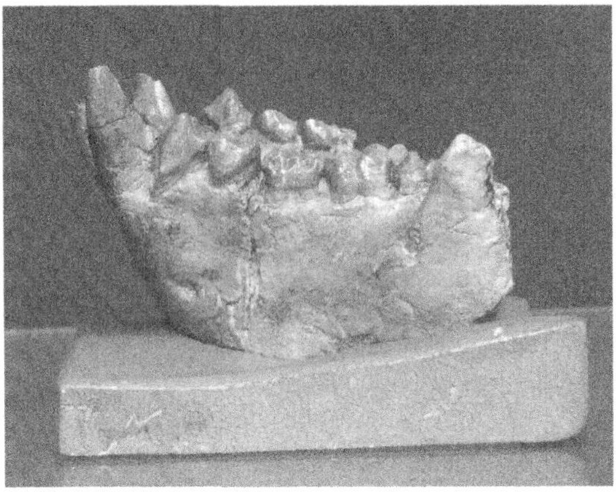

Ghedoghedo, Museum of Natural History, Paris

Restoration of D. fontani with an orangutan-like build.

Pierolapithecus catalaunicus (13 Mya)

Pierolapithecus catalaunicus is an extinct species of primate which lived during the Miocene in what is now Hostalets de Pierola, Catalonia, Spain, giving it its scientific name.

It is believed by some to be a '**common ancestor**' of both modern humans and the other great apes, or at least a species that is closer to a '**common ancestor**' than any previous fossil discovery.

The species was described by a team of Spanish paleoanthropologists led by Salvador Moyà-Solà on the basis of a fossil specimen discovered in December 2002. The finding was first reported in the journal Science on 19th November, 2004.

The question of whether *Pierolapithecus* would be ancestral to modern great apes is debated largely because this great ape was found in the Iberian Peninsula, while most of the fossil evidence of the evolution of *hominids* and *hominins* has been located in East Africa and Southeast Asia.

Because, however, the Mediterranean Sea contracted several times in the past, permitting migration of terrestrial fauna between Africa and Europe, it is possible that *Pierolapithecus*, or its descendants, could have lived on both continents.

Rather than a full '**common ancestor**', it has been suggested that the species may be ancestral to humans, chimpanzees and gorillas but not orangutans, given certain characteristics of the face.

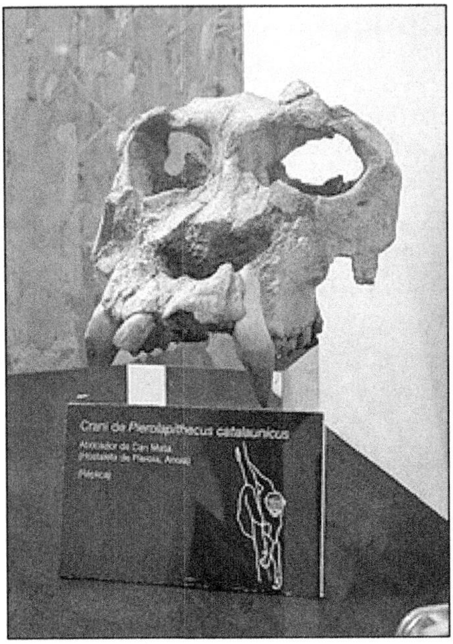

Reconstruction, Museum des Instituto de Paleontología Miquel Crusafont in Sabadell

Samburupithecus kiptalami (9.5 Mya)

Samburupithecus is an extinct primate that lived in Kenya during the middle to late Miocene. The one species in this genus, *Samburupithecus kiptalami*, is known only from a *maxilla* fragment discovered in 1982 and formally described by Ishida & Pickford 1997.

Samburupithecus lived during the so-called '**African ape gap**' 14 to 7 Mya, a period from which very few *hominoid* fossils have been found in Africa until relatively recently.

This apparent gap, however, is now populated by a diversity of apes such as *Nakalipithecus, Chororapithecus abyssinicus, Otavipithecus,* and *Nacholapithecus.*

Sivapithecus indicus
(12.5 – 10.5 Mya)

Sivapithecus sivalensis
(9.5 – 8.5 Mya)

Sivapithecus parvada
(10 Mya)

The first incomplete specimens of *Sivapithecus* were found in northern India in the late 19th century.

Another find was made in Nepal on the bank of Tinau River, in Palpa district, a western part of the country, in 1932. Now it is in Nature Museum, Kathmandu. This find was named '*Ramapithecus*'. The discoverer, G. Edward Lewis, claimed that it was distinct from *Sivapithecus*, as the jaw was more like a human's than any other fossil ape then known, a claim revived in the 1960s.

At that time, it was believed that the ancestors of humans had diverged from other apes 14 million years ago. Biochemical studies upset this view, suggesting that there was an early split between orangutan ancestors and the '**common ancestors**' of chimpanzees, gorillas and humans.

Meanwhile, more complete specimens of *Ramapithecus* were found in 1975 and 1976, which showed that it was less human-like than had been thought. It began to look more and more like *Sivapithecus*, meaning that the older name must take priority. It is also possible that fossils assigned to *Ramapithecus* belonged to the female form of *Sivapithecus.* They were definitely members of the same genus.

It is also likely that they were already separate from the '**common ancestor**' of chimps, gorillas and humans, which may be represented by the prehistoric great ape *Nakalipithecus nakayamai*.

Ramapithecus is no longer regarded as a likely ancestor of humans.

In 1982, David Pilbeam published a description of a significant fossil find, formed by a large part of the face and jaw of a *Sivapithecus*. The specimen bore many similarities to the orangutan skull and strengthened the theory (previously suggested by others) that *Sivapithecus* was closely related to orangutans.

In 2011, a 10.8 million-year old (Neogene period) upper jawbone of *Sivapithecus* was found in Kutch district of Gujarat, India.

The find also extended *Sivapithecus*' southern range in Indian subcontinent significantly. The species can not be identified.

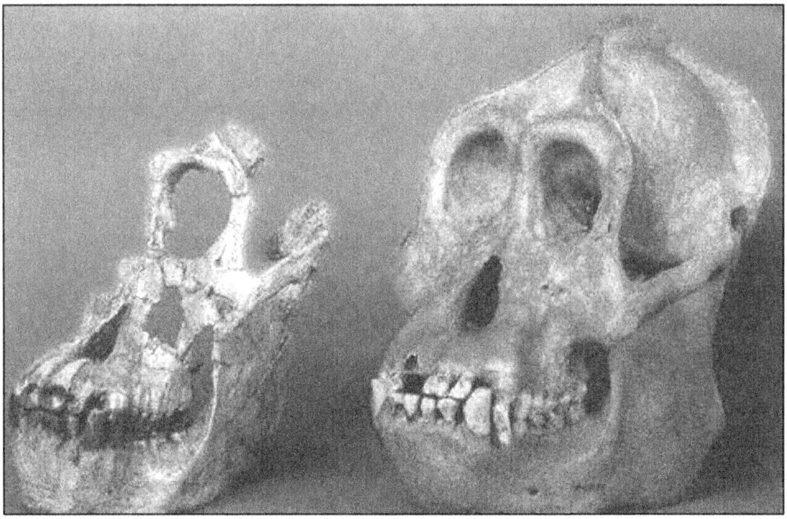

Natural History Museum, London

Ramapithecus
(10 – 14 Mya)

Ramapithecus is a fossil primate dating from the Middle and Late Miocene. For a time in the 1960s and '70s, *Ramapithecus* was thought to be a distinct genus that was the first direct ancestor of modern humans (*Homo sapiens*) before it became regarded as that of the orangutan ancestor *Sivapithecus*. *Ramapithecus* is now considered as being an invalid taxonomic designation for several species of extinct *hominoids*.

The first remains of the now-abolished *Ramapithecus* family were found in the early 20th century.

The new family name *Ramapithecus* was proposed only in 1934 on the basis of fragments of jaws. The preserved teeth with their morphology resembled the teeth of advanced *hominins*.

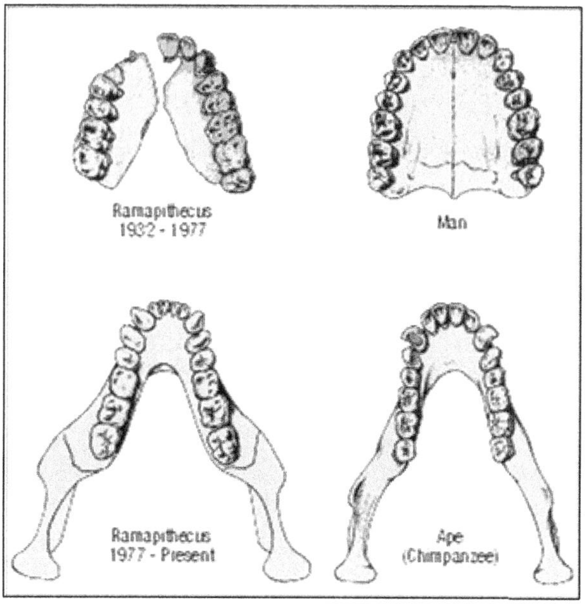

In 1935, the anthropologist Aleš Hrdlička, who assumed that he was an extinct ape, who had no connection to human development, spoke out against this view.

Due to certain morphology, the remains from the Fort Ternan site in Kenya, described by Louis Leakey in 1961 under the species name *Kenyapithecus wicker*i, were also assigned to the genus *Ramapithecus*. They therefore appear as *Ramapithecus wickeri* in older literature. Similarly, other Miocene *hominoids*, such as some species of the genus *Dryopithecus* (*Ramapithecus hungaricus*), *Lufengpithecus* (*Ramapithecus hudienensis*) or Ankarapithecus, have been considered for *Ramapithecus*.

Ramapithecus was considered in the 1960s and 1970s to be the oldest ancestor of modern man and a direct ancestor of the *genus Australopithecus*. The age of the fossils, intended for 10-14 million years ago, corresponded well to the period considered at the time of separation of the separate development line of the genus *Homo*.

At that time, this separation was supposed to be about 15 million years ago, whereas it is currently being put until about 6-8 million years ago. Already during the 1970s, doubts arose about the importance of the genus *Ramapithecus* in human evolution.

Based on further findings, the theory of the origin of man from the genus *Ramapithecus* was abandoned in the early 1980s. This was also helped by the rapid development of genetic studies, in particular the so-called '***molecular clock method***' and the related refinement of the time of formation of individual hominid lines.

At the same time, a considerable similarity of the *Ramapithecus* remains to the findings, classified in the genus *Sivapithecus*, was recognized. At present, the prevailing view is that *Ramapithecus* is identical to *Sivapithecus*, or it is a female and a male of the same genus.

This only confirms the assumption that *Ramapithecus* was not of special significance to modern man, since the genus *Sivapithecus* is more related to contemporary orangutans.

Evolution of Early Homo

Homo habilis, dated between 2.0 and 1.9 Mya, may be ancestral to modern humans.

Skulls suggest portions of the brain associated with speech were enlarged. The ability to speak, moreover, may have led to hunting cooperatively and to the advent of culture.

Homo erectus and similar fossils are found in Africa, Asia, and Europe and are dated between 1.9 and 0.3 Mya.

- Larger brain and flatter face than *Homo habilis*.
- Much taller than previous hominids.
- Believed to have first appeared in Africa and then migrated into Asia and Europe.
- First hominid to use fire.

Evolution of Modern Humans

Most researchers believe *Homo sapiens* evolved from *Homo erectus*.

- **Multiregional Continuity Hypothesis**
    - Similar evolution occurred in many different places.
- **Out-of-Africa Hypothesis**
    - *H. sapiens* evolved from *H. erectus* only in Africa, and thereafter migrated to Europe.
- **Mitochondrial Eve**
    - The **matrilineal most common ancestor** (MDCA) in a direct, unbroken maternal line. Common female ancestor tentatively dated to about 200,000 years ago.

Multiregional Continuity Hypothesis

The **Multiregional Continuity Hypothesis** is a scientific model that provides an alternative explanation to the more widely accepted **Out of Africa** model of *monogenesis* for the pattern of human evolution.

Multiregional evolution holds that the human species first arose around two million years ago and subsequent human evolution has been within a single, continuous human species. This species encompasses all archaic human forms such as *H. erectus* and Neanderthals as well as modern forms, and evolved worldwide to the diverse populations of anatomically modern humans (*Homo sapiens*).

The multiregional hypothesis was first proposed in 1984, and then revised in 2003. In its revised form, it is similar to the **Assimilation Model**, which holds that modern humans originated in Africa and today share a predominant recent African origin, but has also absorbed small, geographically variable, degrees of admixture from other regional (archaic) hominin species.

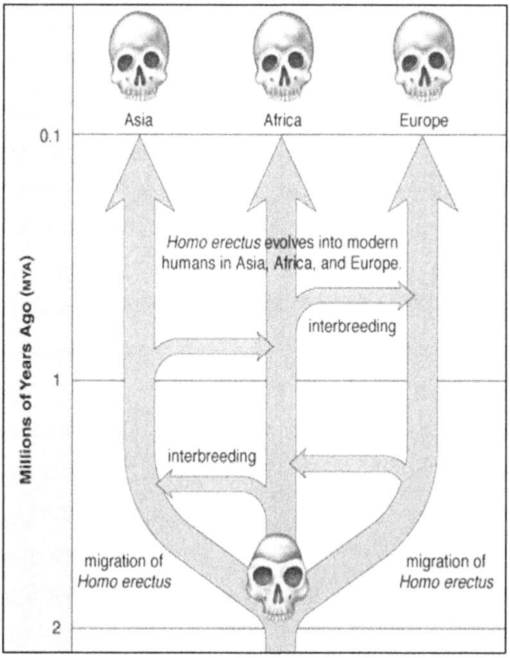

From Wikipedia, the free encyclopaedia

Out of Africa Hypothesis

The **Out of Africa Hypothesis** proposes a 'single origin' of *Homo sapiens* in the taxonomic sense, precluding parallel evolution of traits considered anatomically modern in other regions, but not precluding multiple admixture between *H. sapiens* and archaic humans in Europe and Asia. *H. sapiens* most likely developed in the Horn of Africa between 300,000 and 200,000 years ago. The model proposes that all modern non-African populations are substantially descended from populations of *H. sapiens* that left Africa after that time.

'There were at least several 'Out-of-Africa' dispersals of modern humans, possibly beginning as early as 270,000 years ago. The most significant recent wave out of Africa took place about 70,000–50,000 years ago.

In the 2010s, studies in population genetics uncovered evidence of interbreeding that occurred between *H. sapiens* and archaic humans in Eurasia, Oceania and Africa, indicating that modern population groups, while mostly derived from early *H. sapiens*, are to a lesser extent also descended from regional variants of archaic humans.

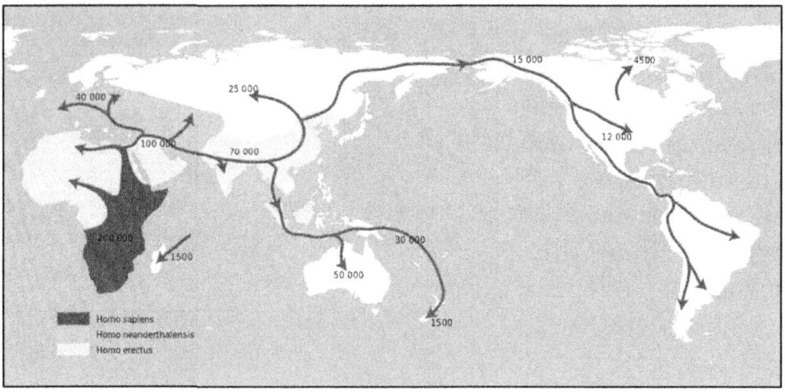

Mitochondrial Eve

Mitochondrial Eve is the **matrilineal most recent common ancestor** (MRCA), in a direct, unbroken, maternal line, of all currently living humans, who is estimated to have lived approximately 200,000 years ago.

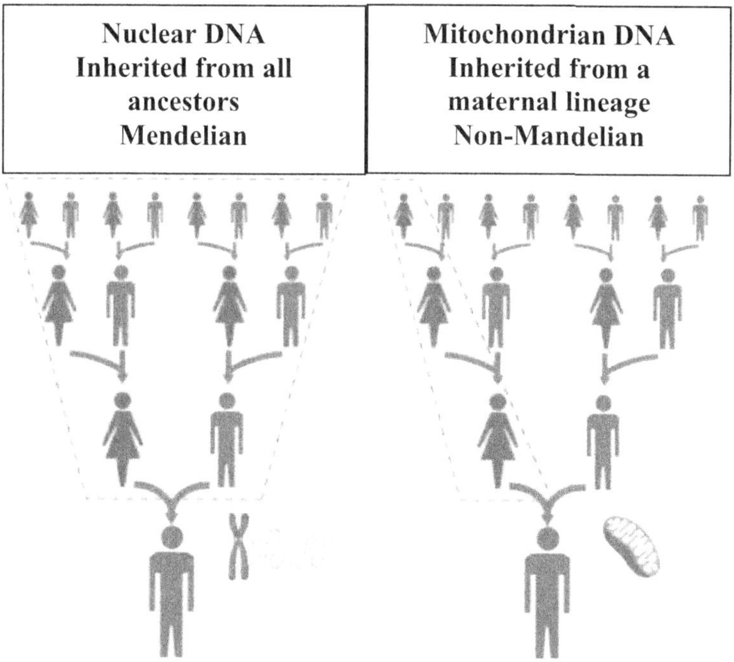

This is the most recent woman from whom all living humans today descend, in an unbroken line, on their mother's side, and through the mothers of those mothers, and so on, back until all lines converge on one person.

Because all mitochondrial DNA (mtDNA) is generally passed from mother to offspring without recombination, all mtDNA in every living person is directly descended from hers by definition, differing only by the mutations that over generations have occurred in the germ cell mtDNA since the conception of the original 'Mitochondrial Eve'.

Mitochondrial Eve is estimated to have lived about 200,000 years ago, most likely in East Africa, when *Homo sapiens* (anatomically modern humans) were developing as a population distinct from other human sub-species. Mitochondrial Eve lived later than *Homo heidelbergensis* and the emergence of *Homo neanderthalensis*, but earlier than the **Out of Africa** migration.

The dating for 'Eve' was contrary to the **Multiregional Continuity Hypothesis** and a support to the theory of the origin and dispersion of modern humans from Africa, replacing more archaic human populations such as Neanderthals.

As a result, a consensus emerged among anthropologists that the latter theory was more plausible.

Analogous to the Mitochondrial Eve is the **Y-chromosomal Adam**, the member of *Homo sapiens* from whom all living humans are descended *patrilineally*. The inherited DNA in the male case is his nuclear Y-chromosome rather than the mtDNA.

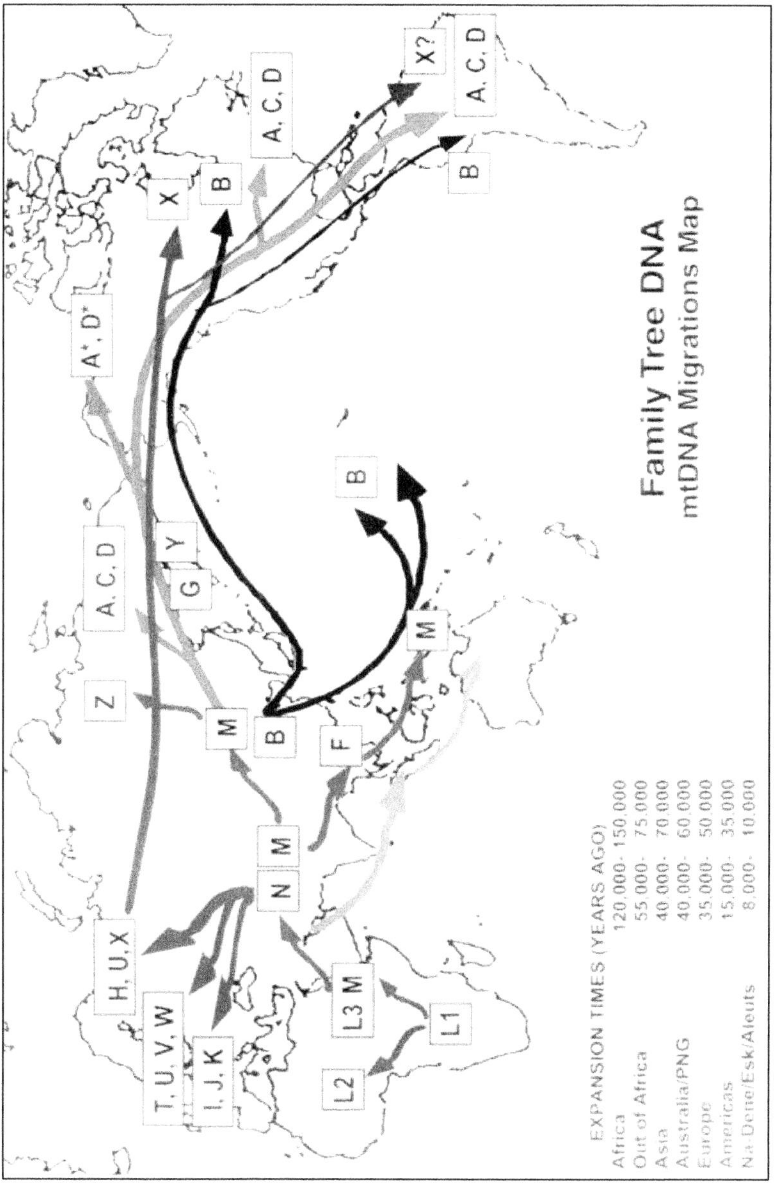
Family Tree DNA
mtDNA Migrations Map
EXPANSION TIMES (YEARS AGO)
Africa 120,000-150,000
Out of Africa 55,000-75,000
Asia 40,000-70,000
Australia/PNG 40,000-60,000
Europe 35,000-50,000
Americas 15,000-35,000
Na-Dene/Esk/Aleuts 8,000-10,000
L1
L2
L3 M
N
M
H,U,X
T,U,V,W
I,J,K
M
B
F
Z
A,C,D
G
Y
A*, D*
M
B
X
B
A,C,D
X?
A,C,D
B

Homo Neanderthalensis (230,000 to 28,000 years ago)

Homo neanderthalensis are an extinct species or subspecies of archaic humans who lived in Eurasia. They most likely went extinct due to assimilation into the modern human genome (bred into extinction), great climatic change, disease, or a combination of these factors.

It is unclear when the line of *Neanderthals* split from that of modern humans. The time of divergence of Neanderthals from their ancestor *H. heidelbergensis* is also unclear. For much of the early 20th century, researchers depicted *Neanderthals* as primitive, unintelligent, and brutish. Although knowledge and perception of them has markedly changed in the scientific community since then, the image of the caveman archetype remains prevalent in popular culture.

Skeletons dating back 200,000 years indicate:

- Massive brow ridges with protruding nose, jaws, and teeth.
- Heavily muscled.
- Culturally advanced.
- Manufactured variety of tools.

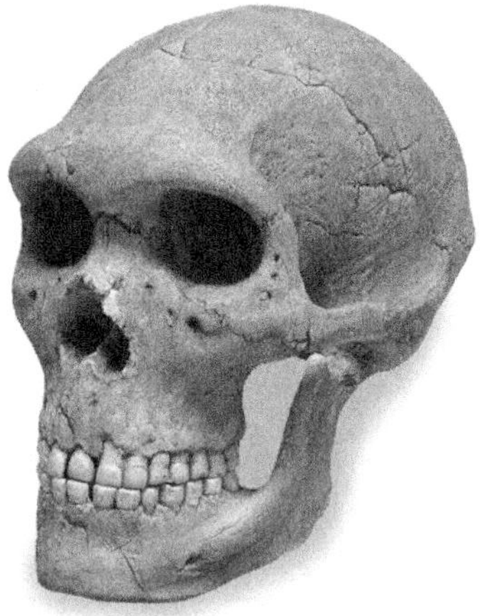

(*See also page 210*)

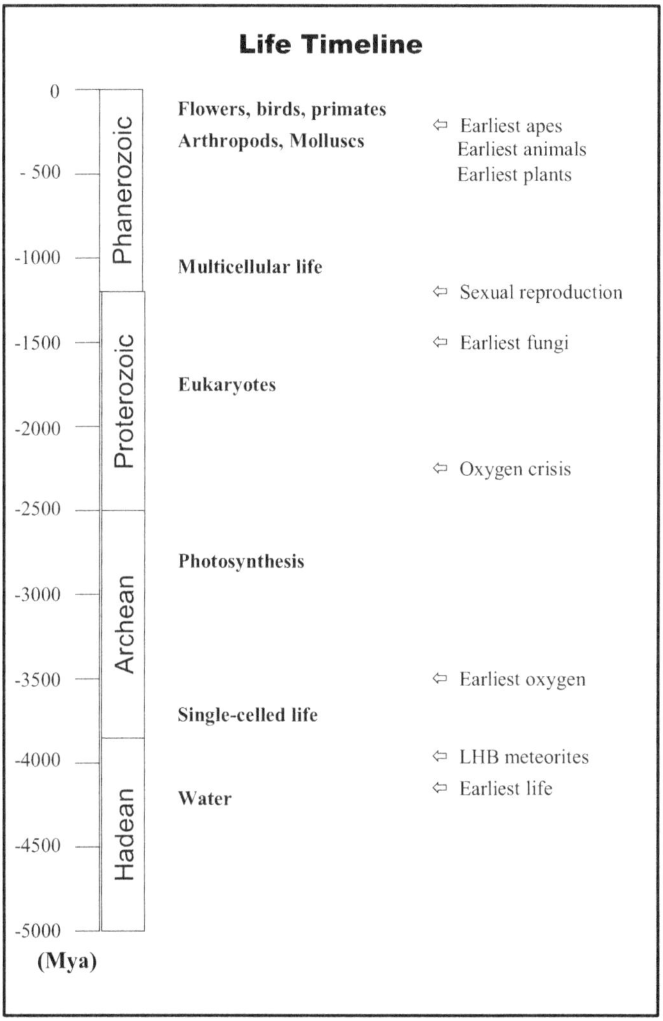
Life Timeline
0
- 500
-1000
-1500
-2000
-2500
-3000
-3500
-4000
-4500
-5000
(Mya)
Phanerozoic
Proterozoic
Archean
Hadean
Flowers, birds, primates
Arthropods, Molluscs
Multicellular life
Eukaryotes
Photosynthesis
Single-celled life
Water
⇦ Earliest apes
Earliest animals
Earliest plants
⇦ Sexual reproduction
⇦ Earliest fungi
⇦ Oxygen crisis
⇦ Earliest oxygen
⇦ LHB meteorites
⇦ Earliest life

Sahelanthropus tchadensis (6 – 7 Mya)

Sahelanthropus tchadensis is an extinct species of the *Homininae* (African apes) during the Miocene.

This species was named in July 2002 from fossils discovered in Chad in Central Africa (Brunet et al. 2002, Wood 2002). It is the oldest known *hominid* or near-*hominid* species. It lived close to the time of the chimpanzee–human divergence, possibly related to *Orrorin*, a species of *Homininae* that lived about one million years later. It may have been ancestral to both humans and chimpanzees (which would place it in the tribe *Hominini*), or alternatively an early member of the tribe Gorillini. In 2020, the femur was analyzed, and it was found that *Sahelanthropus* was not bipedal, casting doubt on its position as a human ancestor.

This species is known from a nearly complete cranium nicknamed **Toumai**, and a number of fragmentary lower jaws and teeth. The skull has a very small brain size of approximately 350cc.

As stated above, it is not known whether it was bipedal. *S. tchadensis* has many primitive ape-like features, such as the small brain-size, along with others, such as the brow ridges and small canine teeth, which are characteristic of later *hominids*. This mixture, along with the fact that it comes from around the time when the *hominids* are thought to have diverged from chimpanzees, suggests it is close to the 'common ancestor' of humans and chimpanzees.

A further possibility is that **Toumaï** is not ancestral to either humans or chimpanzees at all, but rather an early representative of the *Gorillini* lineage. Brigitte Senut and Martin Pickford, the discoverers of *Orrorin tugenensis*, suggested that the features of *S. tchadensis* are consistent with a female proto-gorilla.

Even if this claim is upheld the find would loose none of its significance, because at present, very few chimpanzee or gorilla ancestors have been found anywhere in Africa.

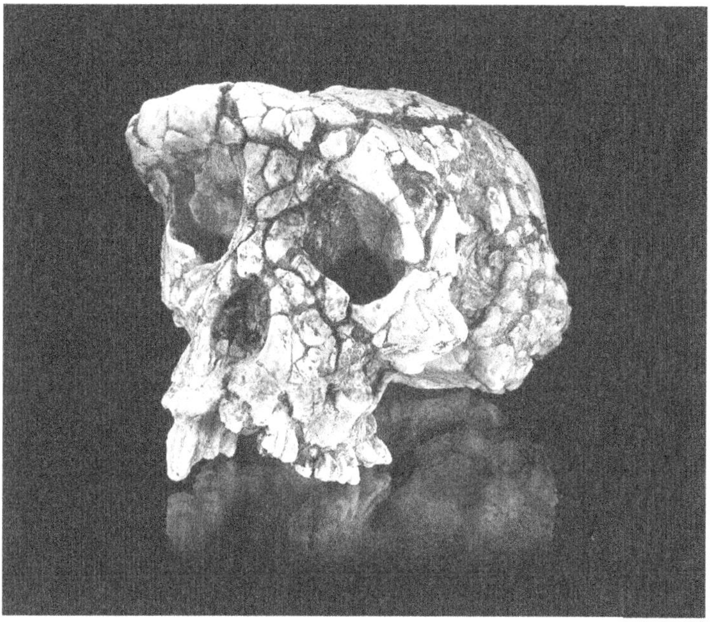

Specimen of Anthropology Molecular and Imaging Synthesis of Toulouse by Didier Descouens

Orrorin tugenensis (6 Mya)

This species was named in July 2001 from fossils discovered in western Kenya (Senut et al. 2001). The fossils include fragmentary arm and thigh bones, lower jaws, and teeth and were discovered in deposits that are about 6 million years old.

The limb bones are about 1.5 times larger than those of **Lucy** (p402), and suggest that it was about the size of a female chimpanzee. Its finders have claimed that *Orrorin* was a human ancestor adapted to both bipedality and tree climbing, and that the *australopithecines* are an extinct offshoot. Given the fragmentary nature of the remains, other scientists have been sceptical of these claims so far (Aiello and Collard 2001). A later paper (Galik et al. 2004) has found further evidence of bipedality in the fossil femur.

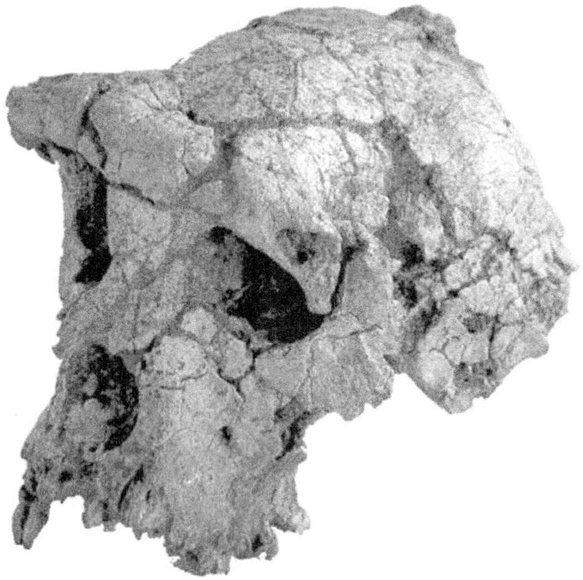

Ardipithecus ramidus (5.8 Mya)

Ardipithecus is a very early hominine genus (subfamily Homininae) which lived during the early Pliocene.

Because this genus shares several traits with the African great ape genera (genus *Pan* and genus *Gorilla*), it is considered by some to be on the chimpanzee rather than human branch, but most consider it a proto-human because of a likeness in teeth with *Australopithecus*.

Ardipithecus ramidus was named in September 1994. The first fossil find was dated to 4.4 million years ago based on its interval between two volcanic strata: the basal Gaala Tuff Complex (GATC) and the Daam Aatu Basaltic Tuff (DABT).

Subsequent discoveries identified as *A. ramidus* and would push the date back as far as 5.8 million years ago.

In 1992-1993 a research team discovered the first *A. ramidus* fossils—seventeen fragments including skull, mandible, teeth and arm bones—from the Afar Depression in the Middle Awash river valley of Ethiopia.

More fragments were recovered in 1994, amounting to 45 percent of the total skeleton. Features of the foramen magnum and leg fragments are indicative of bipedalism.

This species was named *Australopithecus ramidus* in September 1994 (White et al. 1994; Wood 1994) from some fragmentary fossils dated at 4.4 million years. A more complete skull and partial skeleton was discovered in late 1994 and based on that fossil, the species was reallocated to the genus *Ardipithecus* (White et al. 2005). This fossil was extremely fragile, and excavation, restoration and analysis of it took 15 years. It was published in October 2009, and given the nickname '**Ardi**'. *Ar. Ramidus* was about 120cm tall and weighed about 50kg. The skull and brain are small, about the size of a chimpanzee. It was bipedal on the ground, though not as well adapted to bipedalism as the *australopithecines* were, and quadrupedal in the trees. It lived in a woodland environment with patches of forest, indicating that bipedalism did not originate in a savannah environment.

A number of fragmentary fossils discovered between 1997 and 2001, and dating from 5.2 to 5.8 million years old, were originally assigned to a new subspecies, *Ardipithecus ramidus kadabba* (Haile-Selassie 2001), and later to a new species, *Ardipithecus kadabba* (Haile-Selassie et al. 2004). One of these fossils is a toe bone belonging to a bipedal creature, but is a few hundred thousand years younger than the rest of the fossils and so its identification with *kadabba* is not as firm as the other fossils.

Australopithecus anamensis (4.2 – 3.9 Mya)

This species was named in 1995 (Leakey et al. 1995). The material consists of 9 fossils, mostly found in 1994, from Kanapoi in Kenya, and 12 fossils, mostly teeth found in 1988, from Allia Bay in Kenya (Leakey et al. 1995).

Anamensis has a mixture of primitive features in the skull, and advanced features in the body. The teeth and jaws are very similar to those of older fossil apes. A partial tibia (the larger of the two lower leg bones) is strong evidence of bipedality, and a lower humerus (the upper arm bone) is extremely human-like.

Note that although the skull and skeletal bones are thought to be from the same species, this is not confirmed.

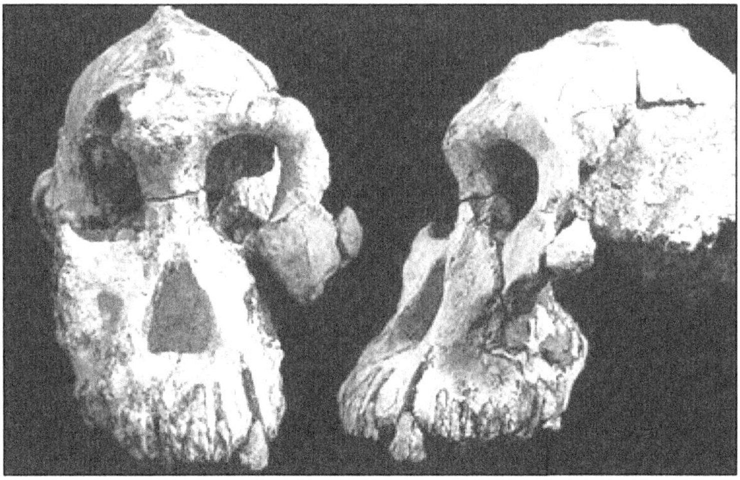

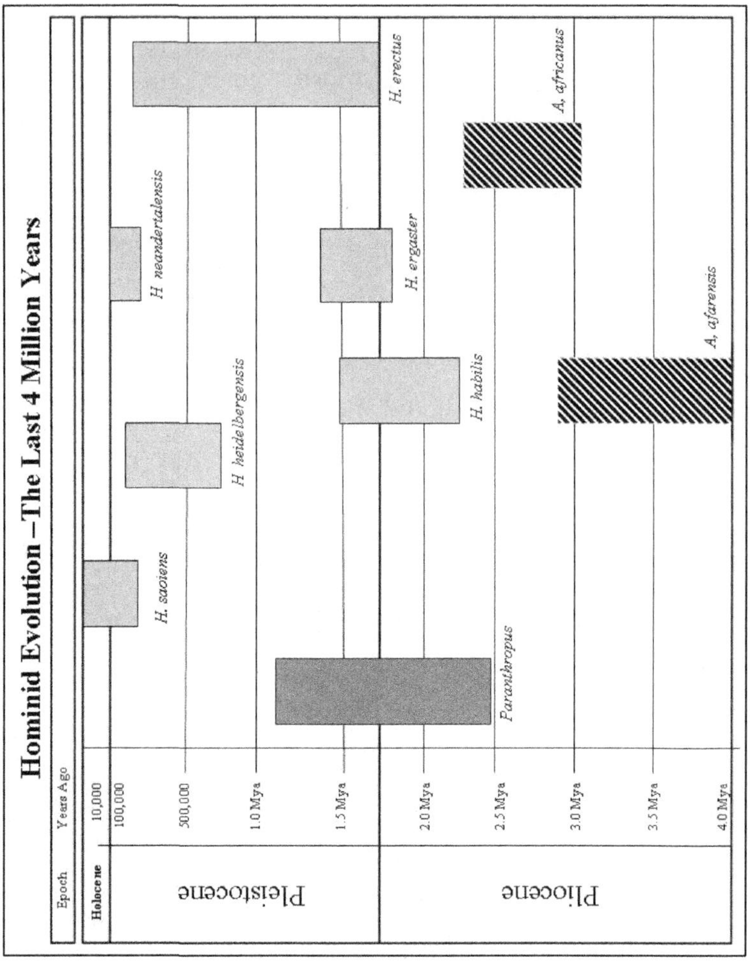
Hominid Evolution –The Last 4 Million Years
Epoch
Years Ago
Holocene
Pleistocene
Pliocene
10,000
100,000
500,000
1.0 Mya
1.5 Mya
2.0 Mya
2.5 Mya
3.0 Mya
3.5 Mya
4.0 Mya
Paranthropus
H. saoiens
H heidelbergensis
H. habilis
A, afarensis
H neandertalensis
H. ergaster
A, africanus
H. erectus

Australopithecus afarensis (Lucy) (3.9 - 3.0 Mya)

Lucy is the common name of AL 288-1 several hundred pieces of fossilized bone representing 40 percent of the skeleton of a female of the *hominin* species *Australopithecus afarensis*. In Ethiopia, the assembly is also known as *Dinkinesh*, which means 'you are marvellous' in the Amharic language. Lucy was discovered in 1974 in Africa, at Hadar, a site in the Awash Valley of the Afar Triangle in Ethiopia, by paleoanthropologists Donald Johanson of the Cleveland Museum of Natural History.

Lucy is ~ 3.5-million-years-old

- *Australopithecus afarensis*
- Adaptations in Lucy's hip, leg and foot allowed a fully bipedal means of locomotion

A. afarensis had an apelike face with a low forehead, a bony ridge over the eyes, a flat nose, and no chin. They had protruding jaws with large back teeth. Cranial capacity varied from about 375 to 550cc. The skull is similar to that of a chimpanzee, except for the more human-like teeth.

The canine teeth are much smaller than those of modern apes, but larger and more pointed than those of humans, and shape of the jaw is between the rectangular shape of apes and the parabolic shape of humans. However their pelvis and leg bones far more closely resemble those of modern man, and leave no doubt that they were bipedal (although adapted to walking rather than running (Leakey 1994)). Their bones show that they were physically very strong. Females were substantially smaller than males, a condition known as sexual dimorphism. Height varied between about 107cm and 152cm. The finger and toe bones are curved and proportionally longer than in humans, but the hands are similar to humans in most other details (Johanson and Edey 1981). Most scientists consider this as evidence that *afarensis* was still partially adapted to climbing in trees, others consider it evolutionary baggage.

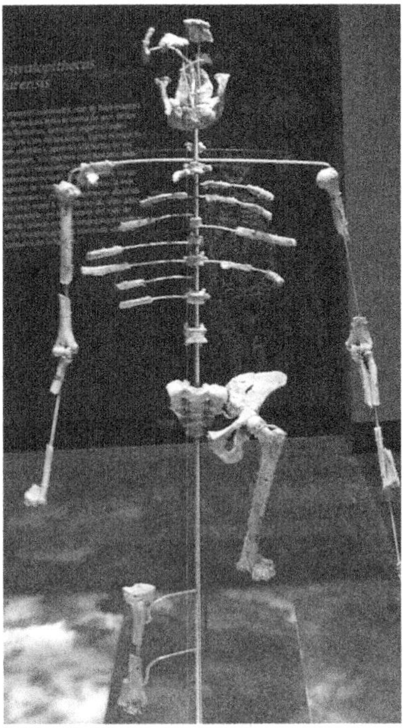

Lucy replica,
Museo Nacional de Antropología, Mexico City

Kenyanthropus platyops (~3.5 Mya)

This species was named in 2001 from a partial skull found in Kenya with an unusual mixture of features (*Leakey et al 2001*).

The size of the skull is similar to *A. afarensis* and *A. africanus* and is most recognizable by an unusually flat face and small teeth for such an early *hominin.*

Multiple *australopithecine* species may have coexisted by foraging for different food items (*niche partitioning*), which may be reason why these apes are anatomically different with respect to areas related to chewing.

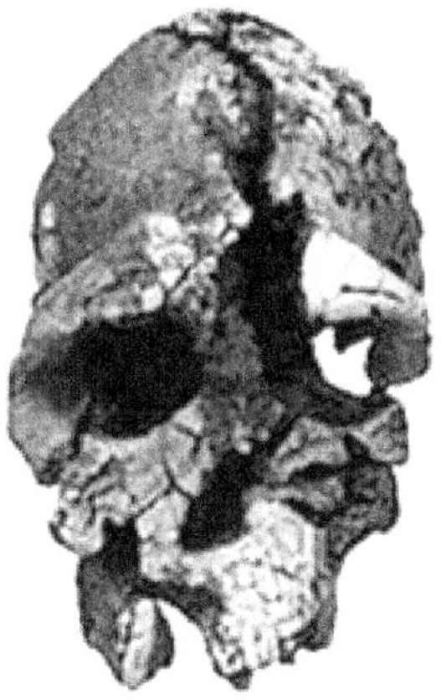

Cast of KNM-WT 40000 Cantonal Museum of Geology, Lausanne

Australopithecus africanus (3 – 2 Mya)

A africanus is similar to *afarensis*, and was also bipedal, but body size was slightly greater. Brain size may also have been slightly larger, ranging between 420 and 500cc. This is a little larger than chimpanzee brains (despite a similar body size), but still not advanced in the areas necessary for speech. The back teeth were a little bigger than in *afarensis*.

Although the teeth and jaws of *africanus* are much larger than those of humans, they are far more similar to human teeth than to those of apes (Johanson and Edey 1981). The shape of the jaw is now fully parabolic, like that of humans, and the size of the canine teeth is further reduced compared to *afarensis*.

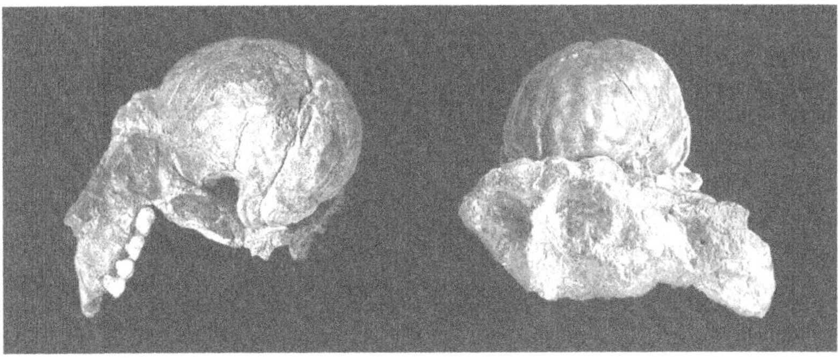

Australopithecus garhi (2.6 – 2.5 Mya)

This species was named in April 1999 (*Asfaw et al. 1999*). It is known from a partial skull. The skull differs from previous australopithecine species in the combination of its features, notably the extremely large size of its teeth, especially the rear ones, and primitive skull morphology.

A. garhi is the first pre-*Homo hominin* postulated to have manufactured tools, using them in butchering. This fact may be counted among a growing body of evidence for pre-*Homo* stone tool industries. The ability to manufacture tools was previously believed to have separated *Homo* from predecessors. *A. garhi* possibly produced the *Oldowan* industry which was previously considered to have been invented by the later *H. habilis*, though this may have been produced by contemporary *Homo*.

Some nearby skeletal remains may belong to the same species. They show a humanlike ratio of the humerus and femur, but an apelike ratio of the lower and upper arm. (*Groves 1999; Culotta 1999*)

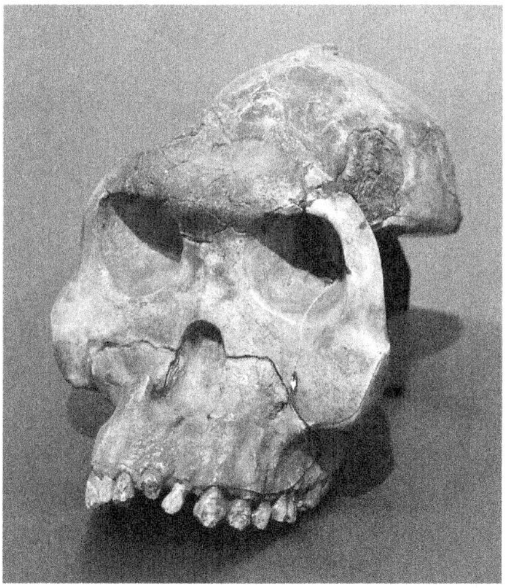

Paleontological collections of the National Museum of Ethiopia

Australopithecus sediba (1.78 – 1.95 Mya)

A. sediba was discovered at the site of Malapa, South Africa in 2008. Two partial skeletons were found of a young boy and an adult female (*Berger et al 2010, Balter 2010*).

Because it is more similar to *Homo* than any other *australopithecine*, it has been claimed to be a possible candidate as the ancestor of *Homo*. *A. sediba* was bipedal with long arms suitable for climbing, but also had a number of human-like traits in the skull, teeth and pelvis. The boy's skull has a volume of 420cc, and both the fossils are short – about 130cm.

A. afarensis and *A. africanus* as well as the other species above, are known as *'gracile' australopithecines*, because their skulls and teeth are not as large and strong as those of the species that followed, which are referred to as the *'robust' australopithecines.* Despite this, they were still more robust than modern humans.

Natural History Museum, London

Australopithecus aethiopicus (2.7 – 2.3 Mya)

Australopithecus aethiopicus is known from one major specimen and a few other minor specimens which may belong to the same species. It may be an ancestor of *A. robustus* and *A. boisei*, but it has a confusing combination of primitive and advanced traits.

The brain size is very small at 420cc and parts of the skull. Particularly the hind portions are very primitive, more resembling those of *A. Afarensis*.

Other characteristics, like the massiveness of the face, jaws and single tooth found, and the largest **sagittal crest** in any known *hominid*, are more representative of *A. Boisei* (*Leakey and Lewin, 1882*).

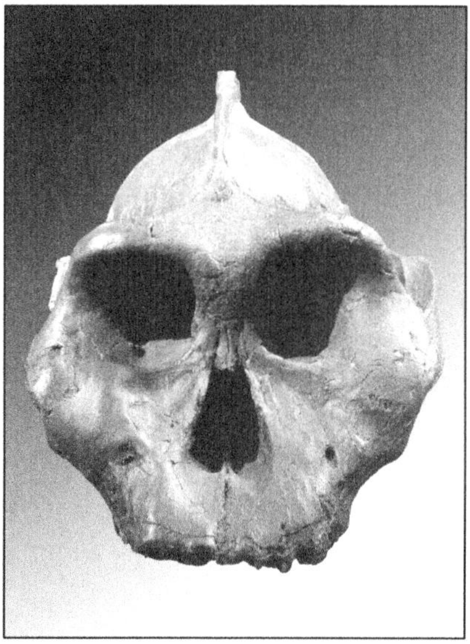

Muséum d'Anthropologie campus universitaire d'Irchel, Université de Zurich (Suisse) CC BY-SA 3.0)

Australopithecus robustus (2.0 – 1.5 Mya)

A robustus had a body similar to that of *africanus*, but a larger and more robust skull and teeth. It existed between 2 and 1.5 million years ago.

The massive face is flat or dished, with no forehead and large brow ridges. It has relatively small front teeth, but massive grinding teeth in a large lower jaw. Most specimens have sagittal crests. Its diet would have been mostly coarse, tough food that needed a lot of chewing.

The average brain size is about 530cc. Bones excavated with *robustus* skeletons indicate that they may have been used as digging tools.

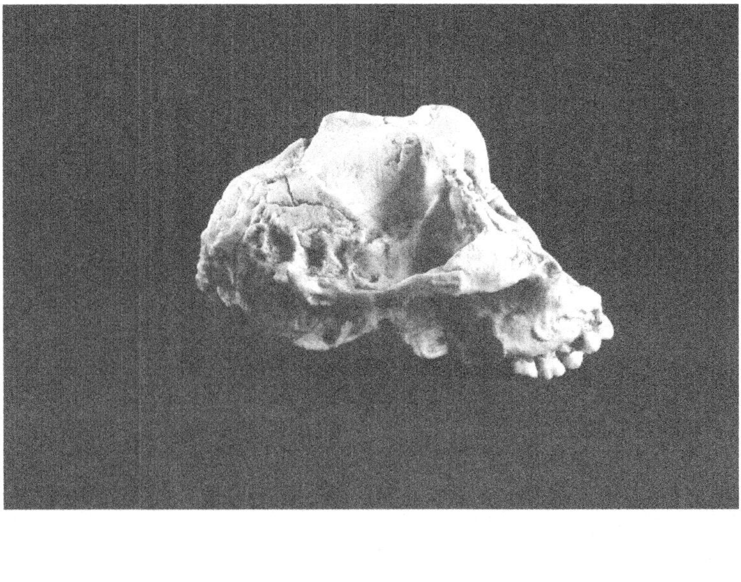

Australopithecus boisei (2.5 – 1.15 Mya)

A. boisei was similar to *robustus*, but the face and cheek teeth were even more massive, some molars being up to 2cm across. The brain size is very similar to *robustus*, about 530cc.

A few experts consider *boisei* and *robustus* to be variants of the same species.

Australopithecus aethiopicus, *robustus* and *boisei* are known as robust *australopithecines*, because their skulls in particular are more heavily built. They have never been serious candidates for being direct human ancestors. Many authorities now classify them in the genus *Paranthropus*.

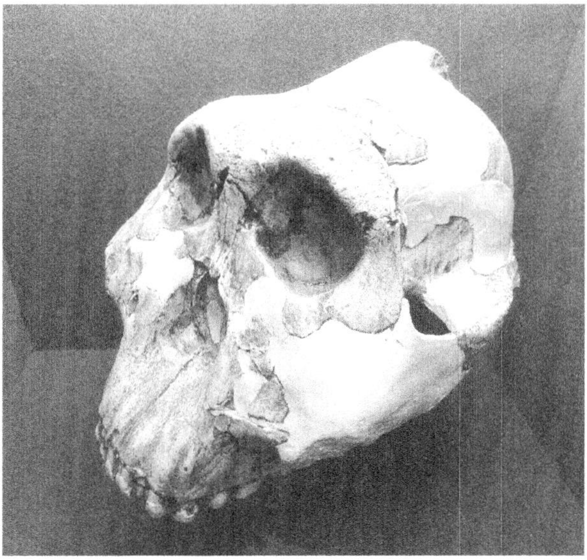

Exhibit in the Springfield Science Museum, 21 Edwards Street, Springfield, Massachusetts, USA.
The museum permitted photography without restriction.
CC0 1.0

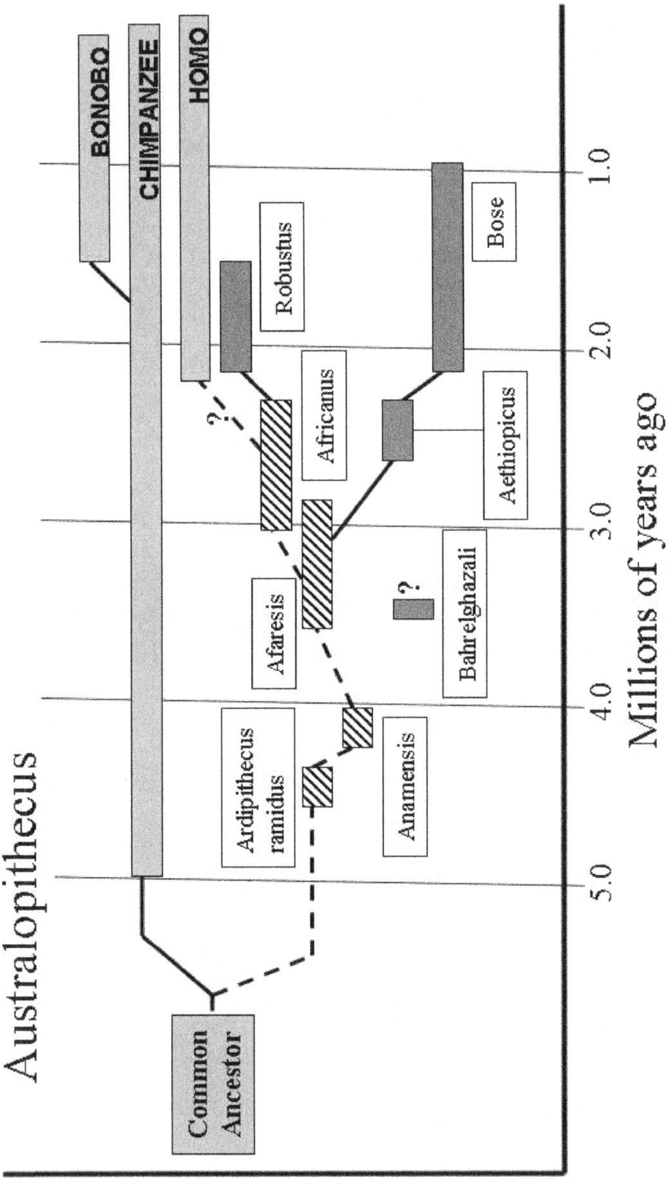

Australopithecus
Common Ancestor
BONOBO
CHIMPANZEE
HOMO
Ardipithecus ramidus
Anamensis
Afaresis
Bahrelghazali
?
Africanus
?
Aethiopicus
Robustus
Bose
5.0
4.0
3.0
2.0
1.0
Millions of years ago

Homo habilis
(2.2 – 1.6 Mya)

Homo habilis ('handy man', 'skillful person') is a species of the genus *Homo*, which lived from approximately 2.2 million to at least 1.6 million years ago at the beginning of the Pleistocene. It was called this on account of evidence of tools found with its remains.

The definition of this species is credited to both Mary and Louis Leakey, who found fossils in Tanzania, East Africa, between 1962 and 1964.

Homo habilis is arguably the first species of the *Homo* genus to appear.

In its appearance and morphology, *Homo habilis* was the least similar to modern humans of all species to be placed in the genus *Homo*, except possibly *Homo rudolfensis*.

Homo habilis was short and had disproportionately long arms compared to modern humans. However, it had a reduction in the protrusion in the face. It is thought to have descended from a species of australopithecine hominid. Its immediate ancestor may have been the more massive and ape-like *Homo rudolfensis*.

Homo habilis had a cranial capacity slightly less than half of the size of modern humans. Despite the ape-like morphology of the bodies, *H. habilis* remains are often accompanied by primitive stone tools.

H. habilis is very similar to *australopithecines* in many ways. The face is still primitive, but it projects less than in *A. africanus*. The back teeth are smaller, but still considerably larger than in modern humans. The average brain size, at 650cc, is considerably larger than in australopithecines. Brain size varies between 500 and 800cc, overlapping the *australopithecines* at the low end and *H. erectus* at the high end. The brain shape is also more human-like. The bulge of Broca's area, essential for speech, is visible in one *habilis* brain cast, and indicates it was possibly capable of rudimentary speech. *Habilis* is thought to have been about 127cm tall and about 45kg in weight, although females may have been smaller.

H. habilis has been a controversial species. Originally, some scientists did not accept its validity, believing that all *habilis* specimens should be assigned to either the australopithecines or *Homo erectus*.

H. habilis is now fully accepted as a species, but it is widely thought that the 'habilis' specimens have too wide a range of variation for a single species, and that some of the specimens should be placed in one or more other species. One suggested species which is accepted by many scientists is *Homo rudolfensis*, which would contain fossils such as ER 1470.

Homo georgicus
(1.8 – 1.6 Mya)

This species was named in 2002 to contain fossils found in Dmanisi, Georgia, which seem intermediate between *H. habilis* and *H. erectus*. Fossils consist of three partial skulls and three lower jaws. The brain sizes of the skulls vary from 600 to 780cc. The height, as estimated from a foot bone, would have been about 1.5m. A partial skeleton was also discovered in 2001 but no details are available on it yet. (*Vekua et al. 2002, Gabunia et al. 2002*)

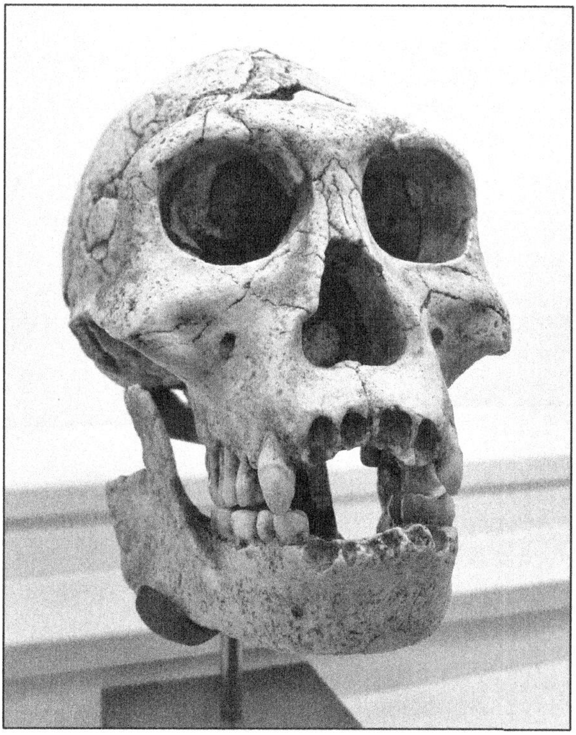

Fossil skull from Dmanisi. Georgia

Homo erectus
(1.8 – 0.3 Mya)

Like *H. habilis*, the face of *H. erectus* has protruding jaws with large molars, no chin, thick brow ridges, and a long low skull, with a brain size varying between 750 and 1225cc. Early *erectus* specimens average about 900cc, while late ones have an average of about 1100cc (*Leakey 1994*). The skeleton is more robust than those of modern humans, implying greater strength. Body proportions vary; the **Turkana Boy** is tall and slender though still extraordinarily strong like modern humans from the same area, while the few limb bones found of Peking Man indicate a shorter, sturdier build.

Study of the **Turkana Boy** skeleton indicates that *erectus* may have been more efficient at walking than modern humans, whose skeletons have had to adapt to allow for the birth of larger-brained infants (*Willis 1989*). *H. habilis* and all the *australopithecines* are found only in Africa, but *erectus* was wide-ranging, and has been found in Africa, Asia, and Europe. There is evidence that *erectus* probably used fire, and their stone tools are more sophisticated than those of *habilis*.

Subspecies

Homo erectus erectus (Java Man 1.6–0.5 Mya)
Homo erectus ergaster (1.7–1.4 Mya)
Homo erectus georgicus (1.8–1.6 Mya)
Homo erectus lantianensis (Lantian Man 1.6 Mya)
Homo erectus nankinensis (Nanjing Man 0.6 Mya)
Homo erectus pekinensis (Peking Man 0.7 Mya)
Homo erectus soloensis (Solo Man 0.546–0.143 Mya)
Homo erectus tautavelensis (Tautavel Man 0.45 Mya)
Homo erectus yuanmouensis (Yuanmou Man 1.7 Mya)

Replica of the skull of Peking Man (Homo erectus pekinensis) at the Paleozoological Museum of China   CC BY-SA 3.0

Homo ergaster
(1.7 – 1.4 Mya)

H. ergaster is an extinct species or subspecies of archaic humans who lived in Africa in the Early Pleistocene.

Whether *H. ergaster* constitutes a species of its own or should be subsumed into *H. erectus* is an ongoing and unresolved dispute within paleoanthropology. Proponents of synonymisation typically designate *H. ergaster* as '**African *Homo erectus***' or '***Homo erectus ergaster***'. The name *Homo ergaster* roughly translates to 'working man', a reference to the more advanced tools used by the species in comparison to those of their ancestors. Though fossils are known from across East and Southern Africa, most *H. ergaster* fossils have been found along the shores of Lake Turkana in Kenya. There are later African fossils, some younger than 1 million years ago, that indicate long-term anatomical continuity, though it is unclear if they can be formally regarded as *H. ergaster* specimens. As a chronospecies, *H. ergaster* may have persisted to as late as 600,000 years ago, when new lineages of *Homo* arose in Africa.

Several features distinguish *H. ergaster* from australopithecines as well as earlier and more basal species of *Homo*, such as *H. habilis*. Among these features are their larger body mass, relatively long legs, obligate bipedalism, relatively small jaws and teeth, indicating a major change in diet, as well as body proportions and inferred lifestyles more similar to modern humans than to earlier and contemporary *hominins*. With these features in mind, some researchers view *H. ergaster* as being the earliest true representative of the genus *Homo*.

Some scientists classify some African *erectus* specimens as belonging to a separate species, *Homo ergaster*, which differs from the Asian *H. erectus* fossils in some details of the skull (e.g. the brow ridges differ in shape, and *erectus* would have a larger brain size).

Skull of Homo ergaster Skull KNM-ER 3733 discovered by Bernard Ngeneo in 1975 (Kenya) CC BY 2.5

Homo rudolfensis (2.5/1.9 – 1.35/1.55 Mya)

Homo rudolfensis is an extinct species of archaic human from the Early Pleistocene. Because *H. rudolfensis* coexisted with several other hominins, it is debated what specimens can be confidently assigned to this species beyond the *lectotype* skull KNM-ER 1470 and other partial skull aspects. No bodily remains are definitively assigned to *H. rudolfensis*. Consequently, both its generic classification and validity are debated without any wide consensus, with some recommending the species to actually belong to the genus *Australopithecus* as ***A. rudolfensis*** or *Kenyanthropus* as ***K. rudolfensis***, or that it is synonymous with the contemporaneous and anatomically similar *H. habilis*.

H. rudolfensis is distinguished from *H. habilis* by larger size, but it is also argued that this species actually consists of male *H. habilis* specimens, assuming that *H. habilis* was sexually dimorphic and males were much larger than females. Because no bodily remains are definitely identified, body size estimates are largely based on the stature of *H. habilis*. Using this, male *H. rudolfensis* may have averaged about 160cm in height and 60kg in weight, and females 150cm and 51kg, KNM-ER 1470 had a brain volume of about 750cc. Like other early *Homo*, *H. rudolfensis* had large cheek teeth and thick enamel.

Early *Homo* species exhibit marked brain growth compared to *Australopithecus* predecessors, which is typically explained as a change in diet with a calorie-rich food source, namely meat. Though not associated with tools, dental anatomy suggests some processing of plant or meat fibre before consumption, though the mouth could still effectively chew through mechanically challenging food, indicating tool use did not greatly affect diet.

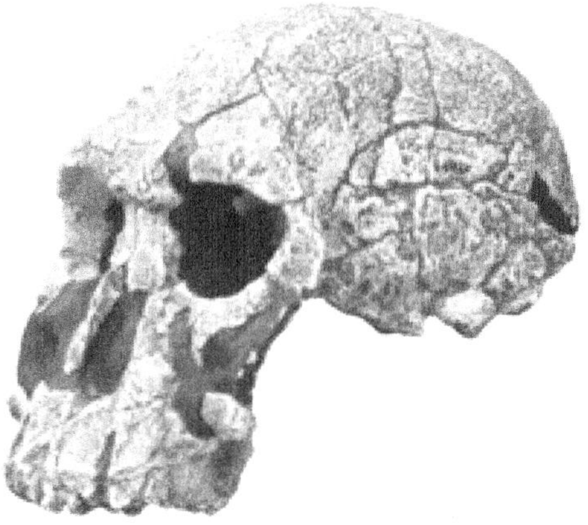

Reconstruction of the KNM-ER 1470 skull

Reconstruction of H. rudolfensis by Mauricio Antón

Homo antecessor
(780,000 years ago)

H. antecessor was named in 1977 from fossils found at the Spanish cave site of Atapuerca, making them the oldest confirmed European *hominids*. The mid-facial area of *antecessor* seems very modern, but other parts of the skull such as the teeth, forehead and brow ridges are much more primitive.

Many scientists are doubtful about the validity of *antecessor*, partly because its definition is based on a juvenile specimen, and feel it may belong to another species. (*Bermudez de Castro et al. 1997; Kunzig 1997; Carbonell et al. 1995*)

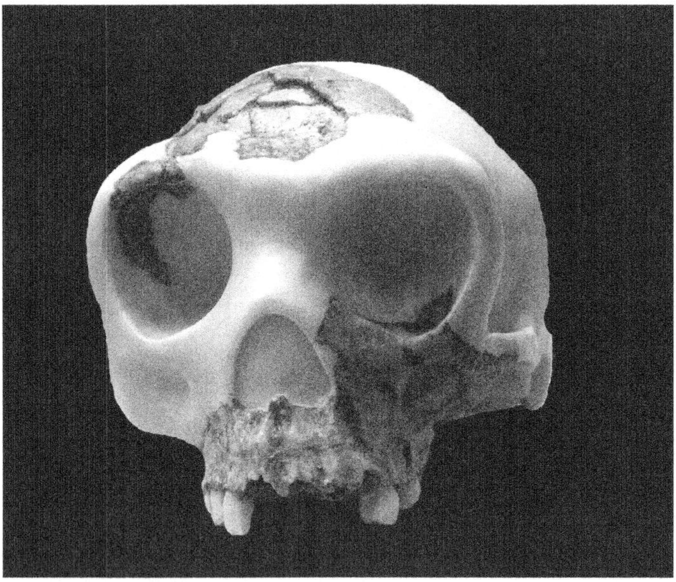

Reconstructed skull of the Boy of the Gran Dolina, Sierra de Atapuerca, Central Spain

Homo heidelbergensis (500,000 years ago)

Archaic forms of *H. sapiens* first appear about 500,000 years ago. The term covers a diverse group of skulls which have features of both *H. erectus* and modern humans. The brain size is larger than *erectus* and smaller than most modern humans, averaging about 1200cc, and the skull is more rounded than in *erectus*. The skeleton and teeth are usually less robust than *erectus*, but more robust than modern humans. Many still have large brow ridges and receding foreheads and chins.

There is no clear dividing line between late *erectus* and archaic *sapiens*, and many fossils between 500,000 and 200,000 years ago are difficult to classify as one or the other.

By convention, *H. heidelbergensis* is placed as the most 'recent common ancestor' between *H. sapiens* and *H. neanderthalensis.* Brain size averaged about 1,200cc, comparable to modern humans. Height in the Middle Pleistocene is estimated as being 169.5cm.

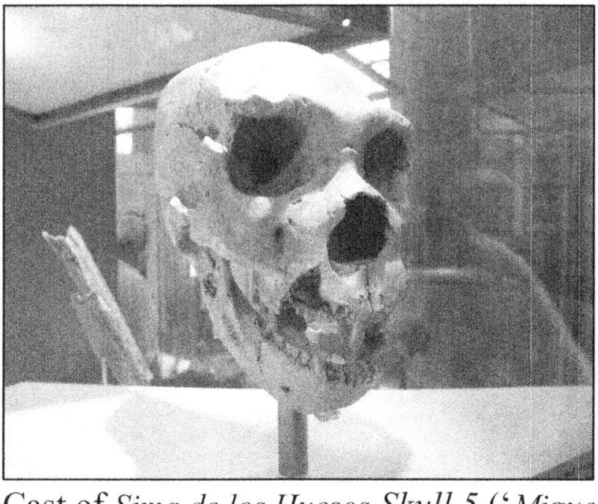

Cast of *Sima de los Huesos Skull 5 ('Miguelón') at the Natural History Museum, London CC BY-SA 2.0*

Homo neanderthalensis (230,000 - 28,000 years ago)

The average brain size of *H. neanderthalensis* is slightly larger than that of modern humans at about 1450cc, but this is probably correlated with their greater bulk. The brain case however is longer and lower than that of modern humans, with a marked bulge at the back of the skull. Like *erectus*, they had a protruding jaw and receding forehead. The chin was usually weak. The mid-facial area also protruded, a feature that is not found in *erectus* or *sapiens* and may be an adaptation to cold.

There are other minor anatomical differences from modern humans, the most unusual being some peculiarities of the shoulder blade, and of the pubic bone in the pelvis. *Neanderthals* mostly lived in cold climates, and their body proportions are similar to those of modern cold-adapted peoples: short and solid, with short limbs. Men averaged about 168cm in height. Their bones are thick and heavy, and show signs of powerful muscle attachments. *Neanderthals* would have been extraordinarily strong by modern standards, and their skeletons show that they endured brutally hard lives.

A large number of tools and weapons have been found, more advanced than those of *H. erectus*. *Neanderthals* were formidable hunters, and were the first people known to have buried their dead, with the oldest known burial site being about 100,000 years old.

They are found throughout Europe and the Middle East. Western European Neanderthals usually have a more robust form, and are sometimes called ‘Classic Neanderthals’.

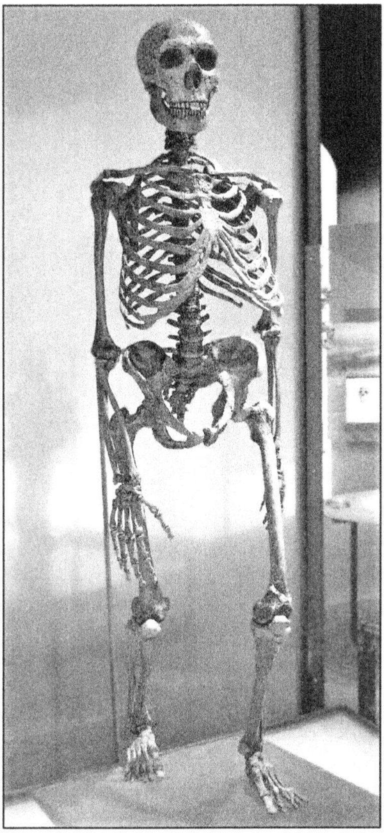

Neanderthal Skeleton, American Museum of Natural History, New York

Reconstruction of Neanderthal by Hermann Schaaffhausen, 1888

Homo floresiensis
(50,000 year ago)

H. floresiensis was discovered on the Indonesian island of Flores in 2003. Fossils have been discovered from a number of individuals. The most complete fossil is of an adult female about 1 metre tall with a brain size of 417cc.

Other fossils indicate that this was a normal size for *floresiensis*. It is thought that *floresiensis* is a dwarf form of *Homo erectus* - it is not uncommon for dwarf forms of large mammals to evolve on islands.

H. floresiensis was fully bipedal, used stone tools and fire, and hunted dwarf elephants also found on the island. (*Brown et al. 2004, Morwood et al. 2004, Lahr and Foley 2004*)

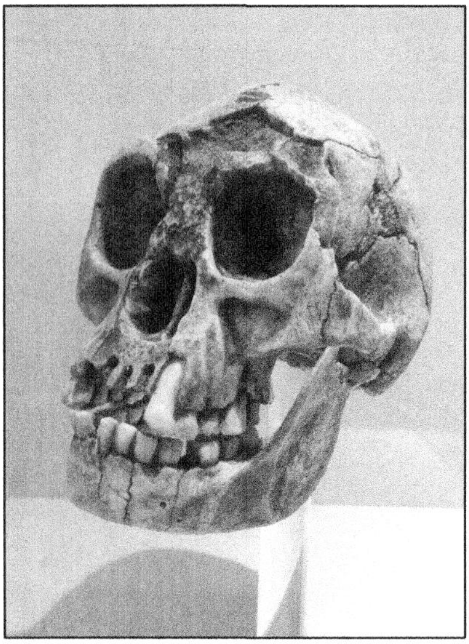

Skull at the Naturmuseum Senckenberg, Germany by Daderot CC0 1.0

Homo sapiens (195,000 years ago – present)

Modern forms of *Homo sapiens* first appear about 195,000 years ago. Modern humans have an average brain size of about 1350cc. The forehead rises sharply, eyebrow ridges are very small or more usually absent, the chin is prominent, and the skeleton is very *gracile.*

About 40,000 years ago, with the appearance of the **Cro-Magnon** culture, tool kits started becoming markedly more sophisticated, using a wider variety of raw materials such as bone and antler, and containing new implements for making clothing, engraving and sculpting.

Fine artwork, in the form of decorated tools, beads, ivory carvings of humans and animals, clay figurines, musical instruments, and spectacular cave paintings appeared over the next 20,000 years. (*Leakey 1994*)

Even within the last 100,000 years, the long-term trends towards smaller molars and decreased robustness can be discerned. The face, jaw and teeth of Mesolithic humans (about 10,000 years ago) are about 10% more robust than ours. Upper Palaeolithic humans (about 30,000 years ago) are about 20 to 30% more robust than the modern condition in Europe and Asia. These are considered modern humans, although they are sometimes termed 'primitive'.

Interestingly, some modern humans (aboriginal Australians) have tooth sizes more typical of archaic *sapiens*. The smallest tooth sizes are found in those areas where food-processing techniques have been used for the longest time. This is a probable example of natural selection which has occurred within the last 10,000 years (*Brace 1983*).

Homo sapiens (Cro-Magnon) (48,000 - 10,000 years ago)

The ***Cro-Magnons***, or **Early European Modern Humans (EEMH),** were the first early modern humans (*Homo sapiens*) to settle in Europe, continuously occupying the continent possibly from as early as 48,000 years ago. They interacted and interbred with the indigenous Neanderthals (*H. neanderthalensis*), who went extinct 40,000 to 35,000 years ago; and from 37,000 years ago onwards all EEMH descended from a single founder population which contributes ancestry to present-day Europeans.

EEMH were anatomically similar to present-day Europeans, but were more robust, having broader and shorter faces, more prominent brow ridges, and bigger teeth.

Compared to most present-day Europeans, EEMH had shorter upper jaws, more horizontally oriented cheekbones, and more rectangular eye sockets, which are more frequent in East Asian populations.

The first EEMH would have probably had dark skin; natural selection for lighter skin would not begin until 30,000 years ago, and whiter skin would not become prevalent in Europe until the Bronze Age.

EEMH are well renowned for creating a diverse array of artistic works, including cave paintings, animal figurines, and geometric patterns.

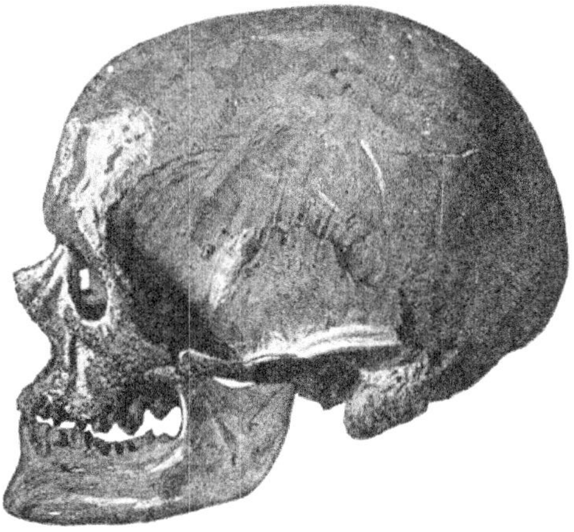

Skull of the elderly man Cro-Magnon CC BY4.0

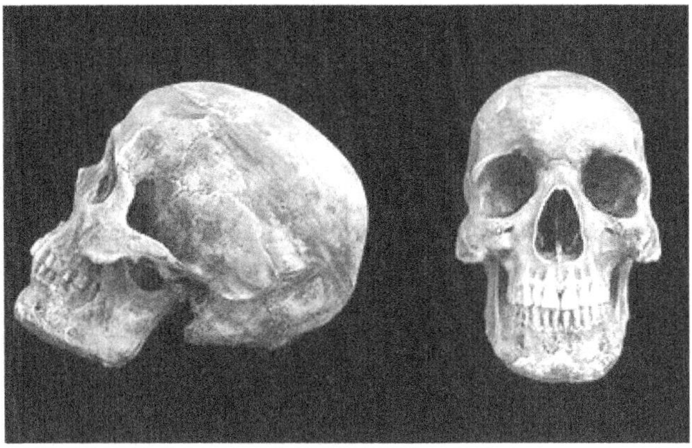

Human Taxonomy

Kingdom	Animalia	Animal
Phylum	Chordate	Chordates
Sub-phylum	Vertebrata	Vertebrates
Class	Mammalia	Mammals
Infra-class	Eutheria	Eutherians
Order	Primates	Primates
Sub-order	Anthropoides	Anthropoids
Infra-order	Catarrhini	Catarrhined

Platyrrhini *(flat nose)* *Catarrhini* *(down nose)*

Super-family	Hominoidea	Hominoids
Family	Himinidae	Hominids
Genus	Homo	Humans
Species	Homo sapiens	
Sub-species	Homo sapiens sapiens	

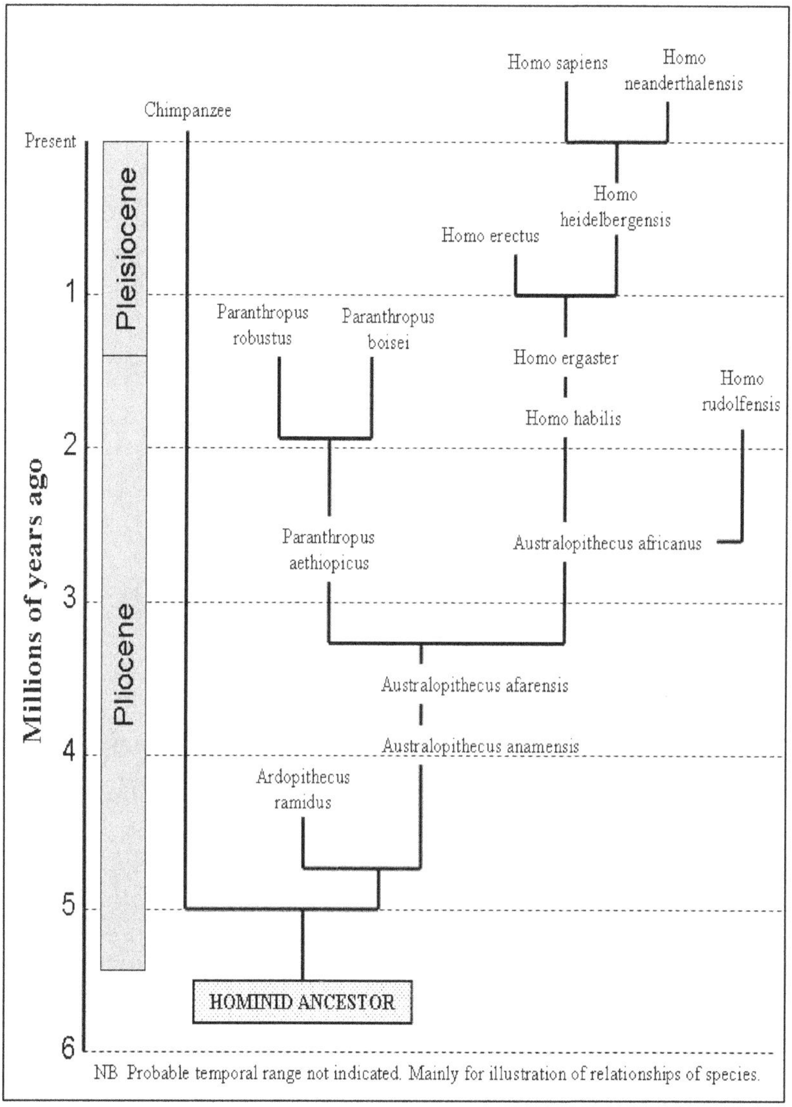

Homo sapiens
Homo neanderthalensis
Chimpanzee
Present
Pleisiocene
Homo heidelbergensis
Homo erectus
1
Paranthropus robustus
Paranthropus boisei
Homo ergaster
Homo rudolfensis
Homo habilis
2
Millions of years ago
Paranthropus aethiopicus
Australopithecus africanus
3
Pliocene
Australopithecus afarensis
4
Australopithecus anamensis
Ardopithecus ramidus
5
HOMINID ANCESTOR
6
NB. Probable temporal range not indicated. Mainly for illustration of relationships of species.

Human Vestigiality

The muscles connected to the ears of a human do not develop enough to have the same mobility allowed to monkeys.

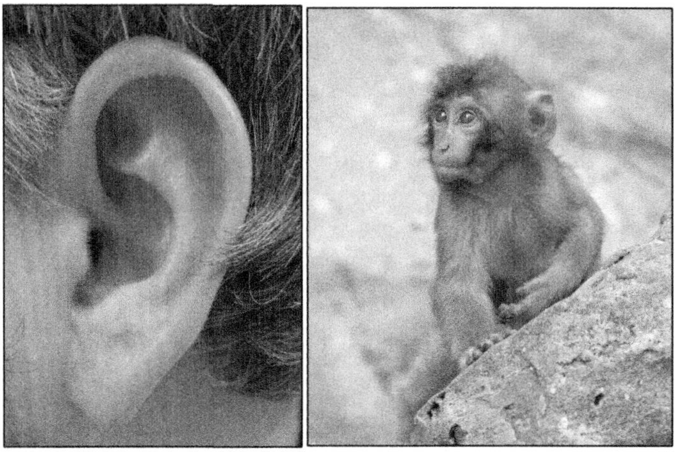

Human vestigiality involves those traits (such as organs or behaviours) occurring in humans that have lost all or most of their original function through evolution. Although structures called *vestigial* often appear functionless, a vestigial structure may retain lesser functions or develop minor new ones. In some cases, structures once identified as vestigial simply had an unrecognized function.

The examples of human vestigiality are too numerous to mention in their entirety here. They include the anatomical (such as the human appendix, tailbone, gill slits, wisdom teeth webbed hands, and inside corner of the eye), the behavioural (goose bumps and palmar grasp reflex), sensory (decreased olfaction), and molecular (non-coding DNA).

Many human characteristics are also vestigial in other primates and related animals.

Appendix

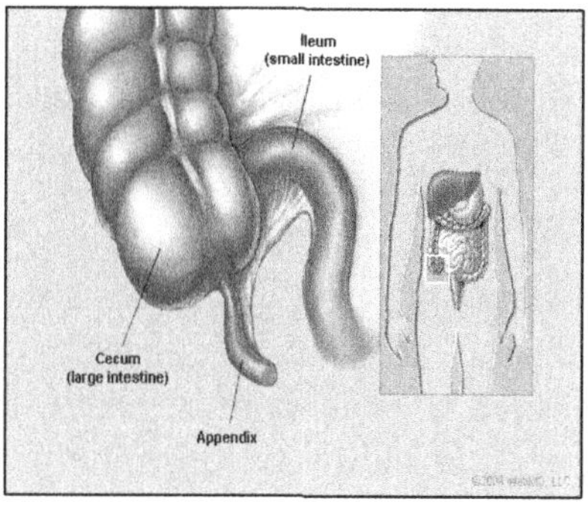

In modern humans, the appendix is a vestige of a redundant organ that in ancestral species had digestive functions, much as it still does in extant species in which intestinal microbiomes hydrolyze cellulose and similar indigestible plant materials.

Some herbivorous animals, such as rabbits, have a terminal vermiform appendix and caecum that apparently bear patches of tissue with immune functions and may also be important in maintaining the composition of intestinal flora. It does not however seem to have much digestive function, if any, and is not present in all herbivores, even those with large *caeca.*

Typically, the human appendix is about comparable to that of the rabbit's in size, though the caecum is reduced to a single bulge where the ileum empties into the colon.

Some carnivorous animals may have appendices too, but seldom have more than vestigial caeca.

Intestinal bacterial populations entrenched in the appendix may support quick re-establishment of the flora of the large intestine after an illness, poisoning, or antibiotic treatment depletes or otherwise causes harmful changes to the bacterial population of the colon.

Wisdom Teeth

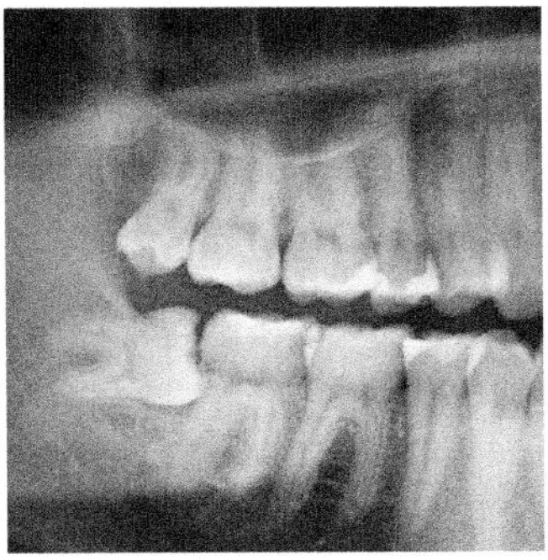

Wisdom teeth are vestigial third molars that human ancestors used to help in grinding down plant tissue.

The common postulation is that the skulls of human ancestors had larger jaws with more teeth, which were possibly used to help chew down foliage to compensate for a lack of ability to efficiently digest the cellulose that makes up a plant cell wall.

As human diets changed, smaller jaws were naturally selected, yet the third molars, or 'wisdom teeth', still commonly develop in human mouths. Currently, wisdom teeth have become useless and even harmful to the extent where surgical procedures are often performed to remove them.

Ear

The ears of a Macaque monkey and most other monkeys have far more developed muscles than those of humans, and therefore have the capability to move their ears to better hear potential threats.

Humans and other primates such as the orangutan and chimpanzee however have ear muscles that are minimally developed and non-functional, yet still large enough to be identifiable.

A muscle attached to the ear that cannot move the ear, for whatever reason, can no longer be said to have any biological function.

Like humans, chimpanzees have ear muscles that are minimally developed and are non-functional

In humans there is variability in these muscles, such that some people are able to move their ears in various directions, and it can be possible for others to gain such movement by repeated trials.

In such primates the inability to move the ear is compensated mainly by the ability to turn the head on a horizontal plane, an ability which is not common to most monkeys.

Coccyx

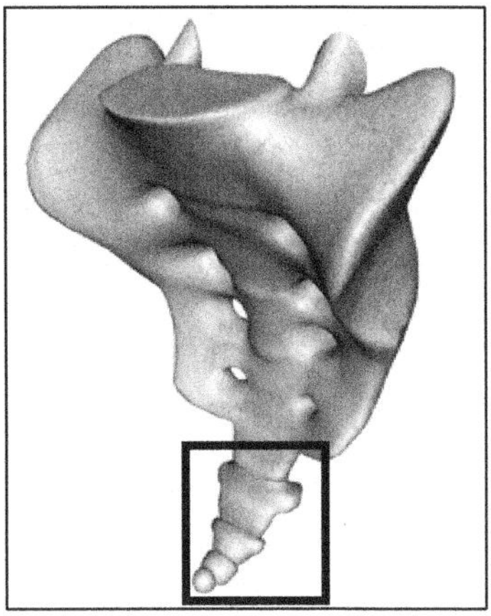

The coccyx, or tailbone, is the remnant of a lost tail. All mammals have a tail at some point in their development; in humans, it is present for a period of 4 weeks, during stages 14 to 22 of human embryogenesis.

This tail is most prominent in human embryos 31–35 days old.

The tailbone, located at the end of the spine, has lost its original function in assisting balance and mobility, though it still serves some secondary functions, such as being an attachment point for muscles, which explains why it has not degraded further.

In rare cases congenital defect results in a short tail-like structure being present at birth. Many cases of human babies born with such a structure have been reported in the medical literature since 1884. In rare cases such as these, the spine and skull were determined to be entirely normal.

The only abnormality was that of a tail approximately twelve centimeters long. These tails were able to be surgically removed, and the individuals have resumed normal lives.

The presence of a tail is evidenced by the following chart, which displays the embryonic development of the human compared to various other animals.

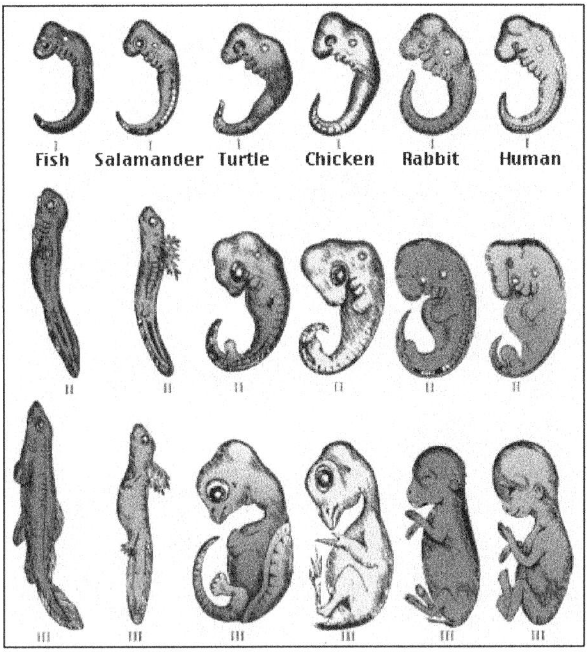

Eyes

The *plica semilunaris* is a small fold of tissue on the inside corner of the eye. It is the vestigial remnant of the **nictitating membrane**, an organ that is fully functional in some other species of mammals.

Its associated muscles are also vestigial. Only one species of primate, the *Calabar angwantibo*, is known to have a functioning nictitating membrane.

Hymen

The hymen is a membrane that surrounds or partially covers the external vaginal opening.

The existence of hymen in some animals, such as horses, prevents semen from leaving the vagina. Due to similar reproductive system development, many mammals, including chimpanzees, elephants, manatees, whales, and horses, retain hymens.

Musculature

A number of muscles in the human body are thought to be vestigial, either by virtue of being greatly reduced in size compared to homologous muscles in other species, by having become principally tendonous, or by being highly variable in their frequency within or between populations.

Head

The ***Occipitalis Minor*** is a muscle in the back of the head which normally joins to the auricular muscles of the ear. This

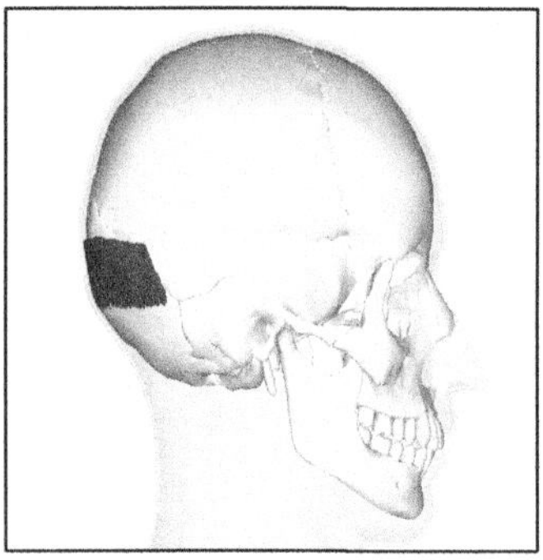

muscle is very sporadic in frequency - always present in Malays, in 56% of Africans, 50% of Japanese, 36% of Europeans, and is nonexistent in the Khoikhoi people of south-western Africa and in Melanesians.

Face

In many non-human mammals the upper lip and sinus area is associated with whiskers or **vibrissae** which serve a sensory function. In humans these whiskers do not exist but there are still sporadic cases where elements of the associated vibrissal capsular muscles or sinus hair muscles can be found.

Sensory

Although the sense of smell, or olfaction, is essential for other animals in avoiding predators, finding food, and other functions, olfaction is greatly decreased in humans as they have, for the most part, no predators and obtain food mostly by agriculture.

There is great variation in olfactory sensitivity from person to person, which is common in vestigial characteristics. It has been observed that native South Americans, native North Americans, and African natives have a highly developed sense of smell, such that they may be able to identify others in the dark by their odor alone.

This does not mean that having any olfactory ability at all is vestigial, for example it may save a person from inhaling toxic fumes. A characteristic may degenerate despite being of some use if there is very little or no selection pressure on the genes associated with it.

Reflexes

Humans also bear some vestigial behaviours and reflexes. For example, the formation of goose bumps in humans under stress is a vestigial reflex a possible function in human evolutionary ancestors was to raise the body's hair, making the ancestor appear larger and scaring off predators.

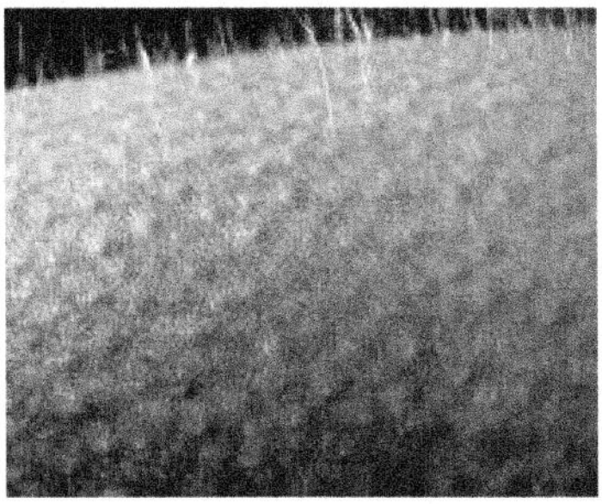

Raising the hair is also used to trap an extra layer of air, keeping an animal warm. Due to the diminished amount of hair in humans, the reflex formation of goose bumps when cold is also vestigial.

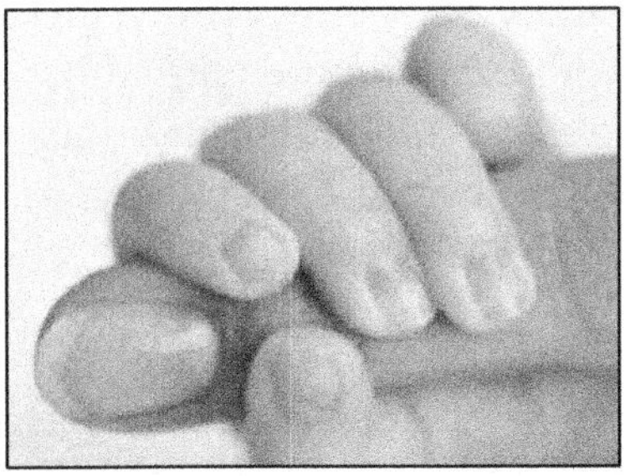

The palmar grasp reflex is supported to be a vestigial behaviour in human infants.

When placing a finger or object to the palm of an infant, it will securely grasp it. This grasp is found to be rather strong. Some infants are able to support their own weight from a rod, although there is no way they can cling to their mother. The grasp is also evident in the feet too. When a baby is sitting down, its prehensile feet assume a curled-in posture, similar to that observed in an adult chimp. An ancestral primate would have had sufficient body hair to which an infant could cling unlike modern humans.

Vestigial Organs

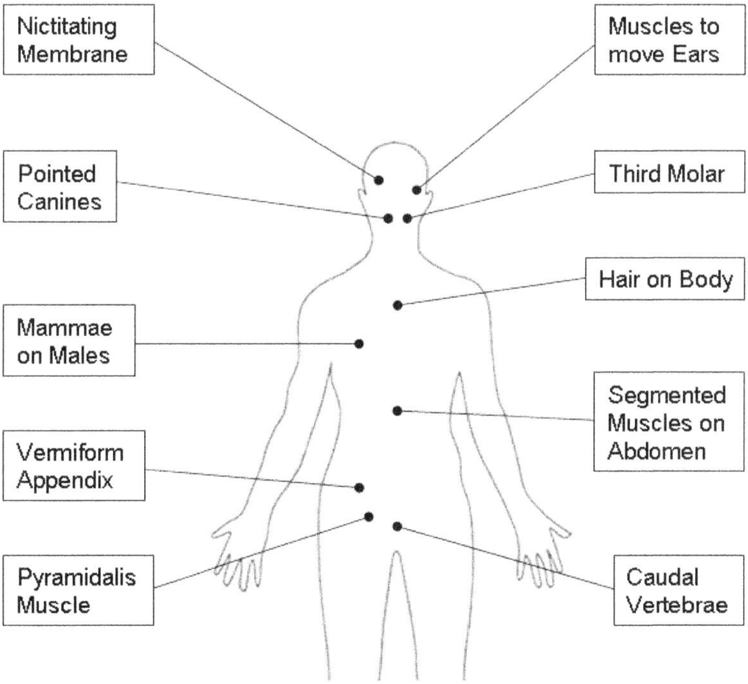

Nictitating Membrane
Muscles to move Ears
Pointed Canines
Third Molar
Hair on Body
Mammae on Males
Segmented Muscles on Abdomen
Vermiform Appendix
Pyramidalis Muscle
Caudal Vertebrae

Early Artwork of Homo

Prehistoric art is all art produced in preliterate, prehistoric cultures. It begins somewhere in very late geological history, and generally continuing until that culture either develops writing or other methods of record-keeping, or makes significant contact with another culture that has, and that makes some record of major historical events.

Blombos Cave, South Africa. (c. 73,000 years old)

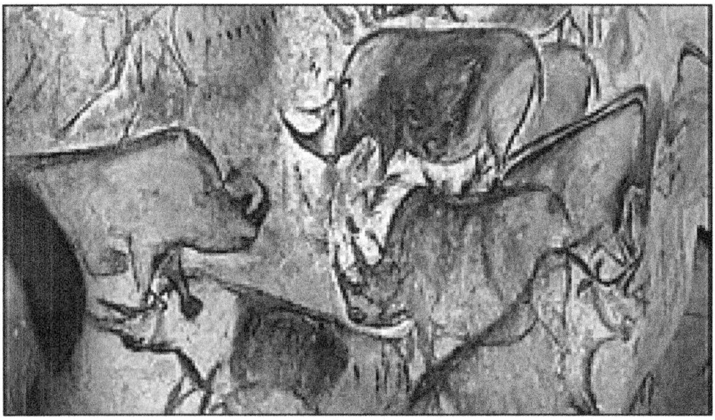

Chauvet Cave, France (35,000 years old)

Chauvet , Rhône-Alpes, France (32,000 years old)

Shimbetka, Madhya Pradesh, India (30,000 yrs old)

Serra da Capivara, Brazil (25,000 yrs old)

Lascaux Dordogne, France (17,000 yrs old)

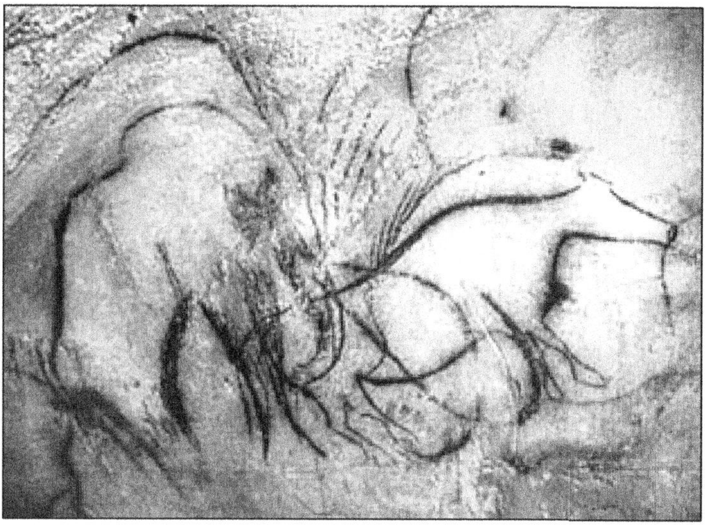

Peche Merle, France, Do (15,000 yrs old)

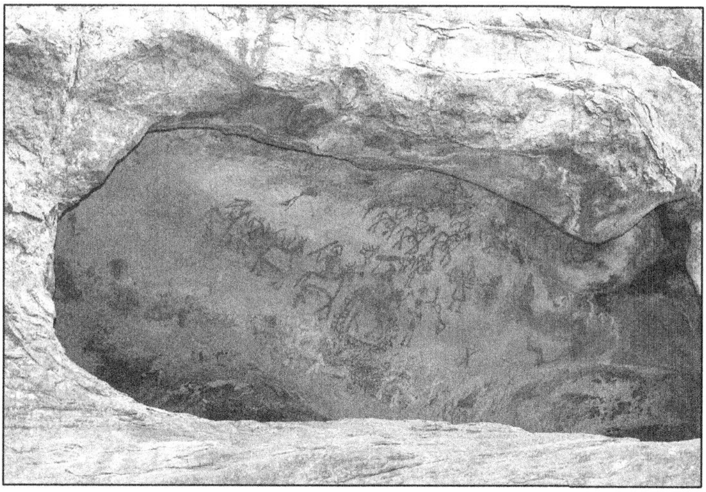

Bhimbetka, Bhopal (12,500 – 13,000 yrs old)

Cuevas de las Manos, Santa Cruz Argentina (9000 – 13,000 yrs old)

Laas Gaal, Somalia (3,000 – 9,000 yrs old)

Animals with Interesting Properties

Charnia (570 – 550 Mya)

Charnia is a genus of frond-like Ediacaran life forms with segmented, leaf-like ridges branching alternately to the right and left from a zigzag medial suture (thus exhibiting glide reflection, or opposite isometry).

The living organism grew on the sea floor and is believed to have fed on nutrients in the water. Despite *Charnia*'s fern-like appearance, it is not a photosynthetic plant or alga because the nature of the fossil beds where specimens have been found implies that it originally lived in deep water, well below the photic zone where photosynthesis can occur.

Charnia is a highly significant fossil because it is the first fossil which was ever described to have come from undoubted Precambrian rocks.

Prior to 1958, the Precambrian was thought to be completely devoid of fossils and consequently possibly devoid of macroscopic life. Similar fossils had been found in the 1930s (in Namibia) and the 1940s (in Australia) but these forms were assumed to be of Cambrian age and were therefore considered unremarkable at the time. *Charnia* has become an enduring image of Precambrian animals.

Originally interpreted as an alga, it was reinterpreted as a sea pen (a sister group to the modern soft corals). From 1966 onwards acceptance of *Charnia* as a Precambrian life form led to recognition of other major Precambrian animal groups, although the sea pen interpretation of *Charnia* has recently been discredited.

An increasingly popular theory has arisen since the mid-1980s, suggesting that *Charnia* belongs to an extinct group of unknown grade which was confined to the Ediacaran. This suggests that almost all the forms that have been postulated to be members of many and various modern animal groups are actually more closely related to one another than they are to anything else.

This new group was termed the *Vendobionta*, a clade whose position in the tree of life remains unclear.

It follows that little is known about the ecology of *Charnia*. It has been established to have been benthic and sessile, anchored to the sea floor.

The growth and development of the Ediacaran biota is the subject of continued research.

Charniodiscus (565 – 555 Mya)

Charniodiscus is an Ediacaran fossil that in life was probably a stationary filter feeder that lived anchored to a sandy sea bed. The organism had a holdfast, stalk and frond.

The '*holdfast*' was bulbous shaped, and the stalk was flexible. The frond was segmented and had a pointed tip. There were two growth forms: one with a short stem and a wide frond, and another with a long stalk, elevating a smaller frond about 50 centimetres above the holdfast. While the organism superficially resembles the *Cnidaria*, it is probably not a *crown-group*. A *Charniodiscus* was first found in Charnwood Forest in England, and named by Trevor D. Ford in 1958. The name is derived from the fact that Ford described a holdfast consisting only of a double concentric circle, his species being named *Charniodiscus concentricus*. Later it was discovered that a frond (*Charnia masoni*) was part of a closely related organism. *Charnia* differs in the branching structure in the frond.

Species are distinguished by the number of segments, the presence or absence of distal spines, and by shape ratios.

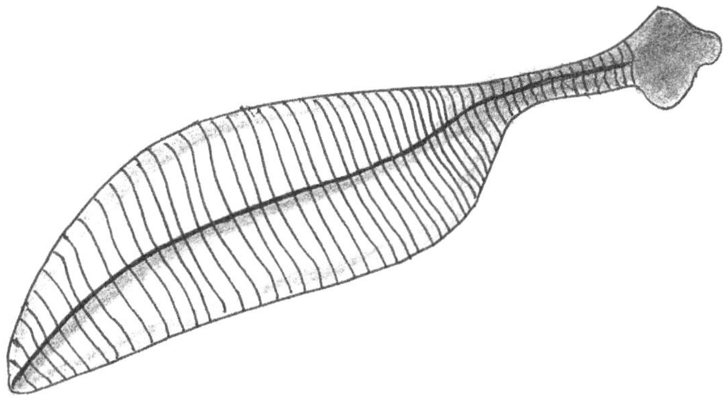

Spriggina floundersi (555 Mya)

Spriggina floundersi is the oldest fossil organism to be described with a 'head'.

The fossil was originally described as a *polychaete* worm (commonly referred to as 'bristle worms'), where subjective conclusions about its worm-like morphology were drawn from the fossil impressions. A current and objective morphological analysis is overdue. *Spriggina* shares some morphological characters with *arthropods*, such as a broadly segmented body plan, possibly implying a relationship with that group.

Two Spriggina floundersi specimens. Large adult specimen (actual size ~ 5cm long), with a juvenile to its left. South Australia. Image: Dr Alex Liu

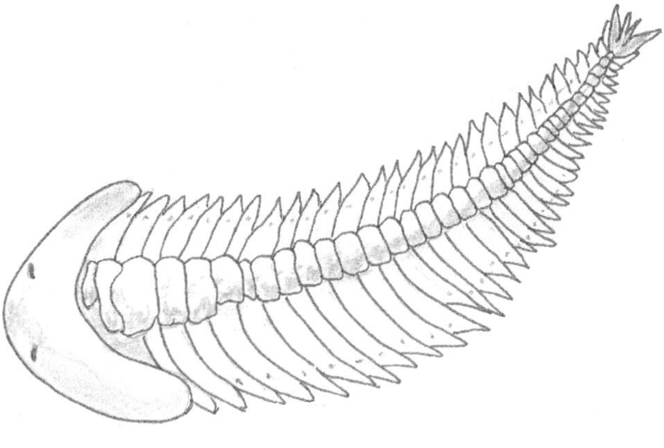

Ctenophora (540 Mya – present)

Ctenophora from Ancient Greek κτείς *(kteis)* 'comb', and φέρω *(pherō)* 'to carry', comprise a phylum of marine invertebrates, commonly known as **comb jellies**. They are notable for the groups of *cilia* they use for swimming (commonly referred to as 'combs'), and they are the largest animals to swim with the help of *cilia*.

Depending on the species, adult *ctenophores* range from a few millimetres to 1.5m in size. Only 100 to 150 species have been validated, and possibly another 25 have not been fully described and named.

Almost all *ctenophores* function as predators, taking prey ranging from microscopic larvae and rotifers to the adults of small crustaceans.

Comb Jellies are any of the species of jellyfish belonging to the taxonomic phylum *Ctenophora*. They are almost completely radially symmetric and normally completely colourless.

The body is made up of two clear cell layers, which make up its outer skin, or *ectoderm*, and its inner skin, or *gastroderm*. The outer layer is two layers thick and is coated in a protective slime that has been discharged from the body through special glands. The inner layer surrounds a pocket in the *Ctenophora* which is used as the stomach of this organism.

The food is caught with the tentacles and drawn up into the stomach. The food is pre-digested with very strong enzymes in a long, narrow channel that connects the stomach to the opening, which it first passes through. It then passes into the stomach where it is completely broken down into nutrients for the organism to use. If there is any waste that cannot be digested, then it is emitted from the body through the mouth.

The way that the Ctenophora usually move is by drifting with the current, although, they can swim if the need arises. The way that they can do that is by spinning their tentacles and using them as a propeller; they then open their mouths and use the opening as a rudder.

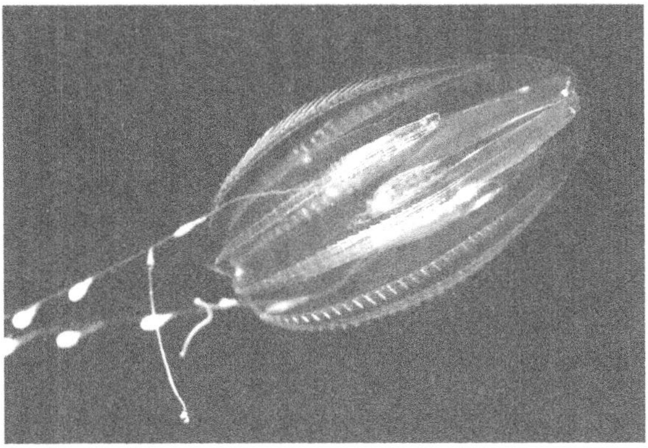

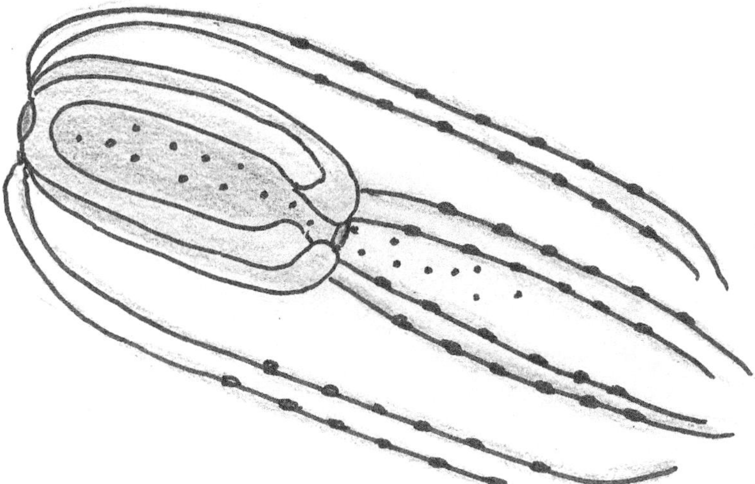

Xenusion auerswaldae (534 – 524 Mya)

Xenusion auerswaldae is an early *lobopodian* known from two specimens found in glacial debris in Germany. The older specimen is 10cm or so in length with a narrow, weakly segmented body. A depression runs up the bottom on all but the rearmost segments. There is a slightly bulbous termination, and each segment beyond that seems to have a single pair of tapering annulated legs similar to the modern *onychophoran*, but without claws. Nine segments are present.

There is a spine on each body bump and faint transverse parallel striations on the annulations on the legs. The legs of what is possibly the foremost segments are either missing or not preserved. The head is believed to be missing or is poorly preserved.

If *Xenusion* is truly a *lobopodian*, it is one of the oldest currently known fossils of a mobile, modern animal with legs. It has been said to have a long narrow *proboscis*, but this is probably a preservational artefact.

Assuming that the creature is actually a *lobopodian*, the original specimen would appear to be part of an animal about 20cm in length.

Museum für Naturkunde, Berlin

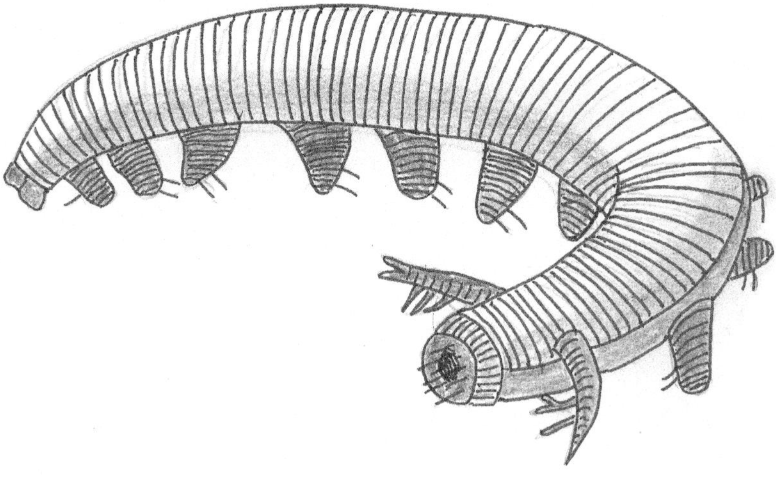

Halkieriids (541 – 513 Mya)

The **halkieriids** are a group of fossil organisms from the Lower to Middle Cambrian. Their eponymous genus is ***Halkieria***, which has been found on almost every continent in Lower to Mid Cambrian deposits, forming a large component of the small shelly fossil assemblages. The best known species is *Halkieria evangelista*, from the North Greenland Sirius Passet Lagerstätte, in which complete specimens were collected on an expedition in 1989.

The animals looked like slugs in chain mail - 1.5cm to 8cm long, bilaterally symmetric, flattened from top to bottom and un-armoured on the bottom. Very near each end there is a shell plate with prominent growth lines rather like the growth rings of trees. The rest of the upper surface was covered with about 2,000 *sclerites* that overlapped each other like tiles and formed three zones with *sclerites* of different shapes.

As the animals grew, the shell plates grew by adding material to the outer edges. Individual *sclerites* stayed the same size. Since the cultrate *sclerites* form a pattern that is constant in all fairly complete specimens, the old ones that were too small may have been shed and replaced by larger ones as the animals grew. The *sclerites* seem to have grown by basal secretion. There are traces of thin ribs between the *sclerites* and the skin.

The shell plates and the *sclerites* were probably made of calcium carbonate originally. It has been suggested on the basis of how they were preserved that they may have been wholly organic, but this is less likely since fossils of non-calcified organisms are usually thin films while *Halkeieria* fossils are three-dimensional like those of trilobites and hyoliths - in fact several specimens show curvature in the horizontal plane, which suggests that the muscles associated with the *sclerites* were still present at the time of burial.

The sole was soft and probably muscular. Since *Halkieria* was unsuited to swimming and had no obvious adaptations for burrowing, it must have lived on the sea-floor, 'walking' by making its muscular sole ripple.

The backward-projecting siculate *sclerites* may have improved its grip by preventing it from slipping backwards. Some specimens have been found partially rolled up, rather like a pillbug, and in this position the cultrate *sclerites* projected outwards, which probably deterred predators.

It is difficult to determine the functions of the cap-shaped shells at either end of the animal, as the sclerites appear to have offered adequate protection. Scars on the inner surface of the front shell may indicate that it provided an attachment for internal organs. In one specimen the rear shell appears to have rotated by about 45^0 before fossilization, which suggests there was a cavity underneath, which may have housed gills.

Traces of a gut have been found in the rear halves of some fossils. Parts of one specimen have been interpreted as a radula, the toothed chitinous tongue that is the signature feature of molluscs.

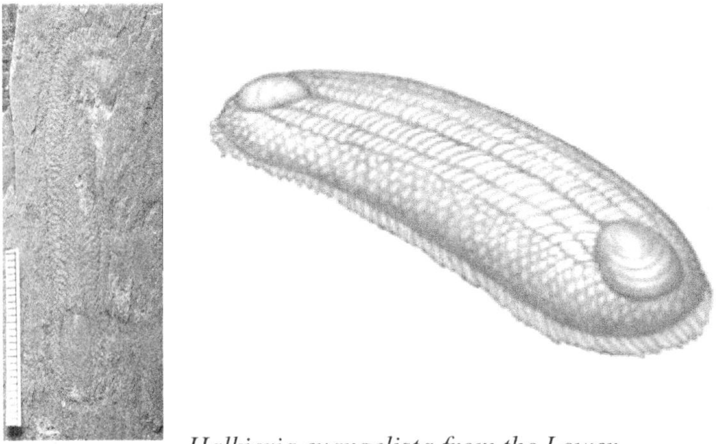

Halkieria evangelista from the Lower Cambrian Sirius Passet, North Greenland CCY-SA 3.0

Trilobite (521 – 252 Mya)

Trilobites are a group of extinct marine *arthropods* that form the class **Trilobita**. Trilobites form one of the earliest-known groups of *arthropods*.

The last extant *trilobites* finally disappeared in the Mass Extinction at the end of the Permian. Trilobites were among the most successful of all early animals, existing in oceans for almost 270 million years, with over 20,000 species having been described.

By the time *trilobites* first appeared in the fossil record, they were already highly diversified and geographically dispersed. Because they had wide diversity and an easily fossilized exoskeleton, they left an extensive fossil record. The study of their fossils has facilitated important contribution to the study of Plate Tectonics.

Trilobites evolved into many ecological niches; some moved over the seabed as predators, scavengers, or filter feeders and some swam, feeding on plankton.

Some even crawled onto land. Most lifestyles expected of modern marine arthropods are seen in trilobites, with the possible exception of parasitism. Some are even thought to have evolved a symbiotic relationship with sulphur-eating bacteria from which they derived food. The largest trilobites were more than 45cm long and may have weighed as much as 4.5kg.

Walliserops trifurcatus, from Jebel Oufatene mountain near *<u>Fezzou, Morocco</u>*

Kainops invius Cravat Member, Bois d'Arc formation, Lower Devonian. Clarita, Coal Co., Oklahoma, U.S.A.

Cheirurus Middle Ordovician, Volkhov River, Russia

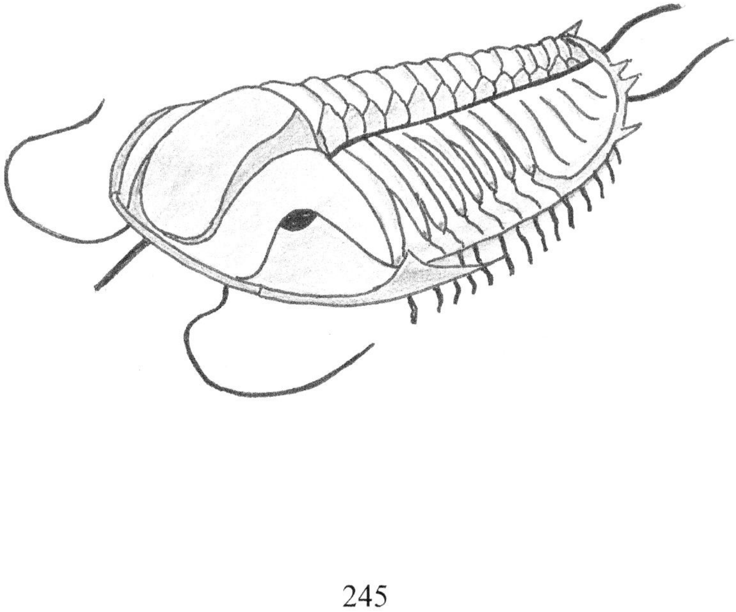

Anomalocaris (520 – 299 Mya)

Anomalocaris ('unlike other shrimp', or 'abnormal shrimp') is an extinct genus of *radiodont* (*anomalocaridid*), an order of animals thought to be closely related to ancestral *arthropods*.

The first fossils of *Anomalocaris* were discovered in the Ogygopsis Shale by Joseph Frederick Whiteaves, with more examples found by Charles Doolittle Walcott in the Burgess Shale.

Originally several fossilized parts discovered separately (the mouth, frontal appendages, and trunk) were thought to be three separate creatures, a misapprehension corrected by Harry B. Whittington and Derek Briggs in a 1985 journal article. *Anomalocaris* is thought to be one of the earliest examples of an 'apex predator', though others have been found in older Cambrian Lagerstätten deposits.

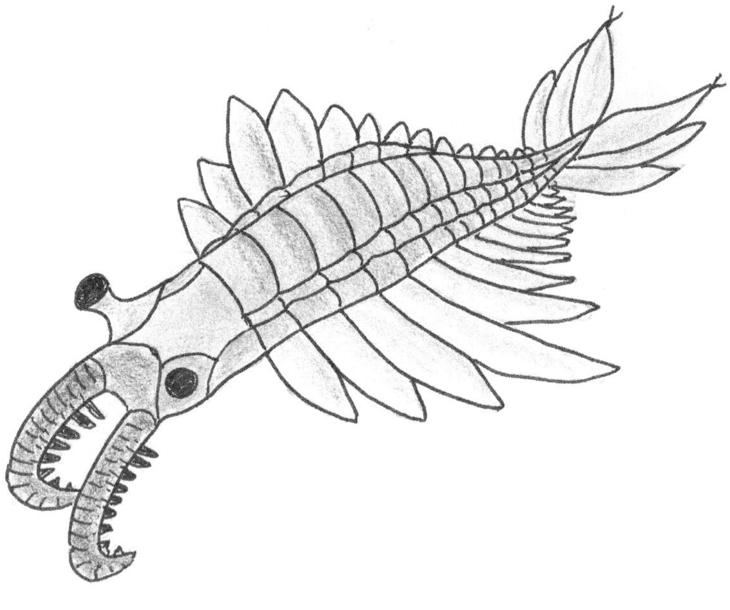

Frontal appendage of Anomalocaris canadensis

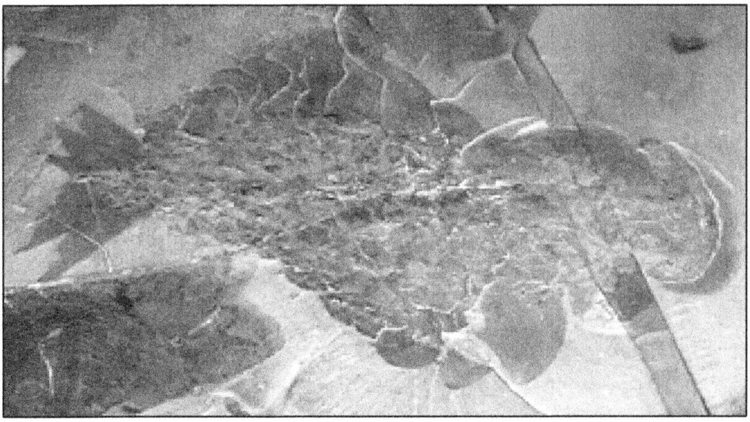

Image of the first complete Anomalocaris fossil residing in the Royal Ontario Museum, Toronto

Helicoplacus (525 Mya)

Helicoplacus is the earliest studied fossil *echinoderm*. The animal was a cigar-shaped creature up to 7cm long that stood upright on one end. Unlike more typical echinoderms such as sea stars, *Helicoplacus* does not have five-fold symmetry. Instead, there is a spiral food groove on the outside along which food was moved to a mouth that is thought to be on the side.

The respiratory system appears to be primitive. Although the animal does not look like a typical *echinoderm*, the plates are composed of the characteristic calcareous plates known as *stereom* that are common to all echinoderms.

Helicoplacus is thought to have been a suspension feeder living at moderate depths in highly oxygenated water with strong enough currents to ensure a steady food supply. It is typically found in greenish shales and, rarely found in shallow water sandstones and limestones. The helically spiralling rows of plates radiate from the base, which in life probably was anchored in the muddy substrate.

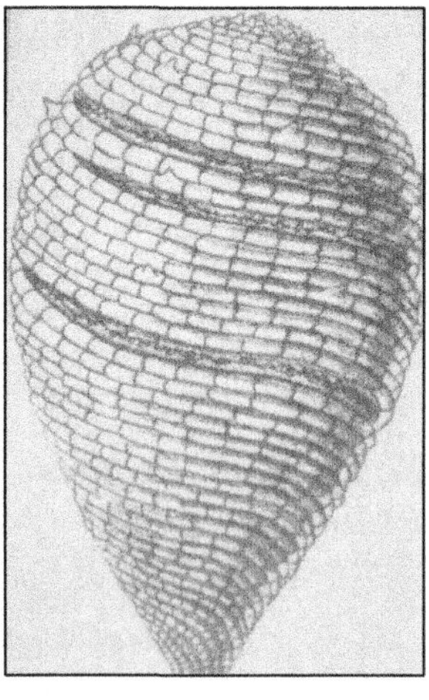

Helicoplacus guthi

Microdictyon (513 – 505 mya)

Microdictyon is an extinct armoured worm-like animal coated with net-like *scleritic* plates, known from the Early Cambrian Maotianshan Shale of Yunnan, China and other parts of the world. *Microdictyon* is part of the ill-defined taxon – *Lobopodia.* This includes several other odd worm-like animals that resembling worms with legs, such as *Hallucigenia*, *Onychodictyon*, *Cardiodictyon*, *Luolishania*, and *Paucipodia.*

The isolated *sclerites* of *Microdictyon* are known from other Lower Cambrian deposits. *Microdictyon* sclerites appear to have molted; one *sclerite* seems to have been preserved during *ecdysis.*

Microdictyon sinicum is typical. The wormlike animal has ten pairs of *sclerites* on the sides, matched to a pair of tentacle-like feet below. The head and posterior are tubular and featureless.

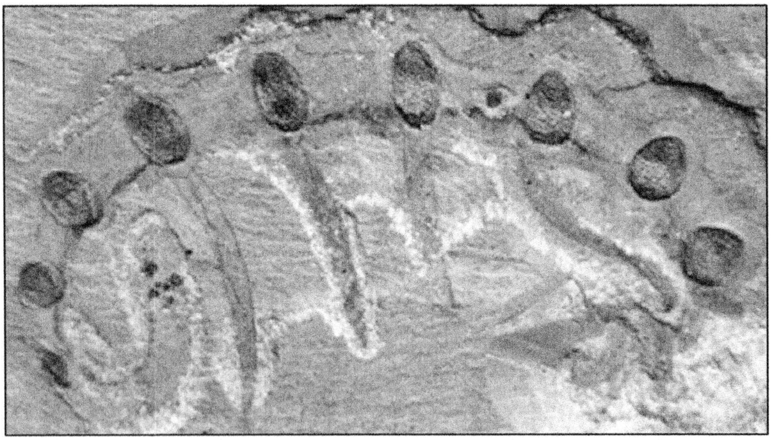

Fossil of Microdictyon on display at the Chengjiang fossil site museum CC BY-SA 4.0 (Detail of image on previous page)

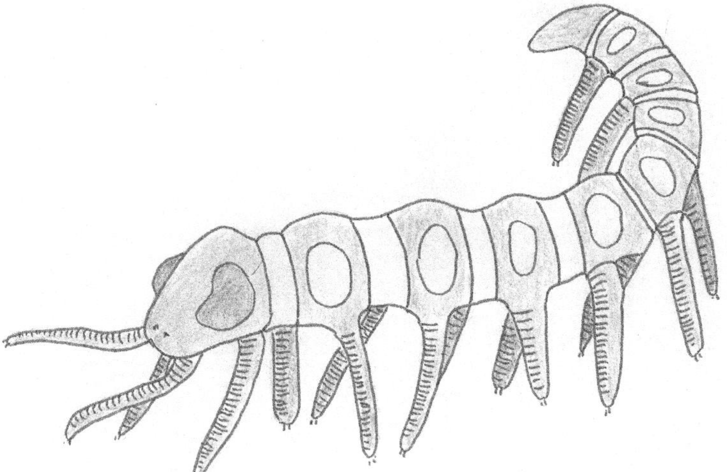

Orthocone nautiloid (470 - 440 mya)

An ***orthocone*** is an unusually long straight shell of a *nautiloid cephalopod.*

An *orthocone* can be thought of as like a *nautilus*, but with the shell straight and uncoiled. It was previously believed that these represented the most primitive form of *nautiloid*, but it is now known that the earliest *nautiloids* had shells that were slightly curved.

Orthocones existed from the Late Cambrian to the Late Triassic, but they were most common in the early Paleozoic. Revivals of the *orthocone* design later occurred in other *cephalopod* groups, notably *baculitid ammonites* in the Cretaceous. *Orthocone nautiloids* range in size from less than 25mm to, in some giant *endocerids* of the Ordovician, 5.2m long. *Orthocone Cephalopod* fossils are known from all over the world

Clearly visible are the ***septae*** *dividing the body chambers, and the tube-like* ***siphuncle*** *running the length of the shell.*
Photo Credit MLF

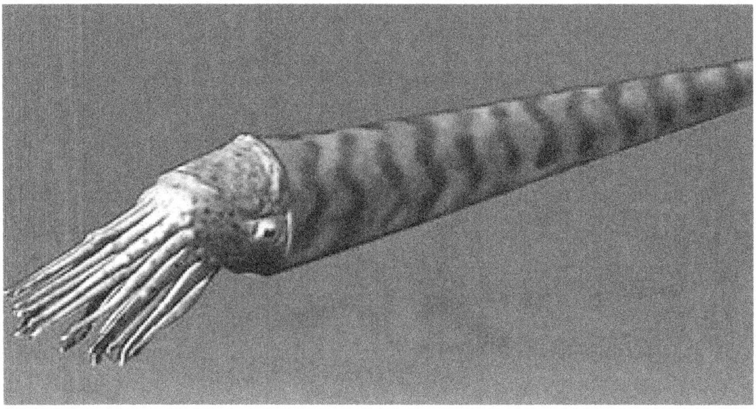

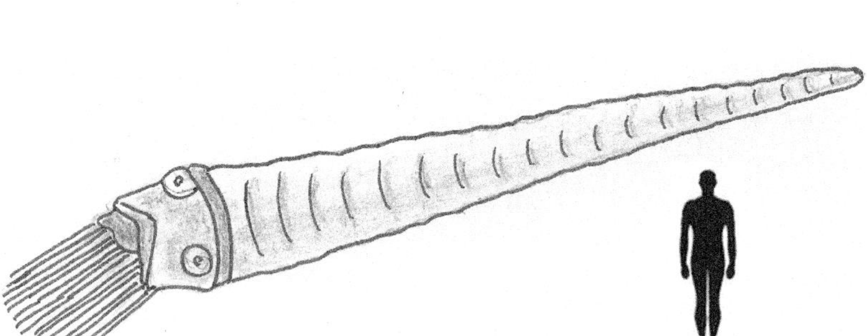

Astraspis (467 – 443 mya)

Astraspis is an *astraspid astraspidiform* jawless fish from the Middle Ordovician-Llandovery of North America, Canada, and Bolivia. It was named in 1982 by Charles Doolittle Walcott (of Burgess Shale fame). It was one of the many jawless fishes to swim in the Ordovician seas, which were advanced at the time.

Astraspis represented the generic jawless fish, a fish with a mobile tail and a large, oval-shaped body. It had eyes positioned on the side of its head, 8 gills on each side of its body, and bony plates on the animal's head with star-shaped projections protruding from them (hence the meaning of its name, 'star shield'). Its body would have been covered in scaly skin, with bony plates covering most of it.

Astraspis was a *detritivore*, sucking up pieces of organic debris suspended in the water. Its small, toothless mouth would have been used to filter detritus from the water.

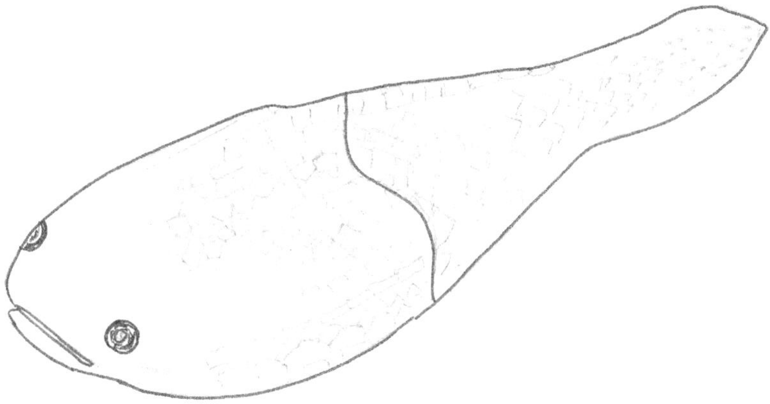

Pterygotus (428 – 372 Mya)

With the largest species, *P. grandidentatus*, reaching a body length of 1.75m *Pterygotus* was among the largest known *eurypterids* to have existed, though some of its close relatives (such as *Acutiramus* and *Jaekelopterus*) surpassed it in length. Though there were a few gigantic species, many species were considerably smaller in size. The smallest species, *P. kopaninensis*, measured just 50cm in length.

Pterygotus is classified as part of the *pterygotid* family of *eurypterids*, to which it lends its name, a group of highly derived *eurypterids* of the Silurian to Devonian periods that differ from other groups by a number of features, perhaps most prominently in the *chelicerae* and the *telson* of the body.

The *chelicerae* of the *Pterygotidae* were enlarged and robust, clearly adapted to be used for active prey capture and more similar to the claws of some modern crustaceans, with well developed teeth on the claws, than to the *chelicerae* of other *eurypterid* groups.

Unlike most of the rest of the body, which was covered in a scale-like ornamentation like other *pterygotid eurypterids*, the claws lacked any type of ornamentation. Additionally, the end points of the claws were round and curved unlike the sharp points present at the ends of the claws of the related *Erettopterus*. The *pterygotid telsons* were flattened and expanded, likely used as rudders when swimming. Their walking legs were small and slender, without spines, and they were likely not capable of walking on land.

Pterygotus is distinguishable from other *pterygotids* by the curved distal margin of the *chelae* claws. The *prosoma* head is *sub-trapezoidal*, with compound eyes located near the edge of the front corners. The *telson* has a pronounced *dorsal carina* running down its centre, terminating in a short spine.

The *Pterygotidae* include the largest known arthropods to have ever lived, with several species surpassing two metres in length (such as *Jaekelopterus rhenaniae* at 2.5m and *Acutiramus bohemicus* at 2.1m. Though *Pterygotus* was not the largest of the *pterygotids*, several species were large, surpassing 1m in length.

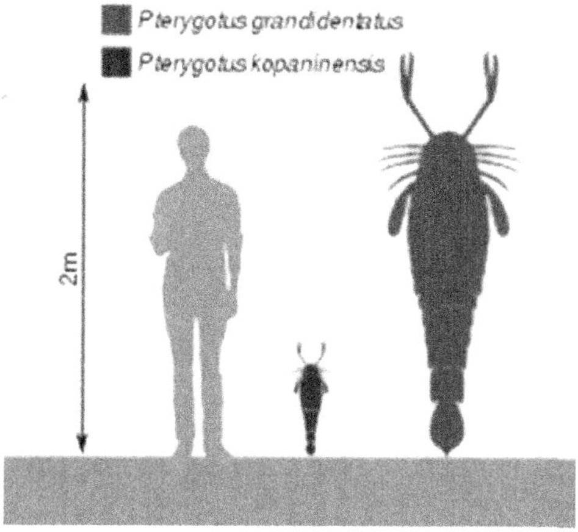

The size of the largest (*P. grandidentatus*) and smallest (*P. kopaninensis*) species of *Pterygotus* compared to a human.

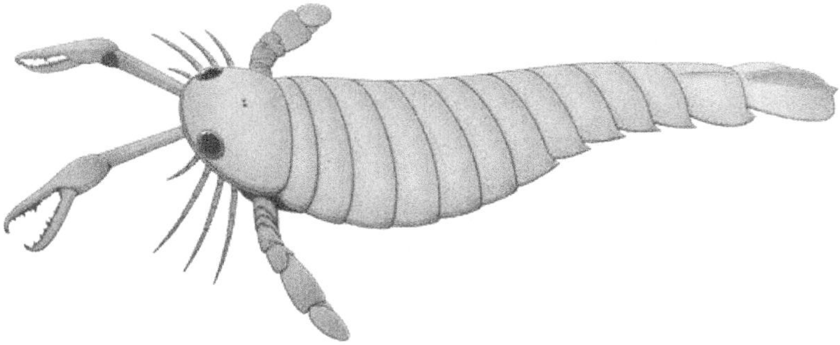

Reconstruction of Pterygotus anglicus, a Devonian pterygotid eurypterid (Chelicerata: Eurypterida: Pterygotidae). Appendage II (pedipalps) are conjectural and based on the suggestion of Selden 1986.

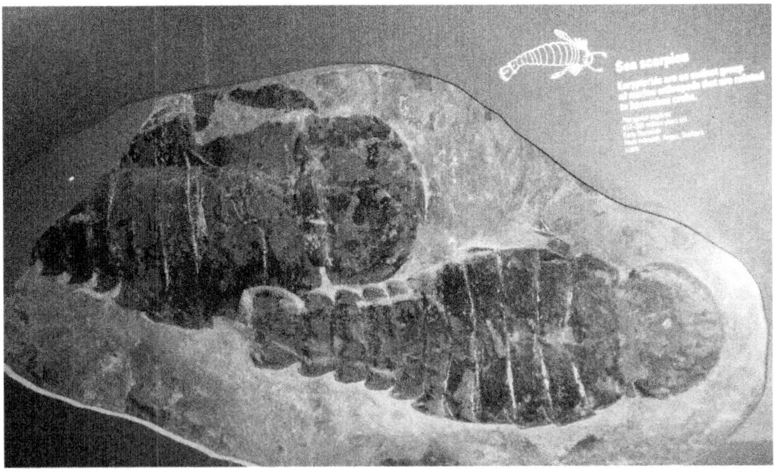

Drepanaspis (419 – 393 mya)

Drepanaspis is an extinct genus of primitive jawless fish from Early Devonian.

It was a flattened creature with a heavily armoured body, superficially ray-like in appearance. Its mouth faced upwards, unlike most other *Heterostracans*, which had downward-facing mouths. *Drepanaspis* also had small, widely spaced eyes. It is presumed to have foraged the ocean floor for food.

This 'frying-pan' shaped fish may have been the ancestor of the giant, metre-long, metre-wide *Psammosteid heterostracans* of the Late Devonian.

Fossil of Drepanaspis sp. in the Field Museum of Natural History

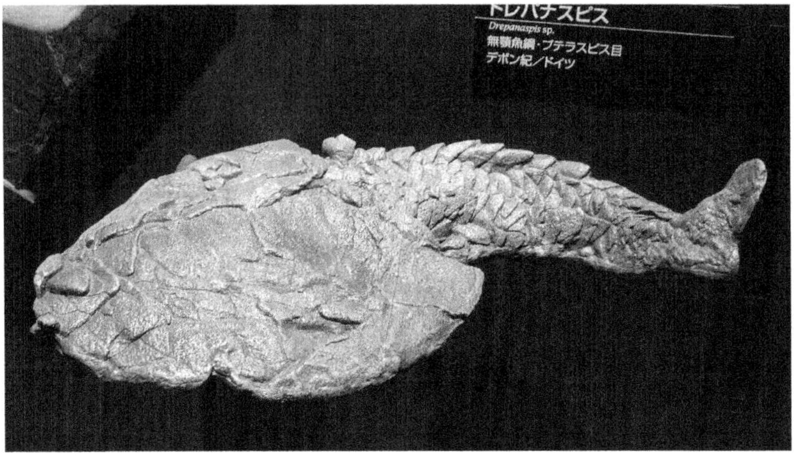

National Museum of Nature and Science, Tokyo, Japan

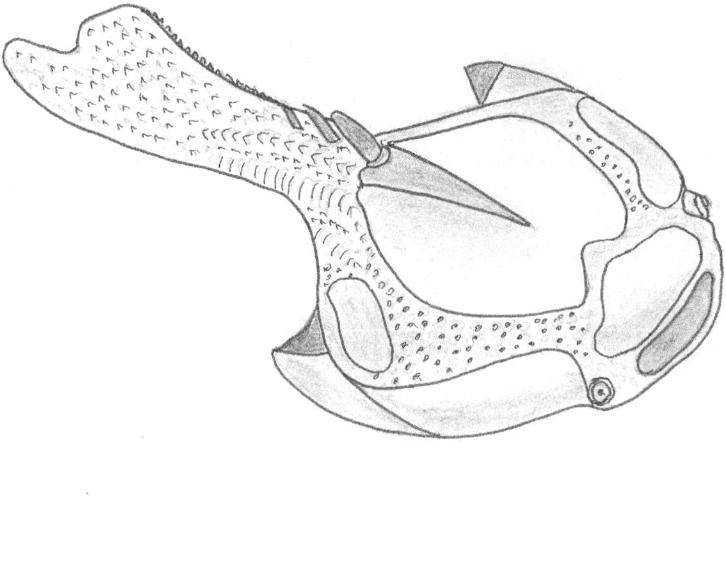

Pteraspis (416 – 386 mya)

Pteraspis is an extinct genus of *pteraspidid heterostracan agnathan vertebrate* that lived from the Lochkovian to Eifelian epochs of the Devonian period in what are now Brazil, Britain, Ukraine and Belgium.

Reconstruction of Pteraspis, Estonian Museum of Natural History

Like other *heterostracan* fishes, *Pteraspis* had protective armoured plating covering the front of its body. Though lacking fins other than its lobed tail, it is thought to have been a good swimmer thanks to stiff, wing-like protrusions derived from the armoured plates over its gills. This, along with the horn-like *rostrum*, made *Pteraspis* very streamlined in shape - a perfect quality for a good swimmer. *Pteraspis* also had some stiff spikes on its back, possibly an additional form of protection against predators. It is thought to have fed from shoals of plankton just under the ocean surface, and is found in association with marine fossils. *Pteraspis* grew to an estimated length of 20cm.

Coelacanth (420 Mya – Present)

Latimeria chalumnae and ***Latimeria menadoensis*** are the only two known living *coelacanth* species. Coelacanths are large, plump, lobe-finned fish that can grow to more than 2m and weigh around 90kg. They are estimated to live up to 100 years, based on analysis of annual growth marks on scales, the oldest known specimen was 84 years old at the time of its capture in 1960. They are nocturnal *piscivorous* drift-hunters.

Coelacanths have eight fins – two dorsal fins, two pectoral fins, two pelvic fins, one anal fin and one caudal fin. The tail is very nearly equally proportioned and is split by a terminal tuft of fin rays that make up its caudal lobe. The eyes of the coelacanth are very large, while the mouth is very small. The eye is acclimatized to seeing in poor light by rods that absorb mostly short wavelengths. Two nostrils, along with four other external openings, appear between the *premaxilla* and lateral *rostral* bones. The nasal sacs resemble those of many other fish and do not contain an internal nostril.

Externally, several characteristics distinguish *coelacanths* from other lobe-finned fish. They possess a three-lobed caudal fin. A secondary tail extending past the primary tail separates the upper and lower halves of the coelacanth. *Cosmoid* scales act as thick armour to protect the coelacanth's exterior.

Several internal traits also aid in differentiating *coelacanths* from other lobe-finned fish. At the back of the skull, the coelacanth possesses a hinge, the intracranial joint, which allows it to open its mouth extremely wide.

Additionally, *coelacanths* retain an oil-filled *notochord,* a hollow, pressurized tube which is replaced by a vertebral column early in embryonic development in most other vertebrates. The coelacanth's heart is shaped differently from that of most modern fish, with its chambers arranged in a straight tube.

The coelacanth's braincase is 98.5% filled with fat and only 1.5% of the braincase contains brain tissue. Also unique to extant coelacanths is the presence of a 'fatty lung' or a fat-filled single-lobed vestigial lung, homologous to other fishes' *swim bladders*. The parallel development of a fatty organ for buoyancy control suggests a unique specialization for deep-water habitats.

According to the fossil record, the divergence of *coelacanths,* lungfish and *tetrapods* is thought to have occurred during the Silurian. The oldest identified coelacanth fossils are around 420-410 million years old, dating to the early Devonian.

Coelacanth locomotion is unique. To move around they most commonly take advantage of up- or down-swells of current and drift. Their paired fins stabilize movement through the water. While on the ocean floor, they do not use the paired fins for any kind of movement. *Coelacanths* generate thrust with their *caudal* fins for quick starts. Due to the abundance of its fins, the *coelacanth* has high manoeuvrability and can orient its body in almost any direction in the water.

Holophagus penicillatus (Undina penicillata)
Münster 1834 from the Jurassic of Painten, Germany

Preserved Latimeria menadoensis,
Tokyo Sea Life Park, Japan

Ammonoidea (409 – 65 Mya)

Ammonoids are a group of extinct marine mollusc animals in the subclass *Ammonoidea* of the class *Cephalopoda.* These molluscs are commonly referred to as **ammonites.** The earliest ammonites appeared during the Devonian, and the last species either vanished in the **Cretaceous–Paleogene Extinction Event**, or shortly after, during the Danian epoch of the Paleocene.

The name '*ammonite*', from which the scientific term is derived, was inspired by the spiral shape of their fossilized shells, which somewhat resemble tightly coiled rams' horns. Pliny the Elder (d.79 AD near Pompeii) called fossils of these animals, *ammonis cornua* ('horns of Ammon'), because the Egyptian god Ammon (Amun) was typically depicted wearing ram's horns. Often, the name of an ammonite genus ends in *-ceras*, which is from κέρας (*kéras*) meaning 'horn'.

Asteroceras, a Jurassic ammonite from England

Many *ammonoids* probably lived in the open water of ancient seas, rather than at the sea bottom, because their fossils are often found in rocks laid down under conditions where no bottom-dwelling life is found. Many of them (such as *Oxynoticeras*) are thought to have been good swimmers, with flattened, discus-shaped, streamlined shells, although some ammonoids were less effective swimmers and were likely to have been slow-swimming bottom-dwellers.

Analysis has revealed remains of isopod and mollusc larvae in its *buccal cavity*, indicating at least the kind of ammonite which fed on plankton. They may have avoided predation by squirting ink, much like modern *cephalopods*. Ink is occasionally preserved in fossil specimens.

Inside the *ammonite*, there were numerous body chambers which the animal would have pumped air into and out of. This would have helped it to move up and down through the water column. To travel quickly away from predators *ammonites* moved by '*jet propulsion*', expelling water through a funnel-like opening to propel them in the opposite direction.

Ammonites were devastated by the **end-Triassic extinction**, with only a handful of genera belonging to the family *Psiloceratidae* of the suborder *Phylloceratina* surviving and becoming ancestral to all later Jurassic and Cretaceous ammonites. Ammonites explosively diversified during the early Jurassic, with many orders, all appearing during the Jurassic.

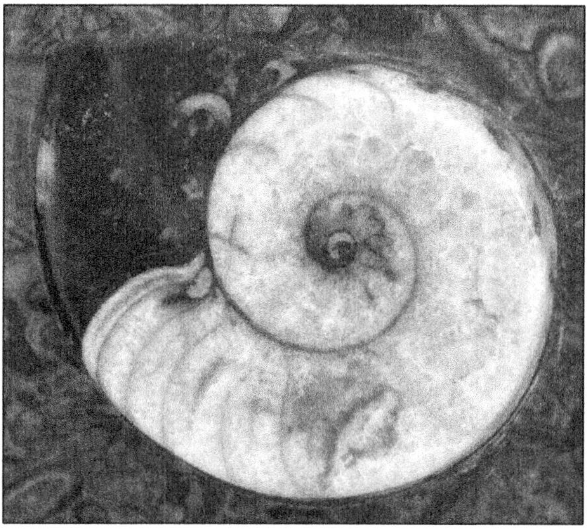

Photo credit MLF

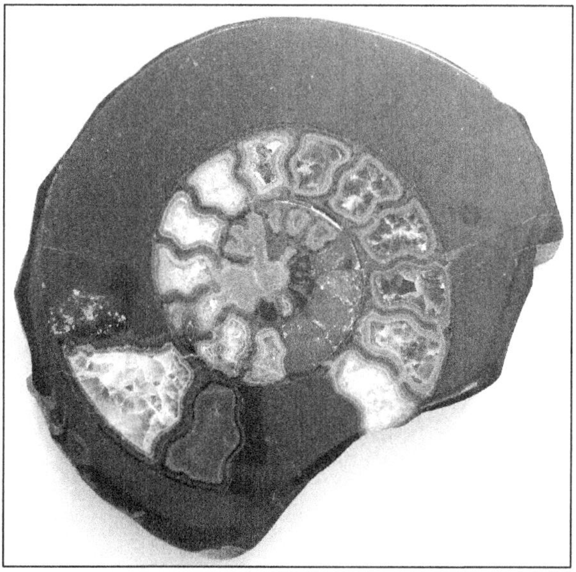

Hildoceras shell viewed in section, revealing the petrified internal chambers and septa.
Whitby, UK Photo credit MLF

Osteolepis (393 – 382 mya)

Osteolepis ('bone scale') is an extinct genus of lobe-finned fish from the Devonian. It lived in the Lake Orcadie of northern Scotland.

Osteolepis was about 20cm long, and covered with large, square scales. The scales and plates on its head were covered in a thin layer of spongy, bony material called *cosmine*. This layer contained canals which were connected to sensory cells deeper in the skin. These canals ended in pores on the surface, and were probably for sensing vibrations in the water.

Osteolepis was a *rhipidistian*, having a number of features in common with *tetrapods* and was *probably* close to the base of the *tetrapod* family tree.

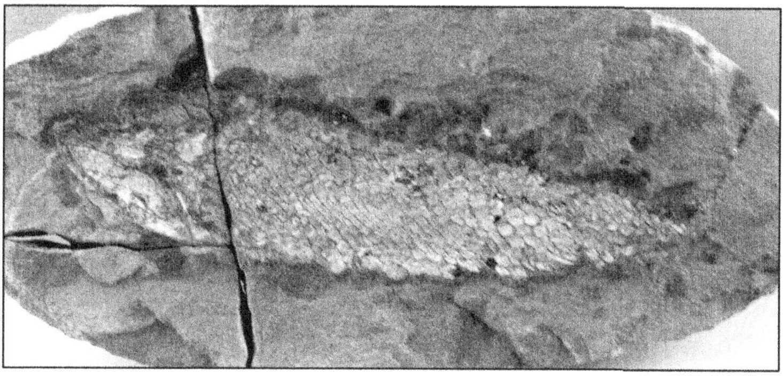

Osteolepis macrolepidotus AGASSIS, Devon, Scotland

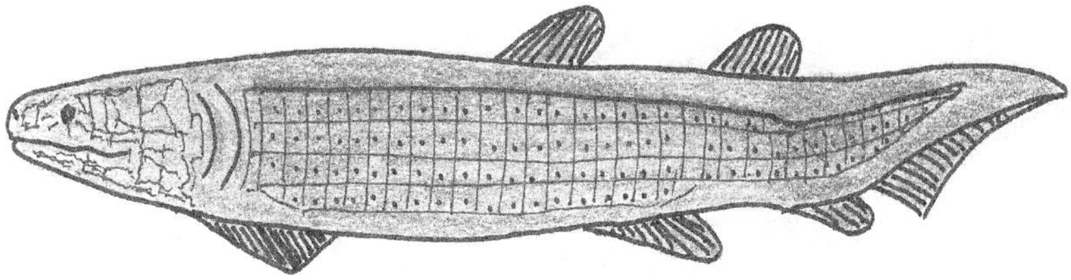

Eusthenopteron (385 Mya)

Eusthenopteron is a genus of lobe-finned fishes being known from several species that lived during the Late Devonian.

The earliest-known fossilized evidence of **bone-marrow** has been found in *Eusthenopteron*, which may point to the origin of bone-marrow in *tetrapods*.

Eusthenopteron shares many unique features in common with the earliest-known *tetrapods*. It shares a similar pattern of skull roofing bones with forms such as *Ichthyostega* and *Acanthostega*.

What is more is that, along with other *tetrapodomorph* fishes, it had *choana*, which are one of the defining traits of *tetrapodomorphs*, including *tetrapods*. It also had *labyrinthodont* teeth, characterized by infolded enamel, which characterizes all of the earliest known *tetrapods*.

Like other lobe-finned fishes, *Eusthenopteron* possessed a two-part cranium, which hinged at mid-length along an intracranial joint.

Particularly noteworthy is the fact that the pattern of this fish's fin endoskeleton bears a distinct *humerus, ulna*, and *radius* in the fore-fin, and *femur, tibia*, and *fibula* in the pelvic fin.

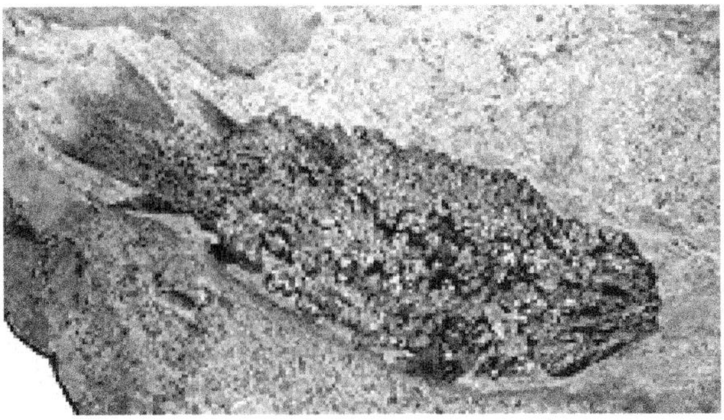

Eusthenopteron foordi
Ghedoghedo
CC BY-SA 3.0

Head of Eusthenopteron (model at State Museum of Natural History Stuttgart, Germany). by Dr. Günter Bechly

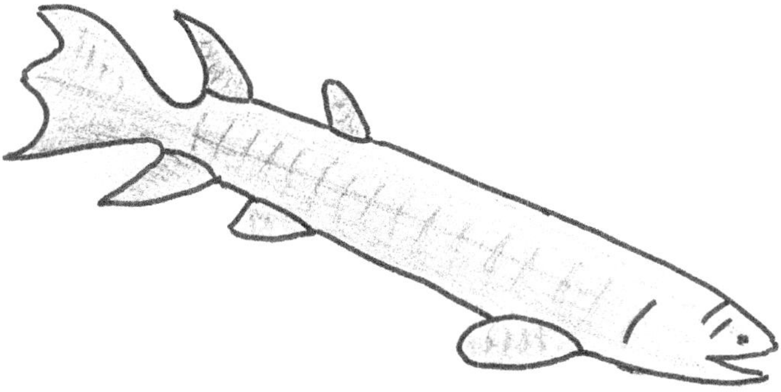

Panderichthys (385 – 374 Mya)

Panderichthys is a genus of extinct lobe-finned fish from the late Devonian. Possible *tetrapod* tracks dating back to before the appearance of *Panderichthys* in the fossil record were reported in 2010, which suggests that *Panderichthys* is not a direct ancestor of *tetrapods*, but nonetheless shows the traits that evolved during the fish-tetrapod evolution.

Panderichthys is a 90–130cm long fish with a large tetrapod-like head that is flattened, narrow at the snout and wide in the back. The intracranial joint, which is characteristic of most lobe-fin fishes, has been lost from the external elements of the skull, but is still present in the braincase. The patterns of external bones in the skull roof and cheeks are more similar to those of early *tetrapods* than those of other lobe-fins. The vertebral column is ossified throughout its length and the vertebrae are comparable to those of early tetrapods. On the other hand, the distal parts of the front fins are unlike those of *tetrapods*.

Panderichthys has many features that can be considered an intermediate form during the fish-tetrapod evolution and displays some features that are more derived than its phylogenetic position indicates, while others that are more basal. The body form of both *Panderichthys* and *Tiktaalik* represents a major step in the transition from fish to *tetrapods* and they were even able to haul out on land.

A rise in global oxygen content allowed for the evolution of large, predatory fish that were able to exploit the shallow tidal areas and swamplands as top predators. Being a shallow-water fish, the *Panderichthys* evolved many of the basic adaptations, apart from those already mentioned, that later allowed the *tetrapods* in general to become terrestrial animals. The most important ones were the shift of main propulsion apparatus from the tail fin to the pectoral and pelvic fins, and a shift to reliance on lungs rather than gills as the main means of obtaining oxygen.

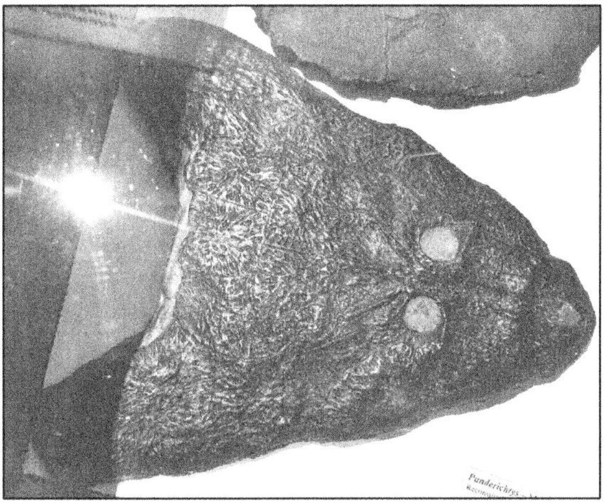

Panderichthys - taken from original by Dmitry Bogdanov (dmitrchel@mail.ru) CC BY 3.0

Musee d'Histoire Naturelle, Lille
Taken from photo by Ghedoghedo
CC BY-SA 4.0

Dunkleosteus (382 – 358 mya)

Dunkleosteus is an extinct genus of large armoured, jawed fishes that existed during the Late Devonian. It consists of ten species, some of which are among the largest *placoderms* to have ever lived. The largest and most well known species is *D. terrelli*, which grew up to 8.79m long and 4 tonnes in weight.

The secret of the success of *Dunkleosteus* was in its mouth. The evolution of a movable lower jaw marked the start of its rapid rise to dominance in the seas.

Instead of teeth, *Dunkleosteus* had **razor-sharp sheering plates** made from bone, which would flash past each other in a scissor-like motion. The jaws were powerful and anything caught between them would have been sliced in two.*

The lack of teeth meant that it could not chew and so had to swallow large pieces of food in their entirety. Sometimes the stomach could not cope with such large chunks of meat and it would be forced to vomit onto the seabed. Deposits of this fossilized vomit are common in Late Devonian rocks.

Dunkleosteus could quickly open and close its jaw, like modern-day suction feeders, and had a bite force of 6,000N (612kg) at the tip and 7,400N (755kg) at the blade edge.

Some major historians believe that scissors were invented in Mesopotamia about 3,000-4,000 years ago.

Although the ancient Egyptians are believed to have crafted a scissor-like tool somewhere around 1,500 B.C.

* *It took around 350 million years for scissors to be invented, thus replicating the sheering plates of Dunkleosteus!*

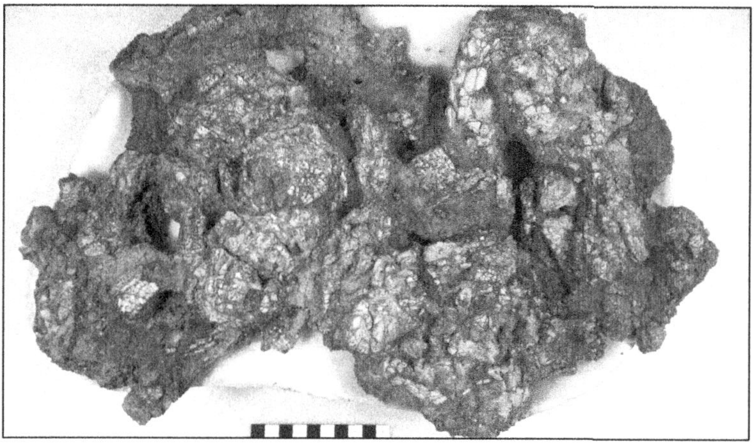

Sample of fossilized vomit

D. marsaisi skull Musee des Confluences, Lyon

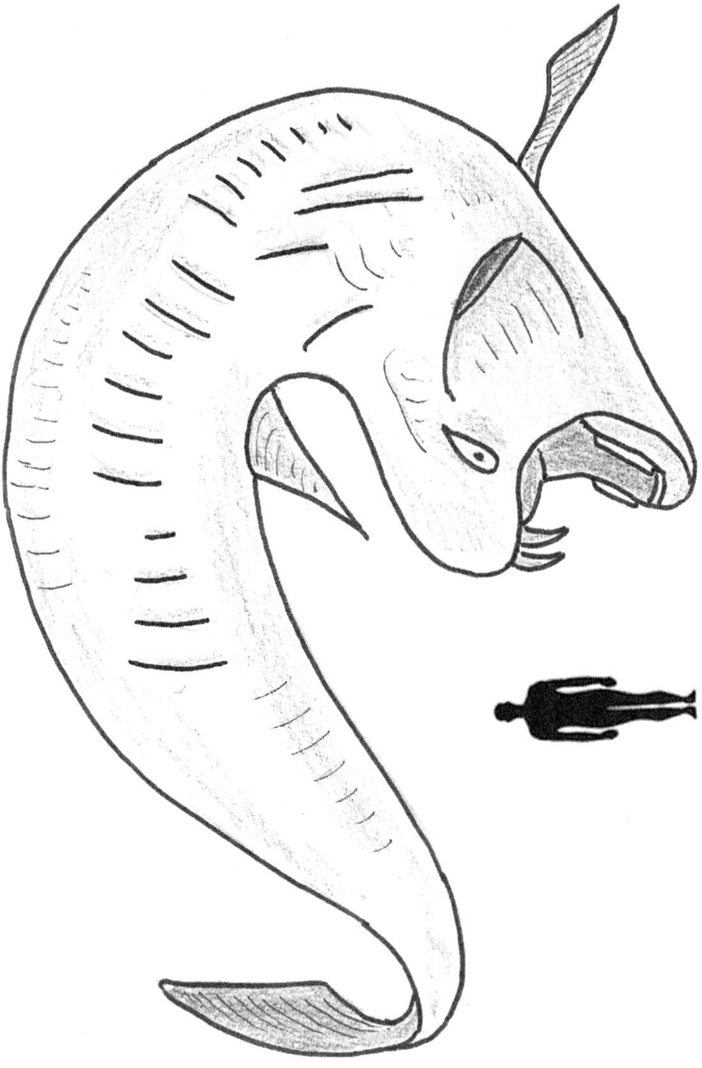

Tiktaalik (375 Mya)

Tiktaalik is a monospecific genus of extinct lobe-finned fish from the Late Devonian, having many features akin to those of *tetrapods*.

Tiktaalik is a non-tetrapod *Osteichthyes*, complete with scales and gills, but has a triangular, flattened head and unusual cleaver-shaped fins. Its fins have thin ray bones for paddling like most fish, but they also have sturdy interior bones that would have allowed Tiktaalik to prop itself up in shallow water and use its limbs for support as most four-legged animals do. Tiktaalik has a combination of features that show the evolutionary transition between swimming fish and their descendants, the four-legged vertebrates.

This animal, and similar animals, may possibly be the common ancestors of the broad swath of all vertebrate terrestrial fauna of amphibians, reptiles, birds, and mammals.

Tiktaalik provides insights on the features of the extinct closest relatives of the *tetrapods*. Unlike many previous, more fishlike transitional fossils, the '*fins*' of *Tiktaalik* have basic wrist bones and simple rays reminiscent of fingers. The bones of the fore-fins show large muscle facets, suggesting that the fin was both muscular and had the ability to flex like a wrist joint. These wrist-like features would have helped anchor the creature to the bottom in fast moving current.

Also notable are the *spiracles* on the top of the head, which suggest the creature had primitive lungs as well as gills. This attribute would have been useful in shallow water, where higher water temperature would lower oxygen content. The more robust ribcage of *Tiktaalik* would have helped support the animal's body any time it ventured outside a fully aquatic habitat. *Tiktaalik* also lacked a characteristic that most fishes have, which are bony plates in the gill area that restrict lateral head movement.

This makes *Tiktaalik* the earliest known fish to have a neck, with the *pectoral girdle* separate from the skull. This would give the creature more freedom in hunting prey either on land or in the shallows.

Tiktaalik in the Field Museum, Chicago
by Eduard Solà   CC BY-SA 3.0

Elginerpeton (368 Mya)

Elginerpeton is a genus of *stem-tetrapods*, the fossils of which were recovered from Scat Craig, Morayshire in the UK, from rocks dating to the late Devonian. The only known fossil has been given the name *Elginerpeton pancheni.*

Elginerpeton is known from skeletal fragments including a partial shoulder and hip, a femur, tibia (lower hind limb), and jaw fragments. The holotype is a lower jaw fragment estimated at 40cm in total length. The total body is estimated to have measured about 1.5m in length.

A biomechanical analysis of *stegocephalian* jaws has indicated that *Elginerpeton* had an unusual feeding habit among tetrapod relatives. Its jaws were thin, and plotted as the most susceptible to high stresses among the sample group. However, the heavy sculpturing of the bone may have reduced these stresses. It also had a high bite force, third overall compared to *Crassigyrinus* (second) and *Megalocephalus* (first). These two features combined indicated that the jaw was best suited for quick, strong bites for hunting small yet fast prey.

Elginerpeton pancheni
An early tetrapod from the Late Devonian of Scotland

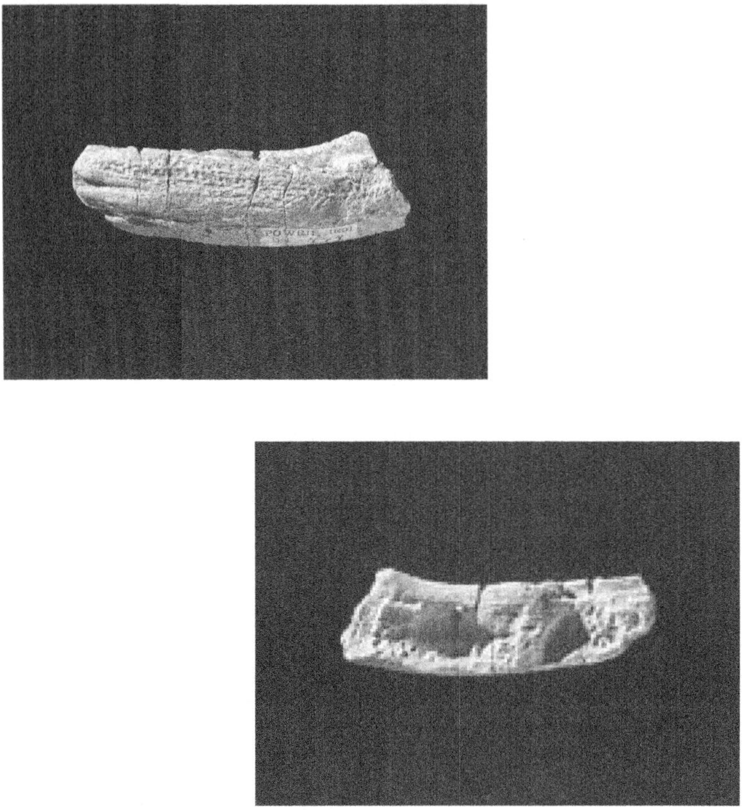

Fossil incomplete right premaxilla of Elginerpeton pancheni, from Scaat Craig, Morayshire, Scotland National Museum, Scotland

Acanthostega (365 Mya)

Acanthostega is an extinct genus of *stem-tetrapod*, among the first vertebrate animals to have recognizable limbs and was anatomically intermediate between lobe-finned fishes and those that were fully capable of coming onto land.

The 60cm *Acanthostega* had **eight digits on each hand** (the number of digits on the feet is unclear) linked by webbing. It lacked wrists, and was generally poorly adapted for walking on land. It also had a remarkably fish-like shoulder and forelimb.

The front limbs of *Acanthostega* could not bend forward at the elbow, and therefore could not be brought into a weight bearing position, appearing to be more suitable for paddling or for holding on to aquatic plants. It had internal gills that were covered like those of fish. It also had lungs, but its ribs were too short to support its chest cavity out of water.

Acanthostega probably lived in shallow, weed-choked swamps, its legs apparently being adapted for these specific ecosystems. The animal was not adapted in any way for walking on land. It appears that *Acanthostega* was primarily an aquatic animal descended from fish that never left the sea, and that the specializations in the *tetrapod* lineage **developed features which would later be useful for terrestrial life**!

Its *humerus* also exhibits traits that resemble those of later fully terrestrial *stem-tetrapods*. This could indicate that vertebrates evolved terrestrial traits earlier than previously assumed, and numerous times independently from another.

Acanthostega is seen as part of widespread evolutionary radiation in the late Devonian, starting with purely aquatic finned *tetrapodomorphs*, with their successors showing increased air-breathing capability and related adaptations to the jaws and gills, as well as more muscular neck thus allowing freer movement of the head, and use of modified fins to raise the body.

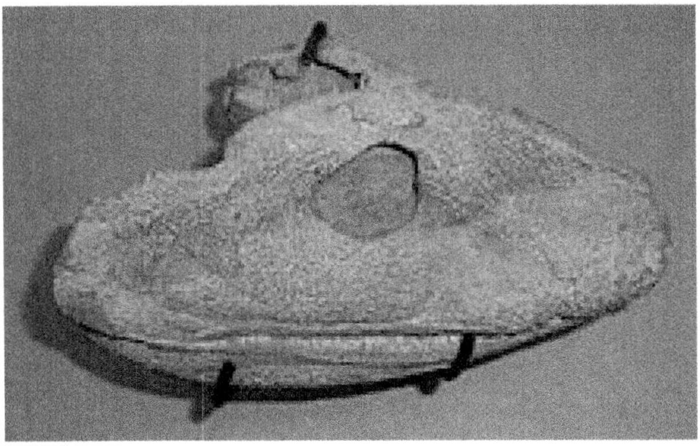

Fossil of Acanthostega gunnari from Musee d'Histoire Naturelle, Brussels (Ghedoghedo) CC BY-SA 3.0

Ichthyostega (365 – 360 mya)

Ichthyostega was a fairly large animal, broadly built and about 1.5m long. The skull was flat with dorsally placed eyes and armed with large *labyrinthodont* teeth. The posterior margin of the skull formed an *operculum* covering the gills. The *spiracle* was situated in an optic notch behind each eye.

The limbs were large compared to contemporary relatives, and it had seven digits on each hind limb. The exact number of digits on the forelimb is not yet known, since fossils of the *manus* (hand) have not been found. It had a fin containing fin rays on its tail.

Ichthyostega is related to *Acanthostega gunnari*, also from East Greenland. *Ichthyostega*'s skull seems more fish-like than that of *Acanthostega*, but its girdle (shoulder and hip) morphology seems stronger and better adapted to life on land. *Ichthyostega* also had more supportive ribs and stronger vertebrae with more developed *zygapophyses*. Whether these traits were independently evolved in *Ichthyostega* is debated. It does, however, show that *Ichthyostega* may have ventured onto land on occasions, unlike contemporaneous limbed vertebrates such as *Elginerpeton* and *Obruchevichthys*.

In Late Devonian vertebrate speciation, descendants of pelagic lobe-finned fish – like *Eusthenopteron* – exhibited a sequence of adaptations. *Panderichthys*, suited to muddy shallows not on land, *Tiktaalik* with limb-like fins that could take it onto land, fully limbed vertebrates in weed-filled swamps, such as *Acanthostega* which had feet with eight digits and then *Ichthyostega* with an oval-shaped neck and large limbs.

Descendants also included pelagic lobe-finned fish such as *Coelacanth* species.

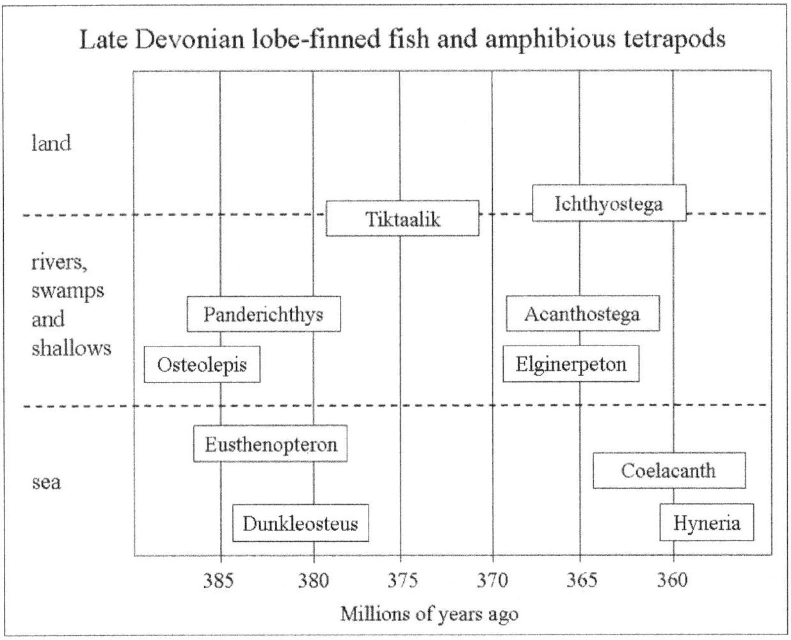

Adapted from CC BY-SA 4.0 Dave Sousa

Ichthyosaur about 10 metres long and dating back 180 million years discovered at Rutland Water

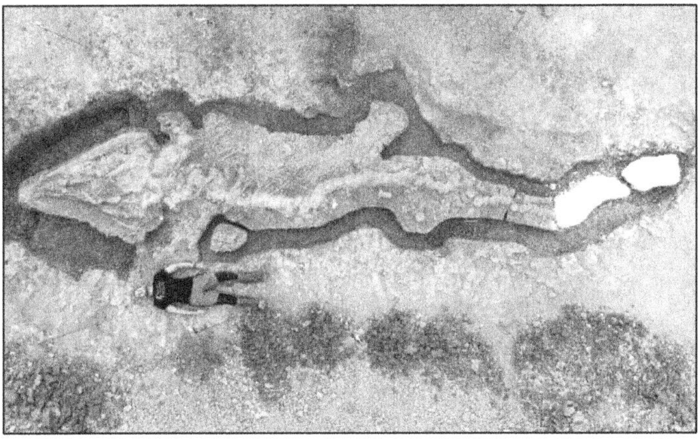

A gigantic prehistoric 'sea dragon' discovered in the Midlands has been described as one of the greatest finds in the history of British palaeontology.

The *ichthyosaur*, which is about 180m years old with a skeleton measuring about 10 metres in length and a skull weighing about a tonne, is the largest and most complete fossil of its kind ever found in the UK.

Joe Davis of the Leicestershire and Rutland Wildlife Trust discovered it during the routine draining of a lagoon island at the Rutland Water reservoir in February 2021.

The first *ichthyosaurs*, which are called sea dragons because they tend to have very large teeth and eyes, were discovered by the fossil hunter and palaeontologist Mary Anning in the early 19th century.

ref: The Guardian newspaper (January, 2022)

Hyneria (360 Mya)

Hyneria is a genus of large prehistoric predatory lobe-finned fish which lived in freshwater during the Devonian.

Hyneria was a large fish, estimated at 2.5 – 3.7m in total length. Its skull had heavy, ornamented dermal bones and its lower jaw was relatively long and shallow. The teeth were stout with those of the *premaxilla* forming fangs upwards of 5cm \9see photo below). Its body was covered by cycloid scales. It had large sensory canals to aid in detection of possible prey, as the freshwater environment it inhabited was probably murky and had low visibility.

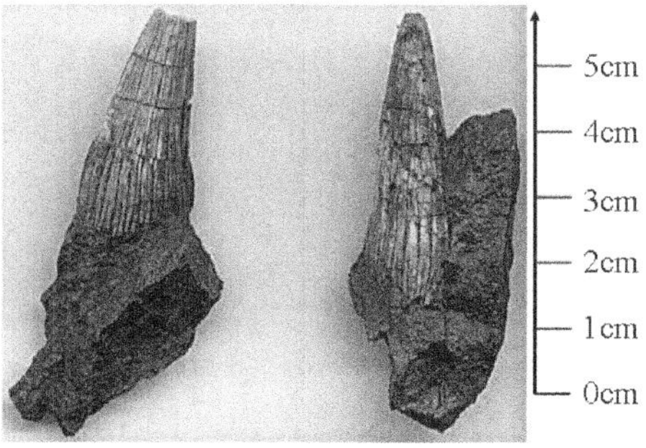

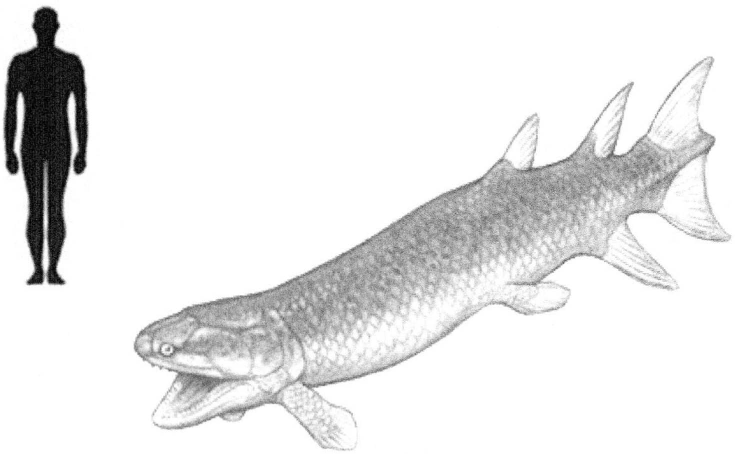

Thelyphonus (359 to 299 Mya – present)

Thelyphonida is an *arachnid* order comprising invertebrates commonly known as **whip scorpions** or **vinegaroons.** The name 'whip scorpion' refers to their resemblance to true scorpions and possession of a whip-like tail.

Whip scorpions range from 25 to 85mm length, with most species having a body no longer than 30mm. Because of their legs, claws, and rear-end 'whip', though, they can appear much larger.

Like the related orders *Schizomida* and *Amblypygi*, the *vinegaroons* use only six legs for walking, with the first two legs serving as antennae-like sensory organs.

All species also have very large scorpion-like *pedipalps* (pincers), but there is an additional large spine on each *palpal tibia*.

They have one pair of eyes at the front of the *cephalothorax* and three on each side of the head, a pattern also found in scorpions.

Vinegaroons have no venom glands, but they have glands near the rear of their abdomen that can spray a combination of acetic acid and caprylic acid when they are bothered. The acetic acid gives this spray a vinegar-like smell, giving rise to the common name *vinegaroon*.

Vinegaroons are carnivorous, nocturnal hunters feeding mostly on insects, millipedes, scorpions, and terrestrial isopods, but sometimes on worms and slugs. The prey is crushed between special teeth on the inside of the *trochanters* (the second segment of the 'legs') of the front appendages.

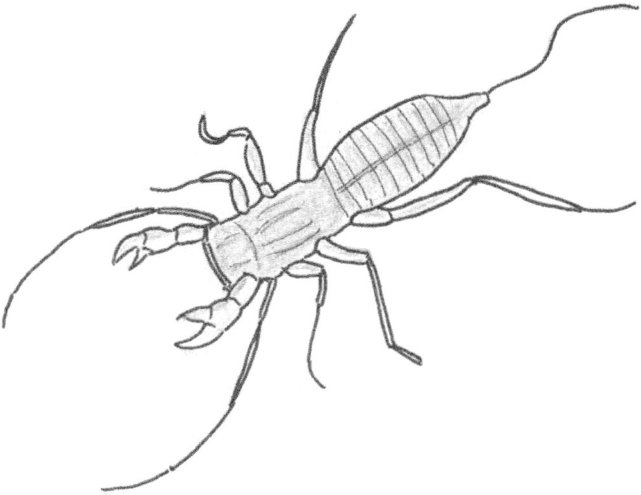

Crassigyrinus (345 -329 mya)

Crassigyrinus is an extinct genus of carnivorous *stem tetrapod* from the Early Carboniferous.

This animal had a streamlined body up to 2m in length. Its limbs were tiny and virtually useless, implying that the animal was almost completely aquatic. *Crassigyrinus* had unusually large jaws, equipped with two rows of sharp teeth, the second row having a pair of palatal fangs.

Studies have shown that *Crassigyrinus* may have been able to open its mouth as wide as 60 degrees, which suggests that it was a powerful predator with a strong bite. This strongly suggests that it was ideally suited for catching fish, and the animal was probably a fast-moving predator.

Several thickened bony ridges ran along the dorsal midline of the snout and between the eyes, and several palaeontologists have suggested that they helped the skull to withstand stress when the animal bit prey. *Crassigyrinus* had large eyes, suggesting that it was either nocturnal, or lived in very murky water.

Its peculiar stunted forelimbs were tiny and the humerus was only 35mm long (the whole animal was about 1.5m long). The hind limbs were much larger than the forelimbs, and in the pelvis the *ileum* lacked a bony connection to the vertebral column. The tail, only known from a few vertebrae fragments, is assumed to have been long and laterally compressed.

Skull of Crassigyrinus shown in dorsal view

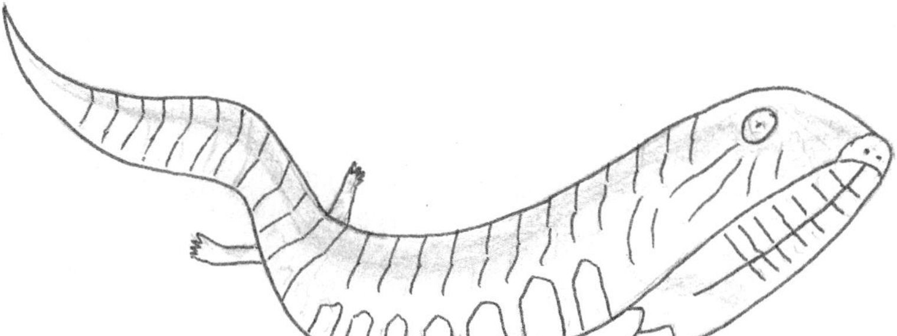

Hylonomus lyelli (315 - mya)

Hylonomus is an extinct genus of reptile that lived during the Late Carboniferous. It is the earliest unquestionable reptile (*Westlothiana* is older, but in fact it may have been an amphibian, and *Casineria* is rather fragmentary). The only species is the type species ***Hylonomus lyelli***.

Hylonomus was 20–25cm long (including the tail). Most of them are 20cm long and probably would have looked rather similar to modern lizards. It had small sharp teeth and it likely ate small invertebrates such as millipedes or early insects.

Fossilized footprints found in New Brunswick have been attributed to *Hylonomus*, at an estimated age of 315 million years.

While it has traditionally been included in the group *Protorothyrididae*, later studies have shown that it is probably more closely related to *diapsids*.

Helicoprion (290 -270 Mya)

Helicoprion is an extinct genus of shark-like *eugeneodont* fish. Almost all fossil specimens are of spirally arranged clusters of the individuals' teeth, called 'tooth whorls', which in life were embedded in the lower jaw. As with most extinct cartilaginous fish, the skeleton is mostly unknown.

Fossils of *Helicoprion* are known from a 20 million year time-span during the Permian period from the Artinskian of the Cisuralian (Early Permian) to the Roadian of the Guadalupian (Middle Permian).

The closest living relatives of *Helicoprion* (and other *eugeneodonts*) are the *chimaeras*, though their relationship is very distant. The unusual tooth arrangement is thought to have been an adaptation for feeding on soft bodied prey, and may have functioned as a de-shelling mechanism for hard bodied *cephalopods* such as *nautiloids* and *ammonoids*.

In 2013, systematic revision of *Helicoprion* via morphometric analysis of the tooth whorls found only *H. davisii, H. bessonowi* and *H. ergassaminon* to be valid, with some of the larger tooth whorls being outliers.

Helicoprion individuals could reach 5 to 8m in length.

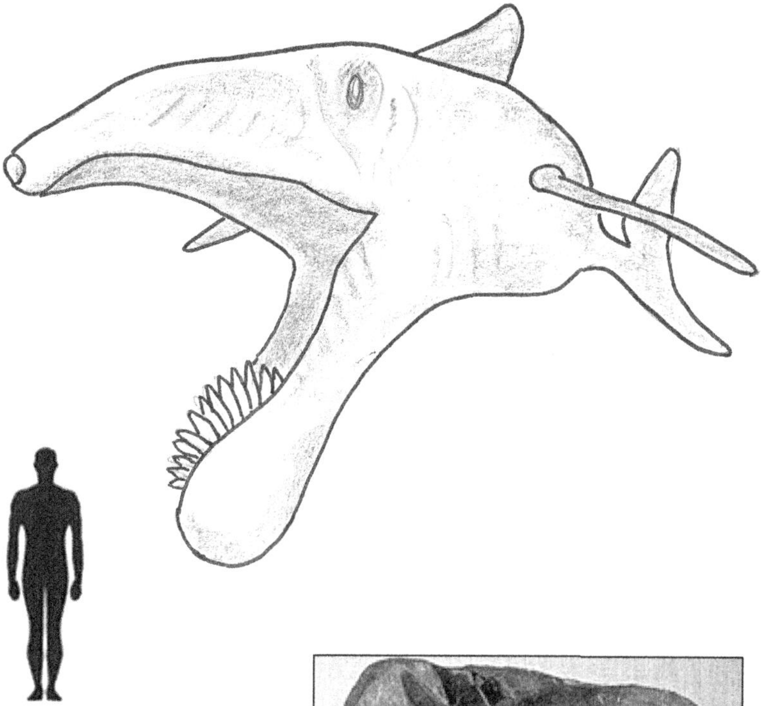

Helicoprion davisii tooth-whorl from the Phosphoria Formation of Idaho Utah Field House of Natural History

Mesosaurus (299 –280 mya)

Mesosaurus is an extinct genus of reptile from the Early Permian of southern Africa and South America. Along with it, the genera *Brazilosaurus* and *Stereosternum*, it is a member of the family *Mesosauridae* and the order *Mesosauria. Mesosaurus*. It was long thought to have been one of the first marine reptiles, although new data suggests that at least those of Uruguay inhabited a hyper saline water body, rather than a typical marine environment. In any case, it had many adaptations to a fully aquatic lifestyle. It is usually considered to have been *anapsid*, although Friedrich von Huene considered it to be a *synapsid*, and this hypothesis has been revived recently.

Fossil in Milan

Mesosaurus had a long skull that was larger than that of *Stereosternum* and had longer teeth. The teeth are angled outwards, especially those at the tips of the jaws.

The bones of the postcranial skeleton are thick, having undergone *pachyostosis*. *Mesosaurus* is unusual among reptiles in that it possesses a cleithrum. A cleithrum is a type of dermal bone that overlies the scapula, and is usually found in more primitive bony fish and tetrapods.

The head of the interclavicle of *Mesosaurus* is triangular, unlike those of other early reptiles, which are diamond-shaped.

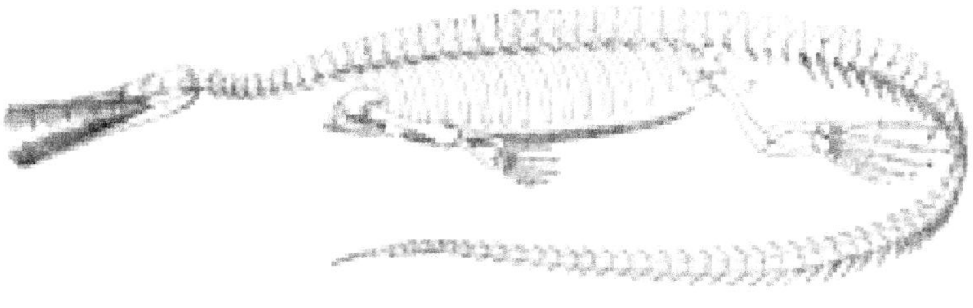

Early reconstruction of the skeleton of M. brasiliensis showing many small teeth in the jaws (MacGregor, 1908).

Mesosaurus was one of the first reptiles known to have returned to the water after early tetrapods came to land in the Late Devonian or later in the Paleozoic. It was around 1 metre in length, with webbed feet, a streamlined body, and a long tail that may have supported a fin.

It probably propelled itself through the water with its long hind legs and flexible tail. Its body was also flexible and could easily move sideways, but it had heavily thickened ribs, which would have prevented it from twisting its body.

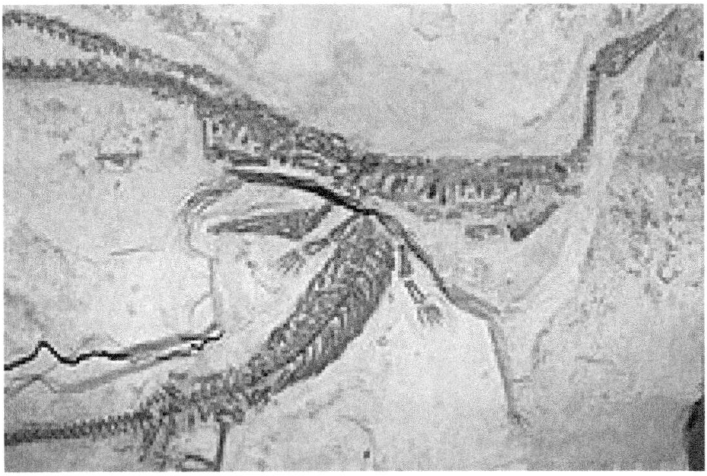

Fossil in Louisiana

Moschops capensis (265 – 260 mya)

Moschops is an extinct genus of therapsids that lived in the Guadalupian epoch. They were heavily built plant eaters, and they may have lived partly in water, as hippopotamuses do. They had short, thick heads and might have competed by head-butting each other. Their elbow joints allowed them to walk with a more mammal-like gait rather than crawling.

Their remains were found in the Karoo region of South Africa, belonging to the *Tapinocephalus* Assemblage Zone. *Therapsids*, such as *Moschops*, are *synapsids*, the dominant land animals in the Permian.

An artist's conception of Moschops capensis, based on the reconstruction of a skeleton found in a semi-desert region of South Africa. The skeleton is displayed at the American Museum of Natural History.

Moschops were heavy set *dinocephalian* *synapsids* that were roughly 2.7m in length. They had small heads with broad orbits and heavily-built short necks. Like other members of *Tapinocephalidae*, the skull had a tiny opening for the *pineal gland*. The *occipital* was broad and deep, but the skull was narrower in the dorsal border. Furthermore, the *pterygoid arches* and the angular region of the jaw with heavily-built jaw muscles. Due to that and the possession of long-crowned, stout teeth, it is believed that *Moschops* was a herbivore feeding on nutrient-poor and tough vegetation, like cycad stems. Due to the presumably nutrient-poor food, it is likely they had to feed for long periods of time. The anatomy of the *taxa* allowed them to open the elbow joints more widely, enabling them to move in a more mammal-like posture than some other animals at the time. This helped to carry their massive bodies more easily while feeding, as well as allowing them short bursts of speed. It has also been proposed that *Moschops* were possibly sub-aquatic. *Moschops* had rather thick skulls, prompting speculation that individuals could have competed with one another by head-butting. A 2017 published study would later confirm this by synchrotron scanning a *Moschops capensis* skull, which revealed numerous anatomical adaptations to the central nervous system for combative behaviour. They were likely preyed upon by *titanosuchids* and larger *therocephalian* species.

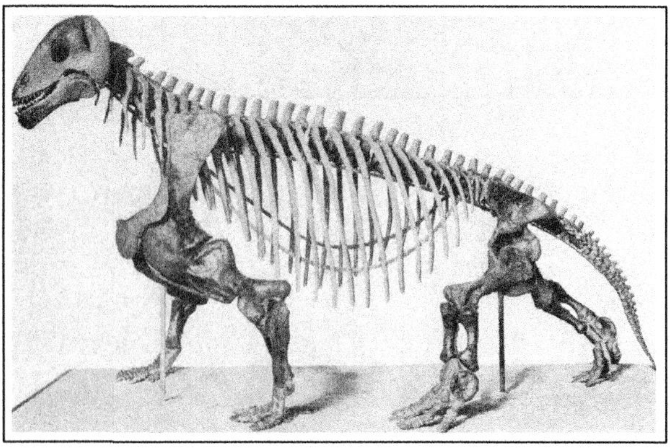

Tanystropheus (251 – 230 mya)

Tanystropheus is an extinct 6m long reptile that dates from the Middle to Late Triassic. It is recognizable by its extremely elongated neck, which measured 3m long - longer than its body and tail combined. The neck was composed of 12–13 extremely elongated vertebrae. With its very long but relatively stiff neck, *Tanystropheus* has been often proposed and reconstructed as an aquatic or semi-aquatic reptile, a theory supported by the fact that the creature is most commonly found in semi-aquatic fossil sites wherein known terrestrial reptile remains are scarce.

The diet of *Tanystropheus* has been controversial in the past, although most recent studies consider it a *piscivorous* reptile. The teeth at the front of the narrow snout were long, conical, and interlocking, similar to those of *nothosaurs* and *plesiosaurs*. This was likely an adaptation for catching aquatic prey. Additionally, hooklets from *cephalopod* tentacles and what may be fish scales have been found near the belly regions of some specimens, further support for a *piscivorous* lifestyle.

The animal is seen to have been poorly equipped for aquatic life, with the only adaptation being a lengthened fifth toe, which suggests that it visited the water some of the time, though was not wholly dependent on it. Research has also shown that *Tanystropheus* would have hunted prey like a heron.

The most likely lifestyle for *Tanystropheus* was that the animal was a shallow-water predator that used its long neck to stealthily approach schools of fish or squid without disturbing its prey due to its large body size. Upon selecting a suitable prey item, it would have dashed forward by propelling itself along the seabed or through the water, with both hind limbs pushing off at the same time.

However, this style of swimming is most common in amphibious creatures such as frogs, and likewise *Tanystropheus* would also have been capable of walking around on land.

The idea that *Tanystropheus* evolved this form of swimming over much more efficient, yet specialized, styles is evidence that it did not live an exclusively aquatic life as in most other marine reptiles such as ichthyosaurs or plesiosaurs.

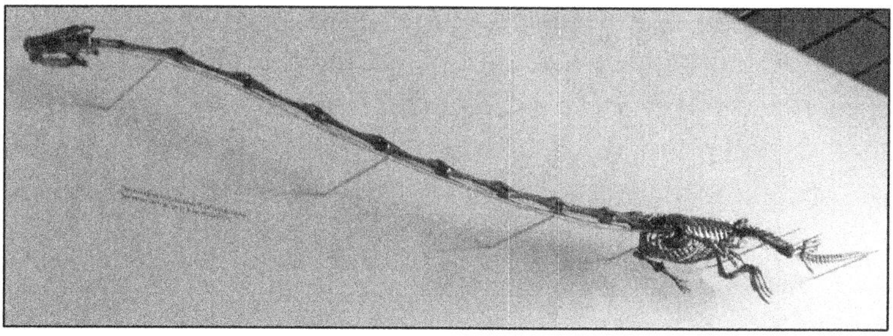

Cymbospondylus (249 – 237 Mya)

Cymbospondylus was a basal early *ichthyosaur* that lived between the early and middle Triassic. The largest species of *Cymbospondylus* may have reached lengths of 17m.

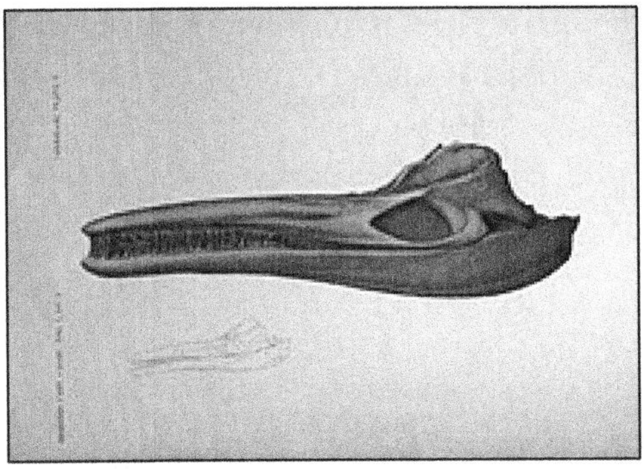

Skull illustration of Cymbospondylus petrinus by John C. Merriam (1908) PD

Unlike other groups of *ichthyosaurs*, *Cymbospondylus* had an elongated, more cylindrical body. The skull of *Cymbospondylus* is overall wedge-shaped and tapering evenly towards the tip of the snout. Most of the *rostrum* is made from the *pre-maxilla* and nasal bones, as typical in *ichthyosaurs*. The robustness varies between the species, with *C. youngorum* having the most massive. The eyes in *Cymbospondylus* are relatively small for an *ichthyosaur* and appear to not have grown in relation to the body size increase observed in the genus. Most species in the genus, with the exception of *C. youngorum* and *C. nichollsi*, have a very pronounced *sagittal crest*. It is currently unknown if *Cymbospondylus* had a dorsal fin similar to those seen in more derived *taxa*.

C. duelferi and *C. buchseri* are among the smallest *Cymbospondylus* species, reaching lengths of 4.3-5m and 5.5m respectively. Both *C. nichollsi* and *C. petrinus* are notably larger, with estimated total body lengths of 7.6m and 9.1m.

When calculating body length based on the *humerus* rather than the skull length, *C. petrinus* may have even reached a length of 12.5m. The largest species is *C. youngorum*, with the holotype skull of LACMDI 15787 measuring a total of 1.97m for the lower jaw length). Based on the size of the *humerus* (the second largest *humerus* recorded in any *ichthyosaur*), *C. youngorum* may have reached a length of 17.65m.

Of particular interest is the rapid increase in body size undergone by *ichthyosaurs* early in their evolutionary history. *Ichthyosaurs* evolved from small (skull length 55mm) ancestors such as *Cartorhynchus* to giant forms like *C. youngorum* in the span of only 2.5 million years. *Cetaceans* meanwhile, which originated under similar conditions (following the **mass extinction** at the end of the Cretaceous eradicating much of marine tetrapod diversity), took notably longer to obtain similar sizes.

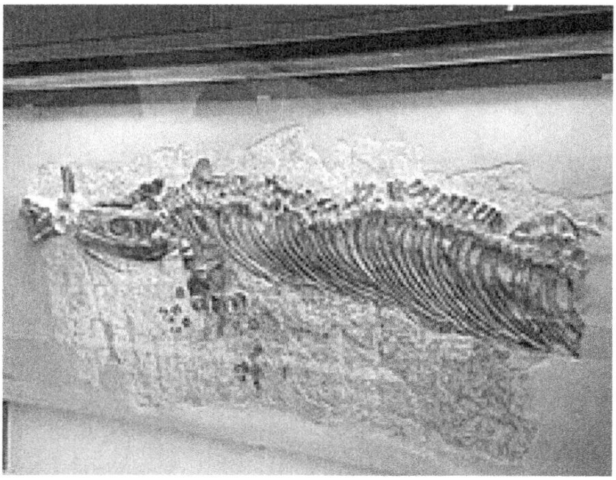

PIMUZ T 4351, a complete skeleton of Cymbospondylus buchseri. The specimen was found at Cava Tre Fontane, an outcrop on Monte San Giorgio preserving the late Anisian (Middle Triassic) Besano Formation. Photo taken at the Paleontological Museum of Zurich.

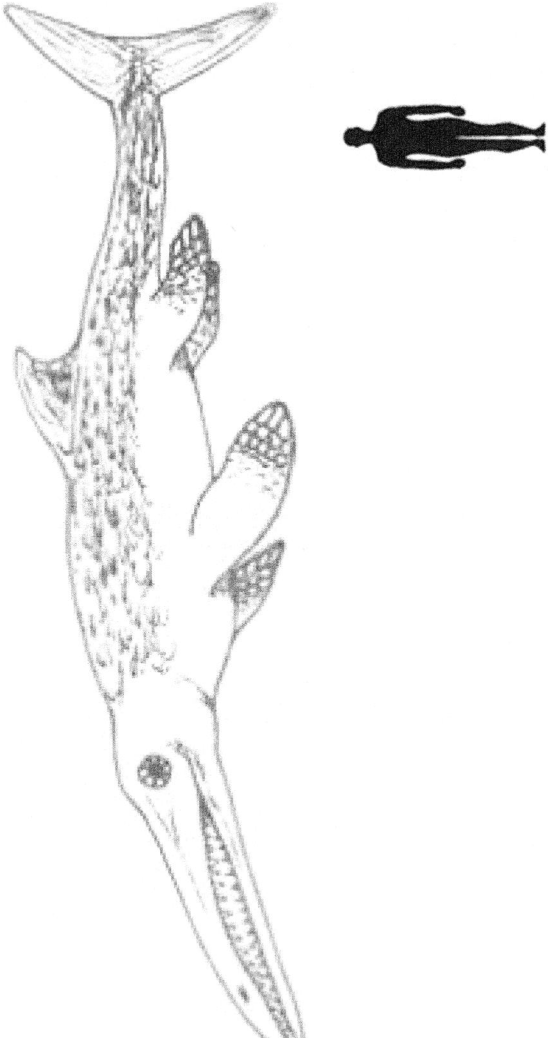

Longisquama (247 – 237 Mya)

Longisquama lived in the Middle Triassic and is characterized by distinctive *integumentary* structures along its back. The holotype (specimen PIN 2584/4) is the only known fossil preserving these appendages projecting from the back of an associated skeleton.

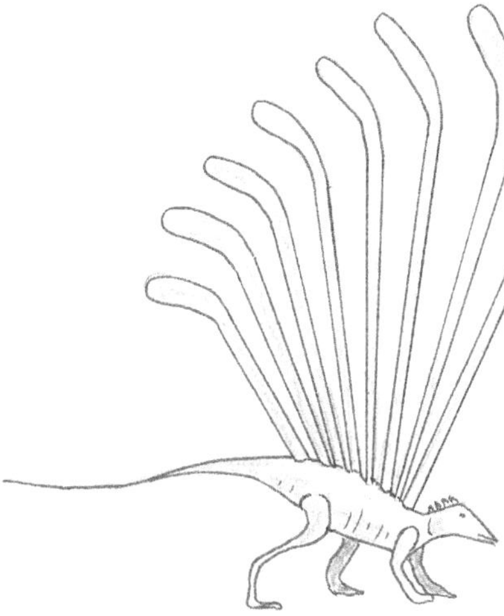

These structures are long and narrow throughout most of the animal's length, and angle backward near the tip to give the appearance of a hockey stick. The proximal straight section is divided into three longitudinal lobes: a smooth lobe on either side and a transversely ridged lobe running between them. The distal section is thought to be an extension of the middle and anterior lobes of the proximal section.

The holotype skeleton shows each structure attaching to a vertebral spine. These anchorage points are visible as raised knobs. The base of each appendage is slightly convex, unlike the flattened shape of the rest of the structure. The convex shape may be evidence that the base of each structure was tubular in life, anchoring like other *integumentary* structures such as mammalian hair or avian feathers into a follicle.

Moreover, the proximity of each structure to its corresponding vertebra suggests that a thick layer of soft tissue, possibly including a follicle,

Longisquama insignis fossil CC BY-SA 4.0

A consensus of palaeontologists agrees that birds evolved from *theropod* dinosaurs. The scenario for this hypothesis is that early *theropod* dinosaurs were *endothermic*, and evolved simple filamentous feathers for insulation. These feathers later increased in size and complexity and then adapted to aerodynamic uses. Ample evidence for this hypothesis has been found in the fossil record, specifically for such dinosaurs as *Kulindadromeus*, *Sinosauropteryx*, *Caudipteryx*, *Microraptor* and many others.

Longisquama is thus regarded as a *diapsid* with strange scales, ambiguous skeletal features and no real significance to bird evolution.

Liopleurodon (166 – 165 Mya)

Liopleurodon is a genus of large, carnivorous marine reptile belonging to the *Pliosauroidea*, a clade of short-necked *plesiosaurs*. The two species of *Liopleurodon* lived from the Middle to Late Jurassic. The largest species, *L. ferox*, is estimated to have grown up to 6.4m in length.

Estimating the size of *pliosaurs* is difficult because not much is known of their postcranial anatomy. It has been suggested that their total body length can be estimated from the length of their skull which he claimed was typically one-seventh of the former measurement, applying this ratio to *L. ferox* suggests that the largest known specimen was a little over 10m while a more typical size range would be from 5 to 7m. The body mass has been estimated at 1 and 1.7 tonnes for the lengths 4.8 and 7m respectively.

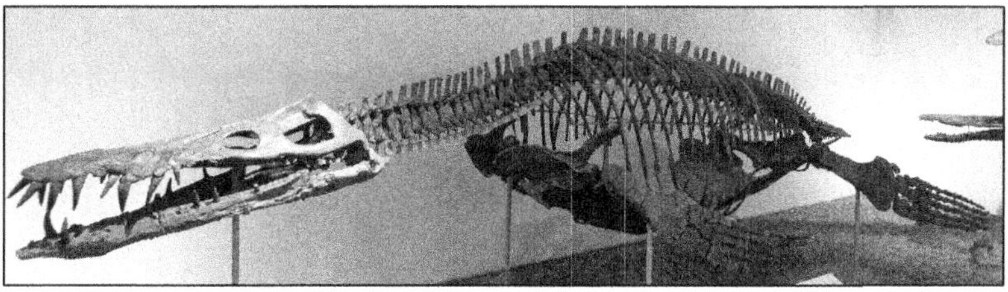

Fossil of Liopleurodon, an extinct reptile - Museum of Palaeontology, Tuebingen CC BY-SA 3.0

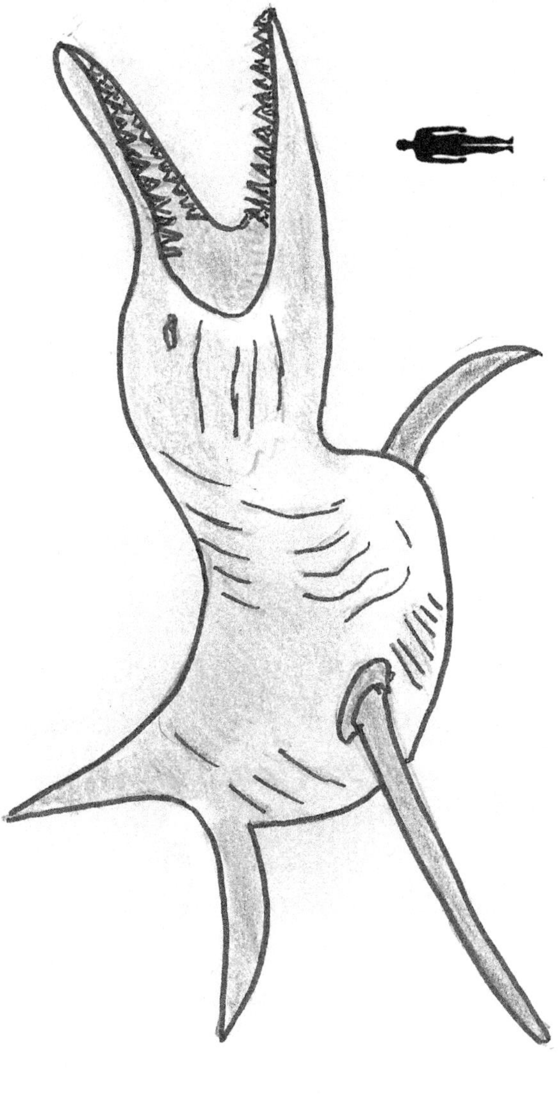

Leedsichthys (168-152 Mya)

Leedsichthys is an extinct genus of *pachycormid* fish that lived in the oceans of the Middle to Late Jurassic. It is the largest *ray-finned* fish known to have ever existed.

As the vertebrae are among the parts that have not been preserved, it is hard to determine the total body length. Estimates have varied significantly. At the beginning of the twentieth century a length of 9m was seen as plausible, but by its end *Leedsichthys* was sometimes claimed to have been over 30m long. Recent research has lowered this to about 16m for the largest individuals. Skull bones have been found indicating that *Leedsichthys* had a large head with bosses on the skull roof. Fossilized bony fin rays show large elongated pectoral fins and a tall vertical tail fin. The gill arches were lined by gill rakers, equipped by a unique system of delicate bone plates that filtered plankton from the sea water, the main food source.

Along with its close *pachycormid* relatives *Bonnerichthys* and *Rhinconichthys*, *Leedsichthys* is part of a lineage of large-sized filter-feeders that swam the Mesozoic seas for over 100 million years, from the middle Jurassic until the end of the Cretaceous. *Pachycormids* might represent an early branch of *Teleostei*, the group most modern bony fishes belong to. In that case *Leedsichthys* is the largest known *teleost* fish.

Isolated elements from various specimens showed that a maximum size of just over 16m is not unreasonable.

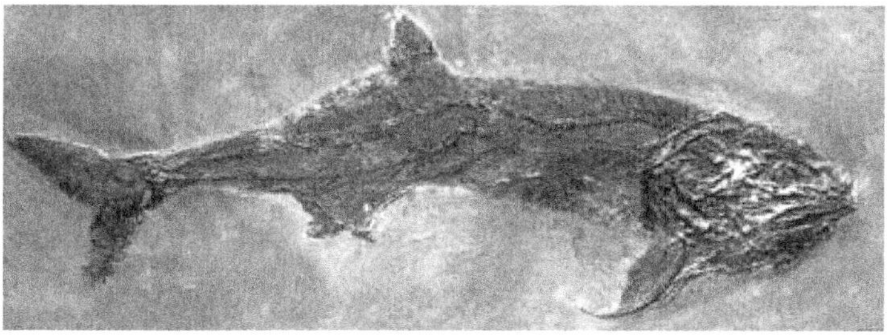

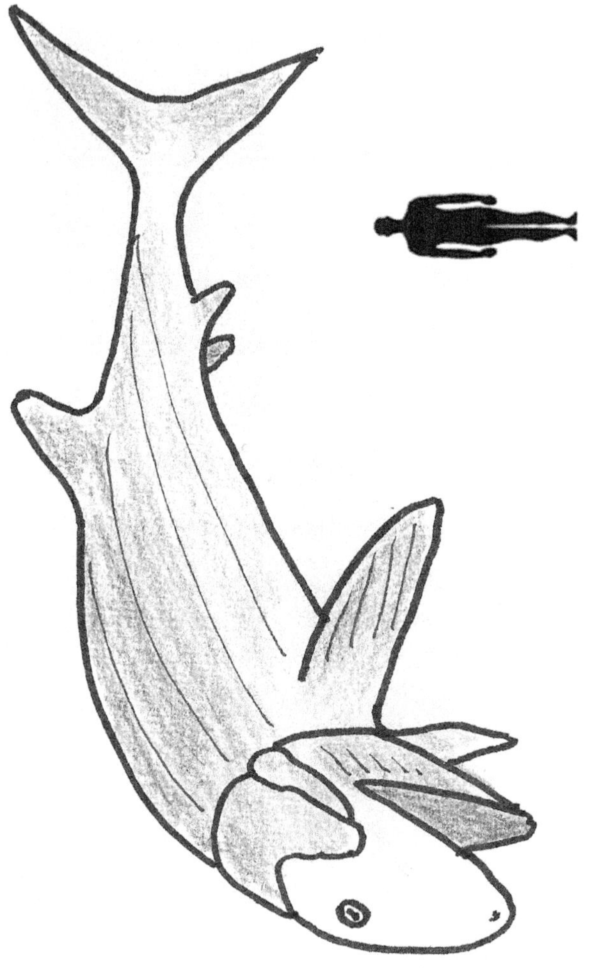

Architeuthis dux (c144 Mya – present)

The **giant squid** (*Architeuthis dux*) is a species of deep-ocean dwelling squid in the family *Architeuthidae*. It can grow to a tremendous size, offering an example of deep-sea gigantism. Recent estimates put the maximum size at around 12–13m for females and 10m for males, from the posterior fins to the tip of the two long tentacles (longer than the colossal squid at an estimated 9–10m but substantially lighter, due to the tentacles making up most of the length. The mantle of the giant squid is about 2m long (more for females, less for males), and the length of the squid excluding its tentacles (but including head and arms) rarely exceeds 5m. Claims of specimens measuring 20m or more have not been scientifically documented.

The number of different giant squid species has been debated, but recent genetic research suggests that only one species exists.

The first images of the animal in its natural habitat were taken in 2004 by a Japanese team.

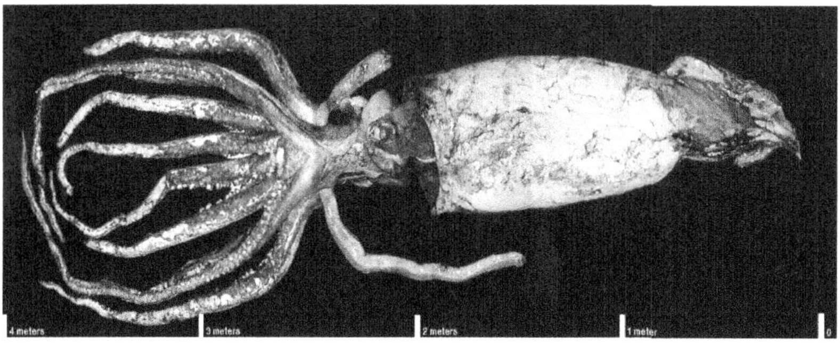

A giant squid specimen measuring over 4 m (13 ft) without its two long feeding tentacles

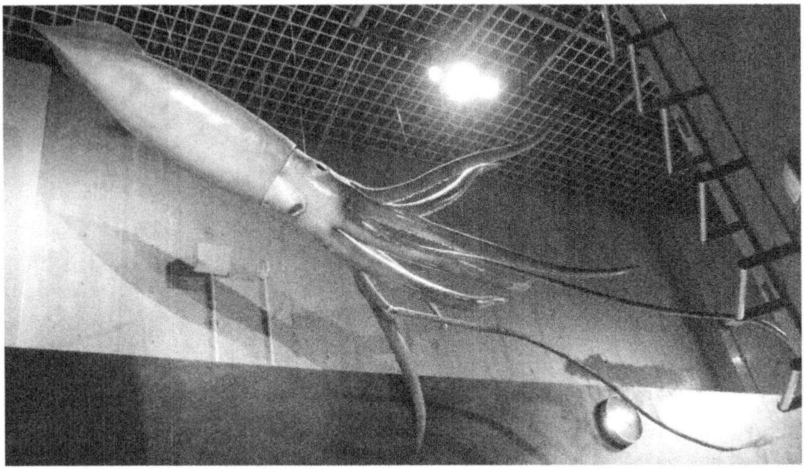

Actual size replica of Giant squid. (Architeuthis dux). National Museum of Nature and Science, Tokyo, Japan. by Momotarou2012 CC 3.0

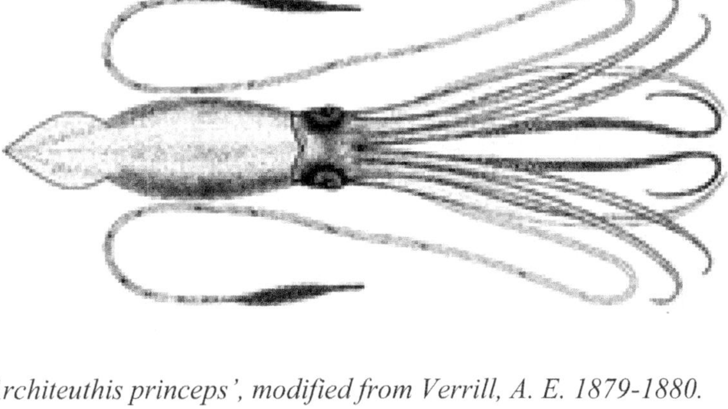

'Architeuthis princeps', modified from Verrill, A. E. 1879-1880.

Confuciusornis (125 – 120 Mya)

Confuciusornis is a genus of basal crow-sized *avialan* from the Early Cretaceous of the Yixian and Jiufotang Formations of China.

It had a toothless beak, but closer and later relatives of modern birds such as *Hesperornis* and *Ichthyornis* were toothed, indicating that the loss of teeth occurred convergently in *Confuciusornis* and living birds. It is the oldest known bird to have a beak.

Confuciusornis shows a mix of *basal* and *derived* traits. It was more 'advanced' or derived than *Archaeopteryx* in possessing a short tail with a *pygostyle* and a bony *sternum*, but more basal or 'primitive' than modern birds in retaining large claws on the forelimbs, having a primitive skull with a closed eye-socket, and a relatively small breastbone.

Many specimens of *Confuciusornis* preserve a single pair of long, streamer-like tail feathers, similar to those present in some modern *birds-of-paradise*. Specimens lacking these feathers include ones that otherwise have exquisitely preserved feathers on the rest of the body, indicating that their absence is not simply due to poor preservation.

The biological meaning of this pattern has been discussed controversially, but it has been suggested that the pattern might reflect *sexual dimorphism*, with the streamer-like feathers only present in one sex.

Cast of a slab with long and short tailed specimens of C. sanctus,
Museum Mensch und Natur, Munchen
Ghedoghedo CC BY-SA 4.0

iC. sanctus, Naturhistorisches Museum, Wien
Tommy from Arad CC BY 2.0

Mitsukurina owstoni (125 Mya - present)

Mitsukurina owstoni (**Goblin Shark**) is a rare species of deep-sea shark. Sometimes called a 'living fossil', it is the only extant representative of the family *Mitsukurinidae*.

This pink-skinned animal has a distinctive profile with an elongated, flat snout, and highly protrusible jaws containing prominent nail-like teeth. It is usually between 3 and 4m long when mature, though it can grow considerably larger such as one captured in 2000 that is thought to have measured 6m.

Goblin sharks are *benthopelagic* creatures that inhabit upper continental slopes, submarine canyons, and seamounts throughout the world at depths greater than 100m.

Various anatomical features of the goblin shark, such as its flabby body and small fins, suggest that it is sluggish in nature. This species hunts for *teleost* fishes, *cephalopods*, and *crustaceans* both near the sea floor and in the middle of the water column. Its long snout is covered with *ampullae of Lorenzini* that enable it to sense minute electric fields produced by nearby prey, which it can snatch up by rapidly extending its jaws.

Dianne Bray / Museum Victoria

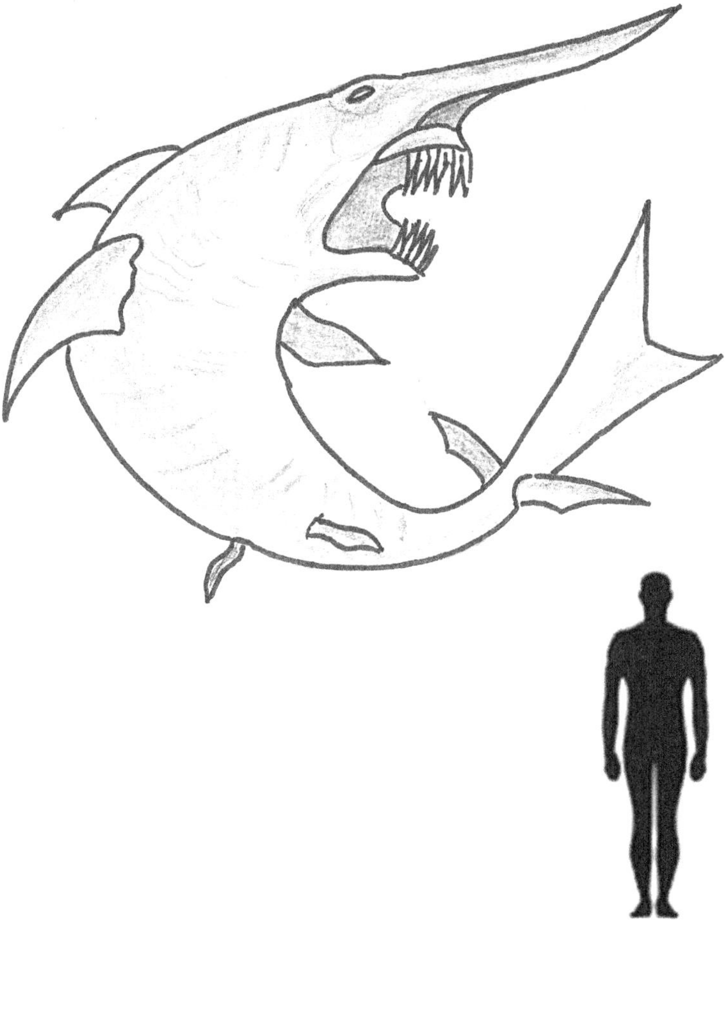

Koolasuchus (120 – 110 Mya)

Koolasuchus is an extinct genus of *brachyopoid temnospondyl* in the family *Chigutisauridae*. Fossils date back 120 million years to the Aptian stage of the Early Cretaceous. *Koolasuchus* is the youngest known *temnospondyl* and is known from several fragments of the skull and other bones such as vertebrae, ribs, and pectoral elements.

Koolasuchus was an aquatic *temnospondyl* with large size, although represented by incomplete material; the skull was likely 65cm long. Body length is sometimes estimated to have been around 4 to 5m in length, with smaller estimation up to 3m long. Its mass has been estimated to be up to 500kg. Like other *chigutisaurids*, it had a wide, rounded head and tabular horns projecting from the backside of the skull.

Koolasuchus inhabited what is now referred to as the Rift Valleys in Southern Australia during the Early Cretaceous. During this time the area was below the Antarctic Circle, and temperatures were relatively cool for the Mesozoic. Based on the coarse-grained rocks in which remains were found, *Koolasuchus* likely lived in fast-moving streams. As a large aquatic predator, it was similar in lifestyle to *crocodilians*.

These *crocodilians* likely displaced *Koolasuchus*, leading to its disappearance in younger rocks.

Koolasuchus, *American Museum of Natural History*
by Liuyo   CC BY 2.0

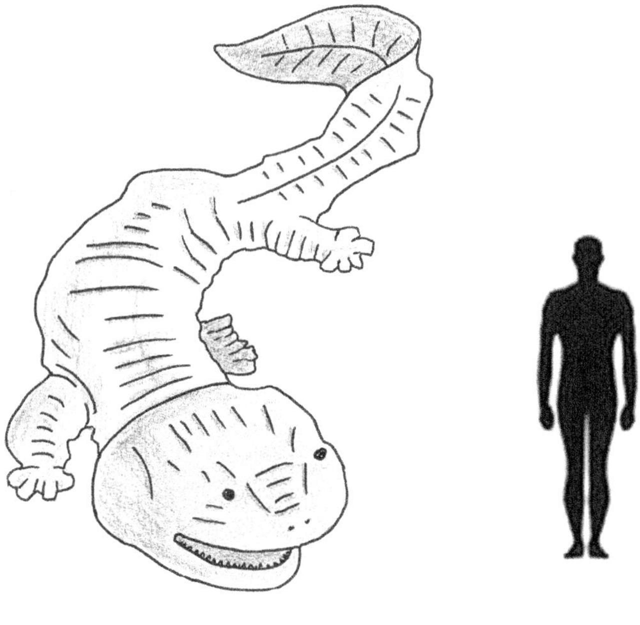

Ornithocheirus (105 – 100 Mya)

Ornithocheirus is a *pterosaur* genus known from fragmentary fossil remains. The type species, *Ornithocheirus simus*, is only known from fragmentary jaw tips. It bore a distinctive convex '*keeled*' crest on its snout similar to its relatives. *Ornithocheirus* had relatively narrow jaw tips compared to the related *Coloborhynchus* and *Tropeognathus*, which had prominently-expanded rosettes of teeth, as well as a more developed 'keeled' crest compared to *Ornithocheirus*. Another feature that made *Ornithocheirus* unique and unlike its relatives, was that its teeth of were mostly vertical, rather than set at an outward-pointing angle.

It was believed in the past that *Ornithocheirus* was one of the largest *pterosaurs* to have existed, with a wingspan possibly measuring 12.2m wide. However, this is a highly exaggerated number, as the animal's wingspan likely measured 4.5 to 6.1m wide, which would make it a medium-sized *pterosaur*. A related species called *Tropeognathus* had a wingspan measuring about 8.2m wide, making it the largest toothed *pterosaur* known.

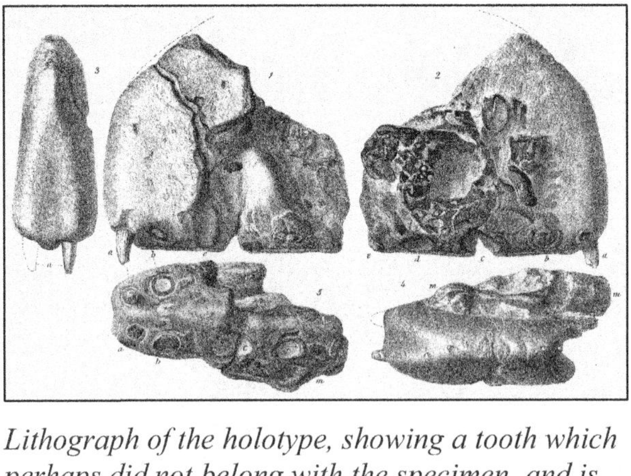

Lithograph of the holotype, showing a tooth which perhaps did not belong with the specimen, and is now lost

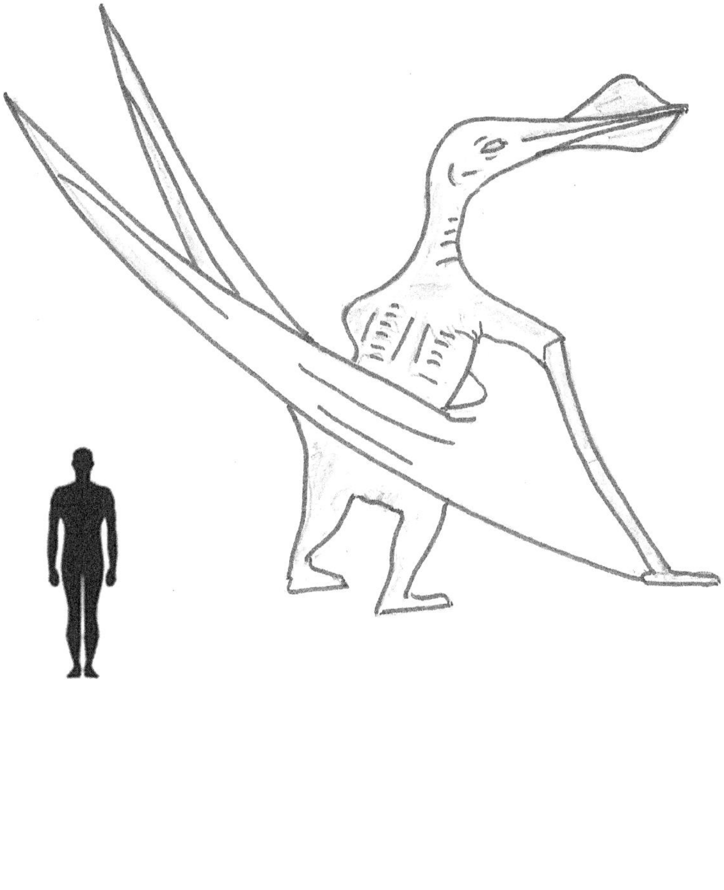

Nodosaurus (100 – 71 mya)

Nodosaurus is a genus of herbivorous *ankylosaurian dinosaur* from the Late Cretaceous, the fossils of which are found in North America.

This **nodosaurid ankylosaur** was about 4 to 6m long. It was an *ornithischian* dinosaur with bony dermal plates covering the top of its body, and it may have had spikes along its side as well.

The dermal plates were arranged in bands along its body, with narrow bands over the ribs alternating with wider plates in between. These wider plates were covered in regularly arranged bony nodules, which give the animal its scientific name. In 2010 it was estimated its length at 6m and its weight at 3.5 tonnes.

It had four short legs, five-toed feet, a short neck, and a long, stiff, clubless tail. The head was narrow, with a pointed snout, powerful jaws, and small teeth. It perhaps ate soft plants, as it would have been unable to chew tough, fibrous ones.

Alternatively it may have processed the latter with gastroliths and its enormous intestinal apparatus.

Giganotosaurus (99.6 – 97 Mya)

Giganotosaurus is a genus of *theropod* dinosaur that lived during the Late Cretaceous.

Giganotosaurus was one of the largest known terrestrial carnivores, but the exact size has been hard to determine due to the incompleteness of the remains found so far. Estimates for the most complete specimen range from a length of 12 - 13m a skull 1.53 - 1.80m in length, and a weight of 4.6 to 15.2 tonnes. The dentary bone that belonged to a supposedly larger individual has been used to extrapolate a length of 13.2m. Some researchers have found the animal to be larger than *Tyrannosaurus*, which has historically been considered the largest *theropod*, while others have found them to be roughly equal in size, and the largest size estimates for *Giganotosaurus* exaggerated.

The skull was low, with *rugose* (rough and wrinkled) nasal bones and a ridge-like crest on the *lacrimal bone* in front of the eye. The front of the lower jaw was flattened, and had a downwards projecting process (or 'chin') at the tip. The teeth were compressed sideways and had serrations. The neck was strong and the pectoral girdle proportionally small.

Giganotosaurus skeleton mount at the Fernbank Museum of Natural History in Atlanta, Georgia

Protopterus aethiopicus (99.7 Mya – Present)

Lungfish are freshwater *rhipidistian* vertebrates belonging to the order *Dipnoi* and represent the closest living relatives of the *tetrapods*. They are best known for their ability to breathe air, and the presence of *lobed fins* with a well-developed internal skeleton.

Fossil record shows that *lungfish* were abundant since the Triassic. While vicariance would suggest this represents an ancient distribution limited to the Mesozoic super continent Gondwana, the fossil record suggests advanced *lungfish* had a widespread freshwater distribution and the current distribution of modern *lungfish* species reflects extinction of many lineages subsequent to the breakup of Pangaea, Gondwana and Laurasia.

All lungfish demonstrate an uninterrupted cartilaginous *notochord* and an extensively developed palatal dentition. Basal ('primitive') lungfish groups may retain marginal teeth and an ossified braincase, but derived lungfish groups, including all modern species, show a significant reduction in the marginal bones and a cartilaginous braincase.

Through convergent evolution, lungfishes have evolved internal nostrils similar to the tetrapods' *choana*, and a brain with certain similarities to the lissamphibian brain (except for the Queensland lungfish, which branched off in its own direction about 277 million years ago and has a brain resembling that of the *Latimeria*).

The dentition of lungfish is different from that of any other vertebrate group. *Odontodes* on the palate and lower jaws develop in a series of rows to form a fan-shaped occlusion surface. These *odontodes* then wear to form a uniform crushing surface. In several groups, including the modern *lepidosireniformes*, these ridges have been modified to form occluding blades.

The modern lungfishes have a number of larval features, which suggest *paedomorphosis*. They also demonstrate the largest genome among the vertebrates.

Lungfish have a highly specialized respiratory system. They have a distinct feature in that their lungs are connected to the larynx and pharynx without a trachea. While other species of fish can breathe air using modified, *vascularized* gas bladders, these bladders are usually simple sacs, devoid of complex internal structure. In contrast, the lungs of lungfish are subdivided into numerous smaller air sacs, maximizing the surface area available for gas exchange.

Most extant lungfish species have two lungs. The lungs of lungfish are homologous to the lungs of *tetrapods*. As in tetrapods and bichirs, the lungs extend from the ventral surface of the esophagus and gut.

Perfusion of Water

Of extant lungfish, only the Australian lungfish can breathe through its gills without needing air from its lungs. In other species, the gills are too atrophied to allow for adequate gas exchange. When a lungfish is obtaining oxygen from its gills, its circulatory system is configured similarly to the common fish. The spiral valve of the *conus arteriosus* is open, the bypass arterioles of the third and fourth gill arches (which do not actually have gills) are shut, the second, fifth and sixth gill arch arterioles are open, the *ductus arteriosus* branching off the sixth arteriole is open, and the pulmonary arteries are closed. As the water passes through the gills, the lungfish uses a *buccal* pump. Flow through the mouth and gills are unidirectional. Blood flow through the secondary lamellae is counter-current to the water, maintaining a more constant concentration gradient.

Perfusion of Air

When breathing air, the spiral valve of the *conus arteriosus* closes (minimizing the mixing of oxygenated and deoxygenated blood), the third and fourth gill arches open, the second and fifth gill arches close (minimizing the possible loss of the oxygen obtained in the lungs through the gills), the sixth arteriole's *ductus arteriosus* is closed, and the pulmonary arteries open. Importantly, during air breathing, the sixth gill is still used in respiration; deoxygenated blood loses some of its carbon dioxide as it passes through the gill before reaching the lung. This is because carbon dioxide is more soluble in water. Air flow through the mouth is tidal, and through the lungs it is bidirectional and observes 'uniform pool' diffusion of oxygen.

Lungfish are *omnivorous*, feeding on fish, insects, crustaceans, worms, mollusks, amphibians and plant matter. They have an intestinal spiral valve rather than a true stomach.

African and South American lungfish are capable of surviving seasonal drying out of their habitats by burrowing into mud and estivating throughout the dry season. Changes in physiology allow it to slow its metabolism to as little as $1/60^{th}$ of the normal metabolic rate, and protein waste is converted from ammonia to less-toxic urea (normally, lungfish excrete nitrogenous waste as ammonia directly into the water).

Burrowing is seen in at least one group of fossil lungfish, the *Gnathorhizidae*.

As lobe finned fish were adapting to live in partial water or on land, 420 million years ago during the Devonian, they seem to have split off into multiple groups. Two such branches are known to survive to the present day, the *coelacanths* and the *lungfish*.

It is worth noting that, despite the name 'lungfish', fish evolved lungs before lungfish, and even lobe-finned fish.

The common ancestor of lobe-finned and ray-finned fish had lungs, but in most surviving branches of ray-finned fish these evolved into *swim bladders* used for floatation, instead of breathing. Some, like the bichirs, do retain their lungs, and several other traits that appear to have been common to lobe-finned and ray-finned fish.

Marbled lungfish

The marbled lungfish, *Protopterus aethiopicus*, is found in Africa. The marbled lungfish is smooth, elongated, and cylindrical with deeply embedded scales. The tail is very long and tapers at the end. They are the largest of the African lungfish species as they can reach a length of up to 200cm. The pectoral and pelvic fins are also very long and thin, almost spaghetti-like. The marbled lungfish has the largest known genome of any vertebrate, with 133 billion base pairs in its DNA double helix.

Elasmosaurus (80.5 Mya)

Elasmosaurus is a genus of *plesiosaur* that lived in North America during the Campanian stage of the Late Cretaceous. Only one incomplete *Elasmosaurus* skeleton is definitely known, consisting of a fragmentary skull, the spine, and the pectoral and pelvic girdles, and a single species is recognized today. Other species are now considered invalid or have been moved to other genera.

Measuring 14m long, *Elasmosaurus* would have had a streamlined body with paddle-like limbs, a short tail, a small head, and an extremely long neck. The neck alone was around 7m long and had 70 vertebrae compared with the mere 5 in humans. The skull would have been slender and triangular, with large, fang-like teeth at the front, and smaller teeth towards the back. It had six teeth in each *pre-maxilla* of the upper jaw, and may have had 14 teeth in the maxilla and 19 in the dentary of the lower jaw. Most of the neck vertebrae were compressed sideways, and bore a longitudinal crest or keel along the sides.

Elasmosaurids were well adapted for aquatic life, and used their flippers for swimming. It could move, however, only with its neck stretched out in front; any bends or kinks in it would affect its ability to steer. Contrary to earlier depictions, their necks were not very flexible, and could not be held high above the water surface. It is unknown what their long necks were used for, but they may have had a function in feeding. *Elasmosaurids* probably ate small fish and marine invertebrates, seizing them with their long teeth, and may have used *gastroliths* to help digest their food. *Elasmosaurus* is known from the Pierre Shale formation, which represents marine deposits from the Western Interior Seaway.

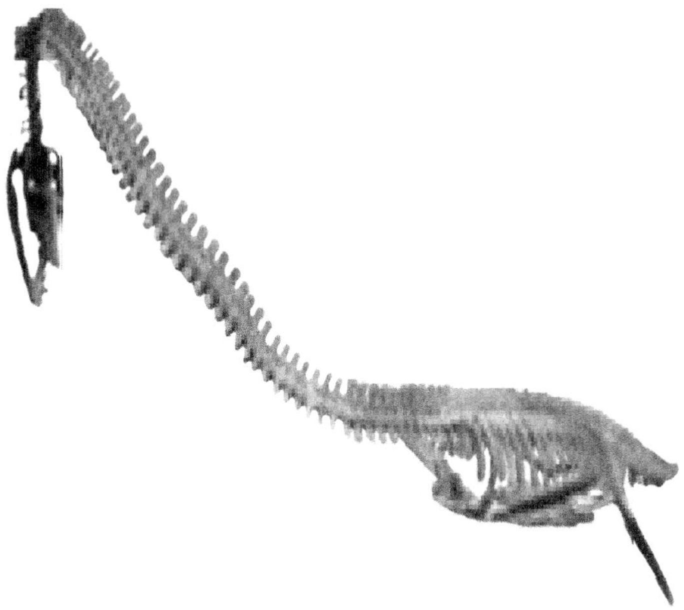

Elasmosaurus platyurus in the Rocky Mountain Dinosaur Resource Centre in Woodland Park, Colorado

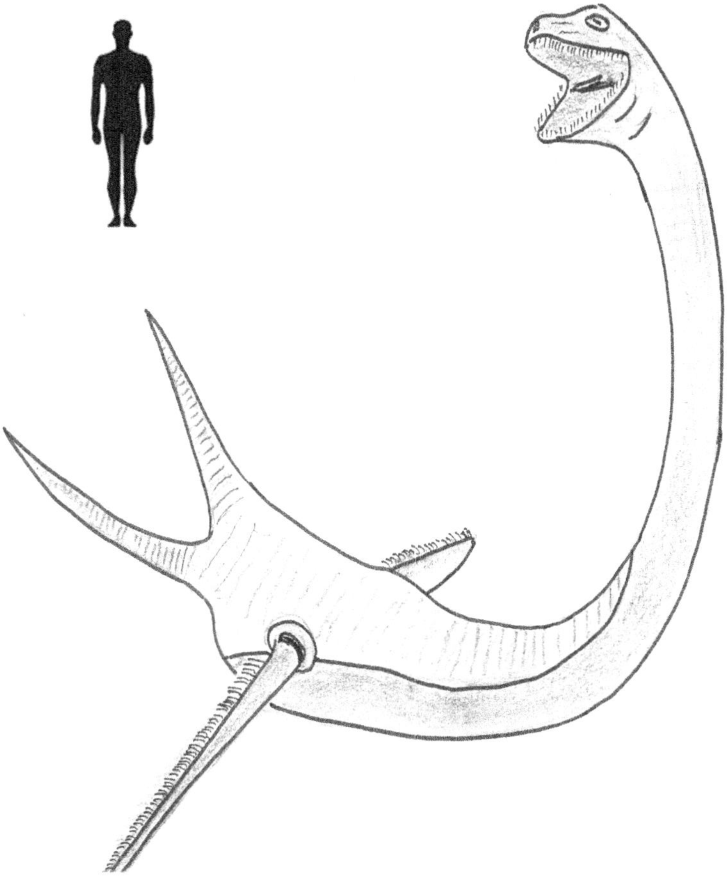

Archelon (80-74 Mya)

Archelon is an extinct marine turtle from the Late Cretaceous, and is the largest turtle ever to have been documented, with the biggest specimen measuring 4.6m from head to tail and 2,200k in weight. It is known only from the **Dakota Pierre Shale** and has one species, ***A. ischyros***.

Archelon had a leathery carapace instead of the hard shell seen in sea turtles. It had an especially hooked beak and its jaws were adept at crushing, so it probably ate hard-shelled crustaceans and mollusks while slowly moving over the seafloor. However, its beak may have been adapted for shearing flesh, and *Archelon* was likely able to produce powerful strokes necessary for open-ocean travel.

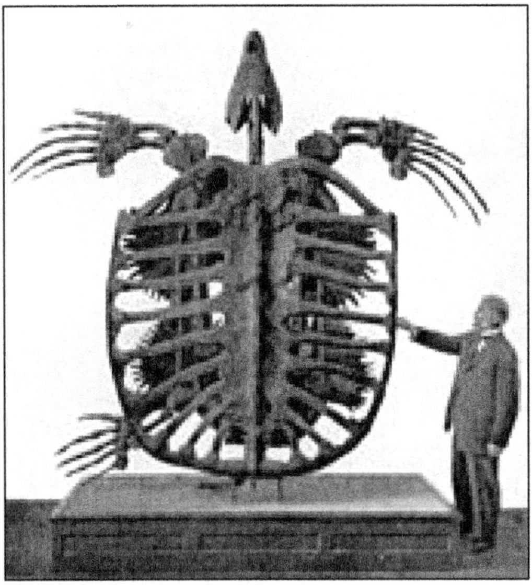

Holotype YPM 3000 at the Yale Peabody Museum

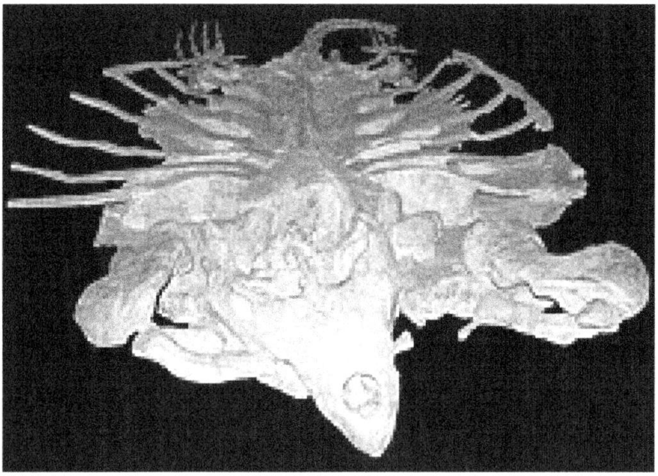

'Brigitta',, the largest specimen, at the Natural History Museum Vienna

The largest specimen, 'Brigitta', measures around 4.6m from head to tail and weighed around 2,200kg.

Brigitta is estimated to have lived to 100 years, and may have died while partially covered in mud *brumating*–a state of dormancy–on the ocean floor. However, the long standing belief that marine turtles *brumate* underwater like freshwater turtles may be incorrect given the high surfacing-frequency needed to prevent drowning.

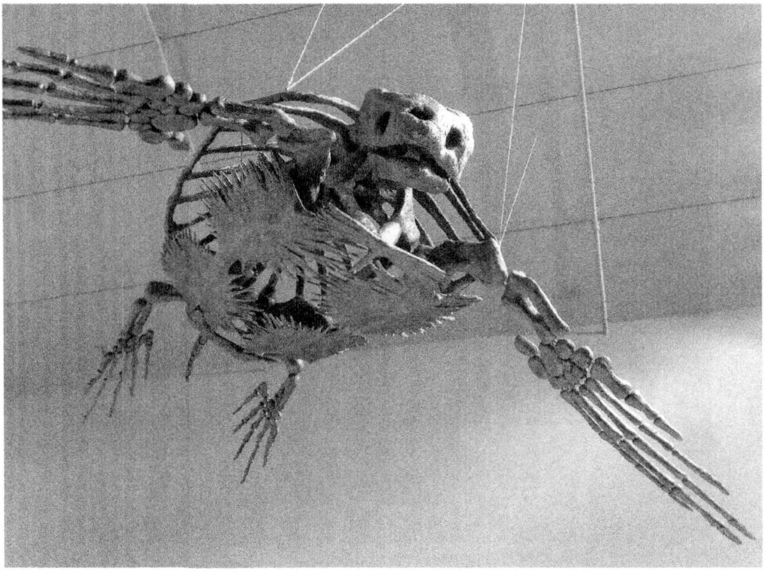

Wallace Building on the University of Manitoba campus, Winnipeg, Manitoba Canada

Styracosaurus (75 mya)

Styracosaurus is a dinosaur which during the late Cretaceous. This animal was approximately 5-6m long, 2m tall at the shoulders and weighed around 3 to 5 tonnes. It was a herbivore that had a frill that emanating from the back of its skull. This frill had 6 spikes that came out of the edge of it. It also had a nose horn, and 2 smaller horns that were over its eyes. All of these horns probably provided this herbivore with the defence capabilities it needed to fend off predators.

Like other herbivores of this time, this dinosaur was more than likely an animal that travelled in herds. This theory has got some traction over the past few years as palaeontologists have found many fossil finds of large groups of this animal together. If this was indeed the case, then this behaviour would have given these dinosaur's enough of an advantage to be quite successful against most predators as travelling in groups allows individual animals to remain safer against predators. Especially since all of the animals in this herd would be equipped with horns.

It is also quite possible that these dinosaurs laid their eggs in nests and took care of the clutches like birds. This behaviour has been shown in other dinosaurs of the time.

Oviraptor (75 – 71 Mya)

Oviraptor is a genus of *oviraptorid* dinosaur that lived in Asia during the Late Cretaceous. The first remains were collected from the Djadokhta Formation of Mongolia in 1923 during a paleontological expedition led by Roy Chapman Andrews, and in the following year the genus and type species ***Oviraptor philoceratops*** were named by Henry Fairfield Osborn.

Oviraptor was a rather small feathered *oviraptorid*, estimated at 1.6m long with a weight between 33-40kg. It had a wide lower jaw with a skull that likely had a crest. Both upper and lower jaws were toothless and developed a horny beak, which was used during feeding along the robust morphology of the lower jaws. The arms were well-developed and elongated ending in three fingers with curved claws. Like other oviraptorids, *Oviraptor* had long hindlimbs that had four-toed feet, with the first toe reduced. The tail was likely not very elongated, and ended in a *pygostyle* that supported large feathers.

Findings of numerous *oviraptorosaurs* in nesting poses have demonstrated that this specimen was actually *brooding* the nest and not stealing nor feeding on the eggs. Moreover, the discoveries of remains of a small juvenile or nestling have been reported in association with the holotype specimen, further supporting parental care.

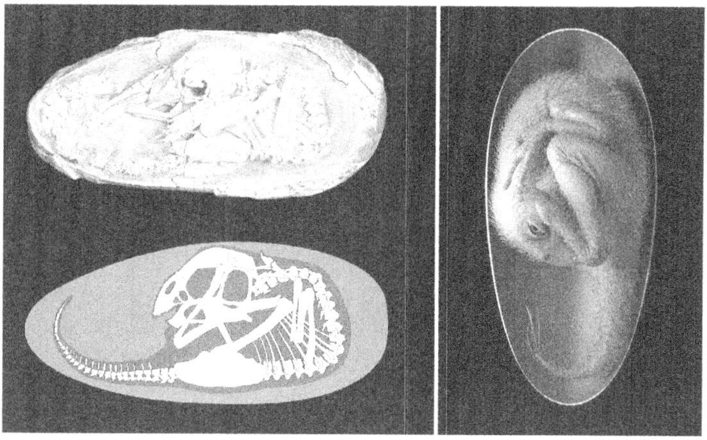

Life restoration of the Cretaceous oviraptorid Oviraptor, from the Djadokhta Form

Preserved dinosaur embryo discovered inside a 72 Million year old egg in China

An exquisitely preserved dinosaur embryo has been found curled up inside a fossilised egg, unearthed in southern China, dating back some 66-72 million years.

The embryo has been dubbed 'Baby Yingliang' and was found in the rocks of the 'Hekou Formation' at the Shahe Industrial Park in Ganzhou City, Jiangxi Province.

Palaeontologists led from the University of Birmingham said that Baby Yingliang belonged to species of toothless, beaked theropod dinosaurs, or 'oviraptorosaurs'.

Oviraptors, which were feathered, are found in the rocks of Asia and North America and had varied beaks and body sizes allowing them to adopt a wide range of diets.

The specimen is one of the most complete dino embryos known and notably sports a posture closer to those seen in embryonic birds than usually found in dinosaurs.

Specifically, Baby Yingliang was close to hatching, and had its head below its body, its back curled into the egg's blunt end and its feet positioned either side of it.

In modern birds, such a posture is assumed during 'tucking' — an embryo behaviour controlled by the central nervous system that is critical for a successful hatching.

The discovery of such behaviour in Baby Yingliang suggests that this is not unique to birds, but may instead have first evolved among the non-avian theropod dinosaurs.

21 December, 2021 Elsevier

Anatotitan (71 – 66 Mya)

Anatotitan is a genus of herbivorous dinosaurs belonging to the *Euornithopoda* from the very end of the Cretaceous. It is one of the largest 'duck-billed dinosaurs' or *Hadrosauridae* that have ever existed with a length of more than twelve metres. It probably had a nasal sac, with which he could warn his peers of danger, by sound signals.

It would walk and graze using all four legs, but could rear up on its muscular hind legs to reach higher intro the trees.

It was a large animal, up to approximately 12m in length, with an extremely long and low skull. *Anatotitan* exhibits one of the most striking examples of the 'duckbill' snout common to *hadrosaurs*.

There were no known defensive features short of its prominent nasal crest. It is thought this gave *Anatotitan* the ability to make loud trumpeting noises to communicate and warn one another. It was, moreover, very large so could only have been attacked by predatory dinosaurs.

(Refer also to Anatotitan Dentition p 570)

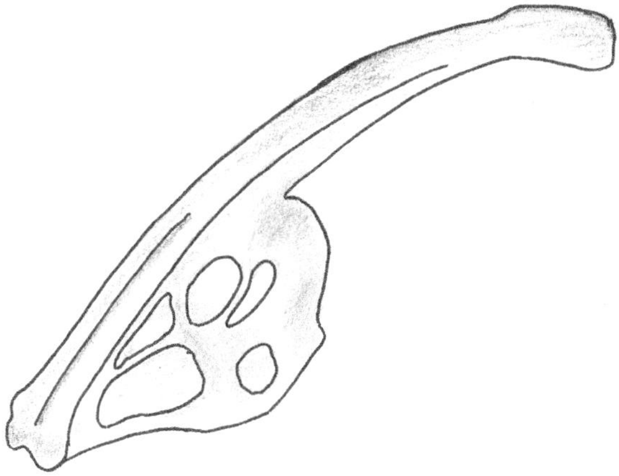

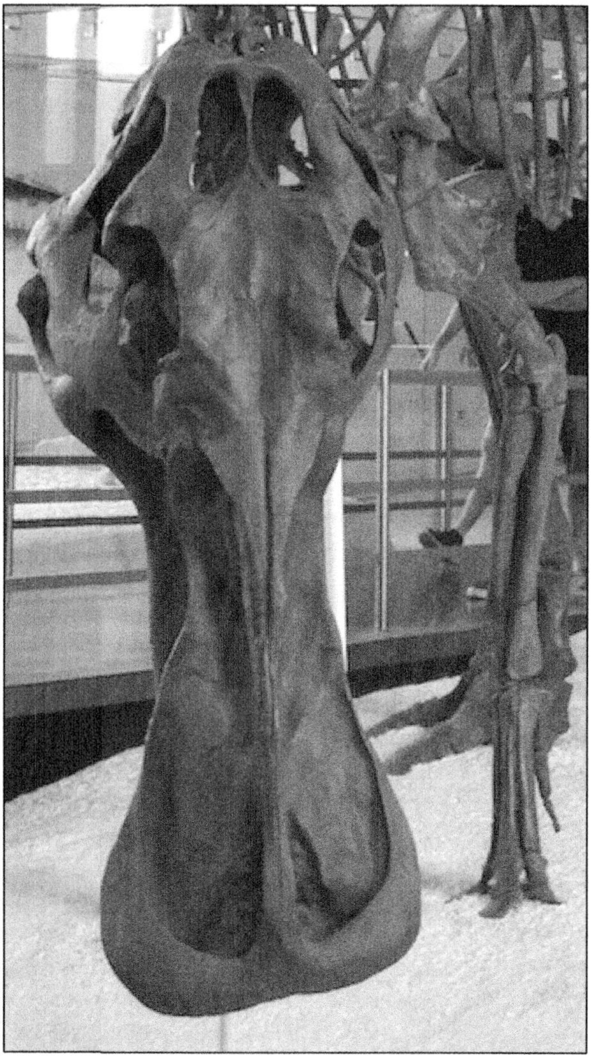

Anatotitan *fossil skeleton at New York American Museum of Natural History*

Therizinosaurus (~ 70 Mya)

Therizinosaurus is a genus of very large *therizinosaurid* that lived during the late Cretaceous. It contains the single type species ***Therizinosaurus cheloniformis***. The genus is known only from a few bones, including gigantic manual *unguals* from which it gets its name, and additional findings comprising fore and hind-limb elements.

Therizinosaurus was a colossal *therizinosaur* that grew up to 9-10m long and weigh possibly over 3,000kg. Like other *therizinosaurs*, it would have been a slow-moving, long-necked high browser equipped with a *rhamphotheca* and a wide torso for food processing. The forelimbs were particularly robust and had three fingers that bore unguals which, unlike other relatives, were stiffened, elongated, and only had significant curvatures at the tips. *Therizinosaurus* had the longest known manual unguals of any land animal, reaching above 50cm in length. Its hind limbs ended in four functionally weight-bearing toes differing from other theropod groups in which the first toe was reduced to a dewclaw and also resembling the unrelated *sauropodomorphs*.

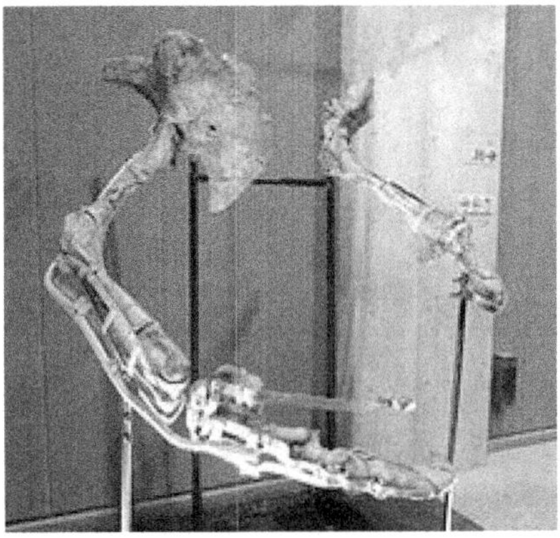

Mounted forelimbs of specimen MPC-D 100/15 at Nagoya City Science Museum CC BY 2.0

Mamenchisaurus (70 – 66 mya)

Mamenchisaurus is a genus of *sauropod dinosaur* known for its remarkably long neck which made up nearly half the total body length. Fossils have been found in the Sichuan Basin and Yunnan Province in China. Several species are from the Upper Shaximiao Formation whose geologic age is uncertain. However, evidence suggests that this be no earlier than the Oxfordian stage of the Late Jurassic.

It is probably one of the largest dinosaurs known; estimated at 35m in length and possibly weighed 60-80 tonnes.

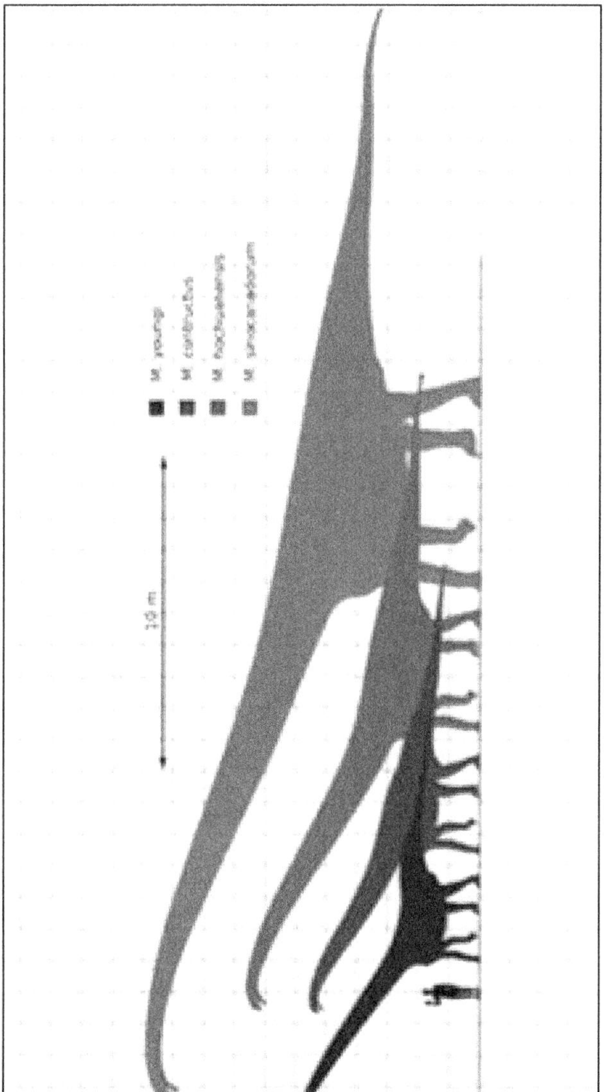
10 m
M. youngi
M. constructus

Quetzalcoatlus (68 – 66 Mya)

Quetzalcoatlus is a *pterosaur* known from the Late Cretaceous of North America (Maastrichtian stage); it was one of the largest known flying animals of all time. *Quetzalcoatlus* is a member of the family *Azhdarchidae*, a family of advanced toothless *pterosaurs* with unusually long, stiffened necks. Its name comes from the Aztec feathered serpent god, Quetzalcoatl, in Nahuatl.

When it was first named as a new species in 1975, scientists estimated that the largest *Quetzalcoatlus* fossils came from an individual with a wingspan as large as 15.9m. In 1981, further advanced studies lowered these estimates to 11–12m.

More recent estimates based on even greater knowledge of *azhdarchid* proportions place its wingspan at 10–11m. Remains found in Texas in 1971 indicate that this *pterosaur* had a minimum wingspan of about 11m. Generalized height in a bipedal stance, based on its wingspan, would have been at least 3m high at the shoulder.

Weight estimates for giant *azhdarchids* are extremely problematic because no existing species share a similar size or body plan, and in consequence, published results vary widely. Generalized weight, based a majority of estimates published since the 2000s have been around 200–250kg.

Quetzalcoatlus was abundant in Texas during the Lancian in a fauna dominated by *Alamosaurus*. The *Alamosaurus-Quetzalcoatlus* association probably represents semi-arid inland plains. *Quetzalcoatlus* had precursors in North America and its apparent rise to wide environment may well represent the expansion of its preferred habitat rather than an immigration event, as some experts have suggested. It co-existed with other *pterosaur* taxons, suggesting relatively high diversity of Late Cretaceous pterosaur genera.

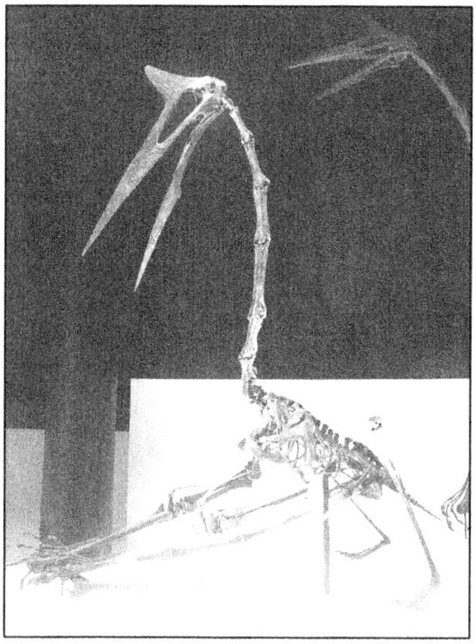

One of the largest flying animals ever, with a 40ft wingspan. It is exhibited in the Houston Museum of Natural Science

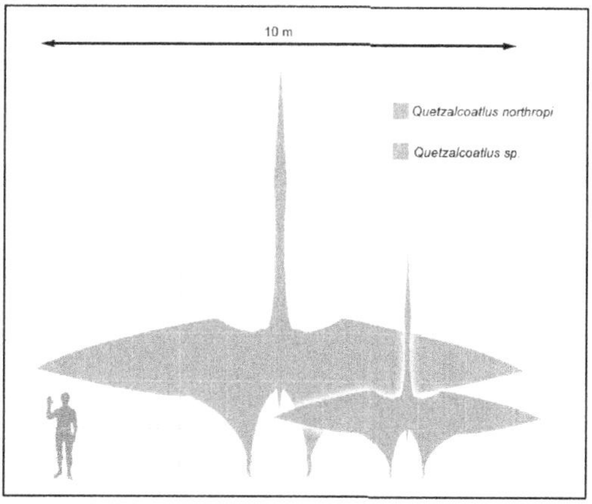

Size comparison of the azhdarchid pterosaurs Quetzalcoatlus northropi and Quetzalcoatlus lawsoni, with a human. Modified from a diagram featured in Witton and Naish (2008). CC BY 3.0

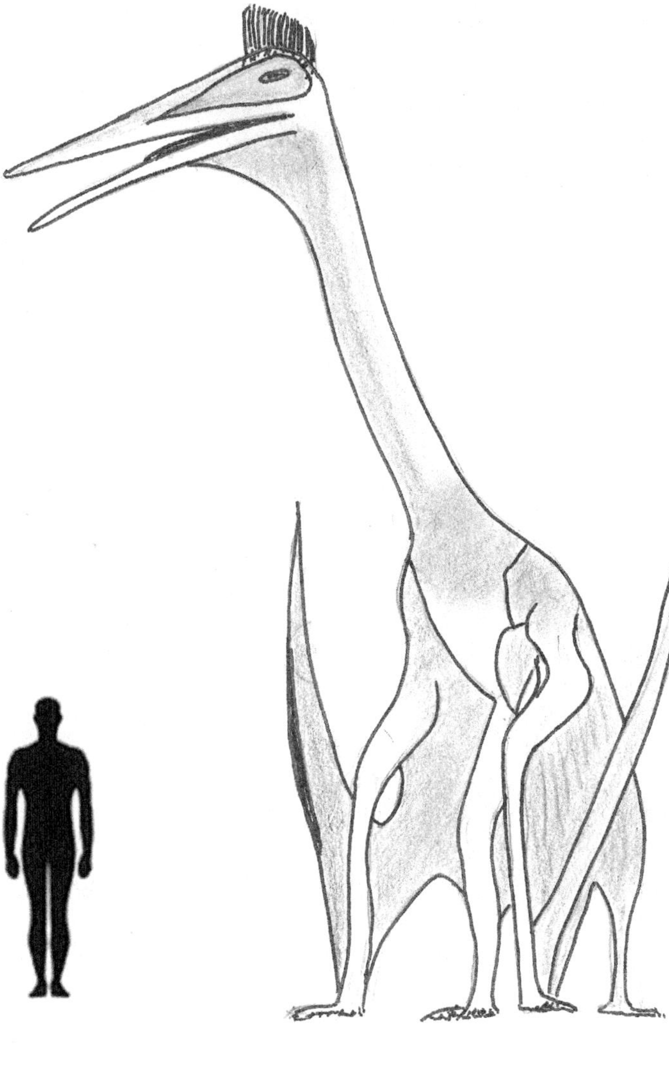

Quetzalcoatlus Northropi

Phorusrhacidae (~62 – 1.8 Mya)

Phorusrhacids, colloquially known as **Terror Birds**, are an extinct clade of large carnivorous flightless birds that were one of the largest species of apex predators in South America during the Cenozoic.

They ranged in height from 1-3m. Their closest modern-day relatives are believed to be the 80cm tall. *Titanis walleri*, one of the larger species, is known from Texas and Florida in North America. This makes the *phorusrhacids* the only known large South American predator to migrate north in the **Great American Interchange** that followed the formation of the Isthmus of Panama land bridge (the main pulse of the interchange began about 2.6 million years ago. *Titanis* at 5 million years ago was an early northward migrant).

It was once believed that *T. walleri* became extinct in North America around the time of the arrival of humans, but subsequent datings of *Titanis* fossils provided no evidence for their survival after 1.8 Mya. However, reports from Uruguay of new findings of a relatively small form (*Psilopterus)* dating to 18,000 and 96,000 years ago would imply that *phorusrhacids* survived there until very recently (i.e. until the late Pleistocene).

Phorusrhacids may have even made their way into Africa. The genus *Lavocatavis* was discovered in Algeria, but its status as a true *phorusrhacid* is questioned. A possible European form, *Eleutherornis*, has also been identified, suggesting that this group had a wider geographical range in the Paleogene.

The closely related *bathornithids* occupied a similar ecological niche in North America across the Eocene to Early Miocene. Some, like *Paracrax*, were similar in size to the largest *phorusrhacids*.

At least one analysis recovers *Bathornis* as sister taxa to *phorusrhacids,* on the basis of shared features in the jaws and coracoid, though this has been seriously contested, as these might have evolved independently for the same carnivorous, flightless lifestyle.

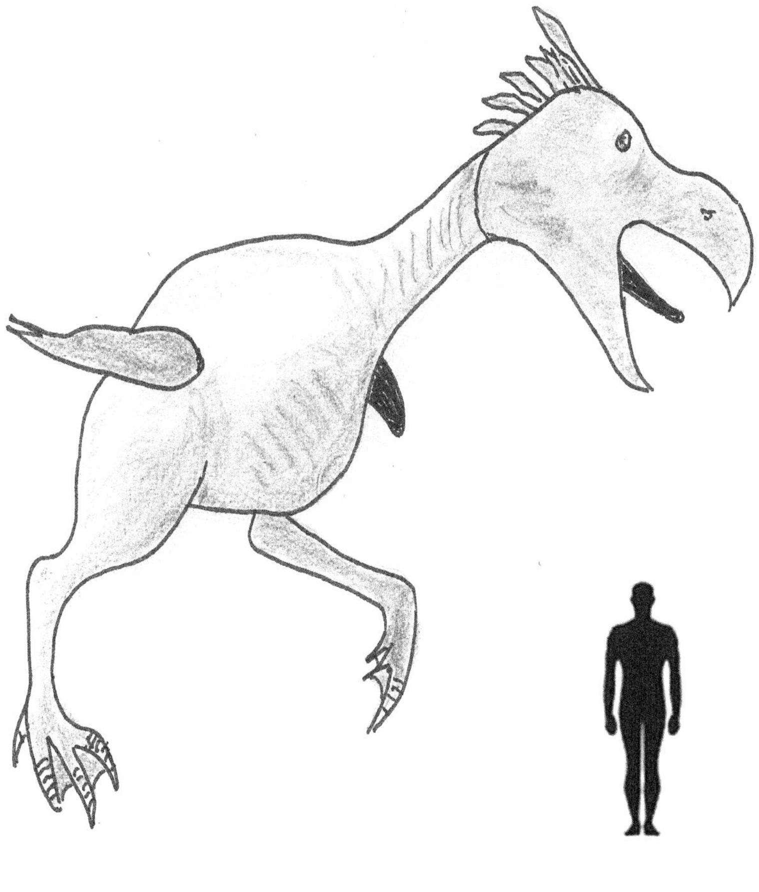

Paraceratherium (34 – 23 Mya)

Paraceratherium is an extinct genus of hornless rhinoceros. It is one of the largest terrestrial mammals that has existed and lived from the early to late Oligocene. It is classified as a member of the *hyracodont* subfamily *Indricotheriinae.*

The exact size of *Paraceratherium* is unknown because of the incompleteness of the fossils. The shoulder height was about 4.8 metres and the length about 7.4m. Its weight is estimated to have been about 15-20 tonnes. The long neck supported a skull that was about 1.3m long. It had large, tusk-like incisors and a nasal incision that suggests it had a prehensile upper lip or *proboscis.* The legs were long and pillar-like.

The lifestyle of *Paraceratherium* may have been similar to that of modern large mammals such as the elephants and extant rhinoceroses. Because of its size, it would have had few predators and a slow rate of reproduction. It was a browser, eating mainly leaves, soft plants, and shrubs. It lived in habitats ranging from arid deserts with a few scattered trees to subtropical forests.

The reasons for the animal's extinction are unknown, but various factors have been proposed.

Skelton of Indricotherium (Indricotherium transouralicum). Exhibit in the National Museum of Nature and Science, Tokyo, Japan.

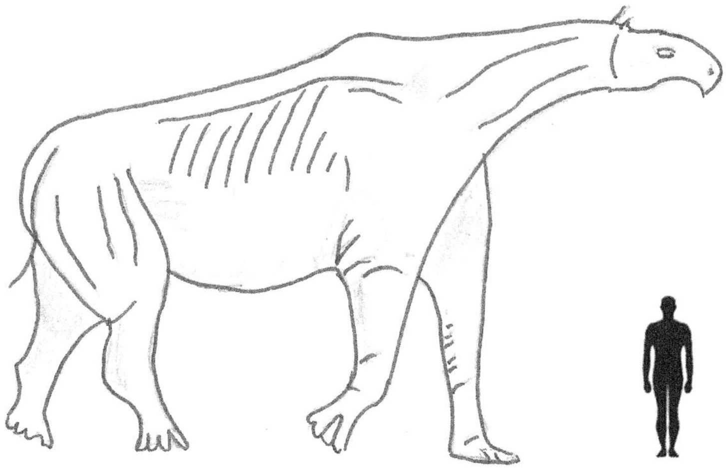

Cryptobranchus alleganiensis (0.8 Mya – Present)

C. alleganiensis (known as the **Hellbender**) is a species of aquatic giant salamander endemic to the eastern and central United States. A member of the family *Cryptobranchidae*, the hellbender is the only extant member of the genus *Cryptobranchus*.

It has a flat body and head, with beady dorsal eyes and slimy skin. Like most salamanders, it has short legs with four toes on the front legs and five on its back limbs, and its tail is keeled for propulsion. The hellbender has working lungs, but gill slits are often retained, although only immature specimens have true gills.

The hellbender, which is much larger than all other salamanders in its geographic range, employs an unusual means of respiration. This involves cutaneous gas exchange through capillaries found in its dorsoventral skin folds.

Megatherium (5 – 0.012 Mya)

Megatherium is an extinct genus of ground sloths that lived from the Early Pliocene through the end of the Pleistocene. It is best known for the elephant-sized type species ***M. americanum***, sometimes called the **giant ground sloth**, or the ***megathere.***

Megatherium is part of the sloth family *Megatheriidae*, which also includes the similarly elephantine *Eremotherium*. Only a few other land mammals equalled or exceeded *M. americanum* in size, such as large *proboscideans* (e.g. elephants) and the giant rhinoceros *Paraceratherium*.

Megatherium became extinct around 12,000 years ago during the Quaternary extinction event, which also claimed most other large mammals in the New World. The extinction coincides with the settlement of the Americas, and a kill site where *M. americanum* were slaughtered and butchered is known, suggesting that hunting could have been a significant factor in the cause for its extinction.

Megatherium americanum skeleton, Natural History Museum, London
CC BY-SA 3.0

Chondrocladia lampadiglobus (2.58 Mya – present)

Chondrocladia sponges (Ping Pong Tree Sponges) are *stipitate*, with a stalk frequently anchored in the substrate by *rhizoids* and an egg-shaped body, sometimes with branches that end in inflatable spheres.

Fossils assignable to this genus are known since the Pleistocene, less than 2 million years ago. But given its deep sea habitat, *Chondrocladia* may well have been around for much longer, perhaps since the Mesozoic, as characteristic *spicules*, almost identical to those of some living *Chondrocladia*, are known from Early Jurassic rocks almost 200 million years old.

Carnivory has since turned out to be common and typical for this sponge family. Unlike their relatives, *Chondrocladia* still possesses the water flow system and *choanocytes* typical of sponges, albeit highly modified to inflate balloon-like structures that are used for capturing prey.

Ambystoma mexicanum (present)

***Ambystoma mexicanum* (axolotl)** is a paedomorphic salamander related to the tiger salamander. The species was originally found in several lakes, such as Lake Xochimilco underlying Mexico City. Axolotls are unusual among amphibians in that they reach adulthood without undergoing metamorphosis. Instead of taking to the land, adults remain aquatic and gilled.

As of 2020, wild *axolotls* were near extinction due to urbanization in Mexico City and consequent water pollution, as well as the introduction of invasive species such as tilapia and perch. They are listed as critically endangered in the wild by the International Union for Conservation of Nature and Natural Resources (IUCN) and are used extensively in scientific research due to their ability to regenerate limbs, gills and parts of their eyes and brains.

Axolotls possess features typical of salamander larvae, including external gills and a caudal fin extending from behind the head to the vent. External gills are usually lost when salamander species mature into adulthood, although the axolotl maintains this feature. This is due to their neoteny evolution, where axolotls are much more aquatic than other salamander species.

Their heads are wide, and their eyes are lidless. Their limbs are underdeveloped and possess long, thin digits. Males are identified by their swollen *cloacae* lined with *papillae*, while females are noticeable for their wider bodies full of eggs. Three pairs of external gill stalks (*rami*) originate behind their heads and are used to move oxygenated water. The external gill *rami* are lined with filaments (*fimbriae*) to increase surface area for gas exchange. Four-gill slits lined with gill rakers are hidden underneath the external gills, which prevent food from entering and allow particles to filter through.

Axolotls have barely visible vestigial teeth, which develop during metamorphosis.

The primary method of feeding is by suction, during which their rakers interlock to close the gill slits. External gills are used for respiration, although buccal pumping (gulping air from the surface) may also be used to provide oxygen to their lungs. Buccal pumping can occur in a two-stroke manner that pumps air from the mouth to the lungs, and with four-stroke that reverses this pathway with compression forces.

Glaucus atlanticus (present)

Glaucus atlanticus **(Sea Slug)** is a species of shell-less gastropod mollusk in the family *Glaucidae.*

These sea slugs are pelagic, they float upside down by using the surface tension of the water to stay up, where they are carried along by the winds and ocean currents. *G. atlanticus* makes use of counter-shading, the blue top-side of its body faces upwards, blending in with the blue of the water while its silver/grey bottom-side is viewed facing upwards underwater.

G.atlanticus feed on other pelagic creatures, including the **Portuguese Man o' War**. The sea slug stores stinging *nematocysts* from the siphonophores within its own tissues as defense against possible predators.

At maturity *G.atlanticus* can be up to 3cm in length, though larger specimens have been found. It can live up to a year under the right conditions It has a flat, tapering body and six appendages that branch out into rayed, finger-like *cerata.*

Cerata, (also known as *papillae*), extend laterally from three different pairs of *peduncles.*

The *radula* of this species bears serrated teeth, to which, paired with a strong jaw and *denticles* allows it to grasp and ‘chip down’ parts of its prey.

G. atlanticus is able to feed on the Portuguese Man o’ War due to its immunity to the venomous *nematocysts.* The slug consumes chunks of the organism and appears to select and store the most venomous *nematocysts* for its own use against future prey.

Sea slugs are *hermaphrodites* and their male reproductive organs have evolved to be especially large and hooked to avoid their partner's venomous *cerata.*

Why were prehistoric animals so large?

During the Jurassic, animals grew very much larger than the animals present today. There are a number of reasons suggested for this:

Their bones were hollow

The bones in many cases are hollowed out and full of air. Consequently, these *pneumatized* bones were not as dense as if they were solid.

Because of this, many prehistoric animals were able to support a very long and tall body without the bone structure collapsing. It is also true of many present-day birds where the same bone structure can be seen.

Prehistoric animals also benefited by using the air inside the bones for breathing. That particular respiratory system would have them blow air into these little holes and the flow of air helped them get more effect out of each breath.

The largest plant-eating *Sauropod* weighed up to 80 tonnes. This is more than ***12 times*** the weight of an African elephant.

Size comparison of selected giant sauropod dinosaurs KoprX CC BY-SA 4.0

They could live on less oxygen

At the time of dinosaurs the oxygen levels in the air were lower. So, as mentioned above, in order for the dinosaurs to survive they developed a more efficient way of breathing.

They could utilize their little holes inside of their bones. Their respiratory systems were better than among humans and the big land animals we find today.

Over time, the levels of oxygen rose and this gave the dinosaurs a distinct advantage over the other animals.

They had a long time to evolve

According to what is often called Cope's Rule, an animal will get a lot larger and larger over time.

Cope's Rule states that evolution tends to **increase body size over geological time in a lineage of populations**. Evolutionary trends towards an increase in body size are common in the fossil record. For example, the Eocene ancestors of modern horses were about the size of a dog.

This is something scientists believed for a long time, but today we have also found signs that point towards animals becoming **smaller** over time.

So even though it sounds plausible, this may not be the case.

They had plenty of food

During the time of the prehistoric animals, the CO_2 levels in the atmosphere were higher than is evident today. This also meant that plants and trees grew higher and bigger.

So in order to eat from the leaves of tall trees the animals had to grow taller themselves (e.g. present-day giraffes).

It also meant they had plenty of food to eat because there were more and bigger trees. A much bigger percentage of the earth was covered with forest.

So if these two facts are combined, the dinosaurs had very good conditions for growing as big as they did.

What is more, they could swallow their food without chewing it first of all. The dentition of prehistoric animals was quite different from modern day carnivores or herbivores (see pages 577 & 578) allowing them to bite off large chunks off their prey or off branches and swallow them whole.

Consequently, their heads were lighter and the long necks were able to support their heads. This also meant that the huge animals were able to eat much more food.

They had few enemies

When an animal is 30 meters long **they do not have many natural enemies**.

The dinosaurs had no natural enemies which meant they could go and sleep where they wanted.

Lions, Tigers, and other predators will always try to hunt animals that are smaller.

Evolution of Teeth

The movement of ancient super-continents meant that there was an opportunity for fauna to move through a great range of different habitats and thus to enable a wide range of new food sources to be exploited. Consequently, this required a development or modification to dentition and the digestive system as a whole to extract the maximum amount of nutrition to meet a creature's needs.

Teeth are present in almost all mammals though a secondary toothless condition is found in some mammals. They have evolved from denticles which are released from armour near the margins of the mouth.

The outer protective layer of a tooth is referred to as the 'enamel'. It is the hardest and heaviest tissue of vertebrates and is composed of crystals of *hydroxyapatite*:

$$\mathbf{3(Ca_3PO_4)_2 \,.\, Ca(OH)_2}$$

It is *ectodermal* in origin and completely *acellular*.

Below the enamel is a hard dermal bony substance layer called 'dentine'. It is harder than bone, but softer than enamel.

Ivory is a specialised dentine and hard creamy-white substance, found in elephant, hippopotamus and walrus tusks.

The human dentine is composed of mainly:

- Calcium phosphate and fluoride 66.72%,
- Organic matter 28.01% and
- Calcium carbonate.

Since teeth are made of very tough Calcium phosphate, they fossilize well and outlast every other part of a mammal's body, even the bones.

The *hominoids* (including *Homo*) generally had 44 teeth. These teeth are arranged in a distinct series, with different shapes and functions:

3 incisors

1 canine

4 premolars and

3 molars

They make up a total of 11 teeth in each half of each jaw.

The root of tooth is covered by a thin layer of cement and a vascular periodontal membrane of strong connective tissue fibres.

The elephant's tusks are the second pair of incisors in the upper-jaw. The lower incisors have disappeared. The upper incisors are made of ivory, have no root and grow to form the tusks. In the wild boar (*Sus scrofa*), the upper canines are enlarged to form stout tusks, whereas the warthog (*Phacochoerus*) has four upward curving tusks; these are transformed canines of both jaws. The male muntjak (*Muntiacus*) and musk deer (*Moschus*) possess tusks which are the enlarged form of upper canine teeth, and walruses have modified forms of upper canines.

The evolution of teeth in primitive fishes from structures similar to the dermal denticles in the skin of modern sharks contributed importantly to the success of vertebrates.

The teeth of fishes led on to amphibians and higher vertebrates and, initially, were in essence, simple pointed cones useful in capturing and holding prey.

Little significant advancement was made before the Permian when the teeth of some *pelycosauran* reptiles and fish began to differentiate by the appearance of canine-like fangs. These are still evident in the *Hydrocynus goliath* which has 32 interlocking teeth. It is also known as the **goliath tiger-fish,** which can be found today in Lake Tanganyika, and the Congo Basin in Africa. Further differentiation followed among the mammal-like *therapsid* reptiles.

Mesozoic mammals are known chiefly from several types of tiny teeth. Among them simple triangular teeth seem to be ancestral to the molars of Tertiary mammals.

Modernized triangular teeth first appeared in the Cretaceous, and from the Palaeocene onward teeth provide important basis concerning the evolution of many mammals.

Generally, the number of teeth decreased, and the molars were progressively specialized with respect to feeding habits. Specialization progressed from small primitive carnivores in two directions:

- to more efficient carnivores with enlarged cutting teeth, and
- to herbivores with teeth adapted to grinding harsh grasses.

The latter passed through an omnivorous stage with square low-cusped teeth like those of pigs and humans.

Prehistoric Carnivore
No pronounced canines or carnassials

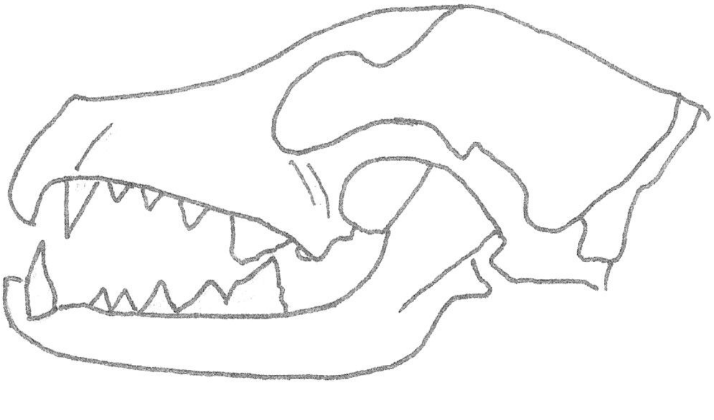

Present-day Dog
Developed canines and carnassials

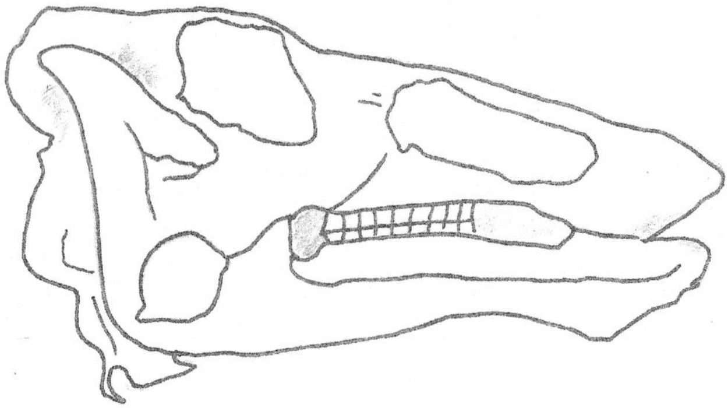

Prehistoric Herbivore
No hard lip or pronounced diastema

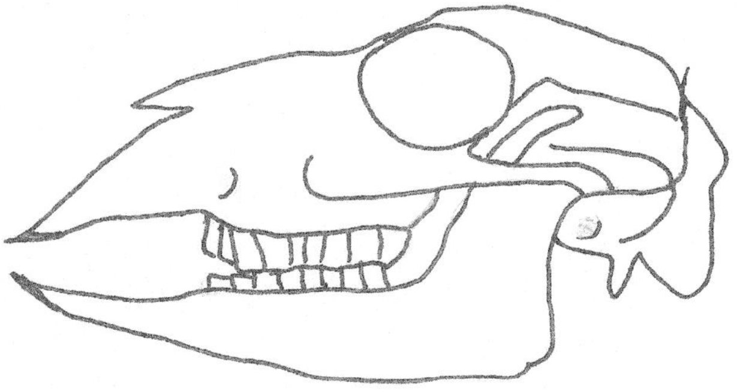

Present-day Sheep
Hard front pad and pronounced diastema

Anatotitan Dentition

Unlike modern lizards, dinosaur teeth grew individually in the sockets of the jawbones. These differ from teeth of other vertebrates, which are directly fused to the bones of the jaw. Teeth that were lost were replaced by teeth below the roots in each tooth socket. Occlusion refers to the closing of the dinosaur's mouth, where the teeth from the upper and lower parts of the jaw meet.

The majority of dinosaurs had teeth that were similarly shaped throughout their jaws but varied in size. A dinosaur that has a variety of tooth shapes is said to have 'heterodont' dentition.

While most dinosaurs had a single row of teeth on each side of their jaws, others had 'dental batteries' where teeth in the cheek region were fused together to form compound teeth. Individually these teeth were not suitable for grinding food, but when joined together with other teeth they would form a large surface area for the mechanical digestion of tough plant materials. This type of dental strategy is observed in the duck-billed *Anatotitan*, which had **more than one hundred teeth** in each' dental battery'.

The *Anatotitan* ripped leaves and plants using its bill, and then, unlike reptiles usually do, chewed the leaves and stems extensively. This caused wear to their teeth, which ground down quickly. The teeth were not only lying next to each other but were also stacked one above the other within the jawbone to form vertical tooth rows. So there were quite a lot of teeth in one jaw and all the densely packed teeth together are referred to as 'tooth battery'.

In the jaw that is shown below, many unworn, keeled, diamond-shaped surfaces of the stacked teeth are visible. Furthermore, the teeth erupted in a way that there was more than one tooth functional in each vertical row.

The teeth rotated during their lifetime around the long axis of the jaw so that a new tooth first reached the mouth cavity on the inner side of the jaw, yet before the older tooth or teeth, sitting closer to the cheek, were entirely worn down. The tooth wear acting on the surfaces of about one hundred functional teeth formed an inclined chewing surface on each tooth battery.

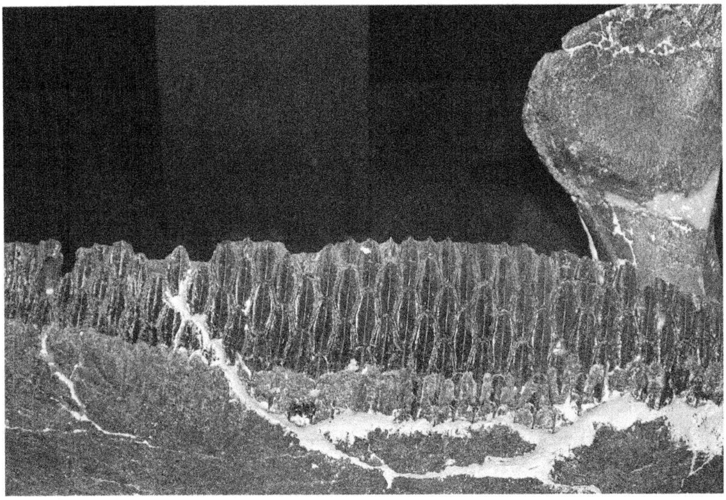

The mandible (lower jaw) of an Edmontosaurus at the Museum of the Rockies in Bozeman, Montana, seen from the inner side (i.e. from the tongue side). CC BY-SA 2.0

Shark's Teeth

The most ancient types of sharks date back to 450 million years ago, during the Late Ordovician, and are mostly known by their fossilized teeth. However, the most commonly found fossil shark teeth are from the Cenozoic (the last 66 million years).

Sharks continually shed their teeth and replace them relatively quickly with replacement teeth.

They are only shed once new teeth are formed underneath and push them out of the connective tissue that was holding them in place.

Elementorum myologiae specimen, 1669 BETC

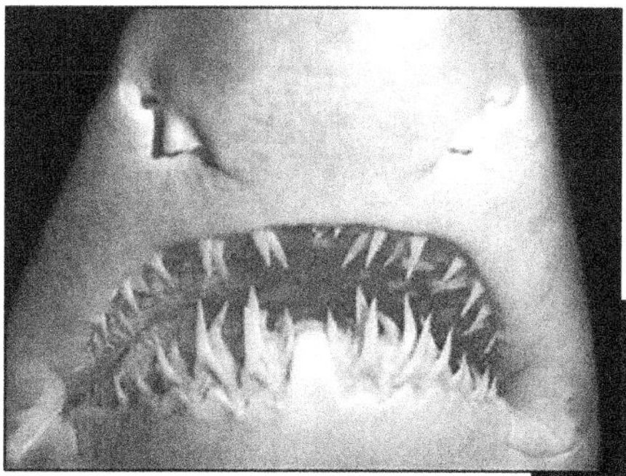

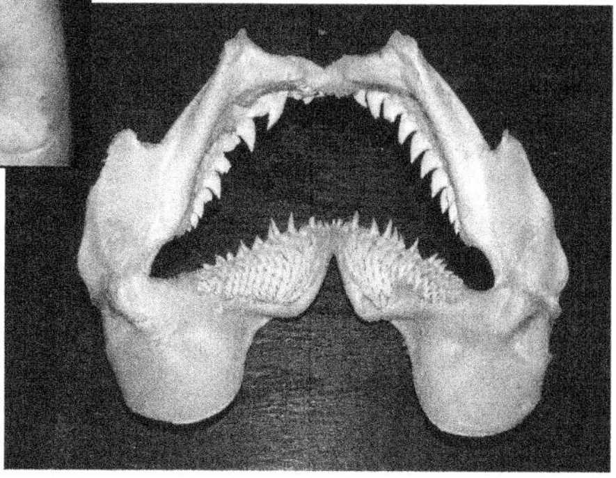

Carcharodon megalodon fossil shark jaw (reconstruction) (late Cenozoic)

Snail’s Teeth

A single snail's jaws contains from 1,000-20,000 teeth, depending on species and age, which are placed in rows in the mouth. The teeth are replaced in the same way that the teeth of a shark are replaced, with new rows sprouting at the back of the mouth and gradually coming forward to replace worn teeth in the front. These rows actually combine to form a *radula*, which looks like a tongue-like pad which is used to grab food by extending it out of its mouth.

When food enters into the snail's mouth, it actually will use this *radula* to scrape off the softer sections of its food, almost like a file. This action wears down their teeth, hence why they change over time. Snails feed using a jaw and a *radula*, a flexible ring of thousands of tiny teeth.

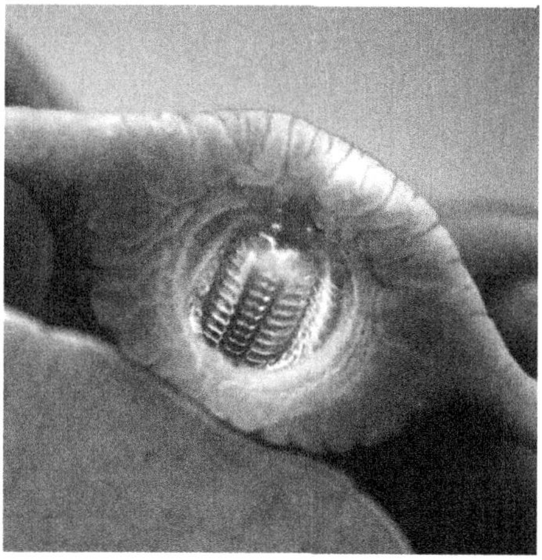

Food particles are scraped using a tongue-tooth arrangement. The inside of its mouth may appear to be long under the microscope, lined with snail teeth close up. The snail's teeth hook inward, hence, grasping food and sliding it inside look easy, unlike other animals.

The snail's teeth are two to five times stronger than spider silk. The teeth are made of robust carbon nanofibres called ***chitin*** *which is* a long-chain polymer of ***N*-acetylglucosamine**.

It is unbreakable and cannot be broken down even with large giga Pascal’s of pressure.

Tomia in Geese

The **tomia** (singular 'tomium') are the cutting edges of the two mandibles. In most birds, these range from rounded to slightly sharp, but some species have evolved structural modifications which allow them to better handle their typical food sources. Granivorous (seed-eating) birds, for example, have ridges in their tomia which help the bird to slice through a seed's outer hull. Geese teeth are arranged along the tongue and can work with the bill to improve cutting. Some geese even have the barbs at the back of the tongue to prevent food they are trying to ingest from being regurgitated.

Tomia exhibited on a young Penguin chick's tongue.

Geese tomia are made of **cartilage**, and while not carrying the enamel of true teeth, the tomia are extremely tough. The serrated protrusions are part of the beak and tongue but act in the same way that regular teeth do. The tomia on their tongue also help clamp down on small mammals and insects.

Tomia exhibited in the mouth of a goose

Tomia in Turtles

Unlike many predators, turtles do not require teeth to eat their food.

This does not mean a turtle's mouth is soft.

Turtles do, however, have a **keratin** edge lining their jaws which is very hard and, sometimes, serrated. These edges can be very sharp and appear as a ***serrated ridge***, making them look a little like rows of teeth. They are not dental structures though as are real teeth.

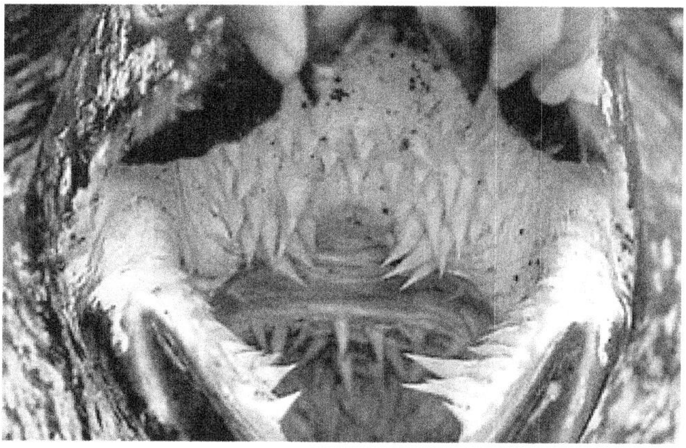

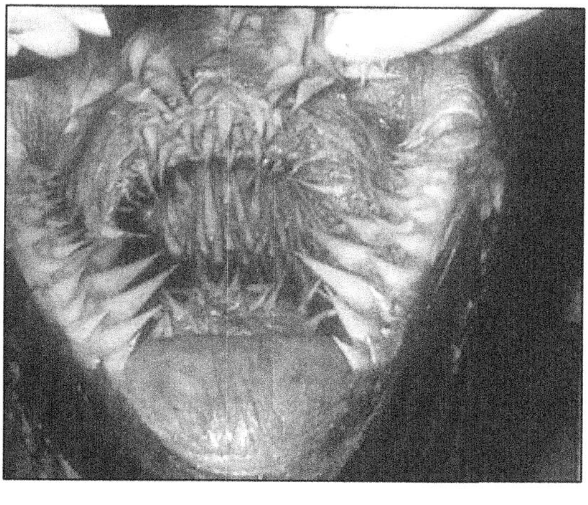

Organisms that use Photosynthesis

Plants are photosynthetic, that is they can create their own energy by harnessing sunlight through chloroplasts or carotenoids.

In recent years, however, a small number of photosynthetic animals have been discovered that process sunlight through symbiosis with algae and even generate their own electric current.

Elysia chlorotica (Eastern Emerald Elysia)

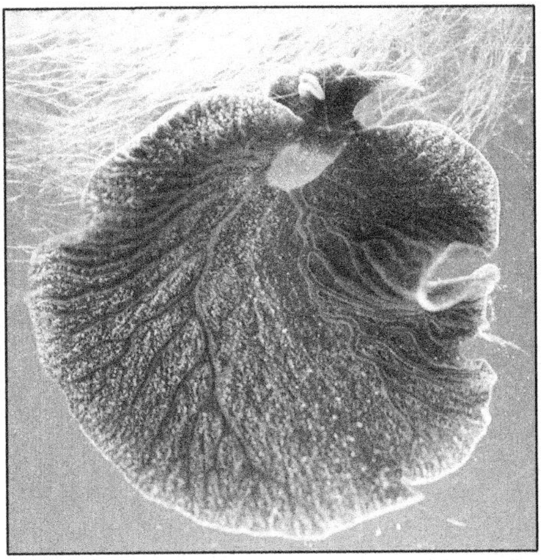

An E. chlorotica individual consuming its obligate algal food Vaucheria litorea
Karen N. Pelletrea et al. - http://journals.plos.org/ *CC BY 4.0*

Elysia chlorotica effectively steals genes from the algae that make up its diet. They eat for photosynthesis, a phenomenon known as *kleptoplasty*, and lives in a symbiotic relationship with chloroplasts of the alga *Vaucheria litorea*.

When *E. chlorotica* eats the algae, it integrates chloroplasts into its own cells. This process is made possible due to the fact that these slugs have a much less complex food breakdown than most animals. Its intestinal lining forms a cell pouch to engulf whole cell parts of whatever it is digesting, allowing the chloroplasts to come through.

Researchers have found that in addition to chloroplasts, *E. chlorotica* can intake other photosynthetic genes in a horizontal genetic transfer, a process in which genes are transferred between organisms where one is not the offspring of another. The stolen chloroplasts can be so efficient that these slugs can live up to nine months without eating and still maintain normal nutritional rates.

Ambystoma maculatum (Spotted Salamander)

http://images.nationalgeographic.co

Ambystoma maculatum is similar to the sea-slug in that it also has a symbiotic relationship with algae. While it has long been known that a relationship existed between the salamander and the algae, it was presumed to be a relationship in which both organisms worked separately. However, it has now been established that the mitochondria of the salamander were directly consuming oxygen and carbohydrates that are created through photosynthesis.

Vespa orientalis (Oriental Hornet)

http://www. Wikipedia.de 15 Nov 2006

Vespa orientalis, in contrast to the sea slug and spotted salamander, was discovered to conduct electricity through the cuticle of its exoskeleton, as well as through silk surrounding the hornet pupae and the colony's comb walls. As opposed to stealing chloroplasts from algae, this photosynthetic insect's yellow band contains **xanthoperin**, which actively absorbs light and converts it to electricity.

Microscopic grooves in the hornet's exoskeleton trap sunlight, and as the photons reach the yellow pigment, they build up voltage. This voltage is released as current when the hornet is in darkness, and seems to be important for the development of the hornet pupae.

Acyrthosiphon pisum (Pea aphid)

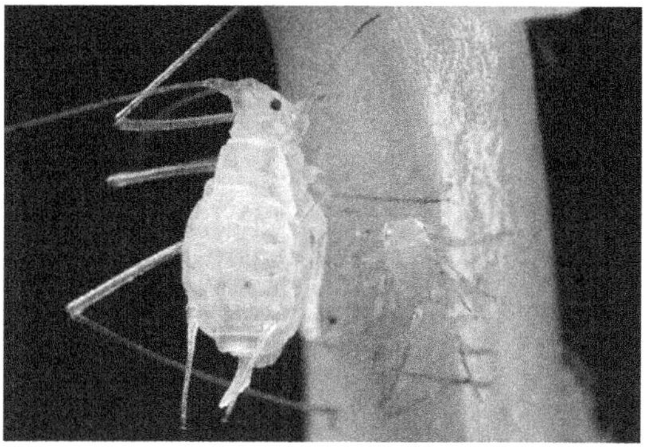

http://www.wired.com/

Acyrthosiphon pisum takes advantage of its food source for photosynthetic powers but it does not make use of chloroplasts. A fungal gene is copied within the aphid's cells, but its purpose is for the production of carotenoids.

In this regard, it is clear that carotenoids can absorb light and pass that energy on to the aphids in the form of Adenosine Triphosphate (ATP).

Mastigias papua (Golden Jellyfish)

Monterey Bay Aquarium, Monterey County, California, USA. CCO 1.0

The **golden jellyfish** are a species of jellyfish most closely related to the spotted jelly (*Mastigias papua*) that inhabit the lagoons nearby Jellyfish Lake, Eil Malk Island. They are similar to their ancestors in that they derive part of their nutrition from symbiotic algae (*Zooxanthellae*) that live in their tissues and part of their nutrition from captured zooplankton.

However, the golden jellyfish are morphologically, physiologically, and behaviourally distinct from the spotted jellyfish. They are easily distinguished from the spotted jellyfish by the almost complete loss of spots on the exumbrella and the almost complete loss of their clubs, an appendage attached to the oral arms.

This evolution started millions of years ago when Jellyfish Lake became isolated, leading to their loss of most of their stinging capabilities to focus on the cultivation of algae. This transformation led to them beginning to migrate and follow the sun in order to feed the algae in question and thereby feed themselves.

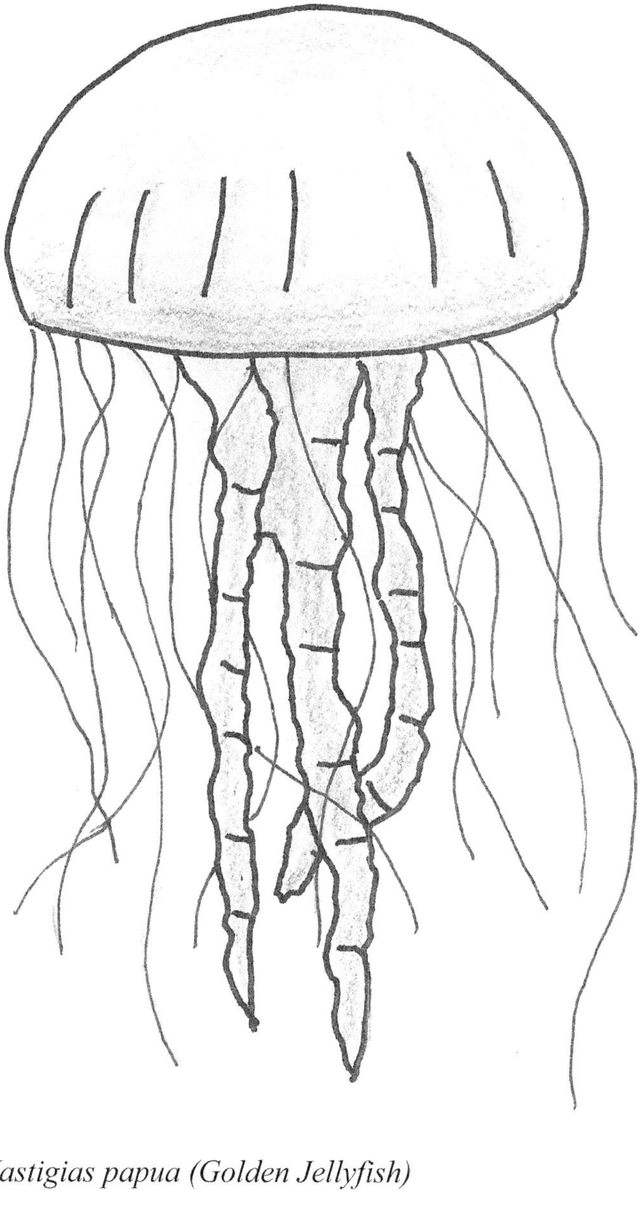

Mastigias papua (Golden Jellyfish)

Symbioses between animals and photosynthetic symbionts

Porifera

Cyanobacteria in many marine sponges,
Symbiodinium in clionid (boring) marine sponges,
Chlorella in freshwater sponges, e.g. *Spongilla*

Cnidaria

Symbiodinium in benthic marine corals, sea anemones etc.
Scripsiella spp. in pelagic taxa, e.g. *Velella*
Chlorella in freshwater hydra

Platyhelminthes

Various in marine turbellarians,
e.g. *Tetraselmis* (prasinophyte)
in *Symsagittifera* (=*Convoluta*) *roscoffensis;*
Licmophora (diatom) in *Convoluta convoluta*
Chlorella in freshwater turbellarians,
e.g. *Dalyella* spp

Mollusca

Dinoflagellates, usually *Symbiodinium* in marine gastropods and bivalves, including tridacnid clams; *Chlorella* in few freshwater clams, e.g. *Anodonta*

Ascidia

Cyanobacteria, usually *Prochloron* in various ascidians

Evolution of Bacteria

Evidence of *microfossils* of early *prokaryotes* was discovered in the Australian Apex Chert rocks, dating back roughly 3.5 billion years ago during the time period known as the Precambrian, suggesting that an organism in of the phylum *Thermotogae* was the most recent 'common ancestor' of modern bacteria.

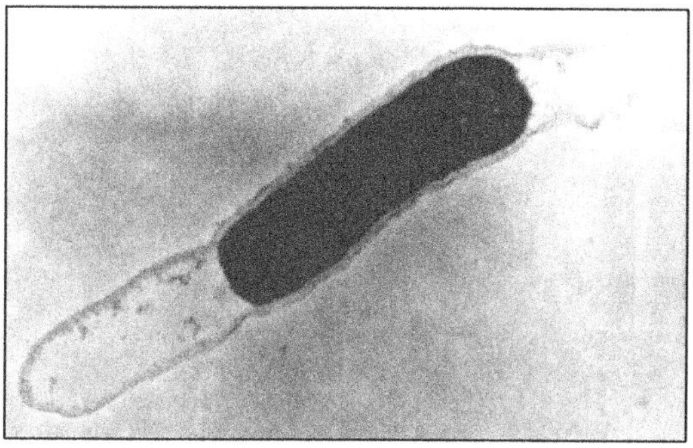

Thermotoga

Further chemical and isotopic analysis of ancient rock reveals that by the Siderian, roughly 2.45 billion years ago, after oxygen had appeared. This indicates that oceanic, photosynthetic *cyanobacteria* evolved during this period insofar as they were the first microbes to produce oxygen as a byproduct of their metabolic process.

However, some scientists argue they could have lived as early as 2.7 billion years ago, as this was roughly before the time of the **Great Oxygenation Event**, meaning oxygen levels had time to increase in the atmosphere before it altered the ecosystem during this event.

The rise in atmospheric oxygen led to the evolution of *proteobacteria*.

Proteobacteria

Today, this phylum includes many nitrogen fixing bacteria, pathogens, and free-living microorganisms. This phylum evolved approximately 1.5 billion years ago during the Paleoproterozoic.

Proteobacteria is a major phylum of Gram-negative bacteria.

They include a wide variety of pathogenic genera, such as Escherichia, Salmonella, Vibrio, Helicobacter, Yersinia, Legionellalas and many others.

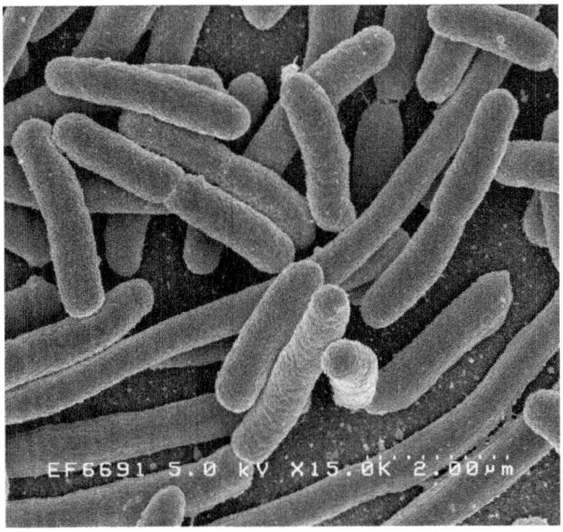

Scanning electron micrograph of Escherichia coli.

However, there are still many conflicting theories surrounding the origins of bacteria.

Bacteria are *prokaryotic* microorganisms that can either have a *bacilli*, *spirilli*, or *cocci* shape and measure between 0.5-20 micrometers.

They were one of the first living cells to evolve and have spread to inhabit a variety of different habitats including hydrothermal vents, glacial rocks, and other organisms.

They share characteristics with eukaryotic cells including the cytoplasm, cell membrane, and ribosomes. Some unique bacterial features include the cell wall (also found in plants and fungi), flagella (not common for all bacteria), and the nucleoid.

Bacteria reproduce through binary fission, though they can still share genetic information between individuals either by transduction, transformation, or conjugation.

Thermotogales

Thermotogale bacteria are typically thermophilic or hyperthermophilic, gram-negative staining, anaerobic organisms that can live near hydrothermal vents where temperatures can range between 55-95^{0}C. They are thought to be some of the earliest forms of life.

Evidence of these organisms has been discovered in the Australian Apex Chert near ancient hydrothermal vents. These rocks date back 3.46 billion years and these fossils are thought to have belonged to early *thermophilic* bacteria.

This is because these organisms do not require oxygen to survive, which was not present in large quantities in Earth's early atmosphere. Furthermore, this phylum still has living species such as *Thermotoga neapolitana*, which still largely resemble their ancestral form and still live around these vents, which some scientists have used as evidence to support this theory.

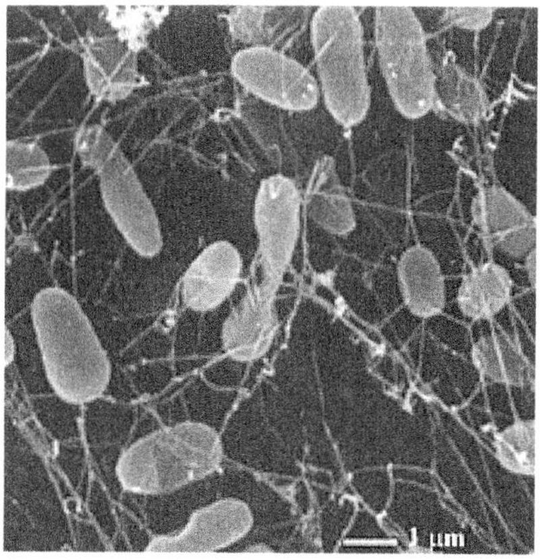

More recent evidence has emerged, which suggests that *Thermotogales* evolved roughly between 3.2 to 3.5 billion years ago. This evidence was collected via gene sequencing of bacterial nucleoids to reconstruct their phylogeny. The first major divergence within the *Thermotogales* phylum was between *Thermotogaceae* and *Fervidobacteriaceae,* however it is yet to be determined as to when this occurred. The family of *Thermotogaceae* then diverged into the genus *Thermotoga* and the genus *Pseudothermotoga.* The genus *Thermotoga* represents the majority of existing hyperthermophiles, and is unique in that members of this genus are wrapped in an outer membrane that is referred to as a 'toga'. Some extant *Thermotoga* species include *T. neapolitana*

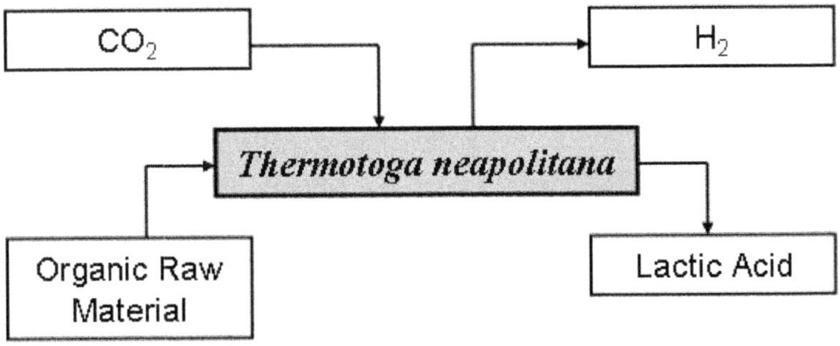

Cyanobacteria

Cyanobacteria or blue green-algae are gram negative bacteria, a phylum of photosynthetic bacteria that evolved between 2.3-2.7 billion years ago. This prokaryote produces oxygen as a byproduct of its photosynthetic processes. They have made a distinctive impact in pharmaceutical and agricultural industry due to their potential of making bioactive compounds with antibacterial, anti-fungal, antiviral, and anti-algal properties.

Typically they form motile filaments referred to as hormogonia, which can form colonies and then bud and travel to colonize new areas. They have been located in environments including freshwater, oceans, soil and rock (both damp and dry), as well as arctic rock.

These organisms had evolved photosynthetic reaction centres and became the first oxygen producing autotrophs to appear in the fossil record.

They utilize sunlight in order to drive their metabolic processes which remove carbon dioxide from the atmosphere and releases oxygen. Due to this trait some scientists credit this phylum to causing the **Great Oxygenation Event** roughly 2.45 billion years ago.

However, the closest known relatives of oxygen producing Cyanobacteria did not produce oxygen. These relatives are Melainabacteria and Sericytochromatia, neither of which can photosynthesize.

Through genetic sequencing, scientists discovered that these two groups did not have any remnants of the genes required for the functioning of photosynthetic reactions. This suggests that *Cyanobacteria*, *Melainabacteria*, and *Sericytochromatia* evolved from a non-photosynthetic common ancestor.

Beneficial Effects of Normal Bacteria Flora

The 'normal flora' merely refers to the population of microorganisms like bacteria, fungi and protists, which typically colonize at specific sites of the human body.

The overall beneficial effects of normal bacterial flora are;

1. They synthesize and excrete vitamins in excess of their own needs, which can be absorbed as nutrients by their host.
For example, in humans, intestinal bacteria secrete Vitamin K and Vitamin B12.

2. They prevent colonization by pathogens by competing for attachment sites or for essential nutrients.
This has been demonstrated in the oral cavity, the intestine, the skin, and the vaginal epithelium.

3. They may antagonize other bacteria through the production of substances which inhibit or kill.

4. The normal flora stimulates the development of certain tissues.
The caecum and certain lymphatic tissues in the GI tract are examples.

5. They stimulate the production of natural antibodies.
Since the normal floras behave as antigens, they induce an immunological response, in particular, an antibody-mediated immune response.

Key Facts – Bacteria Flora

- Normal flora within a human body contains more than **200 bacterial species,**
- The factors influencing the normal flora include age, diet, nutrition, sex, and immune conditions of a person,
- Unlike bacteria, viruses and parasites do not constitute the normal flora,
- Under normal conditions, bacterial flora is harmless or even beneficial,
- Any disturbances in the normal flora may harm the host through the consequence of **opportunistic microorganisms** that may eventually cause disease or an infection,
- A human body is colonized with the normal flora once a newborn body is passed through the **mother's vaginal tract** or exposed to the environment,
- A new born baby establishes the **oral and nasopharyngeal flora** within few hours,
- After one day, resident flora establishes in the **lower intestinal tract** of the neonate.

Sulphate-reducing Bacteria

Sulphate-reducing bacteria share a group along with **sulphate-reducing archaea**, both of which can perform **anaerobic respiration** utilizing sulphate as terminal electron acceptor, reducing it to hydrogen sulfide (H_2S). Therefore, these sulphidogenic microorganisms 'breathe' sulphate rather than molecular oxygen, which is the terminal electron acceptor reduced to water in aerobic respiration.

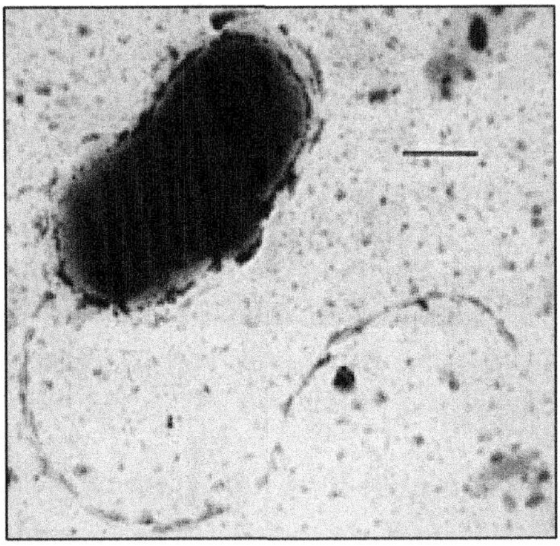

Desulfovibrio vulgaris *is the best-studied sulphate reducing microorganism species; the bar in the upper right is 0.5 micrometre long.*

Most sulphate-reducing microorganisms can also reduce some other oxidized inorganic sulphur compounds, such as sulphite.

Sulphate-reducing microorganisms can be traced back to **3.5 billion years ago** and are considered to be among the oldest forms of microbes, having contributed to the **Sulphur Cycle** soon after life emerged on Earth.

Many organisms reduce small amounts of sulphates in order to synthesize sulphur-containing cell components; this is known as *assimilatory sulphate reduction*.

By contrast, the sulphate-reducing microorganisms considered here reduce sulphate in large amounts to obtain energy and expel the resulting sulfide as waste; this is known as *dissimilatory sulphate reduction*. They use sulphate as the terminal electron acceptor of their electron transport chain. Most of them are anaerobes; however, there are examples of sulphate-reducing microorganisms that are tolerant of oxygen, and some of them can even perform aerobic respiration. No growth is observed when oxygen is used as the electron acceptor. In addition, there are sulphate-reducing microorganisms that can also reduce other electron acceptors.

In terms of electron donor, this group contains both organotrophs and lithotrophs. The organotrophs oxidize organic compounds. The lithotrophs oxidize molecular hydrogen (H_2), for which they compete with methanogens and acetogens in anaerobic conditions. Sulphate occurs widely in seawater and is also found in more extreme environments such as hydrothermal vents.

Some sulphate-reducing microorganisms play a role in the anaerobic oxidation of methane:

$$\mathbf{CH_4 + SO^{2-}{}_4 \rightarrow HCO^-{}_3 + HS^- + H_2O}$$

An important fraction of the methane formed by methanogens below the seabed is oxidized by sulphate-reducing microorganisms in the transition zone separating the methanogenesis from the sulphate reduction activity in the sediments. This process is also considered a major sink for sulphate in marine sediments.

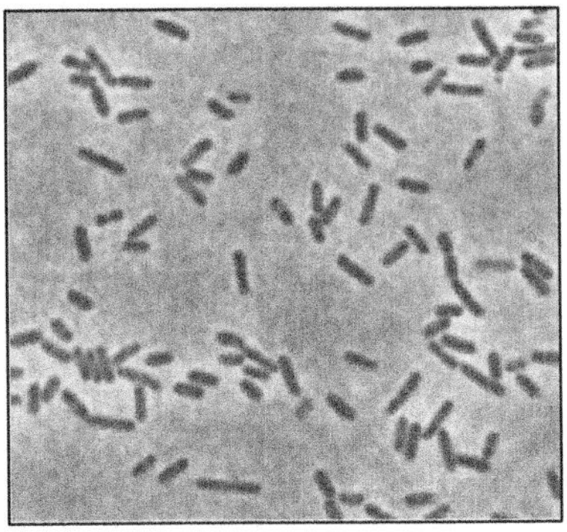

Desulphuromonas acetoxidans is a species of bacteria. It is strictly anaerobic, rod-shaped, laterally flagellated and Gram-negative. It is unable to ferment organic substances; it obtains energy for growth by anaerobic sulphur respiration.

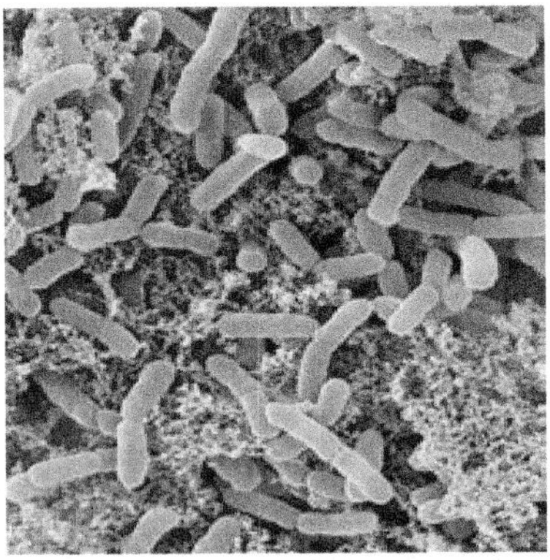

Chlorobium species are thought to have played an important part in mass extinction events on Earth. If the oceans turn anoxic (due to the shutdown of ocean circulation) then *Chlorobium* would be able to out compete other photosynthetic life. They would produce huge quantities of methane and hydrogen sulfide which would cause global warming and acid rain. This would have huge consequences for other oceanic organisms and also for terrestrial organisms.

Beggiatoa-like filaments under a rock in shallow water.
Sorrento Peninsula, Naples, Italy. Fabio Russo

One of the defining features of the genus Beggiatoa is the production of intracellular inclusions of sulphur resulting from the oxidation of reduced sulphur sources (e.g. hydrogen sulfide). In autotrophic Beggiatoa, sulfide is a source of energy and electrons for carbon fixation and growth. The oxidation of sulfide can be aerobic or anaerobic; in fact it can be coupled with the reduction of oxygen or with the reduction of nitrate. Sulphur produced by the oxidation of sulfide is stored into internal globules and can be used when the concentration of sulfide decreases.

Thus, the temporarily storing of elemental sulphur (S^0) increases the adaptability of an organism and its tolerance to changes in the concentrations of sulfide and oxygen.

Sulfide aerobic oxidation:

$$\mathbf{H_2S + \frac{1}{2}O_2 \rightarrow S^0 + \boxed{H_2O}}$$

Sulfide anaerobic oxidation:

$$\mathbf{4H_2S + NO_3 + 2H \rightarrow 4S^0 + NH_4 + \boxed{H_2O}}$$

Limits of known (Bacterial) Life on Earth

(With a special mention for the Tardigrade – an animal with the remarkable ability to cope with extreme environmental stresses!)

Currently we do not have a complete picture of how life originated on this planet. We do have pieces of the puzzle, but the entire picture has not yet been assembled.

Only within the last couple of decades have we been able to place constraints on the limits of life on the Earth, but much still needs explanation as to why those limits exist. These gaps in our understanding of the origin and extent of life on Earth make it especially challenging to explore other planetary bodies in our solar system for life.

The following is a list of those limits to which life-forms have managed to adapt within their particular surrounding environments.

High temperature	113^0C to 122^0C
Low temperature	-20^0C to -25^0C
Alkaline systems	pH > 11
Acetic systems	pH -0.06 to 1.0
Ionising radiation	1,500 to 6,000 Gy
UV radiation	5,000 J/m
High pressure	1,000 bar
Salinity	a_w ~0.6
Desiccation	~60% relative humidity

High temperature 113°C to 122°C

Submarine hydrothermal vents, oceanic crust

Pyrolobus fumarii

Pyrolobus fumarii is a species of archaea known for its ability to live at extremely high temperatures that kill most organisms.

It was first discovered in 1997 in a 'black smoker' hydrothermal vent at the Mid-Atlantic Ridge, setting the upper temperature threshold for known life to exist at 113°C but more recently *Methanopyrus kandleri* has been discovered which can survive temperatures up to 122°C. The species 'freezes' or solidifies and ceases growth at temperatures of 90°C and below.

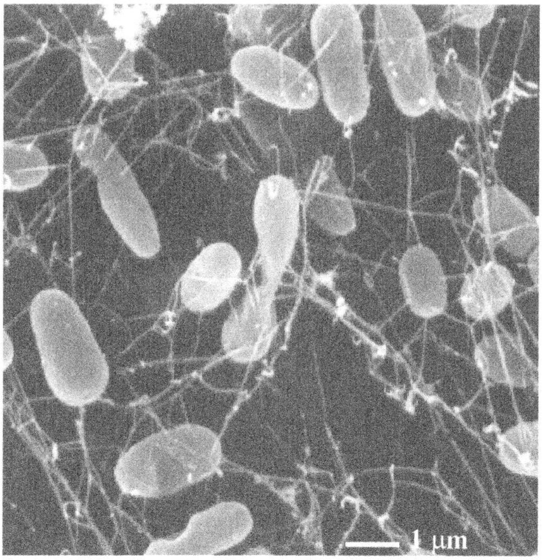

Pyrolobus fumarii

Methanopyrus kanderi

Methanopyrus is a genus of methanogen, with a single described species, *M. kandleri*. It is a rod-shaped *hyperthermophile* living in a hydrogen-carbon dioxide rich environment, and like other methanogens reduces the latter to methane.

It is placed among the *Euryarchaeota,* in its own class.

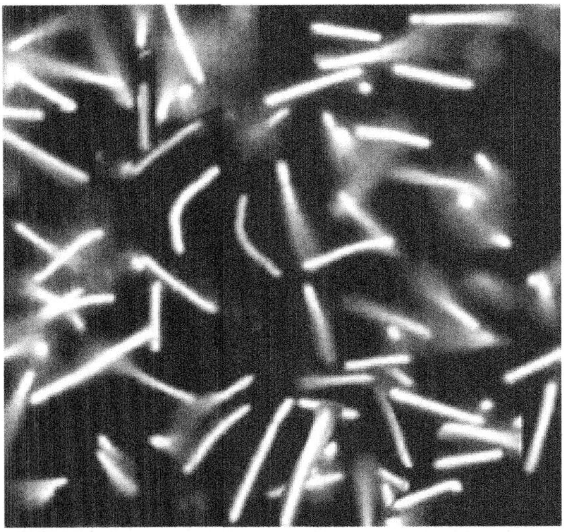

Methanopyrus kanderi

Pyrococcus furiosus

Pyrococcus furiosus is an *extremophilic* species of Archaea. It can be classified as a *hyperthermophile* because it thrives best under extremely high temperatures - higher than those generally preferred of a *thermophile*.

It is notable for having an optimum growth temperature of 100 C (a temperature that would destroy most living organisms), and for being one of the few organisms identified as possessing aldehyde ferredoxin oxidoreductase enzymes containing tungsten, an element rarely found in biological molecules.

Pyrococcus furiosus

Low temperature -20°C to -25°C
Ice

Synechococcus lividus

Synechococcus lividus is one of the most important components of the prokaryotic autotrophic *picoplankton* from arctic to tropical oceans.

The marine forms of *Synechococcus* are *coccoid* cells between 0.6 and 1.6µm in size. They are gram-negative cells with highly structured cell walls that may contain projections on their surface. Cells are known to be motile by a gliding method and a novel uncharacterized, non-phototactic swimming method that does not involve flagellar motion.

While some cyanobacteria are capable of *photo heterotrophic* or even *chemo heterotrophic* growth, all marine *Synechococcus* strains appear to be obligate *photoautotroph* that are capable of supporting their nitrogen requirements using nitrate, ammonia, or in some cases urea as a sole nitrogen source.

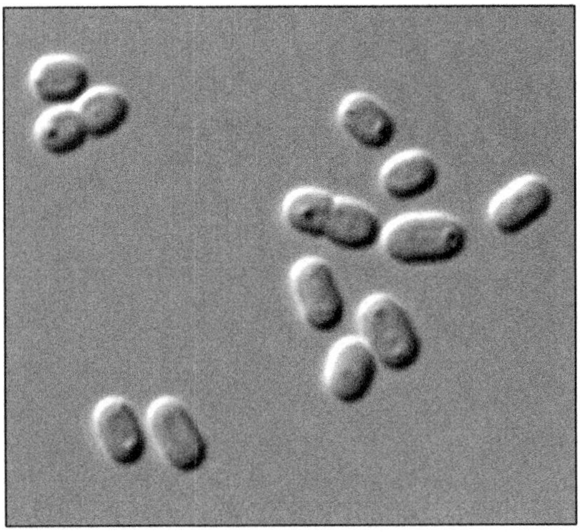

Synechococcus lividus

Alkaline systems pH >11
Soda lakes

Psychrobacter

Psychrobacter is a genus of gram-negative, osmotolerant, oxidase-positive, psychrophilic or psychrotolerant, aerobic bacteria which belong to the family *Moraxellaceae* and the class *Gammaproteobacteria.*

The shape is typically *cocci* or *coccobacilli*. Some of those bacteria were isolated from humans and can cause humans infections such as endocarditis and peritonitis.

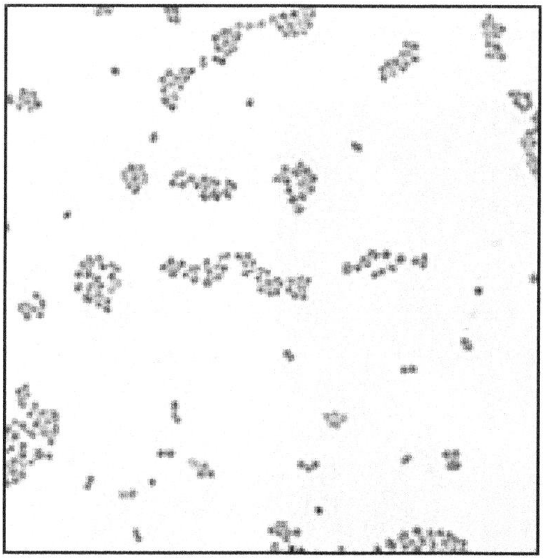

Psychrobacter

Vibrio

Vibrio is a genus of gram-negative bacteria, possessing a curved-rod (comma) shape, several species of which can cause food borne infection, usually associated with eating undercooked seafood.

Typically found in salt water, *Vibrio* species are facultative anaerobes that test positive for oxidase and do not form spores.

All members of the genus are motile. They are able to have polar or lateral flagellum with or without sheaths. *Vibrio* species typically possess two chromosomes, which is unusual for bacteria.

Every chromosome has a distinct and independent origin of replication, and is conserved together over time in the genus.

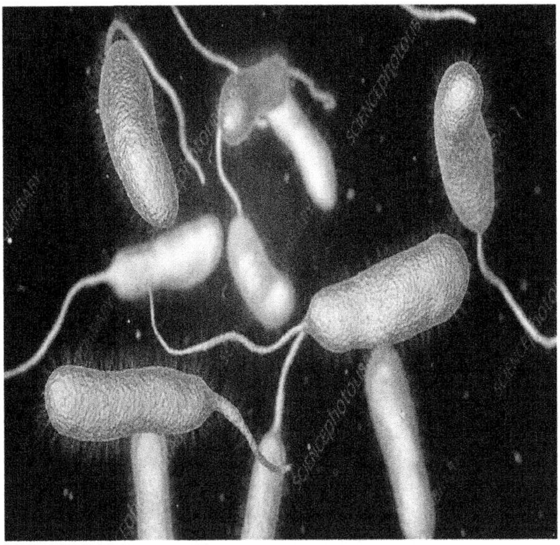

Vibrio

Arthrobacter

Arthrobacter is a genus of bacteria that is commonly found in soil. All species in this genus are Gram-positive obligate aerobes that are rods during exponential growth and cocci in their stationary phase.

Arthrobacter have a distinctive method of cell division called 'snapping division' or 'reversion' in which the outer bacterial cell wall ruptures at a joint.

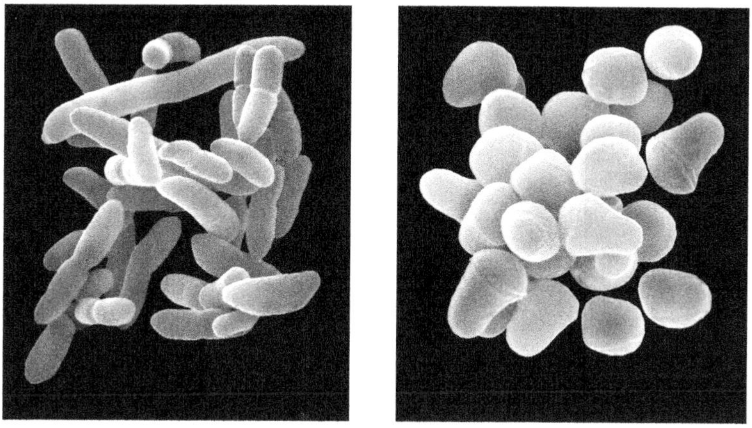

Arthrobacter- Growth and stationary phases

Natronobacterium

In taxonomy, ***Natronobacterium*** is a genus of the *Halobacteriaceae*.

A member of the domain *Archaea*, it is both an extreme *halophile* and *alkaliphile*, thriving at an optimum saline concentration of 20% and optimum pH of 10.

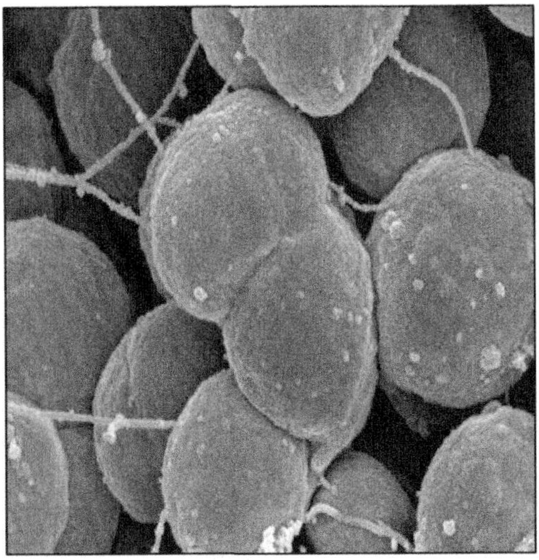

Natronobacterium

Acidic systems pH -0.06 to 1.0
Volcanic springs, acid mine drainage

Bacillus

Bacillus is a rod-shaped bacterium, a member of the phylum *Bacillota*, with 266 named species. *Bacillus* species can be either obligate aerobes: oxygen dependent; or facultative anaerobes: having the ability to continue living in the absence of oxygen.

Bacillus can reduce themselves to oval endospores and can remain in this dormant state for years. The endospore of one species from Morocco is reported to have survived being heated to 420^{0}C. The spores are resistant to heat, cold, radiation, desiccation, disinfectants and acidic conditions.

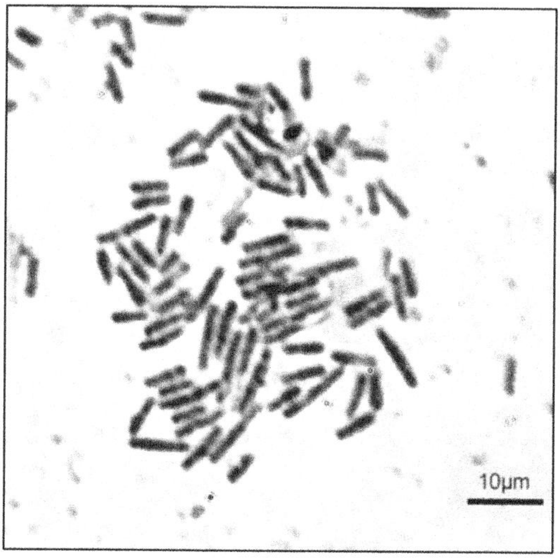

Bacillus

Clostridium paradoxum

Clostridium paradoxum is a moderately thermophilic anaerobic alkaliphile bacterium. It is motile with 2-6 peritrichous flagella and forms round to slightly oval terminal spores.

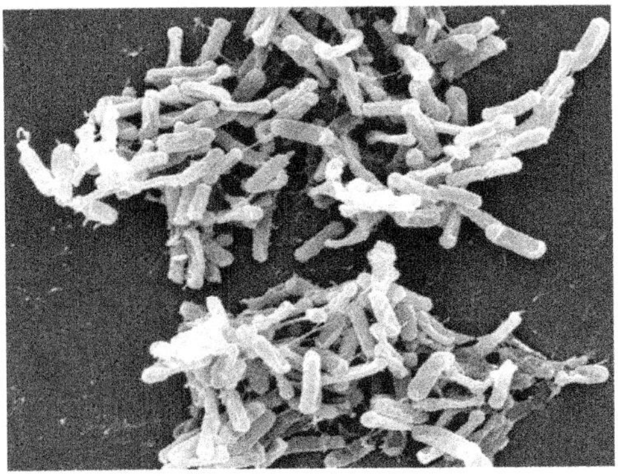

Clostridium paradoxum

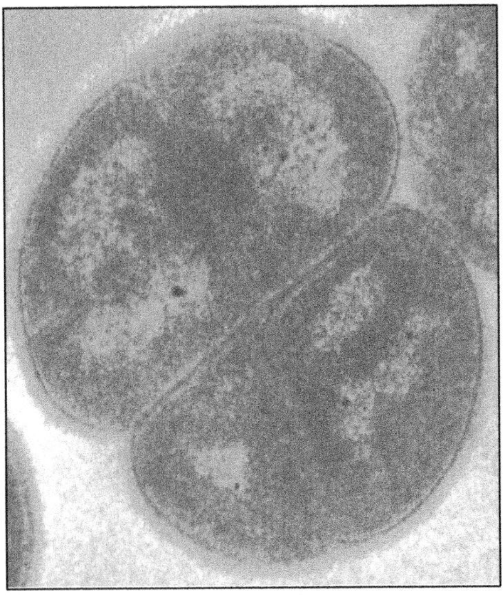

Deinococcus radiodurans

Ionizing radiation 1,500 – 6,000 Gy
Cosmic rays, X-rays, radioactive decay

UV radiation 5,000 J/m
Sunlight

Deinococcus radiodurans

Deinococcus radiodurans is an extremophilic bacterium and one of the most radiation-resistant organisms known. It can survive cold, dehydration, vacuum, and acid, and therefore is known as a *polyextremophile.*

The bacterium has a unique quality in which it can repair both single- and double-stranded DNA. When damage is apparent to the cell, it brings the damaged DNA into a compartmental ring-like structure where the DNA is repaired, and then is able to fuse the nucleoids from the outside of the compartment with the damaged DNA.

In August 2020, scientists reported that bacteria from Earth, particularly *Deinococcus radiodurans* bacteria, were found to survive for three years in outer space, based on studies conducted on the International Space Station (ISS). These findings support the notion of *panspermia*, the hypothesis that life exists throughout the Universe, distributed in various ways, including space dust, meteoroids, asteroids, comets, planetoids, or contaminated spacecraft.

(See above)

Rubrobacter xylanophilus

Rubrobacter xylanophilus is a thermophilic species of bacteria. It is slightly *halotolerant,* short rod- and coccus-shaped.

It is the only true radiation resistant thermophile.

The first strain of the genus *Rubrobacter* was isolated from gamma-irradiated hot spring water samples by Yoshinaka. This organism was found to be extremely gamma-radiation resistant, and was slightly thermophilic with an optimum growth temperature of about 60^0C.[

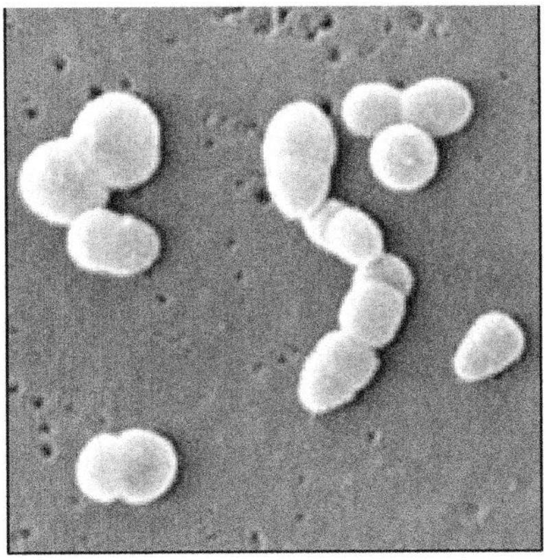

Rubrobacter xylanophilus

Thermococcus gammatolerans

Thermococcus gammatolerans **is** an archaea *extremophile* and the most radiation-resistant organism known to exist.

It is the organism with the strongest known resistance to radiation, supporting a radiation of gamma rays.

The resistance to ionizing radiation of *T. gammatolerans* is enormous. While a dose of 5Gy is sufficient to kill a human, and a dose of 60Gy is able to kill all cells in a colony of *E. coli*, *T gammatolerans* can withstand doses up to 30,000Gy, and an instantaneous dose up to 5,000Gy with no loss of viability.

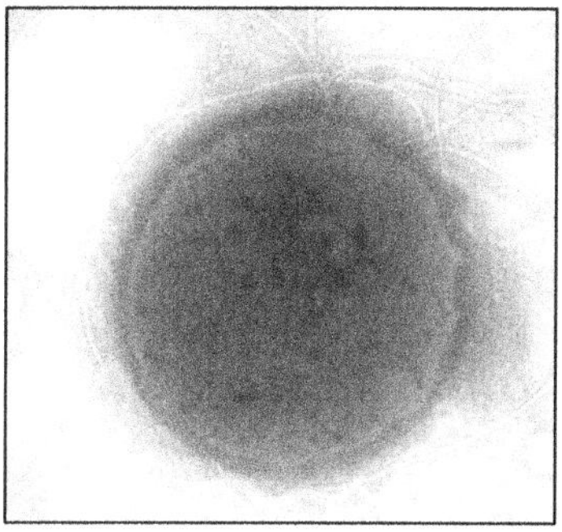

Thermococcus gammatolerans

High Pressure 1,100 bar
Mariana Trench

Pyrococcus (*See page 611*)

Salinity $a_w \sim 0.6$
High salt concentration

Halobacteriaceae

Halobacteriaceae are found in water saturated or nearly saturated with salt.

They are common in most environments where large amounts of salt, moisture, and organic material are available. Large blooms appear reddish, from the pigment *bacteriorhodopsin*. This pigment is used to absorb light, which provides energy to create ATP. *Halobacteria* also possess a second pigment, halorhodopsin, which pumps in chloride ions in response to photons, creating a voltage gradient and assisting in the production of energy from light.

They have certain adaptations to live within their salty environments. For example, their cellular machinery is adapted to high salt concentrations by having charged amino acids on their surfaces, allowing the cell to keep its water molecules around these components. The osmotic pressure and these amino acids help to control the amount of salt within the cell.

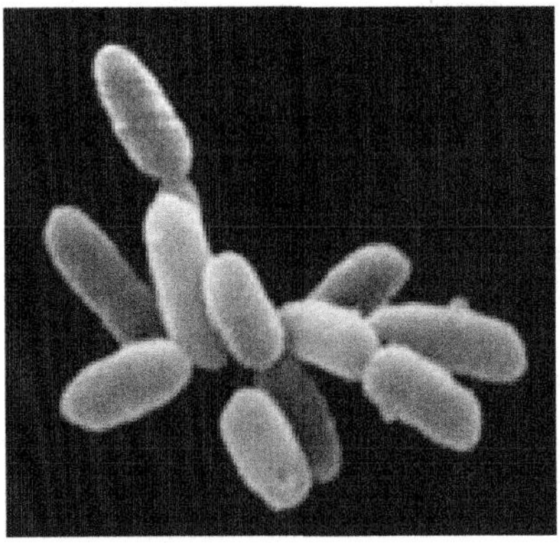

Halobacteriaceae

Dunaleilla salina

Dunaliella salina is a type of halophile green unicellular micro-algae especially found in hypersaline environments, such as salt lakes and salt evaporation ponds. Known for its antioxidant activity because of its ability to create large amount of *carotenoids*.

Dunaliella has two *flagella* of equal length and has a single cup-like *chloroplast* that often contains a central *pyrenoid.* The *chloroplast* can hold large amounts of *β-carotene,* which makes it appear orange-red. The *β-carotene* appears to protect the organism from long-term UV radiation that *D. salina* is exposed to in its typical environments. *D. salina* comes in various shapes and symmetries depending on the conditions in its current environment.

D. salina lacks a rigid cell wall, which makes the organism susceptible to osmotic pressure. Glycerol is used as a means by which to maintain both osmotic balance and enzymatic activity. *D. salina* preserves a high concentration of glycerol by maintaining a cell membrane with low permeability to glycerol and synthesizing large quantities of glycerol from starch as a response to high extracellular salt concentration, which is why it tends to thrive in highly salinic environments.

Desiccation ~ 60% relative humidity
Alacama Desert, Chile
McMurdo Dry Valleys, Antartica

Chroococcidiopsis

Chroococidiopsis is known for their ability to survive harsh environmental conditions, including both high and low temperatures, ionizing radiation, and high salinity.

The ability of *Chroococcidiopsis* to resist **desiccation** in arid environments is due in part because it colonizes the underside of translucent rocks. The underside of these rocks provides enough condensed moisture for growth while the rock's translucent nature allows just enough light to reach the organism for photosynthesis to occur.

Apart from this, *Chroococcidiopsis* is a **photosynthetic**, *coccoidal bacterium.*

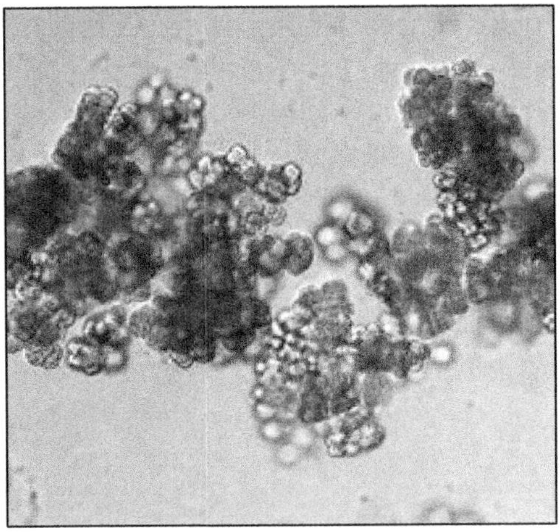

Chroococidiopsis

Mars Exploration

Due to its resistance to harsh environmental conditions, especially low temperature, low moisture, and radiation tolerance, *Chroococcidiopsis* has been thought of as an organism capable of living on Mars.

Scientists have speculated about the possibility of introducing *Chroococcidiopsis* to the Martian environment to aid in the formation of an aerobic environment. In addition to oxygen production, *Chroococcidiopsis* could aid in the formation of soil on the Martian surface.

On Earth, soil is formed by plant, microbial, and geophysical activity on a mineral substrate. The soil produced by chemical weathering of rocks and oxygen produced by photosynthesis could one day provide the conditions necessary for humans to grow food on Mars, possibly allowing for permanent human civilizations on the planet. On a shorter time scale, *cyanobacteria* such as *Chroococcidiopsis* could be used in closed systems to produce resources for human-occupied outposts on Mars without altering the planet's surface or atmosphere.

A space mission called EXPOSE-R2 was launched on 24 July 2014 aboard the Russian Progress M-24M, and was attached on 18 August 2014 outside the ISS on the Russian module Zvezda.

The experiment includes samples of *Chroococcidiopsis* that will be exposed to simulated Martian atmosphere, UVC radiation (range 200nm to 280nm) and temperature extremes.

Tardigrades

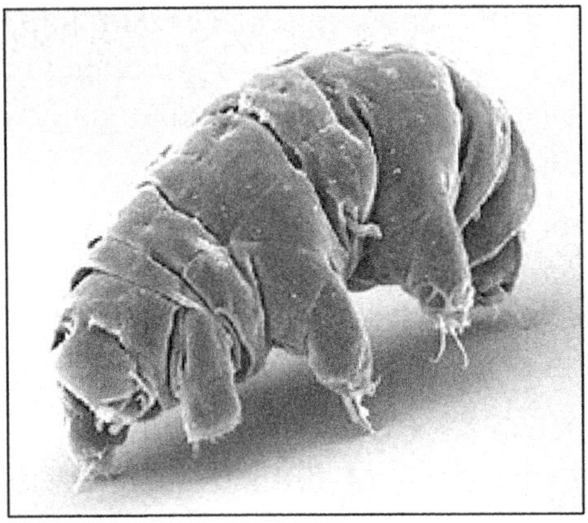

Milnesium tardigradum is a cosmopolitan species of **tardigrade** that can be found in a diverse range of environments. It has also been found in the sea around Antarctica.

M. tardigradum was described by Louis Michel François Doyère in 1840. It contains unidentified *osmolytes* that could potentially provide important information in the process of *cryptobiosis*.

M. tardigradum has a symmetrical body with a total of eight legs; it uses claws, a distinctive feature for this tardigrade species. The total length of the body varies, with some measuring up to 0.7mm in length.

M. tardigradum has been found to have a high level of radio resistance. In 2007, individuals of two tardigrade species, *Richtersius coronifer* and *M. tardigradum*, were subject to the radiation, near-vacuum and near-absolute zero conditions of outer space as part of the European Space Agency's Biopan-6 experiment. Three specimens of *M. tardigradum* survived. The *M. tardigradum* is able to cope with high amounts of environmental stress by initiating cryptobiosis. During this state, the internal organic clock of *M. tardigradum* halts, thus the *cryptobiotic* state does not contribute to the aging process.

Tardigrades - Cryptobiotics

PRESSURE - Tardigrades can withstand the extremely low pressure of a vacuum and also very high pressures, more than 1,200 times atmospheric pressure. Some species can also withstand pressure of 6,000 atmospheres.

IMPACTS – Tardigrades can survive impacts up to about 900 meters per second, and momentary shock pressures up to about 1.14 gigapascals.

DEHYDRATION – The longest that a living tardigrade has been shown to survive in a dry state is nearly 10 years, although there is one report of leg movement, not generally considered "survival", in a 120-year-old specimen from dried moss.

RADIATION – Tardigrades can withstand 1,000 times more radiation than other animals, median lethal doses of 5,000 Gy (of gamma rays) and 6,200 Gy (of heavy ions) in hydrated animals (5 to 10 Gy could be fatal to a human).

ENVIRONMENTAL TOXINS – Tardigrades are reported to undergo chemobiosis, a cryptobiotic response to high levels of environmental toxins.

EXPOSURE TO OUTER SPACE - Tardigrades are the first known animal to survive after exposure to outer space.

TEMPERATURE - They can survive:

- A few minutes at 151 °C
- 30 years at −20 °
- A few days at −200 °C
- A few minutes at −272 °C

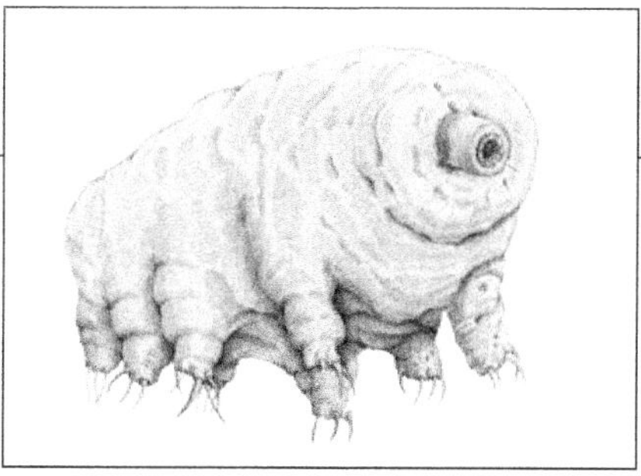

Evolution of Viruses

How did viruses evolve? Are they a streamlined form of something that existed long ago or an ultimate culmination of smaller genetic elements joined together?

The evolutionary history of viruses represents a fascinating, albeit murky, topic for virologists and cell biologists. Because of the great diversity among viruses, biologists have struggled with how to classify these entities and how to relate them to the conventional tree of life. They may represent genetic elements that gained the ability to move between cells. They may represent previously free-living organisms that became parasites. They may be the precursors of life as we know it.

The Basics of Viruses

We know that viruses are quite diverse. Unlike all other biological entities, some viruses, like **poliovirus**, have RNA genomes and some, like **herpesvirus**, have DNA genomes. Further, some viruses (like **influenza virus**) have single-stranded genomes, while others (like **smallpox**) have double-stranded genomes. Their structures and replication strategies are equally diverse. Viruses, do, however, share a few features: First, they generally are quite small, with a diameter of less than 200 nanometers (nm). Second, they can replicate only within a host cell. Third, no known virus contains ribosomes, a necessary component of a cell's protein-making translational machinery.

Are Viruses Alive?

To consider this question, we need to have a good understanding of what we mean by 'life'. Although specific definitions may vary, biologists generally agree that all living organisms exhibit several key properties:
They can grow, reproduce, maintain an internal homeostasis, respond to stimuli, and carry out various metabolic processes. In addition, populations of living organisms evolve over time.

Do viruses conform to these criteria?

'Yes and No. We probably all realize that viruses reproduce in some way. We can become infected with a small number of virus particles — by inhaling particles expelled when another person coughs, for instance — and then become sick several days later as the viruses replicate within our bodies. Likewise we probably all realize that viruses evolve over time. We need to get a flu vaccine every year primarily because the influenza virus changes, or evolves, from one year to the next'. (Nelson & Holmes 2007)

Viruses do not, however, carry out metabolic processes. Most notably, viruses differ from living organisms in that they cannot generate ATP. Viruses also do not possess the necessary machinery for translation, as mentioned above. They do not possess ribosomes and cannot independently form proteins from molecules of messenger RNA. Because of these limitations, viruses can replicate only within a living host cell. Therefore, viruses are obligate intracellular parasites. According to a stringent definition of life, they are non-living. Not everyone, though, necessarily agrees with this conclusion. Perhaps viruses represent a different type of organism on the tree of life - the capsid-encoding organisms, or CEOs.

Where did viruses come from?

There is much debate among virologists on this subject.

Three main hypotheses have been postulated:

1. The **progressive, or escape, hypothesis** states that viruses arose from genetic elements that gained the ability to move between cells;

2. The **regressive, or reduction, hypothesis** asserts that viruses are remnants of cellular organisms; and

3. The **virus-first hypothesis states** that viruses predate or co-evolved with their current cellular hosts.

The Progressive Hypothesis

According to this hypothesis, viruses originated through a progressive process. Mobile genetic elements, pieces of genetic material capable of moving within a genome, gained the ability to exit one cell and enter another. To conceptualize this transformation, let's examine the replication of retroviruses, the family of viruses to which HIV belongs.

Retroviruses have a single-stranded RNA genome. When the virus enters a host cell, a viral enzyme (reverse transcriptase) converts that single-stranded RNA into double-stranded DNA. This viral DNA then migrates to the nucleus of the host cell. Another viral enzyme (integrase) inserts the newly formed viral DNA into the host cell's genome. Viral genes can then be transcribed and translated. The host cell's RNA polymerase can produce new copies of the virus's single-stranded RNA genome. Progeny viruses assemble and exit the cell to begin the process again.

This process very closely mirrors the movement of an important, though somewhat unusual, component of most eukaryotic genomes: retrotransposons. These mobile genetic elements make up an astonishing 42% of the human genome (Lander *et al.*

2001) and can move within the genome via an RNA intermediate. Like retroviruses, certain classes of retrotransposons, the viral-like retrotransposons, encode a reverse transcriptase and, often, an integrase. With these enzymes, these elements can be transcribed into RNA, reverse-transcribed into DNA, and then integrated into a new location within the genome. We can speculate that the acquisition of a few structural proteins could allow the element to exit a cell and enter a new cell, thereby becoming an infectious agent. Indeed, the genetic structures of retroviruses and viral-like retrotransposons show remarkable similarities.

The Regressive Hypothesis

In contrast to the progressive process just described, viruses may have originated via a regressive, or reductive, process. Microbiologists generally agree that certain bacteria that are obligate intracellular parasites, like *hlamydia* and *Rickettsia* species, evolved from free-living ancestors. Indeed, genomic studies indicate that the mitochondria of eukaryotic cells and *Rickettsia prowazekii* may share a common, free-living ancestor (Andersson *et al.* 1998). It follows, then, that existing viruses may have evolved from more complex, possibly free-living organisms that lost genetic information over time, as they adopted a parasitic approach to replication.

Viruses of one particular group, the **Nucleo-Cytoplasmic Large DNA Viruses (NCLDV**s), best illustrate this hypothesis. These viruses, which include smallpox virus and the recently discovered giant of all viruses, Mimivirus, are much bigger than most viruses (La Scola *et al.* 2003). A typical brick-shaped poxvirus, for instance, may be 200 nm wide and 300 nm long. About twice that size, Mimivirus exhibits a total diameter of roughly 750 nm (Xiao *et al.* 2005). Conversely, spherically shaped influenza virus particles may be only 80 nm in diameter, and poliovirus particles have a diameter of only 30 nm, roughly

10,000 times smaller than a grain of salt. The NCLDVs also possess large genomes. Again, poxvirus genomes often approach 200,000 base pairs, and Mimivirus has a genome of 1.2 million base pairs; while poliovirus has a genome of only 7,500 nucleotides total. In addition to their large size, the NCLDVs exhibit greater complexity than other viruses have and depend less on their host for replication than do other viruses. Poxvirus particles, for instance, include a large number of viral enzymes and related factors that allow the virus to produce functional messenger RNA within the host cell cytoplasm.

Because of the size and complexity of NCLDVs, some virologists have hypothesized that these viruses may be descendants of more complex ancestors. According to proponents of this hypothesis, autonomous organisms initially developed a symbiotic relationship. Over time, the relationship turned parasitic, as one organism became more and more dependent on the other. As the once free-living parasite became more dependent on the host, it lost previously essential genes. Eventually it was unable to replicate independently, becoming an obligate intracellular parasite, a virus. Analysis of the giant Mimivirus may support this hypothesis. This virus contains a relatively large repertoire of putative genes associated with translation - genes that may be remnants of a previously complete translation system. Interestingly, Mimivirus does not differ appreciably from parasitic bacteria, such as *Rickettsia prowazekii* (Raoult *et al.* 2004).

The Virus First Hypothesis

The progressive and regressive hypotheses both assume that cells existed before viruses. What if viruses existed first? Recently, several investigators proposed that viruses may have been the first replicating entities. Koonin and Martin (2005) postulated that viruses existed in a pre-cellular world as self-replicating units. Over time these units, they argue, became more organized and more complex. Eventually, enzymes for the synthesis of membranes and cell walls evolved, resulting in the formation of cells. Viruses, then, may have existed before bacteria, archaea, or eukaryotes.

Most biologists now agree that the very first replicating molecules consisted of RNA, not DNA. We also know that some RNA molecules, ribozymes, exhibit enzymatic properties; they can catalyze chemical reactions. Perhaps, simple replicating RNA molecules, existing before the first cell formed, developed the ability to infect the first cells. Could today's single-stranded RNA viruses be descendants of these pre-cellular RNA molecules?

Others have argued that precursors of today's NCLDVs led to the emergence of eukaryotic cells. Villarreal and DeFilippis (2000) and Bell (2001) described models explaining this proposal. Perhaps, both groups postulate, the current nucleus in eukaryotic cells arose from an endosymbiotic-like event in which a complex, enveloped DNA virus became a permanent resident of an emerging eukaryotic cell.

No Single Hypothesis may be Correct

Where viruses came from is not a simple question to answer. One can argue quite convincingly that certain viruses, such as the retroviruses, arose through a progressive process. Mobile genetic elements gained the ability to travel between cells, becoming infectious agents. One can also argue that large DNA viruses arose through a regressive process whereby once-independent entities lost key genes over time and adopted a parasitic replication strategy. Finally, the idea that viruses gave rise to life as we know it presents very intriguing possibilities. Perhaps today's viruses arose multiple times, via multiple mechanisms. Perhaps all viruses arose via a mechanism yet to be uncovered. Today's basic research in fields like microbiology, genomics, and structural biology may provide us with answers to this basic question.

Extract from article by: David R. Wessner, Ph.D. (Dept. of Biology, Davidson College) Nature Education Wessner, D.R. (2010) The Origins of Viruses. *Nature Education 3(9)*:37

Giant Viruses

A **giant virus**, sometimes referred to as a **girus**, is a very large virus, some of which are larger than typical bacteria. All known giant viruses belong to the phylum *Nucleocytoviricota.*

While few giant viruses have been characterized in detail, the most notable examples are the phylogenetically related *mimivirus* and *megavirus*—both belonging to the *Mimiviridae* (aka *Megaviridae*) family, due to their having the largest capsid diameters of all known viruses.

The genomes of many giant viruses encode many unusual genes that are not found in other viruses, including genes involved in glycolysis and the citric acid (Krebs) cycle, fermentation, and the cytoskeleton.

The genomes of these giant viruses are the largest known for all viruses, and contain genes that encode for important elements of translation machinery, a characteristic that had previously been believed to be indicative of cellular organisms.

The two main hypotheses for the origin of these giant viruses are:

- That either they evolved from small viruses, picking up DNA from host organisms, or
- That they evolved from very complicated organisms into the current form which is not self-sufficient for reproduction.

Giant virus name	Capsid diameter (nm)
Bodo saltans virus	~300
Cafeteria roenbergensis virus	300
Klosneuvirus	~300
Mamavirus	500
Megavirus chilensis	440
Mimivirus	500
Pandoravirus	500
Pithovirus	500 x 1500
Tupanvirus	≥450+550

Bodo saltans virus

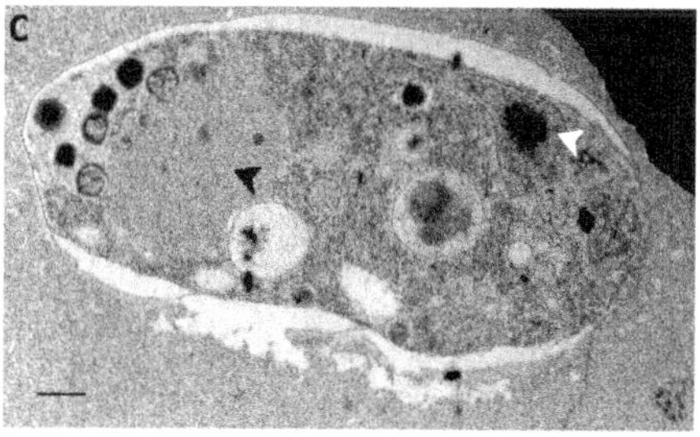

Bodo saltans cell 24 hr post-BsV infection showing degraded intracellular structures and a BsV virus factory (black arrow head)
CC BY-SA 4.0

The **Bodo saltans virus** is a giant virus of the *Mimiviridae* family that infects the protozoa *Bodo saltans*. It has a genome of 1.39 megabases, one of the largest known viral

Cafeteria roenbergensis virus

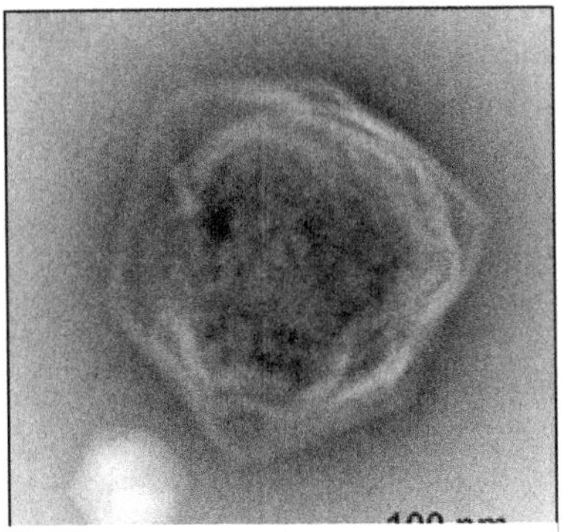

The giant virus CroV with its virophage Mavirus at the lower left

***Cafeteria roenbergensis virus* (CroV)** is a giant virus that infects the marine bicosoecid flagellate *Cafeteria roenbergensis*, a member of the microzooplankton community.

CroV has one of the largest genomes of all marine viruses known, consisting of ~730,000 base pairs of double-stranded DNA. Among its 544 predicted protein-coding genes are several that are usually restricted to cellular organisms. CroV is itself parasitized by a virophage named 'Mavirus'.

Viral protein composition includes 141 encoded proteins that have been identified in CroV, a number believed to be in close proximity to the entirety of the virion proteome. Mature CroV consists of a 300 nm diameter outer protein shell with icosahedral symmetry, an underlying lipid membrane, and an inner core that contains the genome.

The viral genome is primarily a 618,000 base pair strand flanked by large and highly repetitive repeats on both ends of the genome. These large caps are theorized to protect the ends of the protein-coding region, similar to telomeres in eukaryotes. Due to production of transcriptional genes, like that of tRNA synthetase, the virus is able to modify and regulate host translational machinery that results in CroV being less dependent on host-cell components.

Viral reproduction occurs in large constructs known as large cytoplasmic factories or viral factories. This is the site where DNA replication, transcription, and particle assembly are thought to take place.

These factories are also the primary targets of the virophage Mavirus, which utilizes CroV machinery to replicate. Mavirus is a circular double stranded DNA virus. Maviral infection reduces host cell death by interfering with CroV infection and replication. Mavirus integrates into the genome of cells of *Cafeteria roenbergensis*, and thereby confers immunity to the population.

CroV enters cells via phagocytosis. Once inside the cell, the CroV capsid disassembles and the viral proteins and genome are released. CroV does not use the transcription or translation machinery of the host cell. It remains in the cytoplasm, where a 'virus factory' forms and replicates independent of the host cell nucleus.

CroV infects *Cafeteria roenbergensis*, which is a marine zooflagellate. CroV is fatal to the host cell. This impacts coastal ecology because *Cafeteria roenbergensis* feeds on bacteria found in the water. When there are low numbers of *Cafeteria roenbergensis* due to extensive CroV infections, the bacterial latiopopuns rise exponentially.

Klosneuvirus

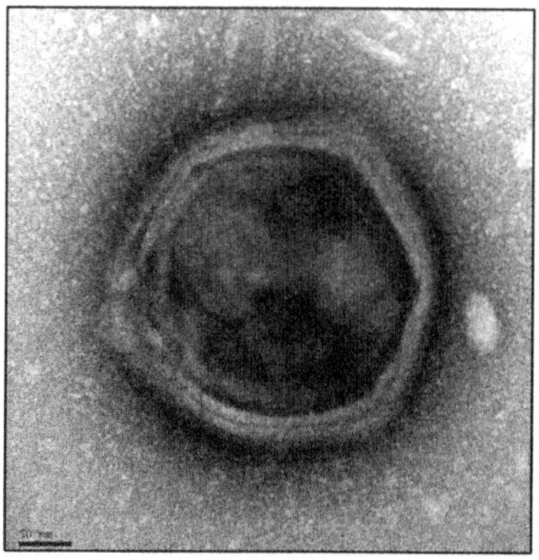

Klosneuvirus (**KNV**, also **KloV**) is a new type of giant virus found by the analysis of low-complexity metagenomes from a wastewater treatment plant in Klosterneuburg, Austria.

It has a 1.57-Mb genome coding unusually high number of genes typically found in cellular organisms, including aminoacyl tRNA synthetases with specificities for 19 different amino acids, over 10 translation factors and several tRNA-modifying enzymes.

Species in this clade include ***Bodo saltans virus*** infecting the kinetoplastid *Bodo saltans*.

Mamavirus

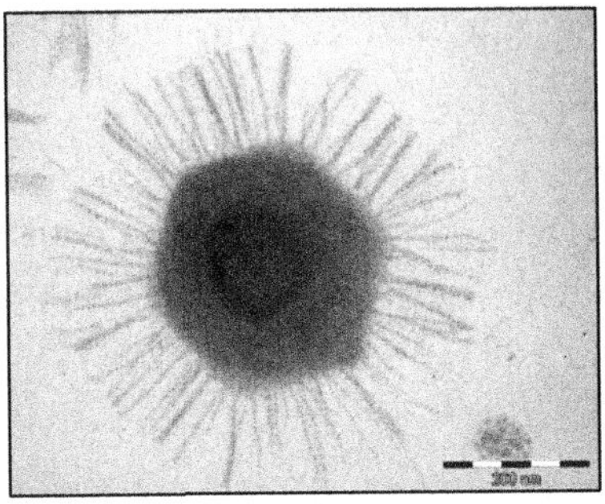

Mamavirus is a large and complex virus in the Group I family Mimiviridae. The virus is exceptionally large, and larger than many bacteria. Mamavirus and other mimiviridae belong to **nucleocytoplasmic large DNA virus** (NCLDVs) family. Mamavirus can be compared to the similar complex virus mimivirus; mamavirus was so named because it is similar to but larger than mimivirus.

Mamavirus, like other mimiviridae, is icosahedral with a core capsid and a peripheral fibre layer. It contains a linear double-stranded DNA genome which has a very high coding density that is characteristic of NCLDVs.

The mimiviridae contain very similar genomes due to gene duplications, and a fair piece of the genome is associated with functions not previously found in a virus.

Mamavirus possesses its own transcription machinery, and it packages transcription proteins in its particles. Transcription is believed to occur in the core particles. The core releases viral DNA and forms a cytoplasmic replication factory where DNA replication begins and transcription of late genes occurs. The replication factory forms around the viral core and expands until it occupies a large fraction of the amoeba cell volume. Later stages of the replication cycle involve partially assembled *procapsids* undergoing DNA packaging.

Sputnik virophage

While the mimiviridae were a surprise themselves, mamavirus contained an even bigger surprise. While looking at mamavirus under the electron microscope, Raoult discovered a second, small virus closely associated with mamavirus which was named Sputnik virophage, a satellite virus. Sputnik contains 21 genes and is tiny compared to mamavirus; however, it is quite powerful in its effects on mamavirus. Sputnik cannot replicate in *acanthamoeba* cells without a simultaneous infection by mamavirus (or mimivirus) so it infects the viral factory that mamavirus creates and hijacks it to replicate its own genome. This causes mamavirus to produce fewer viruses that are often deformed and less effective; there is also evidence of a partial thickening of the capsid. The fact that Sputnik can do this suggests that it is a viral parasite, and thus, was named the first virophage. A virophage is similar to bacteriophage viruses, which infect and sicken bacteria, but virophages infect viruses. Sputnik contains a circular double-stranded DNA of 18,343 base pairs, and is icosahedral in shape. Of the 21 genes it contains, eight encode proteins that have homologues. Of these eight, three are thought to be derived from mamavirus or mimivirus.

This indicates that Sputnik can participate in gene-transfer processes and mediate lateral gene transfer between giant viruses.

Megavirus chilensis

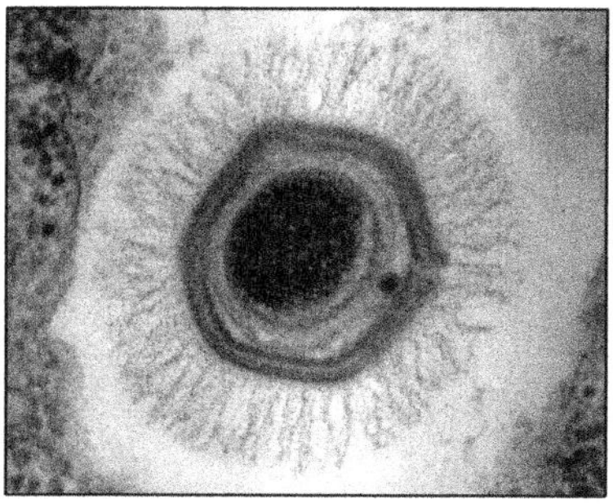

Megavirus is a viral genus containing a single identified species named ***Megavirus chilensis***, phylogenetically related to *Acanthamoeba polyphaga Mimivirus* (APMV). In colloquial speech, Until the discovery of pandoraviruses in

2013, it had the largest capsid diameter of all known viruses, as well as the largest and most complex genome among all known viruses.

The Megavirus particle exhibits a protein capsid diameter of 440nm, enclosed into a solid mesh of bacterial-like capsular material 75nm to 100nm thick. The capsid appears hexagonal, but its icosahedral symmetry is imperfect, due to the presence of the 'stargate', at a single specific vertex of the icosahedron. The stargate is a five-pronged star structure forming the portal through which the internal core of the particle is delivered to the host's cytoplasm. This core is enclosed within two lipid membranes in the particle, also containing a large and diverse complement of viral proteins. Surprisingly, the Megavirus is larger than some bacteria.

The Megavirus chilensis genome is a linear, double-stranded molecule of DNA with 1,259,197 base pairs in length. It exhibits 7 aminoacyl tRNA synthetases, the archetypes of enzymes previously thought only to be encoded by cellular organisms.

While four of these enzymes were known to be present in Mimivirus and Mamavirus (for tyrosine, arginine, cysteine, and methionine), Megavirus exhibits three more (for tryptophan, asparagine, and isoleucine).

Mimivirus

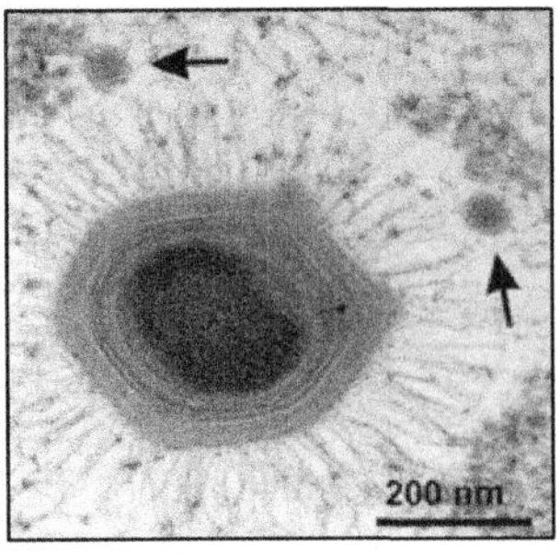

Mimivirus with two satellite Sputnik virophages

Mimivirus is a genus of giant viruses, in the family *Mimiviridae*. Amoeba serve as their natural hosts.

The mimivirus is the fourth-largest virus after *Megavirus chilensis*, *Pandoravirus* and *Pithovirus*. Mimivirus has a capsid diameter of

400nm. Protein filaments measuring 100nm project from the surface of the capsid, bringing the total length of the virus up to 600nm.

Its capsid appears hexagonal under an electron microscope, therefore the capsid symmetry is icosahedral. It does not appear to possess an outer viral envelope, suggesting that the virus does not exit the host cell by exocytosis.

The mimivirus genome is a linear, double-stranded molecule of DNA with 1,181,404 base pairs in length. This makes it one of the largest viral genomes known, outstripping the next-largest virus genome of the *Cafeteria roenbergensis* virus by about 450,000 base pairs.

In addition to the large size of the genome, mimivirus possesses an estimated 979 protein-coding genes, far exceeding the minimum 4 genes required for viruses to exist Analysis of its genome revealed the presence of genes not seen in any other viruses, including aminoacyl tRNA synthetases, and other genes previously thought only to be encoded by cellular organisms. Like other large DNA viruses, mimivirus contains several genes for sugar, lipid and amino acid metabolism, as well as some metabolic genes not found in any other virus.

The stages of mimivirus replication are not well known, but as a minimum it is known that mimivirus attaches to a chemical receptor on the surface of an amoeba cell and is taken into the cell. Once inside, an *eclipse phase* begins, in which the virus disappears and all appears normal within the cell. After about 4 hours small accumulations can be seen in areas of the cell. 8 hours after infection many mimivirus virions are clearly visible within the cell. The cell cytoplasm continues to fill with newly synthesised virions, and about 24 hours after initial infection the cell likely bursts open to release the new mimivirus virions.

Implications for defining 'life'

Mimivirus shows many characteristics which place it at the boundary between living and non-living. It is as large as several bacterial species, possesses a genomic size comparable to that of several bacteria, and codes for products previously not thought to be encoded by viruses (including a kind of collagen). In addition, mimivirus has genes coding for nucleotide and amino acid synthesis, which even some small obligate intracellular bacteria lack. They do, however, lack any genes for ribosomal proteins, making mimivirus dependent on a host cell for protein translation and energy metabolism.

Because its lineage is very old and could have emerged prior to cellular organisms, *Mimivirus* has added to the debate over the origins of life.

Some genes that code for characteristics unique to *Mimivirus*, including those coding for the capsid, have been conserved in a variety of viruses which infect organisms from all domains. This has been used to suggest that *Mimivirus* is related to a type of DNA virus that emerged before cellular organisms and played a key role in the development of all life on Earth. An alternative hypothesis is that there were three distinct types of DNA viruses that were involved in generating the three known domains of life—eukarya, archaea and bacteria. It has been suggested that *Mimivirus* and similar kinds are remnants of a 'fourth domain' of life, and that other giant virus may represent other ancient domains.

Nevertheless, mimivirus does not exhibit the following characteristics, all of which are part of many conventional definitions of life: homeostasis, energy metabolism, response to stimuli, autopoiesis and growth via cellular division (instead of replication via self-assembly of individual components)

Pandoravirus

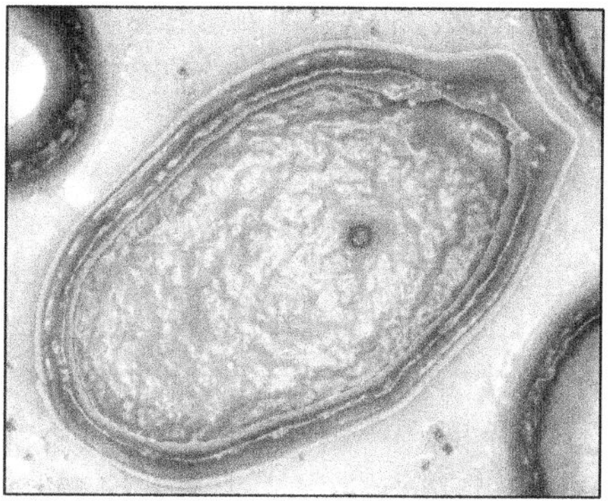

Pandoravirus is a genus of giant virus and the second largest in physical size of any known viral genus. *Pandoraviruses* have double stranded DNA genomes, with the largest genome size (2.5 million base pairs) of any known viral genus.

Pandoraviruses are oval in shape and are about 1μm (1000nm) in length. Other viruses range from 25 to 100nm. In addition to being large physically, Pandoraviruses have a large genome made up of 2,500 genes, compared to only 10 genes on average in other viruses.

For example, the Influenza-A virus contains 7 genes and HIV contains only 9 genes. They are also seemingly capable of moving on their own, unlike other viruses.

Pandoraviruses have double stranded DNA. Like most giant viruses, Pandoraviruses have a viral life cycle. They lack the ability to make their own proteins, rely on the host cells for ATP (energy) and reproduction and also do not contain ribosomes or produce energy to divide. Viral replication and assembly happens simultaneously. In other words, viral DNA is replicated within the cytoplasm of the host cell and assembled into new viral particles followed by lysis of the host cell.

Pandoraviruses do not seem to be harmful to humans. Like other marine viruses, they prey on plankton, which are organisms that live in the water column and form the basis of the food chain for other marine species.

Pithovirus

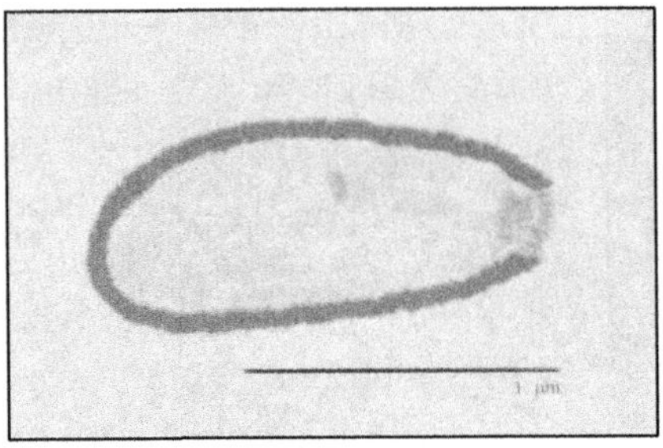

Pithovirus is a genus of giant virus known from two species, ***Pithovirus sibericum***, which infects amoebas, and ***Pithovirus massiliensis***. It is a double-stranded DNA virus, and is a member of the **nucleocytoplasmic large DNA** viruses clade. The 2014 discovery was made when a viable specimen was found in a 30,000-year-old ice core harvested from permafrost in Siberia, Russia.

A specimen of *Pithovirus* measures approximately 1.5μm (1500nm) in length and 0.5μm (500nm) in diameter, making it the largest virus yet found.

It is 50% larger in size than the *Pandoraviridae*, the previous largest-known viruses, is larger than *Ostreococcus* the smallest eukaryotic cell, although *Pandoravirus* has the largest viral genome, containing 1.9 to 2.5 megabases of DNA.

Pithovirus has a thick, oval wall with an opening at one end. Internally, its structure resembles a honeycomb.

The genome of *Pithovirus* contains 467 distinct genes, more than a typical virus but far fewer than the 2556 putative protein-coding sequences found in *Pandoravirus*. Thus, its genome is far less densely packed than any other known virus.

Pithovirus' genome is one circular, double-stranded DNA (dsDNA) chromosome of about 610,000 base pairs, which translate into 467 different proteins. The genome encodes all the proteins needed to produce mRNA. *Pithovirus* therefore undergoes its entire replication cycle in its host's cytoplasm, rather than the more typical method of taking over the host's nucleus.

The rate of mutation of the genome has been estimated to be 2.23×10^{-6} substitutions/site/year. It has been suggested that these viruses evolved at least hundreds of thousands of years ago.

Tupanvirus

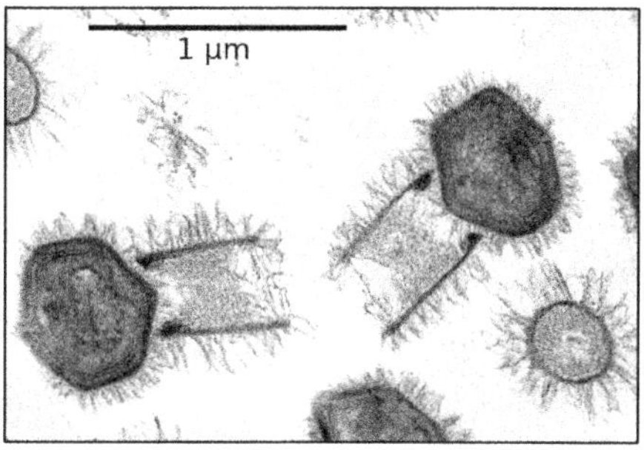

Tupanvirus is a genus of viruses first described in 2018. These are the first viruses reported to possess genes for amino-acyl tRNA synthetases for all 20 standard amino acids.

The genus Tupanvirus was first described in 2018 with the discovery of the two isolates of Tupanviruses found in Soda Lake and deep oceanic sediments samples collected in Brazil. The genus is currently unassigned but hypothesized to be a member of the family *Mimiviridae*, along with the other amoeba-infecting viruses. Unlike the other Mimiviruses in the *Mimiviridae* though, Tupanvirus has a ~550nm long cylindrical tail covered with fibrils that is attached to the base of the capsid. This morphological feature makes tupanvirus the largest described virus (~ 1.2µm in length with the tail) with the longest tail ever observed in a virus.

The genome contains roughly 1.5 million base pairs of double-stranded DNA, coding for 1276–1425 predicted proteins, making it the fourth largest among viral genomes.

As a giant virus, tupanvirus presents the largest translational apparatus within the known virosphere, carrying 20 aminoacyl tRNA synthetase (aaRS) and 70 transfer RNAs (tRNA), while the rest are involved in RNA maturation and splicing, as well as ribosomal protein modification.

Moreover, Tupanviruses contain a number of DNA-independent RNA synthesizing polymerases and enzymes as well as transcription factors that are involved in viral transcription. Furthermore, many genes that encode for processes found in cellular organisms are also found in the Tupanvirus genome, which contains a richer gene set than some bacteria and archaea, and even some eukaryotes.

Viruses have the following characteristics:

- All viruses have either DNA or RNA
- Viruses also have a protein coat which protects the DNA or RNA.
- Viruses cannot multiply outside a host cell
- Viruses are unable to create their own energy
- Viruses are not made of cells and they lack many of the cellular organelles found in other living organisms

Virus Classification

The **Baltimore classification system** can be used to place viruses into one of seven groups based on their manner of mRNA synthesis.

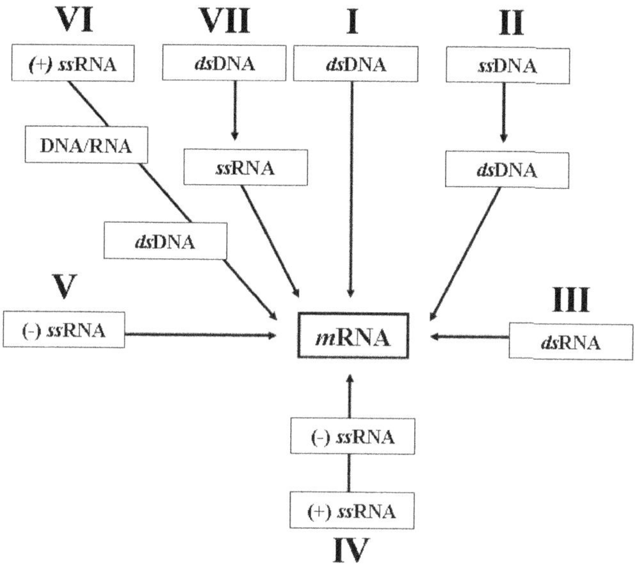

The Baltimore Classification of viruses is based on the method of viral mRNA synthesis.

It is a classification system that places viruses into one of seven groups depending on a combination of their nucleic acid (DNA or RNA, 'strandedness' (single-stranded or double-stranded), sense, and method of replication. These groups are designated by Roman numerals. Classifying viruses according to their genome means that those in a given category will all behave in a similar fashion, offering some indication of how to proceed with further research.

Viruses can be placed in one of the seven following groups:

Baltimore Classification of Viruses

G’p	Nucleic acid	Strandedness and Sense	Examples
I	dsDNA		Adenoviruses, Herpesviruses, Poxviruses
II	ssDNA	+ strand (or ‘sense strand’)	Parvoviruses
III	dsRNA		Reoviruses
IV	(+)ssRNA	+ strand (or ‘sense strand’)	Coronoviruses, Picoviruses, Togaviruses
V	(-)ssRNA	- strand (or ‘antisense’ strand)	Orthomyxoviruses, Rhabdoviruses
VI	ssRNA-RT	+ strand (or ‘sense strand’) RNA with DNA intermediate in life cycle	Retroviruses
V11	dsDNA-RT	- strand (or ‘antisense’ strand) DNA with RNA intermediate in life cycle	Hepadnaviruses

Good Viruses

Biotechnology has been able to convert some viruses into therapeutic agents by reprogramming them to treat diseases. Virotherapy has resulted in the number of good viruses that are being used in virus-based drugs to treat fatal diseases, especially cancer, and to treat certain medical conditions by killing pathogens. Gene over expression adds genetic sequences that compensate for low levels of needed gene expression.

Herpes viruses

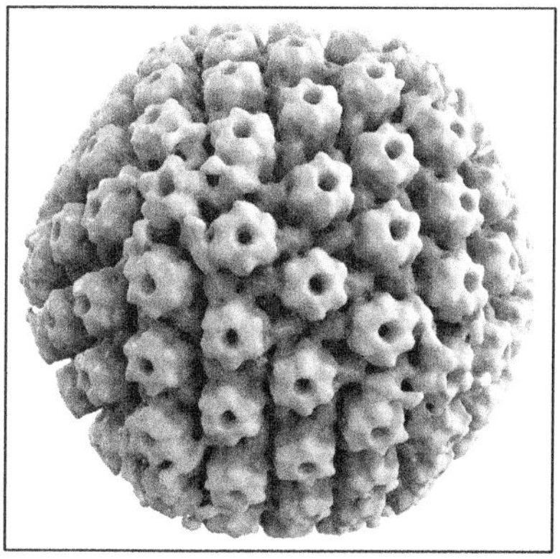

Herpes virus can help human white blood cells to identify cancer cells and cells infected with other pathogenic viruses. They arm white blood cells with antigens that will allow them to identify tumour cells.

This is a virus survival strategy to remain for a longer time within its host and to get rid of competitive viruses to prevent them from harming the host. In the future, modified versions of viruses like these could potentially be used to attack cancer cells.

Pegivirus C

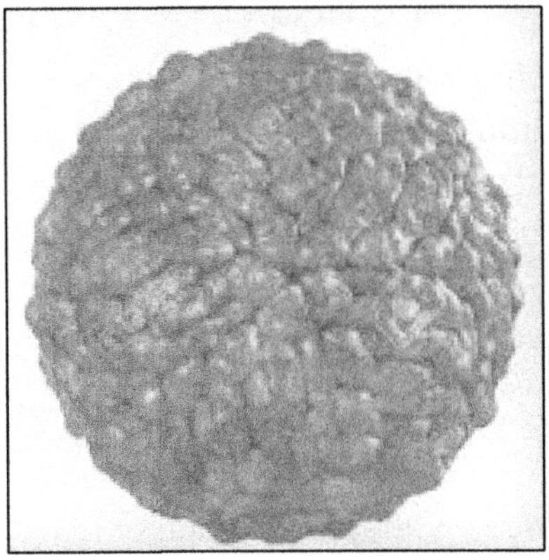

Pegivirus C is a virus that does not cause clinical symptoms. Multiple studies have shown that HIV patients infected with Pegivirus C live longer compared to patients without it.

The virus slows down the progression of the disease by blocking the host receptors necessary for viral entry into the cell and promotes the release of proteins produced by white blood cells that activate inflammation and remove infected cells or pathogens.

Noroviruses

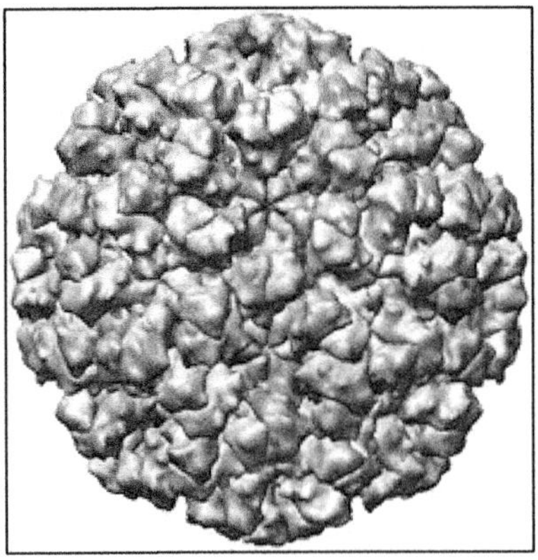

Noroviruses were shown to protect the gut of mice when given antibiotics. The protective gut bacteria that were killed by the antibiotics made the mice susceptible to several gut infections. But in the absence of good bacteria, these *noroviruses* were able to protect their hosts.

Newcastle disease virus

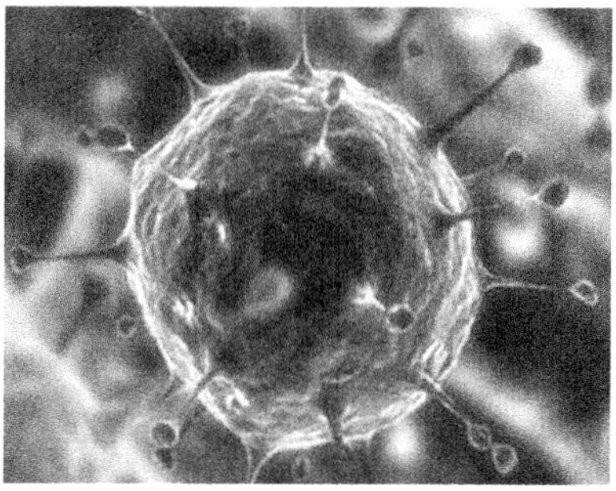

The Newcastle disease virus infects different avian species worldwide, known more generally as Newcastle disease. In the 1850s it was found that Newcastle disease virus (NDV) has cytotoxic effects on certain specific tumor cells. Since then it has been reported that repeated injection of NDV to a patient with acute leukemia treated the disease.

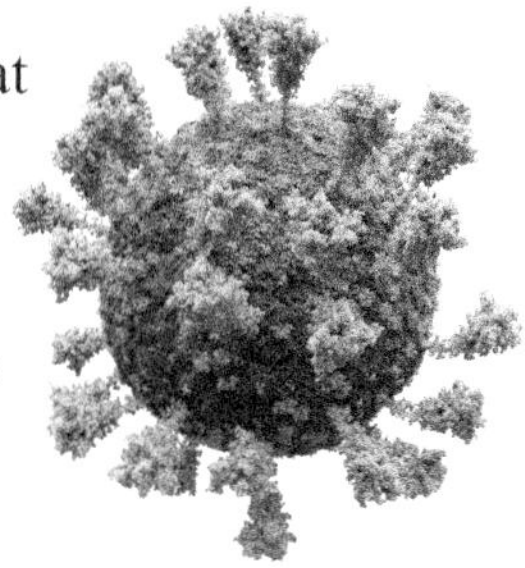

Strains of NDV have been used to treat cancer in humans, since the virus appears to preferentially infect and kill cancerous cells. They have also been used to create viral vector vaccine candidates against **Ebola** and **Covid-19.**

Measles viruses

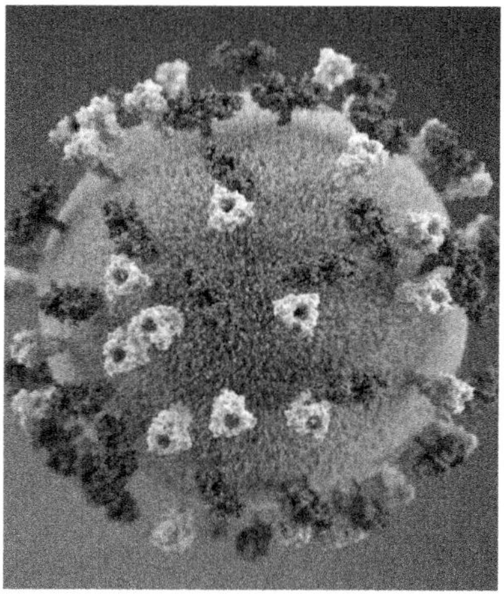

The *Edmonston vaccine strain* of measles *virus* has been effectively used to induce apoptosis via the extrinsic pathway in carcinoma cells. Thus strains of measles have successfully induced necrotic effects in tumour cells resulting in the treatment of cancer. Measles strains work by increasing the apoptotic ability of cells when they become infected cancer cells.

Bacteriophages

'Bacteriophages, or phages, are viruses that infect and destroy germs. These are found in humans in the lining of the mucous membrane of the digestive, respiratory and reproductive systems'

Mucus or mucosa is a thick, amorphous material that provides an anti-bacterial barrier and protects cells below it from infection.

Recent research indicates that the phages living in the in mucus are part of our natural immune system, as they protect the human body from invading the most dangerous germs.

Phages have already been used to treat ***diarrhea*** **and food poisoning caused by** ***Staphylococcus aureus, Salmonella*** **and** ***skin infections*** for nearly a century. Earlier, the primary sources of germs were water, dirt, air, sewage and even body fluids from the infected patients. *Viruses* were isolated from these sources, purified, and then used for treatment.

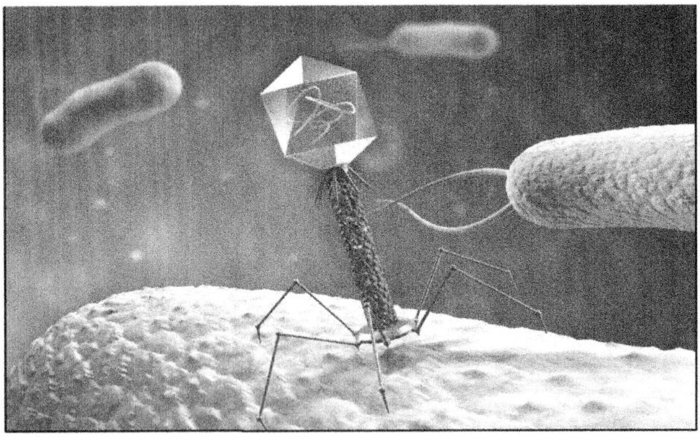

A protein found in bacteriophages — bacterial viruses — has been found to kill E. coli bacteria, offering hope that it could one day fight off antibiotic-resistant bacteria as well. Ref: Medical Diaily.com

DNA	NAKED		ENVELOPED	
ds DNA I	ADENO	Adeno	HERPES	Herpes simplex Varicella zoster
	PAPOVA	Papilloma Polyoma Simian vacuclating	POX	Smallpox Molluscum contagiosum Vaccinia
ss DNA II	PARVO	Parvo B19	*ds* DNA RT VII HEPADNA	Hepatitis B

RNA	NAKED		ENVELOPED	
(+) *ss* RNA IV	ASTRO	ASTRO	CORONA	Covid-19
	CALICI	Norwalk (Noro)		
	HEPE	Hepatitis E	FLAVI	Hepatitis C Dengue Yellow Fever
	PICORNA	Entero Polio Echo Coxsackie Rhino	TOGA	Rubella Alpha
(-) *ss* RNA V			BUNYA	California encephalitis Hanta
			FILO	Ebola Marburg
			ORTHOMYXO	Influenza A Influenza B Influenza C
			PARAMYXO	Measles (Rubeola) Mumps Respiratory syncytial Parainfluenza
			RHABDO	Rabies
ss RNA RT VI	RETRO	HIV		
ds RNA III	REO	Rota		

The gut's 'friendly' viruses

Credit: Maxmen, A. https://doi.org/10.1038/news.2010.353

In the latest exploration into the universe of organisms inhabiting our bodies, microbiologists have discovered new viral genes in faeces. They find that the composition of virus populations inhabiting the tail ends of healthy intestines (as represented in our stools) is unique to each individual and stable over time. Even identical twins — who share many of the same intestinal bacteria — differed in their gut's viral make-up.

More than 80% of the viral genetic sequences found, which included sequences characteristic of both animal and bacterial viruses, have never been reported previously. "This is a largely unexplored world," says Jeffrey Gordon at Washington University in St Louis, Missouri, and an author on the paper, which is published in *Nature* today1. "We are truly distinct life forms — sums of microbial and human parts."

More than 10 trillion bacteria normally inhabit the gastrointestinal tract, where they synthesize essential amino acids and vitamins, produce anti-inflammatory factors and help break down starches, sugars and proteins that people could not otherwise digest. Within and among these bacteria live bacterial viruses, or bacteriophages, which affect bacterial numbers and behaviour as they either prey on bacteria or co-exist with them, shuttling genes from one bacterium to another.

This microscopic dynamic ecosystem affects our lives in ways we still do not fully understand. Indeed, the rise in the incidence of food allergies in Western societies has led to hypotheses that extreme hygiene disrupts the ability of microbes to colonize human guts, resulting in a lack of tolerance to usually harmless foods.

"This study is looking into the genesis of the human body by seeing what viruses within it are up to. … "

To explore this provocative hypothesis, researchers must first understand the complete composition of the microbial ecosystem of the healthy body. To this end, Gordon's group and others are beginning to catalogue the human *'microbiome'*, all the micro organisms living in the human body, using advanced DNA sequencing technologies. Until now, however, such attention has primarily focused on the bacteria rather than viruses.

"This is a wonderful study," says David Relman, a microbiologist at Stanford University in California, who is involved with the US National Institute of Health's Human Microbiome Project. "It could be that viruses are the real drivers of the system because of their ability to modify the bacteria that then modify the human host," he says. "So this study is in some ways looking into the genesis of the human body by seeing what viruses within it are up to."

Microbial truce

According to the new study, bacterial viruses in the terminal gut or colon seem to exist in a more stable state than do similar communities in the environment, such as in the oceans. Faeces from each individual — four pairs of identical twins and their mothers — carried a distinct viral community that varied by less than 5% over the course of a year. The bacterial viruses also appeared to mainly be lying low as *'prophages'* rather than multiplying and killing the bacteria they infect.

"In oceans, the modality of viruses has tended to be predatory," comments Edward DeLong at the Massachusetts Institute of Technology in Cambridge. "Now the interesting thing here is that the system in the faecal micro biota seems to be driven by prophages, which tend to basically integrate their genetic material into the host genome and hide there where it is a much more stable situation."

"This kind of stability implies that there is a symbiosis between bacteria and viruses," comments Martin Blaser at New York University Medical Centre. "This is different from a predator-prey, or an arms race, situation. This is a picture of a more settled existence, in which the different populations are working together."

The team found genes encoding proteins never detected before in bacterial viruses. When in bacteria, these proteins are part of pathways responsible for carbohydrate metabolism and amino-acid synthesis. Viruses carrying such genes might alter them and insert them into gut bacteria, potentially changing a person's metabolism.

Because human nutrition partly depends on the relationship between bacteria and their viruses, understanding the dynamics of that relationship might yield treatments for obesity, allergies and other maladies. "This human ecosystem is quite important because it determines what we can do and what we can eat," says DeLong. "That's why we should care about this."

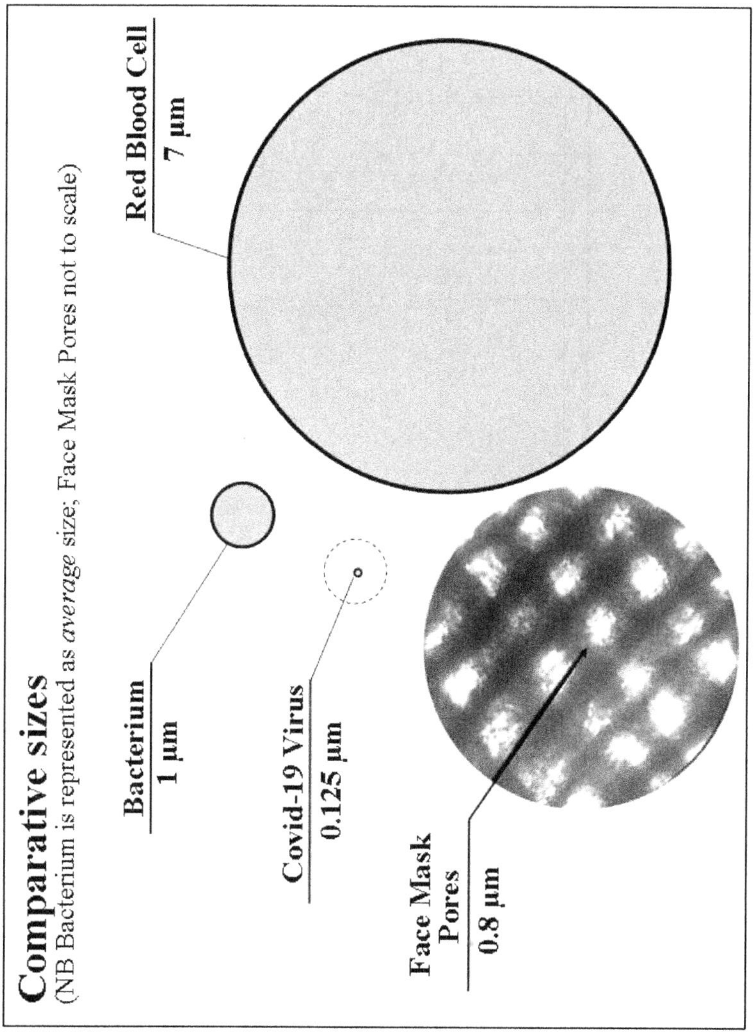

Comparative sizes
(NB Bacterium is represented as *average* size; Face Mask Pores not to scale)
Bacterium
1 µm
Covid-19 Virus
0.125 µm
Face Mask
Pores
0.8 µm
Red Blood Cell
7 µm

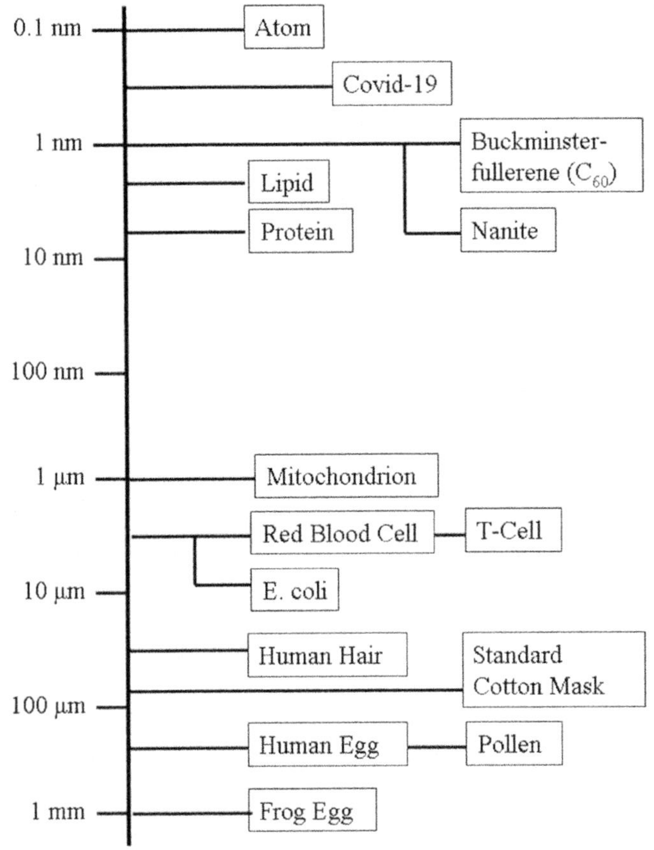

Approximate relative sizes on a logarithmic scale

Glossary

Absorption lines: By measuring the location of lines in astronomical spectra, astronomers can determine the red shift of the receding sources.

Acellular: Life that exists without a cellular structure for at least part of its life cycle.

Accretion: The coming together and cohesion of matter under the influence of gravitation to form larger bodies.

Acritarchs: Organic microfossils, known from approximately 1,800 million years ago.

Actin: A protein that forms (together with myosin) the contractile filaments of muscle cells, and is also involved in motion in other types of cell.

Adenosine Triphosphate: (ATP) An organic compound that provides energy to drive many processes in living cells.

Aerosols: Minute particles suspended in the atmosphere. Dispersal of volcanic aerosols has a drastic effect on Earth's climate.

Agnathan: A group of primitive jawless vertebrates which includes the lampreys, hagfishes, and many fossil fish-like forms.

Albedo Effect: When applied to the Earth is a measure of how much of the Sun's energy is reflected back into space. Overall, the Earth's albedo has a cooling effect.

Algal Reef: An organic reef which has been formed largely of algal remains and in which algae are or were the main lime-secreting organisms.

Allantois: The foetal membrane lying below the *chorion* in many vertebrates, formed as an outgrowth of the embryo's gut. In birds and reptiles it grows to surround the embryo.

Allopatric speciation: Speciation that happens when two populations of the same species become isolated from each other due to geographic changes.

Alvarez Hypothesis: An hypothesis which posits that the mass extinction of the non-avian dinosaurs and many other living things during the Cretaceous–Paleogene extinction event was caused by the impact of a large asteroid on the Earth.

Amiote: An animal whose embryo develops in an *amnion* and *chorion* and has an *allantois*; a mammal, bird, or reptile.

Amnion: The innermost membrane that encloses the embryo of a mammal, bird, or reptile.

Amniotic Egg: An evolutionary invention that allowed the first reptiles to colonize dry land more than 300 million years ago.

Ampullae of Lorenzini: Electroreceptors, sense organs able to detect electric fields. They form a network of mucus-filled pores in the skin of cartilaginous fish. They evolved from the mechanosensory organs of early vertebrates. Most bony fishes and terrestrial vertebrates have lost their Ampullae of Lorenzini.

Anaerobic: Relating to or requiring an absence of free oxygen.

Anapsid: An *amniote* whose skull lacks one or more skull openings (*fenestra*, or *fossae*) near the temples.

Anerobes: A micro-organism that is able to, or can only, live in the absence of oxygen.

Anthropic: Involving or concerning the existence of human life, especially as a constraint on theories of the universe.

Annulated: Having rings; marked with or formed of rings.

Anoxic Event: Period when large expanses of Earth's oceans are depleted of dissolved oxygen (O_2), creating toxic and euxinic waters.

Anthropic: Involving or concerning the existence of human life, especially as a constraint on theories of the universe

Anthropocene: The current geological age, viewed as the period during which human activity has been the dominant influence on climate and the environment.

Apex predator: Usually defined in terms of trophic dynamics, meaning that they occupy the highest trophic levels.

Arboreal: Inhabiting or frequenting trees.

Archaic: Characteristic of an earlier or more primitive time.

Archean: Relating to or denoting the eon that constitutes the earlier (or middle) part of the Precambrian, in which there was no life on the Earth.

Archosaur: Extinct archosaurs include non-avian *dinosaurs*, *pterosaurs*, and extinct relatives of *crocodilians*.

Arroyo: A dry creek, stream bed or gulch that temporarily or seasonally fills and flows after sufficient rain.

Arthropoda: Invertebrates with segmented bodies and jointed limbs. The exoskeleton or cuticles consists of chitin.

Asthenosphere: The upper layer of the Earth's mantle, below the lithosphere.

Astraspidiform: A small group of extinct armoured jawless vertebrates.

Astrobleme: An eroded remnant of a large crater made by the impact of a meteorite or comet.

Astronomical Unit (AU): A unit of length, roughly the distance from Earth to the Sun and equal to 150 million kilometres or 8.3 light minutes.

Atrophied: Having lost effectiveness or vigour due to under use or neglect.

Australopithecine: A fossil bipedal primate with both ape-like and human characteristics, found in Pliocene and Lower Pleistocene deposits (circa 4 million to 1 million years old) in Africa.

Avialan: Any animal belonging to the clade Avialae, including all birds and some dinosaurian relatives.

Axon: A bundle of fibres that uses electrical and chemical signals to transmit sensory and motor information from one body part to another.

Bacillus: A rod-shaped bacterium causing disease.

Baculitidae: A family of extinct ammonoids that lived mostly during the Late Cretaceous.

Basal: Forming or belonging to a bottom layer or base.

Benthic: The collection of organisms living on or in the bottom of a body of water.

Benthopelagic: Relating to species living at the bottom of the sea.

Bifid Claw: A claw which is divided by a deep cleft or notch into two parts.

Bilaterian: An animal having bilateral symmetry. Animals, including humans, with this two-sided symmetry are referred to as being bilaterians.

Black Hole: A region of space having a gravitational field so intense that no matter or radiation can escape.

Bony Fish: *Osteichthyes*, popularly referred to as the bony fish, is a diverse taxonomic group of fish that have skeletons primarily composed of bone tissue. They can be contrasted with the *Chondrichthyes*, which have skeletons primarily composed of cartilage.

Brane: An extended object analogous to the strings of string theory, but having any number of dimensions rather than one dimension.

Brumate: To be in a lethargic state, somewhat analogous to hibernation but not the same. Commonly found in reptiles and in some other animal species.

Buccal Cavity: Relating to the mouth. It has the same meaning as oral. In the context of anatomy, a cavity is a hollow spot inside the body.

Caecum: A pouch connected to the junction of the small and large intestines.

Calcareous: Containing calcium carbonate; chalky.

Capitate: Ending in a distinct compact head.

Carotenoids: Naturally occurring pigments found in plants.

Carpace: The hard upper shell of a tortoise, crustacean, or arachnid.

Cartilaginous: *Chondrichthyes* is a class of jawed fishes having a cartilaginous skeleton. The class includes a diverse group of fishes including sharks, rays, skates and chimaeras. They are mostly marine fishes. The other group of fishes are bony fishes, which are included in the class *Osteichthyes*.

Caudal: At or near the tail or the posterior part of the body.

Centripetal Force: A force that acts on a body moving in a circular path and is directed towards the centre around which the body is moving.

Cephalization: The concentration of sense organs, nervous control, etc., at the anterior end of the body, forming a head and brain, both during evolution and in the course of an embryo's development.

Cephalon: In some *arthropods*, especially *trilobites*, the region of the head composed of fused segments.

Cephalopods: An active predatory mollusc of the large class *Cephalopoda*, such as an octopus or squid.

Chelae: Each of a pair of hinged pincer-like claws terminating the anterior limbs of a crab, lobster, or scorpion, typically curved and sharply pointed and used for feeding, defence, and courtship. Compare with **chelicerae**.

Chelicerae: Either of a pair of appendages in front of the mouth in arachnids and some other arthropods usually modified as pincer-like claws. Compare with **chelae**.

Chimaeras: Any of a family (*Chimaeridae*) of marine cartilaginous fishes with a tapering or threadlike tail and usually no anal fin.

Chironomid: An insect of a family *Chironomidae* that comprises the non-biting midges.

Chloroplasts: In green plant cells which contains chlorophyll and in which photosynthesis takes place.

Choana: Posterior nasal apertures or internal nostrils. They are two openings found at the back of the nasal passage between the nasal cavity and the throat in tetrapods, including humans and other mammals.

Chordates: An animal of the large phylum *Chordata*, comprising the vertebrates together with the *sea squirts* and *lancelets*.

Chorion: The outermost membrane surrounding an embryo of a reptile, bird, or mammal. In mammals it contributes to the formation of the placenta.

Chromophore: The part of a molecule responsible for its colour. The colour that is seen by our eyes is the one not absorbed by the reflecting object within a certain wavelength spectrum of visible light.

Chronospecies: Defined as a single lineage whose morphology changes with time. At some point, it is judged that enough change has occurred that two forms, separated in time and anatomy, once existed.

Cicada: A large *homopterous* insect with long transparent wings, found chiefly in warm countries. The male *cicada* makes a loud, shrill droning noise by vibrating two membranes on its abdomen.

Cilia: A short microscopic hair-like vibrating structure found in large numbers on the surface of certain cells, either causing currents in the surrounding fluid, or, in some *protozoans* and other small organisms, providing propulsion.

Circadian Rhythm: Essentially a 24-hour cycle that runs in the background of the brain, and cycles between sleepiness and alertness at regular intervals to carry out essential functions and processes.

Clade: A group of organisms that are composed of a 'common ancestor' and all its lineal descendants.

Cladistics: A method of classification of animals and plants. It aims to identify and take account of only those shared characteristics which can be deduced to have originated in the common ancestor of a group of species during evolution, not those arising by convergence.

Cloacae: A common cavity at the end of the digestive tract for the release of both excretory and genital products in vertebrates (except most mammals) and certain invertebrates.

Coacervate: A colloid-rich viscous liquid phase that may separate from a colloidal solution on addition of a third component.

Coccus: Any spherical or roughly spherical bacterium.

Columbia: About 1.6 billion years ago Columbia, also known as Nuna or Hudsonland, was one of Earth's ancient supercontinents.

Continental Drift: Hypothesis that the Earth's continents have moved over geologic time relative to each other, thus appearing to have 'drifted' across the ocean bed.

Cornea: The transparent front part of the eye that covers the iris, pupil, and ommatidium when these and others are present.

Corus arteriosus: Also known as *infundibulum*, the *conus arteriosus* is a conical pouch formed from the upper and left angle of the right ventricle in the chordate heart, from which the pulmonary trunk arises.

Cosmine: A spongy, bony material that makes up the dentine-like layers in the scales of the lobe-finned fishes of the class *Sarcopterygii*.

Cosmoid: Fish scales that include layers of cosmine are known as cosmoid scales.

Craniate: An animal that possesses a skull.

Crinoids: An *echinoderm* of the class *Crinoidea*, which comprises the sea lilies and feather stars.

Crown Group: A living monophyletic group, or clade, consisting of the last common ancestor of all living examples, plus all of its descendants.

Cryptobiosis: A metabolic state of life entered by an organism in response to adverse environmental conditions such as desiccation, freezing, and oxygen deficiency.

Ctenoid: Scales that have a variously developed spiny posterior margin.

Ctenii: Spinules or teeth on the posterior margin of a ctenoid scale.

Cultrate: Sharp-edged and pointed; knifelike

Cuticula: A *cuticula*, or cuticle, is any of a variety of tough but flexible, non-mineral outer coverings of an organism, or parts of an organism, that provide protection.

Cycloid: Scales have a smooth posterior margin lacking *ctenii*.

Dark Energy: A theoretical form of energy postulated to act in opposition to gravity and to occupy the entire universe, accounting for most of the energy in it and causing its expansion to accelerate.

Einstein's theories allow for the possible existence of dark energy.

Deccan Traps: A large igneous province of west-central India. It is one of the largest volcanic features on Earth, taking the form of a large shield volcano. It consists of numerous layers of solidified flood basalt that together are more than about 2,000m thick, cover an area of about 500,000 square kilometres, and have a volume of about 1,000,000 cubic kilometres.

Dentine: Hard dense bony tissue forming the bulk of a tooth, beneath the enamel.

Dermal: Of or relating to the skin.

De Sitter Universe: Models the Universe as spatially flat and neglects ordinary matter, so the dynamics of the Universe are dominated by the cosmological constant, thought to correspond to 'dark energy' in our Universe or the 'inflation field' in the early Universe.

Detritivores: Animals which feed on dead organic material, especially plant detritus.

Detritus: Typically includes the bodies or fragments of bodies of dead organisms, and fecal material

Deuterostome: An animals typically characterized by its anus forming before its mouth during embryonic development. Some examples of *deuterostomes* include vertebrates (and thus humans), sea stars, and *crinoids*. In **deuterostomy**, the developing embryo's first opening (the *blastopore*) becomes the anus, while the mouth is formed at a different site later on.

Dewclaw: A digit – vestigial in some animals – on the foot of many mammals, birds, and reptiles (including some extinct orders, like certain *theropods*).

Dimorphic: Occurring in or representing two distinct forms.

Dinosauromorph: A clade of *avemetatarsalian archosaurs* (reptiles closer to birds than to *crocodilians*) that includes the *Dinosauria* (dinosaurs) and some of their close relatives.

Doublet structure: In optics, a doublet is a type of lens made up of two simple lenses paired together.

Ductus arteriosus: A normal foetal artery connecting the main body artery (aorta) and the main lung artery (pulmonary artery). The ductus allows blood to detour away from the lungs before birth. Every baby is born with a *ductus arteriosus*.

Ecdysis: The process of shedding the old skin (in reptiles) or casting off the outer cuticle (in insects and other arthropods).

Echinoderm: A marine invertebrate of the phylum *Echinodermata*, such as a starfish, sea urchin, or sea cucumber.

Ectodermal: The outermost layer of cells or tissue of an embryo in early development, or the parts derived from this.

Ejecta: Material that is forced or thrown out, especially as a result of volcanic eruption, meteoritic impact, or stellar explosion.

Endospore: A resistant asexual spore that develops inside some bacteria cells.

Endothermic: An animal dependent on or capable of the internal generation of heat.

Eponymous: Named after a particular person or group.

Estivate: To spend a hot or dry period in a prolonged state of torpor or dormancy.

Eugeneodont: The meaning of the name Eugeneodont correlates to 'true origin teeth', and comes from the Greek **eu** (good/true), **geneos** (race, kind, origin), and **odon** (tooth). The *Eugeneodontida* disappeared in the Early Triassic.

Eukaryotes: Organisms whose bodies are made up of eukaryotic cells, such as protists, fungi, plants and animals. Eukaryotic cells are cells that contain a nucleus and organelles, and are enclosed by a plasma membrane.

Euxinic: Having a high concentration of hydrogen sulphide and no oxygen.

Event Horizon: As an object approaches the 'point of no return' of a Black Hole, its image appears to freeze and fade away because you cannot see any of the light it emits from that point forward.

Evertible: Capable of being inverted or subjected to inversion.

Exaptation: 'Exaptation' and the related term 'co-option' describe a shift in the function of a trait during evolution. For example, a trait can evolve because it served one particular function, but subsequently it may come to serve another.

Extremophile: A microorganism, especially an archaean, that lives in conditions of extreme temperature, acidity, alkalinity, or chemical concentration.

Eyespots: Photoreceptive organelles found in the flagellate or (motile) cells of green algae and other unicellular photosynthetic organisms such as *euglenids*. They allow the cells to sense light direction and intensity and respond to them, prompting the organisms to either swim towards the light or away from it.

Fimbriae: Small, finger-like projections at the end of the fallopian tubes, through which eggs move from the ovaries to the uterus.

Flagella: Flagella are commonly found in bacteria, but can also be found in *archaea* and *eukaryotic* organisms as well. A flagellum is a lash-like structure that protrudes from the cell body.

Flame cell: A specialized excretory cell found in the simplest freshwater invertebrates, including flatworms, rotifers and *nemerteans*. These are the simplest animals to have a dedicated excretory system. Flame cells function like a kidney, removing waste materials.

Flicker Fusion Rate: The frequency at which an intermittent light stimulus appears to be completely steady.

Foraminifera: Single-celled organisms, members of a phylum or class of *amoeboid protists* characterized by streaming granular ectoplasm for catching food and other uses.

Friedmann expansion: The idea of an evolving universe that contained moving matter.

Ga: Gigaannum or one billion years.

Ganoid: Relating to or being a kind of fish scale that is hard and bony with a shiny surface composed of an enamel-like substance.

Gastroliths: Small stones swallowed by a bird, reptile, or fish to aid digestion in the gizzard.

Glabella: The smooth part of the forehead above and between the eyebrows.

Gluons: Elementary particles that act as 'exchange particles' (or gauge bosons) for the strong force between quarks.

Gondwana: A large landmass often referred to as a supercontinent that formed during the late Neoproterozoic and began to break up during the Jurassic.

Gracile: Having a light, thin body. Used especially in anthropology to describe modern types of human.

Gram negative: Bacteria that have a **thin** *peptidoglycan* layer and **have** an outer lipid membrane.

Gram positive: Bacteria that have a **thick** *peptidoglycan* layer and **no** outer lipid membrane.

Granitoids: A generic term for a diverse category of coarse-grained igneous rocks that consist predominantly of quartz, plagioclase, and alkali feldspar.

Great Dying: The biggest extinction the planet has ever experienced. Happened some 250 million years ago at the time of the Permian-Triassic extinction and was largely caused by greenhouse gases in the atmosphere.

GUT: A **Grand Unified Theory** is a model in particle physics in which, at high energies, the three gauge interactions of the Standard Model comprising the electromagnetic, weak, and strong forces are merged into a single force.

Hadean: A geologic eon preceding the Archean. It began with the formation of the Earth about 4.6 billion years ago.

Halophile: An organism, especially a microorganism, that grows in or can tolerate saline conditions.

Harderian gland: A gland found within the eye's orbit and that occurs in *tetrapods* which possess a nictitating membrane.

Hemibranchs: A gill having lamellae or filaments only on one side.

Hertzprung-Russell: A scatter plot of stars showing the relationship between absolute magnitudes or luminosities versus stellar classifications or effective temperatures.

Heterodont: A set of teeth of various shapes that may serve different functions (e.g. incisors, canines, and molars).

Heterotroph: An organism deriving its nutritional requirements from complex organic substances.

Hipparcos: A scientific satellite of the European Space Agency launched in 1989 and operated until 1993. It was the first space experiment devoted to accurate measurement of the positions of celestial objects on the sky and aimed to collect data centring on an object's speed, velocity, and trajectory.

Holotype: A single type specimen upon which the description and name of a new species is based.

Hominid: A primate of a family *Hominidae* which includes humans and their fossil ancestors, and also (in recent schemes) at least some of the great apes.

Hominini: A primate of a taxonomic tribe (*Hominini*), which comprises those species regarded as human, directly ancestral to humans, or very closely related to humans.

Hominoid: A primate of a group that includes humans, their fossil ancestors, and the anthropoid apes.

Homologous: Similar in position, structure, and evolutionary origin but not necessarily in function.

Humerus: The long bone in the upper arm. It is located between the elbow joint and the shoulder. At the elbow, it connects primarily to the ulna, as the forearm's radial bone connects to the wrist.

Ileum: The third portion of the small intestine, between the jejunum and the caecum.

Impactor: A meteorite impact, occurring when a rocky, metallic (typically iron), or icy body that had been orbiting the Sun passes through the atmosphere to hit the Earth's surface.

Integument: A natural outer covering or coat, such as the skin of an animal or the membrane enclosing an organ.

Kellwasser Event: Event which occurred around the time established by the boundary between the Frasnian and the Famennian stages of late Devonian when 19% of all families and 50% of all genera became extinct.

Kelvin: Although initially defined by the freezing point of water the Celsius scale is now officially a derived scale, defined in relation to the Kelvin temperature scale. Zero on the Celsius scale (0°C) is now defined as equivalent to 273.15K, with a temperature difference of 1^0C equivalent to a difference of 1K, meaning the unit size in each scale is the same. This means that 100°C, previously defined as the boiling point of water, is now defined as the equivalent to 373.15K.

Kleptoplasty: A symbiotic phenomenon whereby plastids, notably chloroplasts from algae, are sequestered by host organisms. The word is derived from *kleptes* (κλέπτης), Greek for thief.

Konservat-Lagerstätte: Sites of deposits known for the extraordinary preservation of fossilized life forms, especially where the soft parts are preserved.

Kuiper Belt: A region of the Solar System beyond the orbit of Neptune, believed to contain many comets, asteroids, and other small bodies made largely of ice.

Labyrinthodont: Labyrinthodont (name meaning 'maze-toothed') was a subclass of amphibian which existed from 395 to 120 million years ago. It is ancestral to all terrestrial vertebrates. This was the first amphibious creature to appear in Primeval.

Lacrimial Bone: A small thin bone making up part of the front inner wall of each orbit and providing a groove for the passage of the lacrimal ducts.

Lamella: A thin layer, membrane, or plate of tissue, especially in bone.

Lapetus Ocean: An ocean that existed in the late Neoproterozoic and early Paleozoic eras.

Lectotype: A biological specimen or illustration later selected to serve as definitive type example of a species or subspecies when the original author of the name did not designate a holotype.

Lepidosireniformes: An order of lungfish with a cylindrical body, paired lungs, and nearly filamentous pectoral and pelvic fins.

Leptons: Subatomic particles, such as electrons, muons, or neutrinos, which do not take part in the strong interaction.

Lissamphibian: Any of the living amphibians, of the subclass *Lissamphibia*, including the frog and salamander families.

Lithology: The study of the general physical characteristics of rocks.

Lithosphere: The rigid outer part of the Earth, consisting of the crust and upper mantle.

Lithospheric Plates: Regions of Earth's crust and upper mantle that are fractured into plates that move across a deeper plasticine mantle.

Lobe-finned: A fish of a largely extinct group having fleshy lobed fins, including the probable ancestors of the amphibians. Compare with ray-finned fish.

Lobopodian: The *lobopodians*, members of the informal group *Lobopodia* (from the Greek, meaning 'blunt feet'), are *panarthropods* with stubby legs called *lobopods*.

Local Group: The galaxy group comprising 54 galaxies and which includes the Milky Way. It has a total diameter of roughly10 million light-years; 9×10^{22} metres and a total mass of the order of 2×10^{12} solar masses.

Metacarpals: Form a transverse arch to which the rigid row of distal carpal bones are fixed.

Metazoan: Any of a group (*Metazoa*) that comprises all animals having the body composed of cells differentiated into tissues and organs and usually a digestive cavity lined with specialized cells.

Methane Clathrate: A solid compound in which a large amount of methane is trapped within a crystal structure of water, forming a solid similar to ice.

Methanogen: A methane-producing bacterium, especially an *Archaean* which reduces carbon dioxide to methane.

Methanogenisis: The production of methane by bacteria or other living organisms.

Microbiome: The microorganisms in a particular environment, including the body or a part of the body. (Replaces old term of 'flora')

Microorganism: A microscopic organism, especially a bacterium, virus, or fungus which may exist in its single-celled form or as a colony of cells.

Microfossils: Fossils that are generally between 0.001mm and 1mm in size, the visual study of which requires the use of light or electron microscopy.

Microvilli: The millions of tiny, hair-fine, finger-like protrusions on the surface cells of *epithelium* which greatly increase the effective surface area so as to facilitate absorption.

Mitochondrion *(pl mitochondria)*: An organelle found in large numbers in most cells, in which the biochemical processes of respiration and energy production occur. It has a double membrane, the inner part being folded inwards to form layers (*cristae*).

Monogenesis: The theory that humans are all descended from a single pair of ancestors. Also called *monogeny*.

Monoplyletic: A group of organisms descended from a common evolutionary ancestor or ancestral group, especially one not shared with any other group.

Multicellular: Having, made up of, or involving more than one and usually many cells especially of living matter. It is probable that, with a few exceptions, all the cells in a *multicellular* organism have the same genetic information encoded in the chains of nucleotide bases that make up their DNA.

Mya: Million years ago.

Myomeres: Blocks of skeletal muscle tissue arranged in sequence, commonly found in aquatic *chordates.*

Nematocyst: A specialized cell in the tentacles of a jellyfish or other coelenterate, containing a barbed or venomous coiled thread that can be projected in self-defence or to capture prey.

Neocortex: A part of the cerebral cortex concerned with sight and hearing in mammals, regarded as the most recently evolved part of the cortex.

Neural Arch: An arch of bone or cartilage of a vertebra that is situated posterior to a vertebral body.

Neutrinos: A neutral subatomic particle with a mass close to zero and half-integral spin, which rarely reacts with normal matter.

Niche Partitioning: Refers to the process by which natural selection drives competing species into different patterns of resource use or different niches.

Nitrogen Fixation: The chemical processes by which atmospheric nitrogen is assimilated into organic compounds, especially by certain *microorganisms* as part of the nitrogen cycle.

Noetics: A branch of metaphysics concerning the study of the mind as well as intellect. It covers the field of thinking and knowing, as well as mental operations.

Notochord: An embryonic midline structure common to all members of the phylum *Chordata*, providing both mechanical and signalling cues to the developing embryo. In vertebrates, the notochord is replaced by the *vertebral column*, and becomes the cartilaginous substance between vertebrae.

Nucleoid: An irregularly shaped region within the prokaryotic cell that contains all or most of the genetic material.

Nucleosynthesis: The fusion of heavy elements from lighter ones.

Occipital: Relating to or situated in the back of the head.

Occlusion: A blockage or closing of a blood vessel or hollow organ, or the position of the teeth when the jaws are closed.

Ocelli: Unlike compound eyes, *ocelli* do not form a complex image of the environment, but are used to detect movement. Most *arthropods* possess *ocelli.* Some species of *arthropod* do not possess compound eyes and only have *ocelli.*

Odontodes: About 500 million years ago, jawed vertebrates evolved exoskeletal body armours. It is believed that teeth of jawed vertebrates evolved by modifications of the ridges of tubercles on vertebrate body armour. These '*dermal teeth*' were hard structures found on the external surfaces of animals or near internal openings.

Oldowan: The Oldowan was a widespread stone tool archaeological industry in prehistory.

Ommatidium: Each of the optical units under the cornea that make up the compound eye of an insect.

Omnivorous: Feeding on a variety of food of both plant and animal origin.

Onychophoran: A terrestrial invertebrate of the small phylum *Onychophora*, which comprises the velvet worms.

Oort cloud: A spherical cloud of small rocky and icy bodies postulated to orbit the Sun beyond the orbit of Pluto and up to 1.5 light years from the Sun, and to act as a reservoir of comets.

Operculum: The covering of the gills of a fish.

Opsin: A group of proteins made light-sensitive via the *chromophore retinal* found in photoreceptor cells of the retina.

Ornithischian: Relating to or denoting herbivorous dinosaurs of an order distinguished by having a pelvic structure resembling that of birds. Compare with Saurischian.

Ortholog: A homologous gene that is related to those in different organisms by descent from the DNA of a 'common ancestor'.

Osmolyte: An *organic solute* that helps cells adapt to dehydration or fluid excess. Osmolytes are generated within cells in response to osmotic stresses.

Ossified: Having turned into bone or bony tissue. (refer to Petrified)

Osteichthyes: Popularly referred to as the 'bony fish'.

Ozone Layer: A layer in the Earth's stratosphere at an altitude of about 10km containing a high concentration of ozone, which absorbs most of the ultraviolet radiation reaching the Earth from the Sun.

Pachyostosis: A non-pathological condition in vertebrate animals in which the bones experience a thickening, generally caused by extra layers of lamellar bone.

Paedomorphosis: Phylogenetic change that involves retention of juvenile characters by the adult.

Palatal Fangs: Any sharp teeth occurring on the palate.

Paleo-Tethys Ocean: An ocean located along the northern margin of the paleo-continent Gondwana.

Pangaea Ultima: The hypothesised future supercontinent, Pangaea is a future supercontinent, earning its name due to its similarities with the previous supercontinent, Pangaea.

Panmixia: Random mating within a breeding population.

Panspermia: The theory that life on the earth originated from microorganisms or chemical precursors of life present in outer space and able to initiate life on reaching a suitable environment.

Papilla: A small rounded protuberance on a part or organ of the body.

Pathogenic: Causing or capable of causing disease.

Patrilineal: Relating to or based on relationship to the father or descent through the male line.

Peduncle: A stalk-like part by which an organ is attached to an animal's body, or by which a barnacle or other sedentary animal is attached to a substrate.

Pelagic: Relating to the open sea.

Pelycosaurs: The *pelycosaurs* appear to have been a group of *synapsids* that have direct ancestral links with the mammals, having differentiated teeth and a developing hard palate.

Perfusion: The passage of blood, a blood substitute, or other fluid through the blood vessels or other natural channels in an organ or tissue.

Pericardial cavity: The pericardial cavity contains the heart, the muscular pump that drives the blood around the cardiovascular system.

Periplast: One of three types of cell-covering of three classes of algae.

Peritrichous: Covered all over with uniformly distributed flagella.

Petrified: Organic matter changed into a stony substance. *(refer to Ossified)*

Photon: A type of elementary particle that serves as the quantum of the electromagnetic field, including electromagnetic radiation such as light and radio waves, and the force carrier for the electromagnetic force.

Photosynthetic: Relating to or involved in the process by which green plants, and some other organisms, use sunlight to synthesize nutrients from carbon dioxide and water:

Phototactic: The bodily movement of a motile organism in response to light, either towards the source of light (positive phototaxis) or away from it (negative phototaxis).

Phototroph: An organism that uses energy from sunlight to synthesize organic compounds for nutrition.

Phyllopod Bed: The most famous fossil-bearing member of the Burgess Shale fossil *Lagerstätte*. It was the source of 95% of the fossils collected.

Phylogeny: A branching diagram or a tree showing the evolutionary relationships among various biological species or other entities based upon similarities and differences in their physical or genetic characteristics.

Phylum: A principal taxonomic category that ranks above class and below kingdom.

Picoplankton: The fraction of plankton composed by cells between 0.2 and 2μm that can be either prokaryotic and eukaryotic *phototrophs* and *heterotrophs*. They have an important role in making up a significant portion of the total biomass of phytoplankton communities.

Pineal Gland: From the point of view of biological evolution, the pineal gland is a kind of atrophied photoreceptor. In some species of amphibians and reptiles it is linked to a light-sensing organ, known as the 'parietal eye'.

Piscivorous: A carnivorous animal that eats primarily fish.

Plate Tectonics: A theory explaining the structure of the Earth's crust and many associated phenomena resulting from the interaction of rigid lithospheric plates which move slowly over the underlying mantle.

Plesiomorphic: An evolutionary trait that is homologous within a particular group of organisms, but is not unique to members of that group.

Pollicis longus: This muscle is unique to humans, being either rudimentary or absent in other primates.

Polychaete: A marine annelid worm of the class Polychaeta. A *'Bristle Worm'*.

Posteriad: Towards the posterior part or surface of the body; to the rear of; posteriorly. *Opposed to anteriad.*

Pre-maxilla: One of a pair of small cranial bones at the very tip of the upper jaw of many animals, usually, but not always, bearing teeth.

Primatomorph: A clade of placental mammals containing two orders: *Dermoptera* and *Primates*.

Proboscis: The nose of a mammal, especially when it is long and mobile such as the trunk of an elephant or the snout of a tapir.

Prokaryotic: A microscopic single-celled organism which has neither a distinct nucleus with a membrane nor other specialized organelles, including the *bacteria* and *cyanobacteria*. Compare with *eukaryote*.

Prosimians: Considered to have characteristics that are more 'primitive' (ancestral or plesiomorphic) than those of *simians* (monkeys, apes, and humans).

Prosoma: The fused head and thorax of spiders and other chelicerate arthropods.

Pseudosuchians: One of two major divisions of *Archosauria*, including living *crocodilians* and all *archosaurs* more closely related to *crocodilians* than to birds.

Pterygoid Arches: A paired bone forming part of the palate of many vertebrates.

Pupae: Insects in their inactive immature form between larvae and adults, e.g. Chrysalides.

Pygidium: The terminal part or hind segment of the body in certain invertebrates. In groups other than insects, it contains the *anus* and, in females, the *ovipositor* and is composed of fused body segments.

Pygostyle: In a bird, a triangular plate formed of the fused caudal vertebrae, typically supporting the tail feathers.

Quadrupedalism: Four-footed; using all four feet for walking and running.

Quarks: Any of a number of subatomic particles carrying a fractional electric charge, postulated as building blocks of the hadrons.

Ramus: (*pl rami*) an arm or branch of a bone, in particular those of the ischium and pubes or of the jawbone.

Ray-finned: The ray-finned fishes are so-called because their fins are webs of skin supported by bony or horny spines (rays), Compare with lob-finned fish.

Red Shift: The displacement of spectral lines towards longer wavelengths (the red end of the spectrum) in radiation from distant galaxies and celestial objects.

Rhamphotheca: The horny sheath composed of modified scales of a bird's bill.

Rhipidistian: Also known as *Dipnotetrapodomorpha*, is a clade of lobe-finned fishes which includes the *tetrapods* and lungfishes.

Right Ascension: The distance of a point east of the '*First Point of Aries*', measured along the celestial equator and expressed in hours, minutes, and seconds.

Robust: The variables between populations, and species of hominoids, all of which reflect great variation in the magnitudes of biomechanical loads and the behaviours that produce them.

Radula: An anatomical structure used by mollusks for feeding, sometimes compared to a tongue. It is a minutely toothed, chitinous ribbon, which is typically used for scraping or cutting food before the food enters the oesophagus.

Roche Limit: The distance within which the gravitational field of a large body is strong enough to prevent any smaller body from being held together by gravity.

Rostral: Situated or occurring near the front end of the body, especially in the region of the nose and mouth.

Rugose: Full of wrinkles.

Sagittal Crest: A bony ridge on top of the skull to which chewing muscles attach.

Sanukitoid: A variety of high-Mg *granitoid* found in convergent margin settings.

Saurischian: Relating to or denoting dinosaurs of an order distinguished by having a pelvic structure resembling that of lizards. Compare with Ornithischian.

Scleritic: A medical condition in which body tissue or organs become harder.

Scute: A bony external plate or scale overlaid with horn, as on the shell of a turtle, the skin of *crocodilians*, and the feet of birds.

Selene: Selene was a Titan goddess in Greek mythology, daughter of the Titans Hyperion and Theia. She had two siblings, Helios and Eos.

Septum: *(pl. septa)* A dividing wall, membrane, or the like, in a plant or animal structure.

Sessile: Lacks the ability of self-locomotion and is predominantly immobile. Those animals which are attached to a substrate.

Shatter Cone: A conical fragment of rock that has striations radiating from the apex and that is formed by high pressure (as from volcanism or meteorite impact).

Shocked Quartz: Found worldwide, and occurs in the thin C-Pg boundary layer, which occurs at the contact between Cretaceous and Paleogene rocks. This is further evidence (in addition to iridium enrichment) that the transition between the two geologic periods was caused by a large impact.

Siberian Traps: A large region of volcanic rock, known as a large igneous province in Siberia, Russia. The massive eruptive event that formed the traps is one of the largest known volcanic events in the last 500 million years.

Sink: Any area that absorbs or holds more carbon than it gives off. A carbon sink absorbs carbon dioxide from the atmosphere.

Siphonophores: Colonial *hydrozoans* that reproduce asexually through a budding process.

Speciation: The formation of new biological species as a result of isolation mutation selection. Once two groups are isolated different mutations occur in each group.

Spherules: Tiny glass spherules are created during an impact, generating such intense heat that the crust melts and sprays into the air. The molten material hardens and falls back down as tiny glass beads.

Spiracles: An external respiratory opening, especially each of a number of pores on the body of an insect, or each of a pair of vestigial gill slits behind the eye of a cartilaginous fish.

Spirilla: (*sing, Spirillum*) are a group of bacteria characterized by a corkscrew (spiral) appearance. They are Gram-negative bacteria and are characterized by motile structures known as flagella.

Standard Candle: A standard candle is an astronomical object that has a known absolute magnitude.

Stegocephalian: A group containing all four-limbed vertebrates.

Stem Group: The classification of fossils that would not otherwise obey systematics based on living organisms.

Stereom: A calcium carbonate material that makes up the internal skeletons found in all echinoderms, both living and fossilized forms.

Sternum: A long, flat bone that protects the underlying muscles, organs, and important arteries within the chest.

Stipitate: Having or borne on a stipe (a stalk or stem).

Subduction: Where the oceanic lithosphere of a tectonic plate converges with the less dense lithosphere of a second plate, the heavier plate dives beneath the second plate and sinks into the mantle.

Sub-trapezoidal: A trapezoid with rounded corners.

Suspensory: Holding and supporting an organ or part.

Swim Bladder: An internal gas-filled organ that contributes to the ability of many bony fish (but not cartilaginous fish) to control their buoyancy.

Synapse: A junction between two nerve cells, consisting of a minute gap across which impulses pass by diffusion of a neurotransmitter.

Synapsid: One of the two major groups of animals that evolved from basal amniotes, the other being the *sauropsids*, the group that includes reptiles (lizards and snakes) as well as *crocodilians* and *dinosaurs* (birds).

Synonymisation: The identification of two taxonomic terms as synonyms, thus equating two potentially disparate categories.

Talon: Hooked claw.

Taxon: A taxonomic group of any rank, such as a species, family, or class.

Tectonic Plates: A massive, irregularly shaped slab of solid rock generally composed of both continental and oceanic lithosphere.

Teleost: A fish of a large group that comprises all ray-finned fishes.

Telson: The last segment in the abdomen, or a terminal appendage to it, in crustaceans, *chelicerates*, and embryonic insects.

Tendonous: Consisting of tendons.

Theia: A hypothesized ancient planet in the early Solar System that, according to the giant-impact hypothesis, collided with the early Earth around 4.5 billion years ago, with some of the resulting ejected debris gathering to form the Moon.

Thermophile (Adj. Thermophylic**):** A bacterium or other microorganism that grows best at higher than normal temperatures.

Theropod: A carnivorous dinosaur of a group whose members were typically bipedal and ranged from small and delicately built to very large.

Therapsid: A fossil reptile of a Permian and Triassic order, the members of which are related to the ancestors of mammals.

Tidal Force: The ***differential force of gravity*** which arises because the force exerted on one body by another is not constant across the diameter in that the side which is the nearest to the second body is subject to more gravitational force compared to the side farther away.

Tomia: (*Sing. Tomium*) are the cutting edges of the two mandibles. In most birds, these range from rounded to slightly sharp.

Traps: Flood basalts forming a step-like landscape. This step-like landscape is the origin of the name 'trap rock' after the Swedish word 'trappa' which means 'stair step.'

Trochanters: Any of a number of bony protuberances by which muscles are attached to the upper part of the thigh bone.

Unguals: (from Latin *unguis*, i.e. nail) A highly modified distal toe bone which ends in a hoof, claw, or nail.

Unicellular: An organism that consists of a single cell, meaning that all life processes, such as reproduction, feeding, digestion, and excretion occur in one cell.

Uniformitarianism: The assumption that the same natural laws and processes that operate in our present-day scientific observations have always operated in the universe in the past and apply everywhere in the universe.

Vascularize: To develop or extend blood vessels or other fluid-bearing vessels or ducts.

Vegetative: Relating to or denoting reproduction or propagation achieved by asexual means, either naturally or artificially.

Vermiform: Resembling or having the form of a worm.

Vestigial: Of organs or parts of the body, degenerate, rudimentary, or atrophied organs, having become functionless in the course of evolution.

Vibrissae: Long stiff whiskers growing around the mouth or elsewhere on the face of many mammals, used as organs of touch.

Vicariance: The geographical separation of a population, typically by a physical barrier such as a mountain range or river, resulting in a pair of closely related species.

Viluy Traps: The Viluy Large igneous province, which includes the Viluy traps. They cover most of the present day north-eastern margin of the Siberian Platform.

Xanthroperin: **A** yellow, crystalline solid that occurs mainly in the wings of butterflies and in the urine of mammals.

Zygapophyses: Any facets of vertebrae that articulate with each other.

Paradigm Shift

Thomas Samuel Kuhn made several claims concerning the progress of scientific knowledge: that scientific fields undergo periodic 'paradigm shifts' rather than solely progressing in a linear and continuous way, and that these paradigm shifts open up new approaches to understanding what scientists would never have considered valid before; and that the notion of scientific truth, at any given moment, cannot be established solely by objective criteria but is defined by a consensus of a scientific community.

Competing paradigms are frequently incommensurable; that is, they are competing and irreconcilable accounts of reality. Thus, our comprehension of science can never rely wholly upon 'objectivity' alone. Science must account for subjective perspectives as well, since all objective conclusions are ultimately founded upon the subjective conditioning/worldview of its researchers and participants.

- A scientific revolution occurs, according to Kuhn, when scientists encounter anomalies which cannot be explained by the universally accepted paradigm within which scientific progress has thereto been made. The paradigm, in Kuhn's view, is not simply the current theory, but the entire worldview in which it exists, and all of the implications which come with it.

- When enough significant anomalies have accrued against a current paradigm, the scientific discipline is thrown into a state of *crisis*... Eventually a new paradigm is formed, which gains its own new followers, and an intellectual 'battle' takes place between the followers of the new paradigm and the hold-outs of the old paradigm. . *Thomas S. Kuhn*

Kuhn used the duck-rabbit optical illusion to demonstrate the way in which a paradigm shift could cause one to see the same information in an entirely different way.

Duck or rabbit?

- "...a new scientific truth does not triumph by convincing its opponents and making them see the light, but rather because its opponents eventually die, and a new generation grows up that is familiar with it." *Max Planck*

    - Newtonian physics to relativistic physics
    - Maxwell's theory of aether to Einstein's universe (spacetime)

- Science is a human endeavour and therefore susceptible to human biases, prejudices, and politics.

    - "Science seems susceptible to dogma, just like religion ... but he holds to the opinion that science has not convincingly shown that one species can evolve into another ... I think there's a lot of problems with evolutionary dogma." *Dr. Gregory J. Brewer*

- **Intelligent Design** could be reconciliation between ultimate reality and physical reality.

The argument in favour of Intelligent Design has two parts:

- Evolutionary theory does not fully explain the origin and development of life on Earth Life on Earth, and more generally:

- The universe shows so much order, purpose and design that there **must** have been a designer.

Intelligent Design holds to the theory that life, or the Universe, cannot have arisen by chance and was designed and created by some intelligent entity.

Intelligent Design

Text summarised from Wikipedia 'Intelligent Design'

Intelligent Design has been defined by its proponents as the idea that "certain features of the Universe and of living things are best explained by an intelligent cause." This 'intelligent cause' is assumed to be the result of actions by one or more omnipotent super agencies often termed as being a 'god-like' entity. Various concepts are at the root of the present understanding of Intelligent Design. These are detailed below:

Irreducible Complexity

The term 'irreducible complexity' was introduced by biochemist Michael Behe in 1996 when he defined it as 'a single system which is composed of several well-matched interacting parts that contribute to the basic function, wherein the removal of any one of the parts causes the system to effectively cease functioning'.

Intelligent design advocates assert that **natural selection** could not create irreducibly complex systems, because the selectable function is present only when all parts are assembled.

Critics point out that the 'irreducible complexity' argument assumes that the necessary parts of a system have always been necessary and therefore could not have been added sequentially. They argue that something that is at first merely advantageous can later become necessary as other components change. Furthermore, they argue, evolution often proceeds by altering pre-existing parts or by removing them from a system, rather than by adding them. This is sometimes called the '*scaffolding objection*' by an analogy with scaffolding, which can support an 'irreducibly complex' building until it is complete and able to stand on its own.

Specified Complexity

In 1986 Charles B. Thaxton, a proponent of *special creation,* used the term 'specified complexity' from **information theory** when claiming that messages transmitted by DNA in the cell were specified by intelligence, and must have originated through the intervention of an intelligent agent.

The **intelligent design** concept of 'specified complexity' was developed in the 1990s by mathematician, philosopher, and theologian William A. Dembski. Dembski states that when something exhibits specified complexity one can infer that it was produced by an intelligent causal agent rather than being the result of natural processes. He states that details of living things can be similarly characterized, especially the *patterns* of molecular sequences in functional biological molecules such as DNA.

Dembski defines **complex specified information** as anything with a less than 1 in 10^{150} chance of occurring by (natural) chance.

Fine-tuned universe

Intelligent design proponents have also occasionally appealed to broader teleological arguments outside of biology, most notably an argument based on the fine-tuning of **universal constants** that make matter and life possible and that are argued not to be solely attributable to chance.

These include the values of:

- **Fundamental physical constants**,
- Relative strengths of **nuclear forces**,
- **Electromagnetism** and **gravity** between fundamental particles,

as well as:

- The **ratios of masses** of such particles.

Intelligent design proponent Guillermo Gonzalez argues that if any of these values were even slightly different, the Universe would be dramatically different, making it impossible for many chemical elements and features, such as galaxies, to form. Thus, proponents argue, an **intelligent designer** of life was needed to ensure that the requisite features were present to achieve that particular outcome.

Critics claim that both **intelligent design** and the **weak form of the anthropic principle*** are essentially a tautology and that these arguments amount to the claim that life is able to exist because the Universe is able to support life. The claim of the improbability of a life-supporting universe has also been criticized as an '*argument by lack of imagination*' for assuming no other forms of life are possible.

Life as we know it might not exist if things were different, but a different sort of life might exist in its place.

Intelligent designer

The contemporary **intelligent design** movement formulates its arguments in secular terms and intentionally avoids identifying the intelligent agent (or agents). Although they do not state that God is the designer, the designer is often implicitly hypothesized to have intervened in a way that only a god could intervene.

But asserting the need for a designer of complexity also raises the question "Who or what designed the designer?"

**Weak Anthropic Principle:* *The observed values of all physical and cosmological quantities are not equally probable but they take on values restricted by the requirement that there exist sites where carbon-based life can evolve and by the requirement that the Universe be old enough for it to have already done so.*

The Anthropic Cosmological Principle (John D Barrow & Frank J Tipler) p16.

SOME RELEVANT QUOTES:

Thomas Nagel (*Philosopher*):
Though not a biologist, proposed a non-Darwinian account of evolution that incorporates impersonal and natural teleological laws to explain the existence of 'life, consciousness, rationality, and objective value'. He is noted as quoting that "The more details we learn about the chemical basis of life and the intricacy of the genetic code, the more unbelievable the standard historical account becomes".

Sir Fred Hoyle (*Cambridge Astrophysicist*) (The Universe: Past and Present Reflections):
"From 1953 onward, Willy Fowler and I have always been intrigued by the remarkable relation of the 7.65 Mev energy level in the nucleus of Carbon-12 to the 7.12 Mev level in Oxygen-16. If you wanted to produce carbon and oxygen in roughly equal quantities by stellar nucleosynthesis, these are the two levels you have to fix, and your fixing would have to be just where these levels are actually found to be.

Another put-up job? … Following the above argument, I am inclined to think so. A common sense interpretation of the facts suggests that a super-intellect has *monkeyed* with physics, as well as with chemistry and biology, and that there are no blind forces worth speaking about in nature."

Sir John Polkinghorne (*Cambridge micro-physicist and theologian*), the Einstein of dialogue on Science & Religion):
"When you realize that the laws of nature must be incredibly finely tuned to produce the Universe we see, that conspires to plant the idea that the universe did not just happen, but that there must be a purpose behind it."

George Ellis *(British Astrophysicist)*:
"Amazing fine tuning occurs in the laws that make this [complexity] possible. Realization of the complexity of what is accomplished makes it very difficult not to use the word 'miraculous' without taking a stand as to the ontological status of the word."

Arno Penzias *(Nobel Prize in Physics)*:
"Astronomy leads us to a unique event, a universe which was created out of nothing, one with the very delicate balance needed to provide exactly the conditions required to permit life, and one which has an underlying (one might say 'supernatural') plan."

Stephen Hawking *(Cambridge Astrophysicist)*:
"Then we shall … be able to take part in the discussion of the question as to why it is that we and the universe exist. If we find the answer to that, it would be the ultimate triumph of human reason – for then we would know the mind of God."

Francisco Ayala (*Evolutionary biologist and philosopher*), suggested that science should focus on the question of whether there is directional change, without regard to whether the change is 'improvement'.

This may be compared to **Stephen Jay Gould's** suggestion of "replacing the idea of progress with an operational notion of directionality".

Michio Kaku (*Theoretical physicist and futurist*) "I have concluded that we are in a world made by rules created by an intelligence. Believe me, everything that we call chance won't make sense anymore. To me it is clear that we exist in a plan which is governed by rules that were created, shaped by a universal intelligence and not by chance."

- **Teleology** is yet another theory which cannot be ignored. Teleology (from τέλος, 'telos', 'end', 'aim', or 'goal,' and λόγos, 'logos', 'explanation' or 'reason') or **finality** is a reason or explanation for something as a function of its end, purpose, or goal, as opposed to as a function of its cause. **Natural teleology** contends that natural entities also have intrinsic purposes, irrespective of human use or opinion. For instance, Aristotle claimed that an acorn's intrinsic *telos* is to become a fully grown oak tree.

Teleology

Natural teleology contends that natural entities also have *intrinsic* purposes, irrespective of human use or opinion. For instance, **Aristotle** claimed that an acorn's intrinsic *telos* is to become a fully grown oak tree. Human cognition and learning often rely on proximal rather than distal causation. Therefore a certain level of teleology might be useful or at least tolerable for practical purposes even by people who reject its cosmologic accuracy.

Its accuracy is upheld by **Barrow and Tipler** (1986), whose citations of such teleologists as Max Planck and Norbert Wiener are significant for scientific endeavour.

Max Planck wrote that *"All matter originates and exists only by virtue of a force... We must assume behind this force the existence of a conscious and intelligent Mind. This Mind is the matrix of all matter"*, whilst **Norbert Wiener** asserted that "*Scientific discovery consists in the interpretation for our own convenience of a system of existence which has been made with no eye to our convenience at all.*"

Plato and Aristotle, depicted here in 'The School of Athens' by Raphael

---

Are other advances in science, mathematics, and cosmology suggesting additional mechanisms at work besides Evolution?

... It is evident that paradigms other than those heretofore adopted with regard to Evolution must be seriously considered.

Epilogue

My granddaughter relates the story of a conversation she recently had with a college friend on 'Evolution'. "Ah yes." said the friend, "That's all about our coming from monkeys, isn't it?" The conversation came to an abrupt end!

The fact is that the subject of 'Evolution' is one that is so broad a topic and covers so many different disciplines, one interlocking with another.

... but what caused the Big Bang?

It is also often difficult to appreciate evolution's real extent and how one aspect is, at the same time, autonomous and dependent of others.

It is hard to accept that the Universe emerged from the singularity of a point of infinite density and gravity

Quantum mechanics attempts to explain the beginning of the Universe through a series of quantum fluctuations which cause the Universe to expand and contract. Another theory predicts a universe being created after the old one is destroyed, each with different universal constants. Yet another theory relies on the fact that the Universe is perhaps one of many in a multi-verse, (*Stephen Hawking's 'no boundary' model ultimately posits that our universe is just one of infinitely many parallel universes.*) and has budded off from another universe as a result of quantum fluctuations, as opposed to our Universe being all that exists.

But interestingly, it has now been reported that a group of three researchers, associate professor at KEK Jun Nishimura, associate professor at Shizuoka University Asato Tsuchiya, and project researcher at Osaka University Sang-Woo Kim, have succeeded in generating a model of the Universe's birth based on superstring theory.

Using a supercomputer, they found that at the moment of the Big Bang, the Universe had 10 dimensions – 9 spatial and 1 temporal – but only 3 of these spatial dimensions expanded.

"*Similar to imagining our Universe (or any three-dimensional space) being enclosed by a two-dimensional boundary, our three-dimensional space may in fact be the boundary around a higher-dimensional space.*" *Bryan Brandenburg*

> One notable feature of string theory and M-theory is that these theories require **extra dimensions** of space-time for their mathematical consistency. In string theory, space-time is *ten-dimensional* (nine spatial dimensions, and one time dimension), while in M-theory it is *eleven-dimensional* (ten spatial dimensions, and one time dimension).

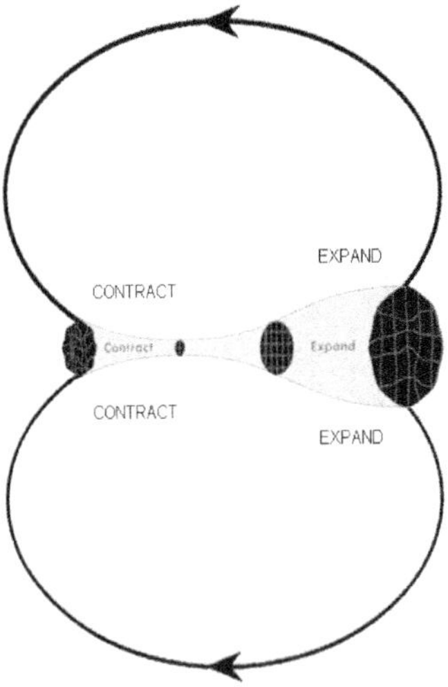

Given all of this, it is not outside the realms of imagination to consider the Universe as being either a **sphere** or a **torus**, because both are curved and closed. The curved/closed model is generally assumed to be a hypersphere, which has a surface volume of $2\pi^2r^3$. Interestingly enough, the surface volume of a torus is also $2\pi^2r^3$, so the spatial geometry of a curved/closed universe could just as easily be **toroidal**.

If this were to be so, it would answer the ever-begging question of 'what happened before the Big Bang'!

Now let us look at some of the figures that pertain to our Universe in general:

The deepest image ever taken, the **Hubble eXtreme Deep Field**, revealed 5,500 galaxies over an area that took up just 1/32,000,000th of the sky. But today, scientists estimate that there are more than ten times as many galaxies that Hubble, even at its limits, is capable of seeing. All told, there are some ~2 trillion galaxies within the **observable** Universe. However, the **James Webb Space Telescope** promises to significantly increase this number now that it has begun to send data back from its orbit one million miles away.

Carl Sagan once stated that "*there are more stars in our Universe than there are grains of sand on all the beaches on Earth*". Such a statement not only leaves one to estimate the number of stars in the Universe but also a meaningful estimate of the number of grains of sand there are on Earth.

Firstly, the Milky Way galaxy has been estimated to contain between 100 and 400 billion stars. There are some ~2 trillion galaxies in the Universe with the high probability that this figure will increase significantly (*see above*). The lowest number of stars that can be found in the Universe based on the estimate of stars in the Milky Way galaxy is therefore between 2.0×10^{14} and 2.0×10^{16} stars.

Secondly, there is the question of the grains of sand … A single grain of sand found on the beach is half a millimetre in diameter. Twenty grains make up about a centimetre, and 8,000 make up one cubic centimetre. To calculate the volume of sand, you need to determine the amount of coastline that consists of sandy beaches. Dr. Jason Marshall '*The Math Dude*' estimates the volume of the beaches to be 700 trillion cubic meters. Mathematically, the figure amounts to 5×10^{21} grains of sand.

The mathematician suggests that this is just an estimate and the number could change by a factor of two to a low of 2.5 and a high of 10 sextillions.

A mathematical conclusion can be made that the least number of stars is equal to the highest number of sand grains. However, it is likely that there are five to ten times more stars than sand on the beaches. In 2016 researchers, observing images from the Hubble Space Telescope stated that there could be more than 2 trillion galaxies in the observable universe, which is ten times more than the highest number expected. This is in addition to the fact that the entire universe cannot be observed by any telescope on the earth. *ref: Worldatlas.com*

But how large is the Universe?

The Sun is one astronomical unit (AU) away from us. One astronomical unit is 149,598,000km.

The Universe is 93 billion light-years across and is **expanding at the speed of light**. Just one light-year, is equivalent to 63,000 AU, or the equivalent to 9 trillion kilometres. So that works out as:

$$\underbrace{9.3 \times 10^{10}}_{\text{Light years}} \cdot \underbrace{6.3 \times 10^{4}}_{\text{AU}} \cdot \underbrace{1.49598 \times 10^{8}}_{\text{km in one AU}} \approx 8.8 \times 10^{23}\ \text{km}$$

or

8,800,000,000,000,000,000,000,000km (or 8.8 septillion km)

That is how large our Universe is, and that is not even the end of it. The 93 billion years is just the **observable** Universe, the Universe which we can currently see. It has been suggested that the whole Universe might very well be 250 times larger than that which is observable by us.

Finally we must look at the number of possible universes, or multiverses, there may be in the greater firmament. That is not to suggest that all, of even a fair proportion of these universes are 'live' universes. They may be dead and totally void of any form of life, and then there are those which may be alive but dependent on entirely different astronomical and physical constants; their chemistry and bases for life may be quite different from those in our universe.

In a recent study, Stanford physicists Andrei Linde and Vitaly Vanchurin have calculated the number of all possible universes, coming up with an answer of 10^10^16.

If that number sounds large, the scientists explain that it would have been even greater except for the fact that we, as observers, are limited in our ability to distinguish more universes. Otherwise, there could be as many as 10^10^10^7 universes.

Somewhere within the Universe is the Solar System, insignificantly small when compared to the size of the Universe, but very significant insofar as it has appeared that life has been produced in a variety of forms on one of its planets – a singular event, or so it would seem.

The search for extraterrestrial intelligence (SETI) is a collective term for scientific searches for intelligent extraterrestrial life, for example, monitoring electromagnetic radiation for signs of transmissions from civilizations on other planets.

Scientific investigation began shortly after the advent of radio in the early 1900s, and focused international efforts have been ongoing since the 1980s.

The Ohio State SETI program gained fame on 15th August, 1977, when Jerry Ehman, a project volunteer, witnessed a startlingly strong signal received by the telescope. He quickly circled the indication on a printout and scribbled the exclamation 'Wow!' in the margin. Dubbed the *Wow! signal*, it is considered by some to be the best candidate for a radio signal from an artificial, extraterrestrial source ever discovered, but it has not been detected again in several additional searches.

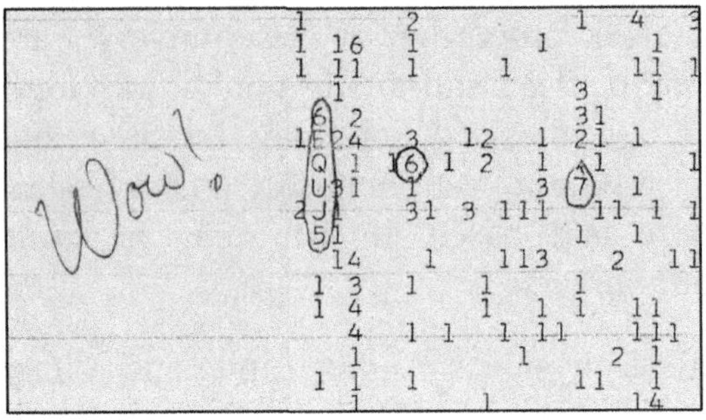

The Wow! Signal

Credit: The Ohio State University Radio Observatory and the North American Astro Physical Observatory (NAAPO).

In the meantime, however, a hint to the existence of extra terrestrial intelligence, albeit very slim, came in the form of a meteorite in 1969. In that year1969 a 100kg meteorite fell in Australia near the settlement of Murchison, Victoria. It belongs to a group of carbonaceous chondrites which are rich in organic compounds.

The age of this meteorite has been determined to be ~7 billion years old, about ~2.5 billion years older than the 4.54 billion year age of our Earth and the 4.6 billion year age of our Solar System.

Murchison samples contain common amino acids such as glycine, alanine, and glutamic acid as well as unusual ones such as isovaline and pseudoleucine. (A complex mixture of alkanes was also found to be similar to that found in the Miller–Urey experiment). Serine and threonine, usually considered to be earthly contaminants, were conspicuously absent in the samples.

The meteorite contained a mixture of left-handed and right-handed amino acids, where most amino acids used by living organisms on Earth are left-handed in chirality, and most sugars used are right-handed.

A 2010 study of one of the samples using **high resolution analytical tools including spectroscopy** identified no less than 14,000 molecular compounds, including ~70 amino acids.

The limited scope of the analysis by mass spectrometry though provided for a potential 50,000 or more unique molecular compositions, with an estimate of the possibility of millions of distinct organic compounds in this single meteorite.

So what implications has all this got to do with Evolution?

Firstly, considering the age of the Murchison meteorite, non-terrestrial life may well have begun at least ~7 billion years ago well beyond the realms of our Solar System.

Secondly, measured purine and pyrimidine compounds were found in the meteorite, and carbon isotope ratios for uracil and xanthine indicate, without a doubt, a **non-terrestrial origin** for these compounds.

Thirdly, that the vast number of molecular compounds and amino acids might even point to the basis of a system of life far more complex and advanced compared to anything witnessed on Earth throughout its 4.54 billion year history.

This meteorite demonstrates that many organic compounds may well have been delivered by early **extra terrestrial bodies** and might well have played a key role in life's origin and development.

Nor did the meteorite originate from either the Kuiper Belt or the Oort Cloud. The origin of the meteorite remains a complete mystery.

Kuiper Belt
Approximately 50 AU from the Sun, it is similar to the asteroid belt, but is far larger - 20 times as wide and 20-200 times as massive. Most short-period comets form their origins in the Kuiper Belt, and there are comets there with orbital periods of 200 years or less. In fact, it has been suggested that there could be more than a trillion comet nuclei in the main body of the Kuiper Belt. The largest **Kuiper Belt Objects** are Pluto, Eris, Haumea, Makemake, Quaoar, Sedna, Ceres, Ixion, Varda,

Gonggong and Orcus. These are often also referred to as Trans-Neptunian Objects (TNOs), Dwarf Planets.

Oort Cloud

The inner limits of the Oort Cloud begin at about 2,000 AU (0.032 ly) from the Sun. The cloud itself stretches out almost a quarter of the way to the nearest star, Proxima Centauri. It is spherically shaped and consists of an outer cloud and a torus inner cloud.

It is an extended shell of icy objects that exist in the outermost reaches of the Solar System and is thought to be the origin of most of the long-period comets that have been observed.

This cloud of particles is theorized to be the remains of the disc of material that formed the Sun and planets. The most likely theory is that the material now in the Oort Cloud probably formed closer to the young Sun in the earliest epochs of Solar System formation. As the planets grew, and in particular as Jupiter coalesced and migrated to its present position, its gravitational influence is thought to have scattered many icy objects out to their present position in the Oort Cloud.

Insofar as the cloud is very far away from the Sun, it can be easily disrupted by the nearby passage of a star, nebula, or by actions in the disk of the Milky Way. Those actions knock cometary nuclei out of their orbits, and send them on a headlong rush toward the Sun.

If we now come to the present day, we are faced with answering the transgressions of those who came before us and our present errors. The whole world is in crisis … the clock is slowing down. If nothing drastic happens in the very short time, we will be faced with the very stark reality of a Sixth Mass Extinction.

More than 500 species of land vertebrates have disappeared over the last 100 years. Many more animals will join those that have already gone. During the decade that has just ended (2010-2019), the International Union for the Conservation of Nature (IUCN) declared the extinction of **160 species**. Mankind has brought this about, and only mankind can make it right.

It is not only the extinction of species which is happening. No person on the face of this planet cannot help but notice the occurrence of global warming and the ensuing wide-scale destruction of forests and arable land. The rise in global temperature has been instrumental in floods throughout the world. As a gradual change in global warming, this may well have triggered mass migrations both on land and in the oceans and in turn initiating evolutionary changes.

Carbon emissions have not helped and, on top of this, it has been estimated that the world's oxygen will run out in a million years. But no one is doing anything really radical to address carbon emissions or depleting oxygen levels.

It is pure ignorant fallacy to insist that electric cars, for example, are the answer to the question of carbon omissions … IT IS NOT!

"Electric cars may run on clean, green electricity, but purchasing millions of electric vehicles to replace our fossil-fuelled vehicles means overseas factories will pour out tonnes upon tonnes of greenhouse gas.

Although they produce just one-third the lifetime emissions of a petrol car, electric vehicles aren't completely clean. Carbon is created in the mining, manufacturing, shipping and recycling of the parts that make up every vehicle."

University of Toronto sustainable transport researcher Alexandre Milovanoff continues by saying: "The emissions from materials and manufacturing are a large chunk of a car's environmental impact".

From his calculations, a Tesla Model 3 emits the equivalent of 16.5 tonnes of carbon dioxide over a lifetime. That's about a third that of the Toyota RAV4, which produces 45.4 tonnes.

"The assembly of the Tesla's battery is the biggest contributor, contributing 6.5 tonnes of carbon dioxide. Furthermore, it takes a lot of energy to mine the lithium, nickel and cobalt metals required," he added "Then there's the battery creation. We need to add heat and electricity in order to change the form of those materials".

The vehicle body adds another 5.7 tonnes. Milovanoff estimates. "Conventional and electric vehicles will be mostly made of steel, cast iron and aluminium. ... Those are quite energy intensive to produce."

Because about 20 per cent of our electricity is generated from burning natural gas or coal, this will also add to an electric car's lifetime carbon footprint – about 4.3 tonnes for a distance of 200,000 kilometres. *Source: Olivia Wannan, 12th March, 2021*

But global warming, carbon emissions and oxygen levels have profound effects on population growth and vice versa.

Based on population growth, the economy doubled every 250,000 years from the Paleolithic until the Neolithic. Then the 'new agricultural' economy doubled every 900 years. Later on, dramatic changes in the rate of growth occurred more so as a consequence of technological advancement beginning with the Industrial Revolution in the 1750's than on any other single factor.

In his *'Essay on the Principle of Population'* which was published in 1798, Thomas Malthus predicted that whilst population grew in a geometrical progression and the supply of food grew through arithmetic progression there would come a time when there would be a drastic food shortage.

In the 'current era' the world's economic output now doubles every fifteen years, sixty times faster than during the 'agricultural era'. "*If the rise of superhuman intelligence causes a similar revolution,*" argues Robin Hanson of George Mason University, "*one would expect the economy to double at least quarterly and possibly on a weekly basis. This would place an intolerable burden to sustain the population*".

The current world population of 7.6 billion is expected to reach 8.6 billion in 2030, 9.8 billion in 2050 and 11.2 billion in 2100, according to a recent United Nations report.

With roughly 83 million people being added to the world's population every year, the upward trend in population size is expected to continue, **even assuming that fertility levels will continue to decline**.

Today, 'persons aged 65 or above' comprise the world's fastest growing of all age groups. Globally, for the first time in 2018, older persons outnumbered children under the age of five, and by 2050, older persons will outnumber adolescents and youth (ages 15 to 24). Some regions, such as Europe and Eastern Asia, already face a considerable challenge in supporting and caring for their older populations. As life expectancy continues to increase, older persons are likely to play more significant roles in societies and economies.

In fact the decline in fertility rates mean nearly every country could have shrinking populations by the end of the century, and 23 nations - including Spain and Japan - are expected to see their populations halve by 2100. Countries will also age dramatically, with as many people turning 80 as there are being born.

If the number falls below approximately 2.1, then the size of the population starts to fall. In 1950, women were having an average of 4.7 children in their lifetime.

Researchers at the **University of Washington's Institute for Health Metrics and Evaluation** showed the global fertility rate nearly halved to 2.4 in 2017 - and their study, published in the *Lancet*, projects it will fall below 1.7 by 2100.

As a result, the researchers expect the number of people on the planet to peak at 9.7 billion around 2064, before falling down to 8.8 billion by the end of the century.

Fertility rates are falling, but this has nothing to do with sperm counts or the usual things that come to mind when discussing fertility. Instead it is being driven by the greater emancipation of women with regard to education and work and acceptable societal norms. This has lead to women choosing to have fewer children.

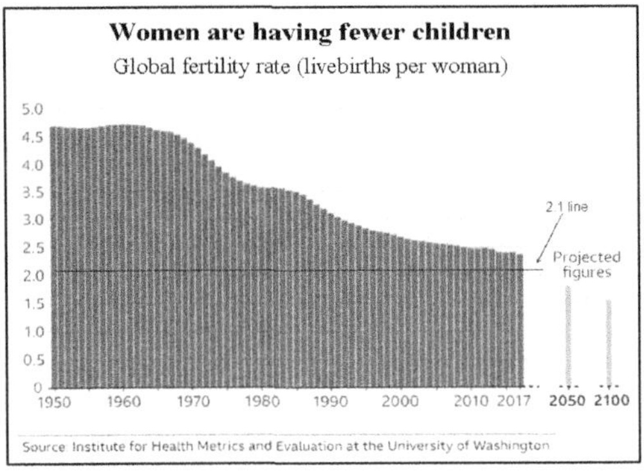

Falling fertility rates can be regarded as a success story, but one that comes with a sting in the tail:

The study projects that the 'number of under-fives' will fall from 681 million in 2017 to 401 million in 2100 whilst the number of over 80-year-olds will increase dramatically from 141 million in 2017 to 866 million in 2100. In other words, demographically, there will be all the uniformly negative consequences of an '*inverted age structure*',

The UK is predicted to peak at 75 million in 2063, and fall to 71 million by 2100. However, globally, 183 out of 195 countries will have a fertility rate below the replacement level.

The growth of human population impacts the Earth's ecological systems and thus evolution in many ways, including:

- **Extraction of resources from the environment.** The process of removing resources, in turn, often releases **pollutants and waste** that reduce **air** and **water quality**, and harm the **health** of humans and other species.
- **Burning of fossil fuels** for energy to generate electricity, and to power transportation and industrial processes.
- **Increase in freshwater use** for drinking, agriculture, recreation, and industrial processes

- **Forests and other habitats** are disturbed or destroyed to construct urban areas. As populations increase, more land is used for **agricultural activities** to grow crops and support livestock, leading to decrease of **species populations,** geographic **ranges, biodiversity,** and **interactions** among organisms.
- **Increasing fishing and hunting**, which reduces **species populations** of the exploited species.
- **Increasing the transport of invasive species**, either intentionally or by accident, as people travel and import and export supplies.
- **Transmission of diseases**. Humans living in densely populated areas can rapidly spread diseases within and among populations.

It is not surprising that humans created 'digital information'... perhaps it was inevitable. But now it has grown to such an extent that it has reached a similar magnitude to biological information in the biosphere. Since the 1980s, the quantity of digital information stored has doubled about every 2.5 years, reaching about 5 zettabytes in 2014 (5×10^{21} bytes).

In biological terms, there are 7.6 billion humans on the planet, each having, on an average, a genome of 6.2 billion nucleotides. Since one byte can encode four nucleotide pairs, the individual genomes of every human on the planet could be encoded by approximately 1.06×10^{19} bytes. The digital realm stored 500 times more information than this in 2014. The total amount of DNA contained in all of the cells on Earth is estimated to be about 5.3×10^{37} base pairs, equivalent to 1.325×10^{37} bytes of information.

> If all the strands of DNA in an average human were to be joined up nose to tail then the resulting strand would stretch to the Sun and back **~610 times**.

If growth in digital storage continues at its current rate of 30 - 38% compound annual growth per year, it will rival the total information content contained in the entire DNA in all of the cells on Earth in about 110 years. This would represent a doubling of the amount of information stored in the biosphere across a total time period of just 150 years".

In the current stage of life's evolution, the carbon-based biosphere has already generated a human cognitive system capable of creating technology that will result in a comparable evolutionary transition.

It is argued that the human species currently dominates other species because the human brain has some distinctive capabilities that other animals lack. If AI surpasses humanity in general intelligence and becomes 'super-intelligent', then it could become difficult or impossible for humans to control.

Public figures such as Stephen Hawking, Bill Gates, and Elon Musk have expressed concern that full **artificial intelligence** could result in human extinction. Others believe that humans will evolve or directly modify their biology so as to achieve radically greater intelligence.

Digital technology has infiltrated the fabric of human society to a degree of indisputable and often life-sustaining dependence.

"*Humans already embrace fusions of biology and technology. We spend most of our waking time communicating through digitally mediated channels... we trust artificial intelligence with our lives through antilock braking in cars and autopilots in planes... With one in three marriages in America beginning online, digital algorithms are also taking a role in human pair bonding and reproduction*". *Trends in Ecology & Evolution (2016).*

Alexa and Siri have also had a not insignificant part to play (with the caveat that they should be turned off when sensitive or private conversations are being held!!)

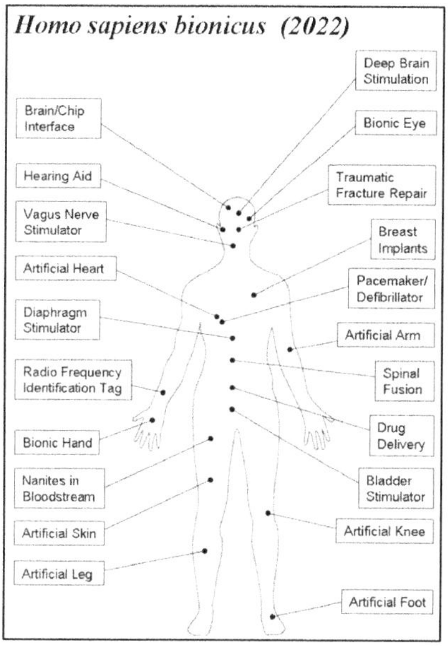

Physical enhancements include cosmetics (plastic surgery and orthodontics), drug-induced (doping and performance-enhancing drugs), functional (prosthetics and powered exoskeletons), Medical (implants (e.g. pacemaker) and organ replacements (e.g. bionic lenses)).

Mental enhancements include nootropics, neuro-stimulation, and supplements that improve mental functions.

Computers, mobile phones, and Internet can also be used to enhance cognitive efficiency. Notable efforts in human augmentation are driven by the interconnected Internet devices, including wearable electronics (e.g. augmented reality glasses, smart watches, and smart textile), personal drones, on-body and in-body nanonetworks.

Many different forms of human enhancing technologies are either on the way or are currently being tested and trialed. A few of these emerging technologies include genetic engineering (gene therapy), neuro-technology (neural implants and brain-computer interfaces), cyberware, strategies for engineered negligible senescence, nanomedicine, and 3D bioprinting.

Mankind has readily adopted these physical and mental enhancements for a variety of different reasons, but what is more to the point is that the more humans become used to these enhancements so the more dependent they will come until a time will come when the panoply of enhancements becomes part and parcel of a new-day *Homo sapiens*.

As has already been stated, humans could well evolve, or directly modify their biology, so as to achieve radically greater intelligence. Many humans in the form which they are currently regarded will be a thing of the past having made way for a fully artificial intelligent being capable of total interface with technology - many, but not all! The fears of Hawking, Gates and Musk would be proved prophetic with the prescient warnings they had made of the future.

But this need not necessarily be the end of *H. sapiens,* or rather it **must not** be the end. Extinction is far too finite for a being such as *H. sapiens* to have journeyed for so long a time from the mud of primordial times.

The ancestors of *H. sapiens*, have demonstrated a remarkable tenacity for life notwithstanding the multitude of extinction events, severe climatic and atmospheric changes, and devastating effects of visiting comets and meteorites.

Surely *H. sapiens* is destined for something greater, more edifying than to mildly accept defeat, roll over and simply die an ignominious passing of an otherwise promising species. Yet it remains the only species throughout the history of life which insists on killing itself *en masse*.

H. sapiens has to 'grow up' and take responsible control of its destiny ... or it will most certainly go extinct and leave its artificial intelligence counterpart to rule the future.

According to a recent survey, the most precise estimates of species presently on Earth total some 8.7 million of which:

6.5 million species are to be found on Earth,
and 2.2 million species dwelling in the world's oceans.

These figures do not include micro-organisms and viruses. Of the 8.7 million estimate, only just over 953,000 have been described and catalogued.

Scientists have, moreover, estimated that over the course of Earth's history, anywhere between 1 and 4 billion species have existed on this planet.

It is rather humbling to realise that *H. sapiens* has been the only sentient being that has been raised to the high levels of consciousness that it now enjoys. It is true that many animals are sentient (... and, in fact, lobsters even have legal status in British courts due to their high level of sentience. Moreover, New Zealand law bans *killing lobsters alive*, with Lacey Act in the USA also making it a federal crime with penalties ranging from $10,000 fines to 5 years in jail per violation). By 'sentience' is meant the faculty by which the external world is able to be perceived through the state of having sensory awareness or conscious sensations.

H. sapiens has gone that one step further in having a 'mind' of its own. By having a 'mind' is meant that humans have a set of faculties responsible for their mental phenomena. These faculties include thought, imagination, memory, will, and of course conscious sensations. They are functionally responsible for various phenomena like perception, pain, belief, desire, intention, and emotion. Ostensibly, it is the mind which raises *H. sapiens* to a level higher than all other species and is the subconscious but ever-present goad behind *Homo's* existence.

H. sapiens has had to travel a very long way along the evolutionary life-line from the closest unicellular living relatives to animals which date back to the *Choanoflagellates* some million odd years ago. Indubitably, a good deal has happened over the time spanning the creation of the first *Choanoflagellate* even to arrive at the putative example of the first primate in the form of the *Purgatorius,* which came to being just after the Cretaceous-Paleogene (K-Pg) extinction event some 66 million years ago.

Human Body

- Everything in this incredible, vast Universe is almost entirely, 99.9999999 percent empty space. If the space between the particles that make up all the atoms (and the spaces between atoms) were removed, i.e. compressed so that all the sub-atomic particles (electrons, protons, neutrons) were pressed together, **a human would fit into a cube 15 micrometres on each edge.** (15 micrometres = 0.015mm).
- The human body contains nearly 37.2 trillion cells. (3.72×10^{13})
- It is estimated that the microbial biome of our bodies, including bacteria and fungi, is around 39 trillion cells. (3.9×10^{13})
- An adult human body is made up of about 7 octillion atoms. (7.0×10^{27})
- The fastest muscles in a human body are the ones that make the eyes blink. They can contract in less than one-hundredth of a second.
- The average body makes about 2 to 3 million red blood cells every second, or about **173 to 259 billion** red blood cells per day.
- The body replaces around 330 billion (3.3×10^{11}) cells per day. At that rate, the body is making over 3.8 million new cells *every second.*
- The human eye can distinguish between approximately 10 million different colours.
- The human brain consists of 100 billion (1.0×10^{11}) nerve cells connected by 100 trillion (1.0×10^{14}) connections, more than the number of stars in the Milky Way galaxy. It uses as much energy as a 10-watt light bulb.
- The total length of the blood vessels in the whole body is **100,000 kilometres**, which can circle the Earth two and a half times.
- If all the neurons found in the human body are lined up together, they would cover a total distance of a 1,000 kilometres.
- The heart is a collection of individual cells, but it is the complex interaction of numerous cell types that give the heart its ability to pump blood. If heart cells were to be placed in a Petri dish some of the cells, called **myocytes**, will be seen to beat independently – and will continue to do so!

H. sapiens is, by any description, a highly sophisticated biological machine, as in fact are many present-day fauna, but in different ways and perhaps to a lesser degree. It is indeed barely credible that such a biological machine as *H. sapiens* is also a species which is sentient and mindful of its existence, perhaps as pure 'accidents' in the course of evolution.

It is true that, throughout evolutionary history, ancestors have had to survive the '*Ravages of Time*', to borrow the idiom from the Hong Kong comic series created by Chan Mou.

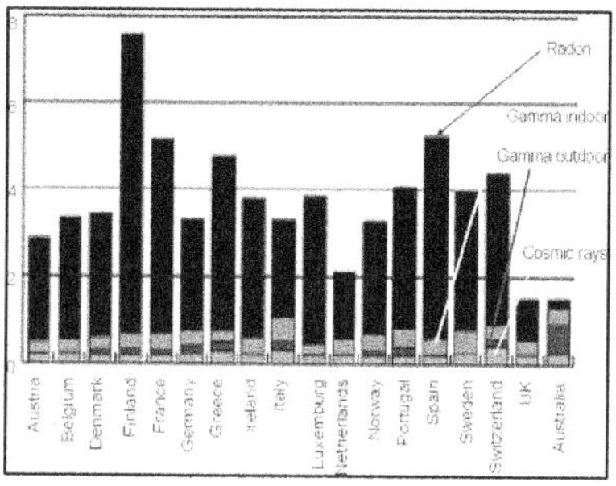

Average annual doses of radiation in different countries (in millisieverts per year). From Encyclopedia of Analytical Science (2005)

There have been extinction events, massive earth movements, volcanic eruptions, global warming, fluctuations in oxygen and ozone levels and greenhouse gas, not to mention background radiation. But perhaps, only perhaps, within the fundamental make-up of humankind, there is the ability to display a probabilistic nature of quantum mechanical phenomena just as particles were seen to do in Young's double-slit experiment in 1802 – everything is, after all, made of the same stuff! Could it be that not necessarily the paths of evolution, but the end scenario, is already pre-ordained for *H. sapiens*. Maybe mankind will develop other faculties; maybe it will be superseded by another more resilient species … and perhaps the class of *H. sapiens* which has readily adopted physical and mental enhancements will evolve into humanoid androids to leave the restrictive confines of Earth and explore the far reaches of the Universe. Pure science fiction? Maybe, but then again maybe not!

Recommended Further Reading

Anthropic Cosmological Principle	1988	Barrow, J D.
Cycles of Time	2011	Penrose, R
Dark Matter and the Dinosaurs	2017	Randall, L
Extinction: Bad Genes / Bad Luck?	1992	Raup, D M
Fossil Identifier	1994	Weidensaul, S
Grand Design	1982	Fay, S
Guide to Prehistoric Life	2005	Haines, T
Human Evolution	2009	Jones, S et al
Life: The First Four Billion Years	1999	Fortey, R
Natural History of Evolution	1993	Whitfield, P
Origin of Humankind	1994	Leakey, R
Origin of Species	2011	Darwin, C
Plundered Planet	2011	Collier, P
Sinking Arc (1980)	1980	Myers, N
Sixth Extinction (1995)	1995	Leakey, R et al
Voyage of the Beagle	1989	Darwin, C
Wonderful Life: (1989)	1989	Gould, S. J.

ed Readers Digest:
Last Two Million Years 1988 (en)
Merveilles et Mystéres de la Nature 1969 (fr)
Bildatlas der Tierwelt * 1971 (ge)

* Original in English:
The Living World of Animals 1971 (en)